Celtic Lore
& Spellcraft
of the
Dark
Goddess

About the Author

Stephanie Woodfield (Brookfield, CT) has been a practicing Witch for over fourteen years and a Priestess for ten years. Her lifelong love of Irish mythology led to a close study of Celtic Witchcraft. A natural clairvoyant and empath, she has worked as a Tarot card reader and is ordained as a minister with the Universal Life Church.

To Write to the Author

If you wish to contact the author or would like more information about this book, please write to the author in care of Llewellyn Worldwide, and we will forward your request. Both the author and publisher appreciate hearing from you and learning of your enjoyment of this book and how it has helped you. Llewellyn Worldwide cannot guarantee that every letter written to the author can be answered, but all will be forwarded. Please write to:

Stephanie Woodfield
℅ Llewellyn Worldwide
2143 Wooddale Drive
Woodbury, MN 55125-2989

Please enclose a self-addressed stamped envelope for reply, or $1.00 to cover costs. If outside the USA, enclose an international postal reply coupon.

STEPHANIE
WOODFIELD

INVOKING
THE
MORRIGAN

Llewellyn Publications
Woodbury, Minnesota

First Edition
Thirteenth Printing, 2022

Book design by Bob Gaul
Cover art © 2011 Chris Down
Cover design by Ellen Lawson
Editing by Nicole Edman
Interior Celtic illustrations from *Celtic Designs CD-Rom and Book* (Dover Publications, 1996–97), *Celtic Designs and Motifs* (Dover Publications, 1991) and Llewellyn art department

Library of Congress Cataloging-in-Publication Data
Woodfield, Stephanie, 1983–
Celtic lore & spellcraft of the dark goddess : invoking the Morrigan / Stephanie Woodfield. — 1st ed.
p. cm.
Includes bibliographical references and index.
ISBN 978-0-7387-2767-7
1. Magic, Celtic. 2. Morrigan (Irish deity)—Miscellanea. I. Title. II. Title: Celtic lore and spellcraft of the dark goddess.
BF1622.C45W66 2011
299'.1612114—dc23
2011021155

Llewellyn Publications
A Division of Llewellyn Worldwide Ltd.
2143 Wooddale Drive
Woodbury, MN 55125-2989
www.llewellyn.com

Printed in the United States of America

Contents

Part Four: *Ancient Goddess, Modern Worship*

Charge of the Morrigan

By Meryt-Meihera

Be still and listen. Enchantment . . . is my name.
Hear my voice in the wind, the sea, the land?
Reach out and embrace me and I will speak.
My familiar is the carrion crow, knower of the
dead, attendee of battles. I am of the land, the
moon, and the sea. I am the cow of fertility, the
hunting wolf, and the eel of electricity. I am
wise, sly, and daring. I am the Queen, the Oracle,
the Warrior, and the Witch. I am the Sorceress
that will not be ruled, the Weaver of Time, the
Teacher of Mysteries. I am kin to the Badb and
Macha, for together we are the Sacred Three.
Come walk with me near the sea's kiss, let me
show you the Old Ways and your innate power.
Come join me under the moonlight and learn the
Ways of the Warrior and the Queen. Let me show
you all that's in between. My ways are dangerous
and difficult, but my gifts are true and blessed.
Swallow your fear and come to me, and you will
discover true beauty, strength, and courage.
Will you take the risks and learn my lessons?
Or will you hide from me and all I have to give
you? Ponder, now, what will you choose?

Introduction: The Call of the Morrigan

The beauty and might of this goddess lie not only in her connection to the cycle of death, but also in her ability to mold her power and gifts to the current situation, to the needs of men and women, to the requirements of the gods.

—*Michelle Skye,* Goddess Alive

The Morrigan flies through the pages of history and myth like an uncontainable whirlwind. Upon ancient battlefields she appeared as a raven, her wild shrieks and battle cry killing men where they stood. She could be a beautiful lusty maiden one minute and a fearsome hag the next. To some she appeared as a phantom, washing the blood-stained clothes of those destined to die along lonely river banks; to others she brought unparalleled victory and protection. The Morrigan is full of mystery, magick, and contradictions. She is powerful and wise but not always benevolent, her nature not always apparent at first glance, her wisdom not easily earned. Is she a tutelary goddess, or a goddess of war? Is she a friend to the Irish hero Cúchulain, or his greatest enemy? Is she loving or spiteful? In Irish mythology, the Morrigan refuses to be boxed into just one role. Just when you think you've figured her out, she changes shape and becomes something else (as a shape-shifter, this seems only fitting). Although she is commonly labeled as a goddess of battle, this is an oversimplification of a very dynamic deity. Like many goddesses of the Celtic pantheon, the Morrigan fills multiple roles: she is a goddess of war, of fertility, of sovereignty, and of magick, all at once.

It isn't surprising that the Morrigan is perhaps one of the most popular Celtic goddesses in modern Paganism. She exudes an air of confidence, power, and magick. She survives in various incarnations within the Celtic tradition, as a goddess, faery woman, ghostly phantom, and mortal queen. Today she remains a popular protagonist in fiction, such as in Marion Zimmer Bradley's *The Mists of Avalon* and Pat O'Shea's *The Hounds of the Morrigan*. Yet despite this, her myths and importance in the Celtic pantheon are often misunderstood. For many, her reputation as a goddess of death and war makes the Morrigan an intimidating figure to work with. Although nineteenth-century scholars interpreted her as a goddess of war, this is not precisely correct. At times she does bring about death, participate in battle, and protect warriors; but she is more accurately called a goddess of sovereignty. She is the patroness of those who wield power, whether it is the power of kingship, prowess on the battlefield, the power over life and death, or personal power.

My own experiences with the Morrigan began a few years after my initiation into Witchcraft. At the time, my life had been very chaotic and a goddess personifying victory over life's battles and inner strength was quite appealing. But even when the Morrigan began to make her presence known in my life, I hesitated to call upon her. Never one to be ignored, the Morrigan then began getting my attention in dramatic ways. Crows, one of her totem animals, began taking an unusual interest in my home, my office, and even my car. When I left for work in the morning, there was always at least one crow perched on top of my car; sometimes it seemed like an entire flock! At first I thought they were attracted to the garbage cans we kept near my usual parking spot, but after moving the cans to the other side of the house and even attempting to park my car elsewhere, my mornings continued to begin with the harsh cries of some very curious birds. At work my boss asked me if I was feeding the crows, since there was almost always one perched on the window ledge next to my desk several times a day. Several people "coincidently" (but we know there are no mere coincidences in a magickal life) lent me books that mentioned the Morrigan or Morgan le Fay, or fantasy novels featuring goddesses that bore a strong resemblance to her. I had remarkably vivid dreams where the Morrigan appeared in both human and animal form.

I had always had an affinity for Morgan le Fay as a child, and when I began to study Celtic mythology, I found it fascinating that—like the goddess Brigid, who survived into Christian times as a saint—the Morrigan had "diminished" in importance over the years. But she had not been completely forgotten, transforming into King Arthur's sorceress sister. While I had found her history interesting, most of the books I read warned against invoking the Morrigan; some even advised against any contact with this goddess. This general discouragement of contact with the Morrigan warred with the inexplicable pull I felt toward her. Finally I decided to follow my instincts.

On the next new moon, I cast a circle and invoked the Morrigan. That first encounter with the Morrigan was one of the most exhilarating experiences I've ever had during ritual work. The Morrigan's presence was so tangible, her voice so clear; it was like nothing I had ever felt before. The beauty of Paganism is that we experience our gods, and after that ritual, there could never be any question for me about the presence and reality of the Divine. The Morrigan's presence radiated power and strength, and I couldn't help but wonder why a goddess who represented personal power and overcoming injustice would ever be described as a divinity to be avoided.

After my initial experience with the Morrigan, I immediately began searching for more information about this powerful goddess, only to find very little that was useful. The more I searched, the more I began to understand the hesitation some felt toward working with her. Besides finding very little information about her history or worship, almost all the information I found was negative. When I spoke to other Pagans who had felt drawn to the Morrigan, our conversations usually revolved around whether or not it was "safe" to work with a goddess of death and war. Eventually I realized that most of what I would learn about the Morrigan would be from the Morrigan herself. For someone who had learned Witchcraft primarily from books, this was a daunting idea.

Now, after more than a decade serving as her Priestess, I can't imagine my life without the strong, reassuring presence of the Morrigan. She has been an invaluable guide, a protector, and a source of strength. The Morrigan stands ready at the edge of our perceptions to challenge our views of the world and of ourselves. She, like the Hindu Kali, is the Terrible Mother, the Dark Goddess, but no less a mother for it. She will not coddle us but will instigate and incite change in ourselves and our lives. The process of change and transformation can be painful, but it is ultimately rewarding. As a goddess of death and war, she is a goddess of hard truths. All living things must one day die in order to sustain new life and be reborn. Sometimes war is necessary to establish peace or retain one's freedom. The Morrigan stands fast next to her children through their battles, guiding them to victory and the peace that is the ultimate goal of any battle. Once she has taught us to battle and conquer our inner demons, she appears as the vibrant goddess of sovereignty, teaching us to embrace the abundance and joy of life.

This book is a guide to working with an ancient goddess in the modern world. It contains information about the Morrigan's myths and her role in the Celtic tradition, and also offers pathworking, exercises, spells, rituals, recipes, and magickal correspondences that you can use to invoke the Morrigan's magick and transformative power into your life. In Part One you will find information about the Morrigan's origins and mythology, along with short retellings of her myths and their hidden spiritual meaning. Parts Two and Three cover the different goddesses that form the Morrigan's triple nature and the many guises she embodies, while Part Four offers information about altars, types of offerings, seasonal and lunar rituals, and how to incorporate the Morrigan into a modern-day spiritual system. I suggest you read the background information in Part I first in order to become familiar with her myths. The other sections do not necessarily need to be read in order, so feel free to begin with whichever of the Morrigan's aspects or guises you feel drawn to work with.

The Great Goddess resides within each of us, her wisdom just as vital to the modern seeker as it was to the ancient Celts who worshipped her. The very first step to answering the call of the Morrigan is to open ourselves to her presence and wisdom. So whether you feel drawn to her as I was or you simply want to know more about this goddess, I invite you to invoke the Morrigan and draw upon the strength and wisdom of this truly powerful goddess!

Part One
Who Is the Morrigan?

Over his head is shrieking
a lean hag, quickly hopping
Over the points of weapons and shields.
She is the grey-haired Morrigu.
—John O'Donovan,
The Battle of Magh Rath

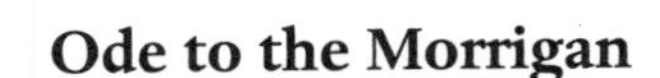

Ode to the Morrigan

By Gwynedd Danu

In olden days she gathered
On battlefields of mist

Chanting, offering golden charms
Granting her champions victory

So they say, so they say

Her shape a crow or raven
Her shield, trickery

She guards the gift of magic
Medicine, wisdom, fertility

Who are you, O Morrigan?
What face in modern times?

Your face shows now its fullness
Not mere war but quiet strength

You gird your women to take their place
A tide of matriarchy

Cleanse time, cleanse space
Bring balance to our human race

The Morrigan is a paradoxical figure. She is young one minute and old the next; she lends her aid to some while cursing others. Her nature is not always apparent at first glance, her wisdom not easily earned. As a shapeshifter, her favorite form was a raven or crow. In this guise the Celts believed the Morrigan flew over battlefields, filling those warriors she favored with an unconquerable battle frenzy and striking fear into the hearts of her enemies. Adept at magick, her spells hindered the enemies of the Túatha Dé Danann (the Irish gods); hence her association with magick and Witchcraft. She appeared in triple form as the sisters Macha, Anu, and Badb. As Macha, she cursed the men of Ulster for failing to aid a woman in her time of need; as Anu, she ruled over fertility and lent her name to the land; and as Badb, she gathered the souls of the dead.

What we know about the Morrigan comes to us from narrative texts written by Irish monks between the eighth and the twelfth centuries, after Christianity had replaced Paganism as the dominant religion in Ireland. She first appears in the *Lebor Gabála Érenn* (also called *The Book of Invasions*), which chronicles the arrival of the Celtic gods, the Túatha Dé Danann, in Ireland and their subsequent battle with the indigenous gods, the Fir Bolgs. She is also a pivotal character in several other narratives, the most well known of which is the *Táin Bó Cuailnge* or *The Cattle Raid of Cooley*, where she acts as both the hero's adversary and his benefactor. These stories were not recorded by the Irish Pagans but by their Christian descendants, who left their own mark on the old myths, adding to the difficulties in understanding the Morrigan's complex nature. While we will be exploring each of her myths and her role in Celtic mythology in greater detail, our first clue to the Morrigan's true nature is in her name.

Like the Morrigan herself, the translation of her name shifts and changes depending on the source. The second part of her name, *rígan,* translates to "queen," and no other alternative translations appear for this part of her name; the dilemma lies with the first half. *Mór* has been attributed several different meanings. In most texts a mark of length appears over the *o* (ō or ó), but in some citations and glosses, the mark of length is omitted. With the mark of length, *mór* means "great" which would make her the "great queen." This translation is the most widely accepted one and probably the most accurate. If we accept this translation as the most accurate, it would suggest that her original function was concerned with sovereignty, making her a tutelary goddess rather than a goddess of war. We see similar names applied to other Celtic goddesses concerned with sovereignty, such as the Welsh Rhiannon, whose name also translates to "great queen" from a similar root, *rigani,* which also means "queen." There are also a surprising number of landmarks and earth works that bear the Morrigan's name or are associated with her, from the twin hills called the Paps of the Morrigan in County Meath to the Cave of Cruachan, which was said to be the Morrigan's dwelling place when she wasn't causing havoc. Her connection to fertility and sexuality also seems more appropriate to a goddess concerned with the land and its continued abundance rather than a goddess concerned solely with battle and strife.

Without the mark of length, *mor* has been connected to the old Irish word *muir,* which translates to "sea" or "water,"[1] making her the "sea queen." This is a more debatable translation, but it is interesting to note that the Morrigan was a river goddess and was associated with bodies of water. It also further connects the Morrigan with Morgan le Fay of Arthurian legends. Again, the *mor* in Morgan le Fay's name is spelled without the mark of length. "Morgans" were also a type of Breton sea nymph, reaffirming the name's connection to water and water spirits.

Whitley Stokes offers an additional translation, connecting *mor* to the Old English *maere,* a word that survives today in the English language as *nightmare.* While in modern English this word refers to a bad dream, *maere* originally referred to a phantom woman who usually bothered horses and cattle at night.[2] According to Stokes, this would make her the "phantom queen." The Morrigan is often equated with the Irish banshee, another spectral woman, making this translation seem appropriate. Yet another translation, suggested by Kim McCone, relates *mor* to the Indo-European word for death, suggesting her name to be the "queen of death." As a goddess of

1. Clark, *The Great Queens,* p. 22.
2. Ibid., p. 22.

battle, this name also seems appropriate. As the queen of death, the Morrigan is a ferrier who bring the souls of fallen warriors to rest in the Celtic Otherworld—not unlike the Norse Valkyrie or the Greek Charon.

No matter which translation you prefer, each meaning works on some level with the Morrigan. Her name provides us with clues to her original nature. She is a phantom queen, a sea queen, and—most important—the great queen, who bestows sovereignty and personifies the land. The only translation that associates her specifically with war is Kim McCone's, making it clear that war was not her sole original function. That is not to say that war and battle do not play a large role in the Morrigan's personality and mythology, but that connection evolved over time and came to overshadow her original role. While the Morrigan is a goddess of battle *par excellence*, it is not her only title.

With a better understanding of her name, and possibly her original place in the Celtic pantheon, we must take a closer look at the culture from which the Morrigan originated. The world we now live in is vastly different from that of the ancient Celts, and we cannot pretend to understand the myths and stories they left behind without first attempting to understand their world.

1

The Celts

The ancient Celts capture the modern imagination as do few other people of classical times. Naked barbarians charging the Roman legions, Druids performing sacrifices ... women fighting beside their men and even leading armies—these ... are the images most of us call to mind when we think of the Celts.

—*Philip Freeman,* War, Women, and Druids

Contrary to popular belief, the Celts were not a unified people. They consisted of small tribes and clans that migrated from what is now eastern Europe sometime around 2000 BCE. They eventually occupied land within twenty-five present-day countries, including parts of Austria, southern Germany, Switzerland, northern Greece, Spain, and northern Italy, and they made their way as far west as Wales, Scotland, England, and Ireland. They were primarily tribal herders, cattle being a very important part of their culture and appearing frequently in their myths as symbols of status and wealth. They spoke a common dialect and enjoyed making war on each other almost as much as they enjoyed fighting with their neighbors.

Unlike the ancient civilizations around them, the Celts did not commit their knowledge to paper, relying instead on their priestly caste, the Druids, to preserve their collective cultural knowledge through memory in what was a purely oral tradition. To the Celts the spoken word held power. Words could be used to curse or heal, or they could summon up the images of the gods through the intricately woven stories of a bard. Words held a potent magick, and when the spoken word was entombed on paper, it lost its mystery. Unfortunately it is because of the nature of this oral tradition that we know so little about the Celts, especially their myths and religion. What we do know comes from archeology, ancient Roman and Greek writers, and the remnants of their oral tradition, which was later committed to paper by the early Irish monks, each text coming to us along with the individual author's cultural baggage and prejudices.

Although viewed by the Greeks and Romans as uncivilized barbarians, the Celts were a very clean people. They used soap, particularly to wash their hair, before the Romans did. (The Romans did not adopt soap for the use of washing until 2 CE, instead using oil for bathing.) They had a great love for ornamental jewelry, which was worn by both men and women. Celtic clothing consisted of trousers and sleeved tunics for men and long sleeveless tunics for women. Both men's and women's clothes were commonly dyed in bright colors. Women made use of cosmetics, which included using the juice from berries to darken their eyebrows and roan as blush. They even painted their nails.[3] Both men and women wore their hair long, and men favored long mustaches. They lived in villages without fortified walls, in circular homes with thatched domelike roofs. During times of war, they built hill forts for protection. Accounts from both the Greeks and Romans claim the Celts loved the consumption of beer and other spirits almost as much as they loved to make war, and it's clear that their contemporary cultures viewed them as a very rowdy bunch.

The legal rights ancient Celtic women enjoyed far exceeded the rights of their contemporaries in other cultures. The Greek historian Plutarch wrote that Celtic women traditionally acted as judges and mediators in both military and political disputes. A Celtic woman could legally own land and inherit property. Marriage was viewed as a partnership, in contrast to Roman law, where women were viewed as the property of their spouses. A Celtic woman could divorce her husband if he did not provide her with enough food or did not satisfy her sexually, and she could even expect the return of her dowry if the union ended in divorce. Other reasons for divorce included the husband striking his wife or if he rejected her for another woman. Celtic marriage was, according to historian Jean Markale, "essentially contractual, social, not at all religious, but based on the freedom of the husband and wife."[4]

Their chief religious leaders were the Druids. We know from Caesar's *The Gallic Wars* (Caesar's firsthand account of his military campaigns against the Gallic tribes) that Druids presided over public rituals and functioned as advisors to kings. They had

3. Conway, *Celtic Magic*, p. 86.
4. Markale, *Women of the Celts*, p. 5.

three groupings—Bards, Ovates, and Druids—each with specific functions and training. "Among all the Gallic peoples, generally speaking, there are three sets of men who are held in exceptional honor: the Bards, the Vates [*sic*], and the Druids. The Bards are singers and poets; the Vates, diviners and natural philosophers; while the Druids, in addition to natural philosophy, study also moral philosophy."[5] The training the Druids underwent was extensive, lasting as long as twenty years according to some claims. As a purely oral culture, it would have been expected that an initiate memorize vast amounts of information, including the genealogies of the gods and kings, and the many myths and teaching stories of their tradition.

Despite historical evidence that places women within their ranks, it is often assumed that the Druids were all men. In classical texts female Druids were referred to as *Bandruaid* (also called *banfhlaith* and *banfhilid*), which meant "Druid woman." In Lampridius's account of the life of Roman Emperor Alexander Severus (d. 235 CE), a prophetic warning is given to the emperor by a Druidess: "As he went to war, a Druid prophetess cried out in the Gallic tongue, 'Go, but do not hope for victory, and put no trust in your soldiers.'"[6] Several Celtic sagas make references to female Druids, usually fulfilling the role of a seer, such as in *The Cattle Raid of Cooley,* where a Druidess named Fidelma foresees doom for Queen Maeve's army. The legendary Druid Mogh Roith was trained by the female Druid Banbhuana. Given that early Celtic women enjoyed equal legal status with men, it is unlikely that women would have been excluded from the Celtic priesthood. According to modern Druid Isaac Bonewits, "The idea that all the ancient druids were men is, in large part, the result of Christian censorship of Classical, Irish, and Welsh references to the female half of the Druidic caste. While there are dozens of such references remaining, they are negative and are vastly outnumbered by the ones referring to male druids. This is in keeping with both Greek and Roman sexism. It also supports the historical Christian preference that women be excluded from positions of spiritual power."[7]

The Celts were renowned for their prowess in battle. Aristotle claimed the Celts feared nothing: "neither earthquake nor waves of the sea."[8] Many of the Celtic sagas left to us today and much of Celtic folklore revolve around epic battles and the bravery—and often tragic demises—of heroes. For the Irish Celts, warfare primarily

5. Jones, *The Geography of Strabo,* p. 247.
6. Lampridius, *The Life of Severus Alexander,* trans. by David Magie, 1924.
7. Bonewits, *Bonewits' Essential Guide to Druidism,* p. 51.
8. Ellis, *A Brief History of the Druids,* p. 27.

consisted of cattle raids. This of course is reflected in the gods they connected to warfare and, as we will discuss later on, the Morrigan enjoyed nothing better than stealing cattle.

War was a common occurrence to the ancient Celts. The clan's security and survival relied heavily on their warriors. Modern warfare is more often than not fought over political and religious interests, which may be why we have such a hard time relating to the Celts' exaltation of war. We no longer live in a time where we have to fear another nation will attack us to steal our food, resources, or land. But to the ancient Celts, it was the ultimate glory to be recognized for one's prowess in battle, since war was necessary to keep one's land and family safe. They honored their warriors for the same reasons we respect our firefighters, armed forces, and police officers—because they keep us safe. Their reverence for warfare can also be seen in the craftsmanship and artwork used to make their weapons. Elaborately decorated weapons, some inlaid with gold and ivory, have been found in lakes and rivers and were most likely offered as a sacrifice to the gods for favorable battles. This tradition remained in later myths of King Arthur, who received his sword from the Lady of the Lake and subsequently threw it into a body of water when he lay dying.

Both men and women could be warriors and fight in battle. According to Tacitus, a philosopher in first-century Rome, "In Britain there is no rule of distinction to exclude the female line from the throne, or the command of armies."[9] Boudicca of the Iceni tribe is perhaps the most well-known woman to have led a Celtic army, but she is not the only example. Onomaris, a cheiftainess of the Galatian Celts, led her people in their battles against the Illyrians of the Balkans.[10] In Celtic mythology we find several examples of female warriors such as Queen Maeve of Connacht, Macha Mong Ruad, and the warrior woman Scáthach who trained the hero Cúchulain. There are many historical references to the ferocity Celtic women displayed on the battlefield. I find it very amusing that we today view women as too weak or too emotional to be allowed to serve in the military whereas ancient military leaders feared Celtic women taking to the battlefield more than their men. Ammianus Marcellinus, a historian of the fourth century, wrote that "a whole band of foreigners will be unable to cope with one [Gaul] in a fight, if he calls in his wife, stronger than he by far and with flashing eyes; least of all when she swells her neck and gnashes her teeth, and poising her

9. Ibid., p. 94.
10. Ellis, *Celtic Women*, p. 80.

huge white arms, begins to rain blows mingled with kicks, like shots discharged by the twisted cords or a catapult."[11]

According to old Irish law, daughters who inherited land were liable for military service or for arming a kinsman on her behalf. Owning land meant one had an obligation to defend it, regardless of the gender of the landholder. If she did not do so, she could only claim half her inheritance. In Tara, the sacred center of Ireland, there was even a mound honoring fallen female heroes called *Cnoc na mBan-Laoch* or The Hill of the Woman-Heroes. It wasn't until 697 CE that women were banned from participating in warfare. A bishop later known as Saint Adamnain was said to have drafted the law at the request of his mother, who had been disturbed by the sight of dead female warriors upon a battlefield.

In 43 CE the Romans began a large-scale invasion of the British Isles. While they were met with several years of resistance, the efficiency of the Roman legion eventually led to their victory over the Celtic tribes in southern England, Wales, and part of Scotland. Many tribes chose to become "client kingdoms," allying themselves with Rome rather than being overrun. The Romans inevitably left their mark on Celtic culture, introducing new developments in agriculture, trade, and urbanization. The Romans began building cities, such as Lodinium (which we know today as London), and importing products from the continent. While the Celts had generally lived in small tribal families prior to the Roman invasion, large trading cities began to build up around Roman forts. The Celts also took up the Roman fashion of worship and began creating statues and carved images of their deities; previously they had connected the identities of the gods to sacred mounds and the features of the land. Although the Druids stoutly refused to commit any of their knowledge to paper, written language was introduced in the form of Latin. In Ireland, Celtic culture remained intact the longest, most likely because of the island's relative isolation. A few Roman forts were established on the Irish coast, but they were primarily used for trade, and the island managed to avoid Roman invasion. Written language wasn't introduced to the Irish Celts until the fifth century with the arrival of Saint Patrick.

Understanding the Celts, their beliefs, and the world and society they lived in is essential to understanding their mythology. The Celtic idolization of warfare, their migrations across Europe, and their social structure and gender norms are all reflected in their myths and sagas, and these influences ultimately show in how they

11. Marcellinus, *The Roman History of Ammianus Marcellinus*, p. 80.

viewed their gods. In the Morrigan we can see their love of warfare, the pride they took in protecting their land and loved ones, and their positive attitude toward women in general. She reflects the Celtic ideal of a woman of power. She is both fierce and beautiful, as likely to share a man's bed as she is to fight beside him on the battlefield. She is a reflection of both Celtic culture and its ideals.

2

The Morrigan in Celtic Mythology

Myths are our maps to the mysteries
codes that unlock their secrets.

—*Edain McCoy,* Celtic Women's Spirituality

Our knowledge of Celtic mythology comes from narrative texts transcribed by Irish monks between the eighth and twelfth centuries CE. By the time these stories were committed to paper, Christianity was the dominant religion in Ireland, and its influence can be seen in the biblical references that were added to the texts. We can only assume that these stories are not the original versions, and that certain aspects of these stories that may have had hidden psycho-spiritual meaning to the Pagan Celts may have been edited or altered by those who were looking at these "teaching stories" in a purely literal sense.

We know from the accounts of Caesar and other ancient historians that the Celtic spiritual tradition was purely oral. Stories were committed to memory and passed down from generation to generation. Druids underwent several years of intensive training to develop the memory and concentration required for learning hundreds of verses, histories, stories, and genealogies. The Celts relied on the Druids as the living repositories of their history and mythology. Bards distributed news from village to village and recited cultural stories and histories; the Druids enacted the seasonal rites and made offerings to the gods, ensuring the turning of the seasons and the spiritual welfare of the tribe.

It is not easy for us today to conceive of a purely oral culture, but the spoken word held great power and mystery for the Celts. The Druids used the spoken word to invoke the gods, cast spells, and perform magick. The myths themselves took on a kind of divine power. In retelling the heroics of the Celtic gods, the listener could gain some of the power the gods exemplified in the story. Repeating these stories may have been seen as an act of magick. According to Edain McCoy, the word *Cath,* which we find in the title of the first two tales we will be exploring, "refers to a type of epic story or myth concerning war which was told as an act of sympathetic magick on the eve of battle. In keeping with the high placement of the art of storytelling in Celtic society, such sessions were referred to until well into the twentieth century as 'the blessing of the story.'"[12]

Although the Druids did have the Ogham, a magickal alphabet that archeologists have found carved onto grave stones and boundary markers, it was not used to record any of the Druids' teachings. Memorization was highly prized, and there was a taboo against writing down any of the Druids' stories or teachings. Whether there was a spiritual belief behind the taboo or a political motivation, we will never know. Unfortunately this has limited our knowledge of the Druids and ancient Celtic spiritual philosophy. What remains today was not recorded by Druids or Pagans, but instead by early Christians. While we owe the monks who preserved these myths a debt of gratitude for preserving some part of the Celtic tradition, we must learn to look at these stories in a much different way than those who recorded them for posterity. In their earliest form, these narratives were used as "teaching stories," rich with symbolism and hidden layers of meaning. Besides acting as oral histories for the Celts, these stories illustrated and taught spiritual lessons. When approached as mere historical events or even inventive fiction, one fails to look past the events described to understand the inner workings of the story.

It is quite evident from the way the monks transcribed these stories that they saw them as literal events. Their motivation for preserving these tales was most likely not to preserve the Pagan traditions of the past, but to record what they thought of as a historical account of Irish pre-history. Throughout these stories, the monks added biblical references to align with what they felt was an accurate historic timeline. In the *Lebor Gabála Érenn* there are several different groups of deities that invade Ireland. For example, Cessair was the first woman to set foot in Ireland. She is most likely an ancestral goddess but is treated as a mortal woman in the first written texts, in which we are told Cessair and her people came to Ireland to escape the biblical flood. (Apparently she couldn't hitch a ride with Noah.) The mention of Noah and the great

---

12. McCoy, *Celtic Women's Spirituality,* p. 43.

flood—which have no real bearing on Cessair's story and have no place in the mythology of the Pagan Celts—was added solely as an indicator of time. If the monks saw these stories as mythology or fiction, there wouldn't have been any reason to relate them to events on "their" timeline, making it obvious that they saw them as actual events that took place in the distant past.

The myths we will be exploring come from a variety of sources. Those concerning the arrival of the Celtic gods in Ireland and the Morrigan's participation in their battles with the rival indigenous gods come from the *Lebor Gabála Érenn,* known in English as *The Book of Invasions.* There are several different versions of *The Book of Invasions* recorded in various surviving manuscripts, the earliest of which dates back to 1150 CE. Like the *Lebor Gabála Érenn,* the *Táin Bó Cúailnge (The Cattle Raid of Cooley),* which details the Morrigan's famous encounters with the hero Cúchulain, can be found in several manuscripts as well, the most complete of which is in *The Book of Leinster,* written sometime between 1151 CE and 1201 CE. It was used as a source book for later Irish manuscripts, such as *The Yellow Book of Lecan,* and contains a variety of Irish myths, poetry, a list of kings for various provinces in Ireland, grammar, and information about the lives of the saints. The Morrigan also appears in the *Dindshenchas,* a series of 176 poems and prose pieces relating the origins of Irish place-names, which was compiled sometime in the twelfth century.

Throughout Irish mythology, the Morrigan appears in several forms and is referred to by several different interchangeable names. She is not simply one goddess but three. In many cases "the Morrigan" is used more or less like a title for the three sisters Badb, Macha, and Anu. In triple form, she is never referred to as "Morrigan"; she is "*the* Morrigan" or "*the* Morrigu," further indicating the name's use as a title for the three goddesses. In some stories, the goddess Nemain is also added to the group, although this is most likely due to Nemain and Badb being confused for one another. All of the Morrigan's names were used interchangeably, showing that the authors of these manuscripts saw the three goddesses as different aspects of the same being. She may be referred to as Macha in one paragraph, then as Badb a few passages later.

The texts to these stories are quite lengthy. *The Cattle Raid of Cooley* itself is over five hundred pages long, making it impossible to present all of the Morrigan's myths here in their entirety. In the following retellings, I have included quotes from the actual texts and a summary of their events.

The First Battle of Moytura
THE CATH MUIGHE TUIREADH

The Tuatha Dé came with a great fleet unto Ireland to take it per force from the Fir Bolg. They burnt their barques ... and the smoke and the mist that came from the vessels filled the neighboring land and air. Therefore it was conceived that they had arrived in clouds of mist.

—*Whitley Stokes,* Cath Maige Tuiread

Like the Celts themselves, their gods, the Túatha Dé Danann, migrated from another land, descending on the shores of Ireland in a cloud of mist. Upon their arrival, the Túatha Dé Danann found the land already inhabited by an older race of deities, the Fir Bolgs. The Fir Bolgs are described as misshapen and ugly, while the Túatha Dé Danann were strong and beautiful. Not unlike the struggle between the Olympians and the Titans, the Túatha Dé Danann represented the new lawful order taking over the old and chaotic one.

After landing, the Túatha Dé Danann sent out one of their champions, the god Bres, to offer the Fir Bolgs peace so long as they gave up half of Ireland to the Túatha Dé Danann. Their offer, of course, was refused. While the Túatha Dé Danann moved to better ground, the Morrigan used her magick to distract the Fir Bolgs, allowing the Túatha Dé Danann the time they needed to prepare for battle. "Badb and Macha and Morrigan went to the Knoll of the Taking of the Hostages, and to the Hill of Summoning of Hosts at Tara, and sent forth magickshowers of sorcery and compact clouds of mist and a furious rain of fire, with a downpour of red blood from the air on the warriors' heads; and they allowed the Fir Bolg neither rest nor stay for three days and nights."[13]

Here the Morrigan acts as both a goddess of war and magick. Her primary weapons in war are almost always spells and incantations. The result of these spells manifest through one of the four elements. In this case, the illusion she creates is connected to water (the mist and blood-colored rain) and fire (showers of fire).

13. Fraser, "The First Battle of Moytura," *Ériu,* p. 34.

The distraction worked, and the Túatha Dé Danann now prepared for the upcoming battle by indulging in a round of boasting about the feats they would perform in the upcoming fight. Amidst the boasting, the Morrigan declared her intention to join the battle: "We will go with you, said the women, that is, Badb, Macha, Morrigan, and Danu."[14]

In the *Cath Muighe Tuireadh* (and in much of the Morrigan's mythology), she is not always referred to as a single being but as a trio of goddesses. The three goddesses that make up the collective being we know as the Morrigan change from story to story or even within the same tale. Each is a facet of a complex personality. Here the Morrigan is associated with the goddess Danu, the mother goddess of the Túatha Dé Danann. She is linked with this goddess in several passages, either as her foster mother or as one of the goddesses in her trinity.

During the battle with the Fir Bolgs, the Morrigan—in her guise as a battle fury—cried out, striking fear into hearts of the Fir Bolgs: "The [B]adba and monsters and hags of doom cried out so that they were heard from the cliffs and waterfalls and in the hollows of the earth."[15] Even in her more terrifying aspects, she is still linked with the land, "the hollows of the earth" and bodies of water, in this case "waterfalls," reminding us that the land and its waters are part of her realm.

Once the battle began, the Morrigan marked the boundaries of the battlefield with magickal pillars, making it impossible for either army to retreat: "The three sorceresses, Badb, Macha and Morrigan; Be Chuille and Danu, their two foster mothers. They fixed their pillars in the ground least anyone flee."[16] Trapping the Túatha Dé Danann may seem counterproductive, but the Morrigan's objective was to instigate change. Change is never easy and we often fight against it, preferring things to stay the way they are. By denying the armies a way to escape the confrontation, she forces the Túatha Dé Danann to overcome their enemy. If they did not fight to the best of their abilities and use all their strength and cunning, they would be doomed. She is reminiscent of a Witch casting her circle, holding control over what happens in her sphere of influence.

In the end, the Túatha Dé Danann defeated the Fir Bolgs and sent them into exile. By defeating the older chaotic order of gods, the Túatha Dé Danann claimed Ireland and established themselves as the supreme deities of the land. As an earth

14. Epstein, *War Goddess*, p. 78.
15. Ibid., p. 78.
16. Fraser, "The First Battle of Moytura," *Ériu*, p. 48.

goddess, the Morrigan is connected to the sovereignty of the land. The battle against the Fir Bolgs is a test in a way: the Túatha Dé Danann had to prove themselves worthy of ruling their new home, in this case by winning the battle, before she would grant them sovereignty over Ireland.

The Second Battle of Moytura
THE CATH MAIGE TUIRED

In the *Cath Maige Tuired* the Morrigan plays several roles. Although she is not always the main protagonist of the story, she influenced the battle from the sidelines. She delivered a prophecy of the future, encouraged the Túatha Dé Danann to go to war, and used her magick to ensure victory.

The Second Battle of Moytura began shortly after Bres became king of the Túatha Dé Danann. Unfortunately power seemed to go to Bres's head and he became a very unpopular king. He lacked generosity, insulted poets, and forced the Túatha Dé Danann to pay humiliating tributes to another race of deities, the Fomorians. He forced the god Ogma to carry firewood for the Fomorians and the god Dagda to dig trenches around their forts.

The Fomorians were a race of seagoing deities who had made several raids against the previous divine inhabitants of Ireland. The name "Fomorian" comes from the Gaelic *faoi-mhuir,* which means "beneath the sea," and this may be why they were thought to live underneath the waves. The Túatha Dé Danann had maintained an alliance with this sea-faring race, which produced several gods with lineages from both races. Bres was born from one of these unions, and after becoming king, he seemed to favor his Fomorian kin more than the Túatha Dé Danann.

Eventually Bres's lack of hospitality caught up with him. After failing to uphold the standards of generosity required of a king, he was dethroned. The enraged Bres then enlisted the aid of his Fomorian kin and began raising an army to take back his throne.

With war imminent, the Túatha Dé Danann gathered to plan the coming battle. Since it had been prophesied that only the god Lugh could defeat the Fomorian leader, the Morrigan confronted him and encouraged him to fight in the coming battle: "Then she said to him, 'Undertake a battle of overthrowing.' The Morrigan said to Lug[h], 'Awake…'."[17] Lugh was also given magickal weapons by the "Three Gods

17. Gray, "The Second Battle of Mag Tuired," verse 83.

of Danu"—Luchar, Lucharba, and Brian—who were named as sons of the Morrigan (instead of from Danu) in one version of the *Lebor Gabála Érenn.*

On the eve of Samhain, while the Túatha Dé Danann were gathering their army, they sent the god Dagda to delay the Fomorian attack and to spy on the enemy. While searching for the Fomorians, Dagda happened upon the Morrigan while she was washing herself in a river: "Nine loosened tresses were on her head. The Dagdae [Dagda] conversed with her, and they make a union. 'The Bed of the Couple' is the name of the stead thenceforward. The woman that is here mentioned is the Morrígan."[18] Dagda had sex with the Morrigan astride the river, and she was so pleased with his performance that she prophesied victory for the Túatha Dé Danann. She also told Dagda where the Fomorians would land and pledged to help in the coming battle, specifically by killing Indech, one of the leaders of the Fomorians. (It is not specifically mentioned how the Morrigan knows where the enemy were planning to land, but as she had a vision of the Túatha Dé Danann emerging from the battle victorious, it can be assumed that she also used her second sight to learn this information.)

The Morrigan's coupling with Dagda is one of her most well-known appearances in Celtic mythology and is rich with symbolism. Dagda, whose name means "the good God," was known for his immense appetite for both food and sex. He is often portrayed as a comical figure, able to laugh at himself and ready to enjoy everything life has to offer. In many ways he was the Morrigan's polar opposite, representing life, mirth, and abundance. Together they represent the full spectrum of the life cycle; life and death meet and join as one through the union of the god of life and abundance with the goddess of death and rebirth.

According to Carl McColman and Kathryn Hinds, this union illustrates the intimate connection the Celts saw between life, death, and rebirth: "Celtic wisdom, however, reminds us that the union of the energies of life and death is closer than most of us would care to admit. Hence the goddess of war couples with the god of abundance at the threshold between the light and dark halves of the year ... Out of the union of death and life comes renewal, expressed through her words of wisdom and foresight from the spiritual realm."[19]

After his union with the Morrigan, Dagda found the enemy camp. The Fomorians offered Dagda an enormous amount of food, hoping he would not be able to finish the portion, thereby insulting the Fomorian's hospitality and giving them an excuse

18. Stokes, "The Second Battle of Moytura," *Revue Celtique* v. 12, p. 85.
19. McColman and Hinds, *Magic of the Celtic Gods and Goddesses,* p. 57.

to kill him: "They fill for him the king's caldron, five fists deep, into which went four-score gallons of new milk and the like quantity of meal and fat. Goats and sheep and swine are put into it, and they are all boiled together with the porridge ... and Indech told him that he would be put to death unless he consumed it all; he should eat his fill so that he might not reproach the Fomorians with inhospitality."[20]

Dagda finished all the food the Fomorians offered him and returned to the Túatha Dé Danann. On his way back, he was mocked by the daughter of one of the Fomorian kings for having such a large belly (from consuming all that porridge). In a surprising twist, Dagda also had sex with her and, like the Morrigan, she also offered to aid him after their coupling: "She said that she would hinder the Fomoire, and she would sing spells against them ... and she alone would take on a ninth part of the host."[21]

Like the Morrigan, this unnamed Fomorian woman used magick as a weapon in battle and we find a reference to the number nine, a number often connected with the Morrigan. In this case the number refers to destroying one-ninth of the Fomorian army, rather than the nine braids in the Morrigan's hair. This woman also offers to kill part of the Fomorian host, mirroring the Morrigan's offer to kill one of the Fomorian kings in battle. Most likely these unions were two separate versions of the same myth that eventually became combined.

When Dagda finally rejoined the Túatha Dé Danann, the gods boasted in turn about what they would do in the upcoming battle with the Fomorians. When asked what the Morrigan will bring to the fray, she answered: "Not hard to say ... I have stood fast; I shall pursue what was watched; I will be able to kill; I will be able to destroy those who might be subdued."[22]

Finally the Túatha Dé Danann and the Fomorians met in battle. Fulfilling the prophecy, Lugh killed the Fomorian king; but even leaderless, the Fomorians proved difficult to defeat. The battle was not won until the Morrigan used her powers to encourage the Túatha Dé Danann into a battle frenzy: "Then the Morrígan, daughter of Ernmas, came, and was heartening the Tuatha Dea to fight the battle fiercely and fervently. So then she sang ... 'Kings arise to the battle.'"[23] Her singing was treated in much the same way as a Witch's spell or incantation. Her words held power and could instill strength into the bodies and souls of the warriors she favored.

20. Stokes, "The Second Battle of Moytura," *Revue Celtique* v. 12, pp. 85–87.

21. Gray, "The Second Battle of Mag Tuired," verse 93.

22. Ibid., verse 107.

23. Stokes,"The Second Battle of Moytura," *Revue Celtique,* v. 12, p. 101.

After defeating the Fomorians, the Morrigan proclaimed the victory for the Túatha Dé Danann and delivered a prophecy. The first part of the prophecy foretold prosperity; the second, the end of the word. That she foresees abundance to be followed by ill fortune may be a reflection of the Morrigan's cyclical nature as a goddess of life, death, and rebirth. Fruitfulness must eventually lead to barrenness and decay. Summer will always give way to fall and winter, and we all must die in order to be reborn. The monks who wrote down these stories had a linear view of the world, with a clear beginning and end to things. In Christian myths there is a distinct beginning and end of the world. There is salvation after death but no rebirth, which would have been a foreign concept to their Pagan ancestors, who viewed everything as part of an unending cycle. Not understanding this, the Irish monks most likely saw the grim second part of the prophecy as a permanent state of doom and interpreted it as the end of the world. Modern critics have claimed that the Morrigan's prophecy predicted the Irish potato famine:

> The Morrigan, the daughter of Ernmas, proceeded to proclaim the battle and the mighty victory which had taken place, to the royal heights of Ireland and to its fairy hosts, to its chief waters and to its rivermouths. And hence it is that Badb also describes high deeds ...
>
> *"Peace high as heaven,*
> *heaven to the earth,*
> *earth under heaven,*
> *strength in everyone,*
> *Cup's great fullness,*
> *Fullness of honey,*
> *mead til satiety.*
> *summer in winter ..."*
>
> Then, moreover, she was prophesying the end of the world ...
>
> *"I shall not see a world that will be dear to me.*
> *Summer without flowers,*
> *Kine will be without milk ..."*[24]

24. Stokes,"The Second Battle of Moytura," *Revue Celtique,* v. 12, pp. 109–11.

Again we see the Morrigan's connection to the land and bodies of water in the list of places to which she proclaims the prophecy, "the royal hills," the "lakes and rivermouths."

While the Morrigan's interactions with her fellow gods led them to victory, her encounters with mortal heroes do not turn out so well. This is mostly because mortal heroes spurned her help and wisdom, only realizing their mistakes after it was too late. Her most famous interaction with a mortal hero was with Cúchulain, whom we will meet in the next myth.

Cúchulain and the Morrigan

TÁIN BÓ REGAMNA AND THE BOYHOOD DEEDS OF CÚCHULAIN

The Morrigan's encounters with Cúchulain (KOO-cull-en) are perhaps her most infamous dealings with the mortal realm. It's no wonder the Morrigan would be interested in the hero—he is the quintessential warrior of Irish mythology. Even in his youth Cúchulain's exploits were legendary. His name meant "Hound of Culann," which he earned as a boy by accidently killing Culann's fierce guard dog, after which he offered to take the hound's place as a guardian of Ulster. When Cúchulain was given his arms, a Druid prophesied his deeds would make his name immortal but that he would die young. He was known for his prowess on the battlefield, having learned from the warrior woman Scáthach, who ran a school for warriors on a mysterious mist-shrouded island. To the Irish, there was no greater warrior.

The Morrigan appeared to Cúchulain at pivotal points in his life, first in his youth, then as an adult when faced with the daunting task of fighting Queen Maeve's army single-handedly, and once more prior to his death. The outcome of each encounter rests solely on Cúchulain's behavior toward the Morrigan. While it is clear she admired the warrior's skill and prowess and wished to aid him in his endeavors, he almost always spurned her aid and ignited her wrath.

There are two versions of Cúchulain's first encounter with the Morrigan. The first occurs in his youth and is told in *The Boyhood Deeds of Cúchulain,* a story that is related in *The Cattle Raid of Cooley,* and gives background information about the hero's early exploits. In *The Boyhood Deeds of Cúchulain,* the young hero encountered a phantom with only half of a head carrying a corpse. The phantom demanded that Cúchulain carry the corpse for him, which he refused to do and proceeded to battle the phantom. When the phantom threw him to the ground, Badb, in the form of a crow, appeared and began to mock him. Furious, Cúchulain knocked off the phantom's head with his hurley stick and then saved the king and his son from a battlefield of corpses. As Badb, the Morrigan prodded Cúchulain into action. The use of ridicule, or *gressacht,* to incite heroic deeds is a common Celt theme.[25]

The second version of their meeting can be found in the *Táin Bó Regamna* and occurs when Cúchulain is an adult. Cúchulain was woken by a terrible shriek coming from the northwest. (The Celts associated the northwest with spirits and the direction hints to the Otherworldly origin of the sound.) He was so startled by the cry that he forgot to dress and rushed outside naked to investigate. Thankfully his wife followed him and brought the hero his clothes and weapons. The Morrigan shakes even seasoned warriors to the core of their being. She strips us of our preconceptions and our self-imposed illusions, seeing us as we truly are, symbolized here by Cúchulain's nakedness.

Cúchulain and his charioteer went to discover the source of the horrible screams, and eventually come to *Ath de Ferta* (The Ford of the Two Chariots Poles). There they found a chariot harnessed to a horse with one leg, one eye, and one ear. In the chariot stood a striking woman with red hair and eyebrows and a red mantle wrapped around her shoulders. Beside her stood a man with a red coat, holding a hazel staff, leading an excellent-looking cow: "Then they saw the chariot come before them, and one red horse on it. The horse was one footed, and the pole of the chariot passed through the body of the horse. A red woman was in the chariot, and a red mantle about her, she had two red eyebrows. A great man was beside her chariot, a red cloak was upon him, and a forked staff of hazel at his back, he drove a cow in front of him."[26]

The Morrigan did not initially reveal who she was, but there were several hints in her description. The color red, which is commonly associated with the Morrigan, is present in both her description and that of her companion. The man's hazel staff is also another clue that this couple is really the Morrigan in disguise. The hazel was the ninth letter in the Ogham alphabet, a number linked to the Morrigan. Cúchulain also remained oblivious to the Otherworldly nature of the horse, which somehow managed to pull a chariot with a single leg. Cúchulain questioned the man about the

25. Rankine and D'Este, *The Guises of the Morrigan,* p. 19.
26. Leahy, *Heroic Romances of Ireland,* p. 132.

cow, telling him it was his job to protect the cattle of Ulster. The man did not respond, and the Morrigan chastised Cúchulain for challenging them, telling the hero he had no right to question her ownership of the cow. Angered, he asked for their names but got a string of nonsense words.

Furious that he is being made to look like a fool, Cúchulain leapt into the chariot and demanded the woman's name at sword point. Still not willing to reveal herself, especially not by force, she lied to Cúchulain, telling him she was a poet and the cow was a prize she won for her verses. Still not convinced, Cúchulain made her recite the poem, which she did once he agreed to remove himself from the chariot. Even after reciting the poem, he still didn't believe her story; as he prepared to jump into the chariot again, the woman, cow, man, and chariot vanished. In their place appeared a crow, and it was only in this form that Cúchulain finally realized who he had been speaking to.

> *"If only I had known is was you," said Cúchulainn, "not thus should we have separated."*
>
> *"What thou hast done," said she, "shall be evil to thee from it."*
>
> *"Thou hast no power against me," said Cúchulainn.*
>
> *"I have power indeed," said the woman, "it is at the guarding of thy death that I am; and I shall be," said she. "I brought this cow out of the fairy-mound of Cruachan, that she might breed by the Black Bull of Cualnge, that is the Bull of Daire Mae Fiachna. It is up to that time that thou art in life, so long as the calf which is in this cow's body is a yearling; and it is this that shall lead to the Tain Bo Cualnge."*
>
> *"I shall myself be all the more glorious for that Tain," said Cúchulainn."*[27]

Angered by Cúchulain's actions and bold statement, the Morrigan vowed to wound him in battle three times, first in the form of an eel, than as a she-wolf, and finally as a heifer. In turn, Cúchulain vowed to deal three wounds to the Morrigan. An identical exchange is repeated in *The Cattle Raid of Cooley*.

Here the cow connects the Morrigan to the wealth of the land. Cúchulain questions her ownership of the cow, and in doing so is questioning her sovereignty over the land. Even after she reveals herself, he questions her power, telling her she has no

27. Ibid, p. 136.

authority over him. Finally she must remind him that she holds his life in the balance. Telling Cúchulain that she is "guarding" his death is a very ambiguous statement. She does not say she will *cause* his demise, but rather *guard* it. This implies that if Cúchulain recognizes her sovereignty and respects her power, he can alter his fate. Like any mortal, Cúchulain has a choice: he can grow past his current limitations or remain stagnant. The Morrigan is warning Cúchulain, foretelling his doom if he does not alter his current life path. Throughout his myths, Cúchulain is arrogant and acts for his own glory and fame, which eventually leads him to kill both his best friend and his own son. Based on his later actions, the Morrigan is clearly giving Cúchulain a wakeup call; alas, he ignores it.

The Cattle Raid of Cooley
The Táin Bó Cúalnge

In the *Táin Bó Cúalnge* we encounter Maeve (also spelled Medb), the queen of Connacht and one of Cúchulain's greatest enemies. As with Cúchulain, the Morrigan's relationship with Maeve is not always clear. The Cave of Cruachan, said to be the Morrigan's home, stood adjacent to Maeve's fortress in Connacht, which seems to indicate she favored Connacht and their queen in some way. At times the Morrigan aids Maeve on the battlefield, usually to spite Cúchulain; on other occasions, she kills hundreds of Maeve's warriors.

Maeve's name means "intoxicating one" or "drunk woman." The root of her name shares the same origins as *mead,* a wine made from honey. She was the daughter of High King Eochu Fedlech. Her father granted her rulership over Connaught, one of the provinces of Ireland, linking her to the sovereignty of the land. She was one of six sisters (a number sacred to the goddess). "I was the goodliest of them in bounty and gift-giving, in riches and treasures. 'Twas I was best of them in battle and strife and combat."[28] Maeve was quite sexual, and it took thirty men to satisfy her in a single night. Both her sexuality and her link to the land are reminiscent of the Morrigan. She survived in later Celtic folklore as the faery queen Madb, similar to the Morrigan's transformation into Morgan le Fay and the banshee.

In some stories, Maeve is the daughter of the Red Woman, Crochan Crogderg, who was the handmaiden of the goddess Étain. Crochan Crogderg was said to have given birth to the queen inside the Cave of Cruachan. While the cave was named

28. Dunn, *The Ancient Irish Epic Tale Táin Bó Cúailnge,* ch. 1.

after Crochan Crogderg, it was also listed as the home of the Morrigan in the *Dindshenchas,* a text detailing the lore of Irish place-names. If the cave is the Morrigan's home, then perhaps the red-skinned Crochan Crogderg is the Morrigan in another form. Both she and Crochan Crogderg are described in Celtic literature as "red" women, a color closely linked with the Otherworlds. If they were in fact the same goddess, then the warrior-queen Maeve may be a daughter of the Morrigan. We can only guess at whether the ancient Celts saw a connection between the two, but the parallels between their stories are interesting.

Maeve's story is certainly rich with goddess symbolism. Most likely she was originally a goddess and was later transformed into a mortal queen as her importance or worship diminished. She had several husbands, none of whom could be granted kingship unless they wed her. In the Celtic tradition, kings symbolically wed the land and its goddess. Only the goddess could make a king, and his union with her linked the ruler to the land in a tangible way. If the king was disfigured or ill, this was believed to manifest in the health and prosperity of the land. The fact that no man could become king without wedding Maeve clearly shows her divine origins. Maeve was also said to run faster than a horse and wore live birds across her shoulders. When she urinated, the water she passed created rivers. This ability to shape the land also marks her as an earth goddess, as does the gigantic stature needed to be able to accomplish such a feat. Many figures in Celtic mythology are described as giants to emphasize their divine nature. It is possible that there was a mortal queen who bore the same name and over time her story and the myths of the goddess merged. I leave to the reader to decide whether she is the Morrigan's daughter, a goddess of sovereignty, or a mortal queen. Nevertheless, Maeve is also a potent symbol of sovereignty and personal power, worthy of more exploration by modern Pagans.

The *Táin Bó Cúalnge* (which I will henceforth refer to as the *Táin*) begins with pillow-talk between Maeve and her husband Ailill, which results in an argument. Ailill comments that she is better off with him as her husband than she was before their marriage.

"'True is the saying, lady, 'She is a well-off woman that is a rich man's wife.'" Maeve disagrees, saying "As well off was I before I ever saw thee."[29] They continue to argue about who is the wealthier of the two, which is synonymous for who is the most powerful in the relationship and thus the true sovereign of the kingdom. If

29. Ibid.

Maeve does in fact have more wealth than Ailill, her claim to the throne of Connacht is legitimate. If Ailill is wealthier than his queen, he, in effect, is the true ruler. This is far more than a petty argument fueled by pride and greed. They are arguing over who is the legitimate sovereign of their realm.

Determined to win the argument, Maeve has all their possessions brought before them. "Then were brought to them the least precious of their possessions that they might know which of them had the more treasures, riches and wealth. Their pails and their cauldrons and their iron-wrought vessels, their jugs and their keeves and their eared pitches were fetched."[30] They were equal in everything until their cattle were brought before them. Ailill has a white bull that Maeve had no equal to. Maeve immediately sets out to find a bull to rival Ailill's in order to reclaim her sovereignty, both over the land and in her relationship with Ailill. When she is told such a bull exists in Ulster, she offers the owner treasures, land, and even an invitation to her bed in exchange for the animal. Her offer is refused, and Maeve—not one to take no for an answer—prepares to take the bull by force.

Fortunately for Maeve, the men of Ulster are under a curse placed on them by the goddess Macha, one of the three goddesses that form the Morrigan's triple nature. Macha was forced to race the king of Ulster's horses while heavily pregnant. She won the race (giving birth to twins afterward) and cursed the men of Ulster to suffer her labor pains when their strength was most needed.

When Maeve's army attacks, the men of Ulster become incapacitated by the curse, leaving Cúchulain to defend Ulster single-handed. In some versions of the *Táin,* Cúchulain is unaffected by the curse because of his semi-divine nature (being the son of the god Lugh); in other versions, he is spared because he was not born in Ulster or because he had a "baby face," not yet having grown a beard, as Macha's curse only affected the bearded men of Ulster.

Impressed with Cúchulain's prowess in battle, the Morrigan appears to Cúchulain while he guards a river crossing. Again she does not immediately reveal her true nature but comes to the hero disguised as the daughter of a king. The Morrigan offers the hero her love, but Cúchulain refuses her affection, telling her "It wasn't for a woman's backside I took on this ordeal!"[31] The Morrigan then offers to help him in the battle instead, but Cúchulain rejects her a second time. Not to be dismissed, she tells him "Then I'll hinder... When you are busiest in the fight I'll come against

30. Ibid., ch. 2.

31. Kinsella, *The Táin,* p. 133.

you."[32] She vows to attack him in battle three times, in the shape of an eel, a she-wolf, and a heifer. Unfazed, Cúchulain promises to wound her three times as well. Because of Cúchulain's divine nature, any wound he inflicted on an enemy could not be healed without his blessing, a blessing he also vows never to give to her. (An identical exchange is given in the *Táin Bó Regamna* after Cúchulain learns the Morrigan's true identity. Most likely this is due to regional variations of the *Táin* and the tales of Cúchulain's exploits, which resulted in different versions of the hero's encounter with the goddess.)

In effect, the Morrigan offers Cúchulain victory, first by offering to mate with him and then by offering her aid in battle. But Cúchulain seems intent on gaining victory without anyone's aid, especially a woman's.

When Cúchulain battles one of Maeve's champions, Loch, the Morrigan fulfills her promise. She attacks him, first in the form of a white red-eared heifer; then as a black eel, coiling around Cúchulain's feet while he fights Loch in a river; and finally in the shape of a grey-red wolf. Although she wounds Cúchulain, he also manages to wound the goddess in each of her animal forms. Unfortunately for the Morrigan, any wounds dealt by the hero could not be healed without his blessing, so she devises a way to trick Cúchulain into healing her.

After the battle, Cúchulain becomes overcome with thirst. Here the Morrigan shape-shifts yet again, this time into an old hag. In this form Cúchulain encounters her leading a three-teated cow and begs for a drink of the cow's milk. The hag gives him milk from each teat. After each drink he blesses the woman, unwittingly healing each of the wounds he inflicted on her.

> *"He will be whole who has brought it," said Cuchulainn; "the blessings of gods and non-gods on you'" said he. Then her head was healed so that it was whole. She gave the milk of the second teat, and her eye was whole; and gave the milk of the third teat, and her leg was whole ...*
>
> *"You told me," said the Morrigan, "I should not have healing from you forever."*
>
> *"If I had known it was you," said Cuchulainn, "I would not have healed you ever."*[33]

32. Ibid., p. 133.
33. Faraday, *The Cattle Raid of Cualnge*, pp. 81–82.

While the Morrigan's attacks seem to be solely in spite, the goddess is really testing Cúchulain. Even though she hinders him, he manages to defeat Loch and fulfills his own promise to wound the goddess. While Cúchulain blesses the Morrigan when she is disguised as the hag and heals her wounds, she too is giving him a blessing. The cow is a symbol of her sovereignty over the land; by giving Cúchulain the cow's milk, she acknowledges his worthiness to be her champion.

The next day the Morrigan appears as the goddess Nemain (this is one of the few places Nemain is mentioned as one of the Morrigan's three faces), this time to help Cúchulain fight Maeve's army. "Then Cúchulain arose ... and sent out the hero's shout from his throat, so the fiends and goblins and sprites of the glen and demons of the air wave answer for the fearfulness of the shout that he lifted on high, until Nemain, which is Badb, brought confusion on the host ... that an hundred warriors of them fell dead that night of fright and of heartbreak."[34]

This is one of many references to the Morrigan's fierce battle cry, which had the dual effect of strengthening the resolve of those she favored and striking fear into the hearts of her enemies. In this case, the fear she instills in the men of Connacht is so great that they drop dead.

In the end, Maeve's army is forced to retreat from Ulster, but in the confusion she manages to capture the brown bull, ensuring her sovereignty over Connacht. Unfortunately when the brown bull meets Ailill's white bull, the two immediately begin to fight. The two bulls rip each other apart, killing one another. Although she loses her prize, Ailill's bull is gone too, restoring equality in their marriage and keeping Maeve's sovereignty intact.

The Death of Cúchulain
Aided Con Culainn

Cúchulain lived for many years after the *Táin*, but the enemies he made during the war between Ulster and Connacht eventually brought about his death. Like her other interactions with the hero, the Morrigan both brings about his doom and attempts to save him from it. In the *Aided Con Culainn*, we see the Morrigan as the phantom death messenger. She appears to Cúchulain, warning him of his coming death and staying with him in his last moments of life. She also bears a striking resemblance to three mortal sorceresses, the daughters of Calatin, who play a pivotal part in the hero's

34. Dunn, *The Ancient Irish Epic Tale Táin Bó Cúailnge*, ch. 17.

demise and may be the Morrigan in another guise. Here she guards the boundaries between life and death and acts for both sides equally.

During the events of the *Táin,* Cúchulain accumulated many enemies. Although Maeve managed to steal the brown bull, Cúchulain had killed a number of her champions. Maeve, along with Lugaid, whose father Cúchulain had slain, conspired to bring about the hero's death. Maeve also enlisted the help of the three daughters of Calatin, whose father had also met his end at Cúchulain's hand. The sisters were hideous in appearance, each being blind in one eye. The queen sent the sisters abroad to learn the arts of magick and Witchcraft. When they returned, versed in the art of sorcery, Maeve gathered an army and began to pillage Ulster. Knowing the men of Ulster would be incapacitated by Macha's curse for several days and unable to come to the hero's aid, she planned to lure Cúchulain into battle to face her forces alone.

Conchubar, the king of Ulster, called Cúchulain to Emain Macha (a fort in the capital of Ulster) and bade everyone to keep watch on the hero and to stop him from going into battle alone against Maeve's army. While Cúchulain waits for the men of Ulster to be free of Macha's curse, the daughters of Calatin use their magick to create the sounds of a phantom battle. The Druid Cathbad manages to convince Cúchulain he is being fooled by an enchantment and stops him from leaving the safety of the fort. Then one of the daughters of Calatin takes on the form of a crow and mocks Cúchulain for staying safely within the walls of Emain Macha while Ulster is being destroyed by Maeve's army. The daughters of Calatin shared many of the same attributes as the Morrigan. They could shape-shift, they appeared as crows, and they assume a triple form. In some versions one of the daughters is even named Badb; in others, she is described as "a Badb." In Cúchulain's youth, the Morrigan, also in the form of a crow, mocked him for failing to fight a phantom, much as Calatin's daughter mocks him for failing to defend his homeland. It is possible that these sisters are the Morrigan in disguise, as she often appeared to the hero disguised as a mortal woman.

Finally Cathbad has Cúchulain brought to Glean-na-Bodhar, The Deaf Valley, where he cannot hear the noise of the phantom battle conjured by the daughters of Calatin. One of the daughters goes into the valley and takes on the appearance of Cúchulain's mistress, Niamh. Thus disguised, she chastises Cúchulain for not going out to face Maeve's army. Not realizing he is being tricked, Cúchulain leaves to face his enemies.

On his way to the battle, Cúchulain encounters the Morrigan as the Washer at the Ford. The Washer at the Ford was a phantom woman who appeared to warriors, washing their bloody clothes in a river, warning them of their impending doom. The Druid Cathbad interprets the encounter as an omen of the hero's death. Although not specifically named as the Morrigan, Cathbad refers to the phantom as "Badb's daughter" suggesting that the woman is either the great queen herself or is connected to her in some way. "'Do you see, Little Hound,' asked Cathbad, 'Badb's daughter yonder, washing your spoils and armour? Mournfully, ever-sorrowfully she executes and tells of your fall, when she signifies your defeat before Medb's [Maeve's] great host.'"[35]

Cúchulain ignores the warning, insisting he will fight Maeve's army regardless of ill omens. Along the road he meets the Morrigan in triple form, disguised as three crones (in some versions it is a single crone), cooking dog flesh on a spit. As he passes by, one of the crones offers Cúchulain a portion of the meat. Cúchulain, like many Celtic kings and heroes, was under a *geis* (also *geas,* plural *geasa*), a prohibition or taboo that the hero was obligated to fulfill. Cúchulain's geis was to never refuse food offered to him and never to eat the flesh of his namesake animal, the dog. Breaking a geis would bring bad luck and in most cases caused the hero's death. A geis was almost always placed on a person by a goddess or a mortal female acting as the representation of the goddess. The hero or king was usually forced to break his geis when he did not live up to the goddess's expectations. In most Celtic stories, the use of a geis becomes a kind of divine system of checks and balances. If the king became unfit to hold his office or committed an act the gods found offensive, he was forced into a situation (usually by an Otherworldly female) that caused him to break one, if not all, of his taboos—an act that ultimately led to his death and removal from power.

No matter what Cúchulain does in this situation, he will break at least one of his taboos. He eats the dog flesh and so seals his fate. In another version of the story, the woman attacks him with the spit she had roasted the dog flesh on. Although Cúchulain does not eat the flesh in this version, the dog's blood mixes with his own through the wound inflicted on him with the spit, thus breaking the *geis*. This seems to be an attempt to make the hero appear blameless for breaking his *geis,* rather than it being a conscious choice. The Morrigan is associated with a cooking spit in other myths as

35. Epstein, *War Goddess,* p. 141.

well. While she does cook with it, more often than not she uses it as a weapon to prod mortals into action.

His encounter with the Washer at the Ford is not the only ill omen Cúchulain encounters. Before leaving for battle, his horse, the Liath Macha, refused to be harnessed to his chariot until Cúchulain himself coaxed the animal. Once harnessed to the chariot, the horse began weeping tears of blood. Both of Cúchulain's horses, the Liath Macha (Gray of Macha) and Dub Sainglend (Black of Saingliu), were said to be a gift from the goddess Macha or possibly the Morrigan. They first appeared out of the pool of Linn Liaith. Then Cúchulain leapt onto their backs; after running across Ireland for an entire day, unable to throw him off their backs, the horses became tame. The Liath Macha seems to share the Morrigan's ability to foresee the future and, as the animal was a gift from the goddess, its crimson tears may have been another way for the Morrigan to warn Cúchulain of his death.

In earlier versions of the *Aided Con Culainn,* the Morrigan smashes Cúchulain's chariot in an attempt to prevent him from fighting in battle, knowing he would die. "On the night before, the Morrigu had broken the chariot, for she liked not Cú Chulainn's going to the battle, for she knew that he would not come again to Emain Macha."[36] But in either version, Cúchulain is determined to go into battle.

In his final battle, Cúchulain is taunted by three of Maeve's bards. He kills them with his three spears, which Lugaid retrieves from the bodies of the bards. The daughters of Calatin had prophesied that the spears were each destined to kill a king. With the first spear Lugaid kills Cúchulain's charioteer (the king of charioteers). With the second, he wounds the Liath Macha (the king of horses). With the final spear, Lugaid strikes Cúchulain (the king of heroes), spilling his intestines. Determined to die a hero's death, Cúchulain ties himself to a standing stone, since dying lying down or sitting was considered dishonorable for a hero. Although wounded, the great horse Liath Macha protects his fallen master, killing fifty warriors with his teeth and thirty with each of his hooves.

As Cúchulain dies, the Morrigan lands on his shoulder in the form of a raven, fulfilling her vow to guard his death. After the hero's death, Liath Macha leads Conall Cernach, one of Cúchulain's comrades, to his body, after which he pursued Cúchulain's killers and avenged his death.

36. Stokes, "The Death of Cú Chulainn," p. 176.

Throughout Cúchulain's myths, he ignores the Morrigan's aid and advice. He is too caught up in his search for personal glory to take her seriously or to recognize her warnings. The Morrigan is often painted as the villain, but it is really Cúchulain's actions that dictate his sorry fate. The Morrigan does aid Cúchulain and warns him several times of his death. Before he insults her, she offers to bring him victory and to help him fight his enemies. If he had accepted her aid and listened to her warnings, he could have avoided his death. Everything that happens to Cúchulain is a reflection of his actions and his personal choices. The Morrigan never forces him to listen to her advice but lets him make his own choices. She only forces him to take responsibility for the consequences of his actions. Even though he ignores her, she forgives him, giving him the chance to change his life's path.

Cúchulain's sad tale teaches us that we reap what we sow. If we open ourselves to the Divine, there is an unlimited source of guidance and wisdom at our disposal; still, it is up to us to listen to that wisdom.

The Dindshenchas

The Dindshenchas is a series of 176 poems and prose pieces concerning the origins of Irish place-names. One version of the *Dindshenchas* can be found in *The Book of Leinster,* which dates back to the twelfth century. Several partial versions also exist within thirteen different manuscripts.

The story of Odras consists of only seventeen lines in the *Dindshenchas* but it illustrates both the Morrigan's function as a goddess of the land and as a goddess of death—two themes that often overlap in the Morrigan's mythology.

Odras's story begins when she is herding cattle with her husband. The Morrigan appears and steals one of Odras's cows with the intentions of mating it with one of her otherworldly bulls, Slemon the Smooth: "Dagda's wife found her: in this wise came the shape-shifting goddess: The envious queen fierce of mood, the cunning raven-caller."[37] The Morrigan brings the cow to the cave of Cruachu (also called the Cave of Cruachan or Oweynagat), her home and an entrance to the Otherworld: "There came to blood-stained Cruachu, according to the weird and terrible tale, the mighty Morrigan, whose pleasure was in mustered hosts."[38]

37. Gwynn, *The Metrical Dindshenchas,* p. 198–99.
38. Ibid., p. 199.

Odras pursues the Morrigan but wearies and falls asleep before reaching the cave. The Morrigan then sings spells over her and turns her into a body of water: "Morrigan out of the cave of Cruachu, her fit abode, came upon her slumbering... chanted over her... every spell of power; she was full of guile... Odras is the sweet-sounding noble name of the sluggish pallid streamlet: it passed from the lady—luckless visitant—to the river Odras."[39]

By defying the Morrigan's judgment (trying to reclaim the cow), Odras is defying fate. Throughout life we pursue our goals and dreams, but death is inevitable; every cycle will end at some point. Here Odras does not physically die; instead her transformation into the river that bears her name becomes symbolic for physical death. When the Morrigan turns Odras into a river, it is not a punishment—Odras is simply returning to the elements. Since the Cave of Cruachan is an entrance to the Otherworlds, Odras must change (pass from life to death) before she can enter it and pass into the Otherworlds. The Celts considered bodies of water, especially rivers, to be doorways to the Otherworlds. Odras's transformation symbolizes her journey from this world to the next. One of the Morrigan's functions is to bring the souls of the dead to the Otherworlds, much like the Norse Valkyries. Odras might not have died on the battlefield, but the Morrigan is still facilitating her journey to the Otherworlds and her eventual rebirth.

The Morrigan's cow thieving represents her ability to both grant and withhold the wealth and the prosperity of the land. She rules over both fertile and barren cycles. Her intention to mate the two animals indicates a cycle of fertility, while Odras's transformation is indicative of the darker cycles of death and rebirth. This story shows the Morrigan's power over both life and death and the natural cycles of life.

The Adventures of Nera
ECHTRA NERAI

The events in *The Adventures of Nera* occur prior to the *Táin* and in part serve to explain the reason behind the conflict. Here the Morrigan engages in her favorite pastime: stealing cattle.

On Samhain, Nera was feasting in the hall of Maeve and Ailill. Being Samhain, the doorways between the worlds were more accessible, and Nera is able to enter the Otherworlds through the Cave of Cruachan, which lay near Maeve's fort and was also the

39. Ibid., p. 201.

Morrigan's home. In the Otherworld, the king of the Sidhe gives Nera a house and a faery wife. He lives happily for a while until his faery wife tells him that the faery king plans to attack Maeve's court on the following Samhain. Nera warns Maeve and Ailill of the coming attack, then returns to the Otherworld to retrieve his wife, child, and cattle from the Otherworld. Maeve attacks the Otherworldly host, keeping her lands safe and gaining several Otherworldly treasures in the process.

Then one day Nera falls asleep while watching his cattle. The Morrigan appears and steals a cow that his wife had given to their son. She mates the cow with the Donn Cúailnge, the brown bull Maeve eventually goes to war to obtain. Nera's wife scolds him for falling asleep, then relates the events that transpired after the cow's abduction.

> *Then while he (Nera) was asleep the Morrigu took his son's cow and the Donn Bull of Cooley bulled her in the east in Cooley. She (The Morrigan) then went again westward with her cow ... Cu Chulainn overtook the Morrigu with her cow, and she said: "This cow must not be taken."*
>
> *Nera went back then to his house with his cows in the evening. "My son's cow is missing," said he.*
>
> *"I did not deserve that thou shouldst go and tend cows in that way," said his wife to him. Thereupon the cow returned.*[40]

(It is never explained exactly how the wife knows what the Morrigan did with the cow; perhaps she allowed the Morrigan to take the cow in order to punish her husband for falling asleep on the job.)

The story relates to the encounter Cúchulain has with the Morrigan in the *Táin Bó Regamna,* where he challenges her right to drive cattle through Ulster and prophesied that the cow's unborn calf would bring about the events of the *Táin.*

Later the same calf fought Ailill's white bull of Connacht. It bellowed three times at the white bull, issuing a challenge and capturing the attention of Queen Maeve with the noise: "Now one time the Morrigu brought away a cow from the hill of Cruachan to the Brown Bull of Cuailnge, and after she brought it back its calf was born. And one day it went out of the Hill and it bellowed three times."[41]

---

40. Meyer, "The Adventures of Nera," *Revue Celtique*, pp. 223–24.
41. Gregory, *Cúchulain of Muirthemne,* p. 158.

The white bull wins the fight with the calf, after which the calf boasts that the white bull could never have won a battle against his father. Hearing this, Maeve swears that she will not eat nor sleep until she sees the two bulls fight. This gives us an alternate reason for the *Táin,* as opposed to Maeve's argument with Ailill over whose possessions are greater. In this version of the story, the Morrigan's actions directly cause the *Táin.* Here she is both a goddess of the land, as seen by her connection to cattle, and a goddess of war, by causing the events that bring about the cattle raid. While she brings fertility with the conception of the magickal calf, she equally brings destruction and death by instigating the battle between Connacht and Ulster.

Children of the Morrigan

According to the *Lebor Gabála Érenn,* Delbaeth was both the Morrigan's father and the sire of her three sons, Brian, Lucharba, and Luchair: "The Morrigan, daughter of Delbaeth, was the mother of the other sons of Delbaeth, that is, Brian, Iucharba [Lucharba], and Iuchair [Luchair]; and it is from her other name 'Danu' the Paps of Ana in Luachair are (so) called, as well as the Túatha Dé Danann."[42]

Brian, Lucharba, and Luchair were gods of craftsmanship. In *The Second Battle of Moytura,* they arm Lugh and the Túatha Dé Danann with magickal weapons after the Morrigan encourages him to fight in the coming battle. They are also referred to as the "Three Gods of Danu," confusing the matter of their parentage. Are they the children of the Morrigan, or of Danu? As with the Morrigan's other names (Badb, Anu, and Macha), the names Morrigan and Danu seem to be used interchangeably, suggesting they were once viewed as the same entity or, at very least, differing aspects of the same goddess.

Despite having a very powerful mother, Brian, Lucharba, and Luchair manage to get themselves into a lot of trouble when they killed Cian, the father of Lugh—the very same god their mother had them craft magickal weapons for. When Lugh found out what the sons had done, he forced them to complete several impossible tasks as punishment for their crime. They completed all of the tasks, but were fatally wounded during the final one.

The story of the Morrigan's fourth son, Méche, can be found in the *Dindshenchas.* Méche had three snakes that lived within his three hearts. We are told that if the snakes were allowed to grow, they would devour every living thing in Ireland. In order to prevent the snakes' growth and Ireland's downfall, Méche must die. He was

---

42. MacAlister, *Lebor Gabála Érenn,* p. 189.

killed on the plain of *Mag Fertaigi* (which afterwards was called *Mag Méchi*). The ashes from his hearts were thrown into the river Berba, making the waters boil and killing every living thing in them. Ireland, however, is spared the snakes' destruction.

Méche's story seems like a corrupted version of a Sacrificial God myth. Méche's death may be more of a willing sacrifice than a necessity. It is also odd that snakes—an animal that represented wisdom in the Druid tradition and was sacred to the Great Goddess—would have been viewed as evil. Of course, the Irish monks transcribing these tales from oral traditions would have seen snakes in a different light, namely, as being the form the devil took in the Garden of Eden. Perhaps they altered this story to represent evil being purged from the world. The fact that Méche has three hearts and three snakes is also significant. Three is a sacred number, which indicates the divine nature of his sacrifice. Méche also bears a resemblance to Mordred, the son of Morgan le Fay, who is also killed for the welfare of the realm, after attempting to steal the crown from his father.

Some have speculated that Brigid, the Irish goddess of smithcraft and fire, was a daughter of the Morrigan and Dagda. Other sources name her as the daughter of Boann, who (like the Morrigan) was associated with rivers and was the goddess of the Boyne River.

Part Two
The Three Morrigans

Badb and Macha and Anand [Anu]
of whom the Paps of Anu in Luachar
were the three daughters of Ernmas.
—R. A. S. MacAlister,
Lebor Gabála Érenn

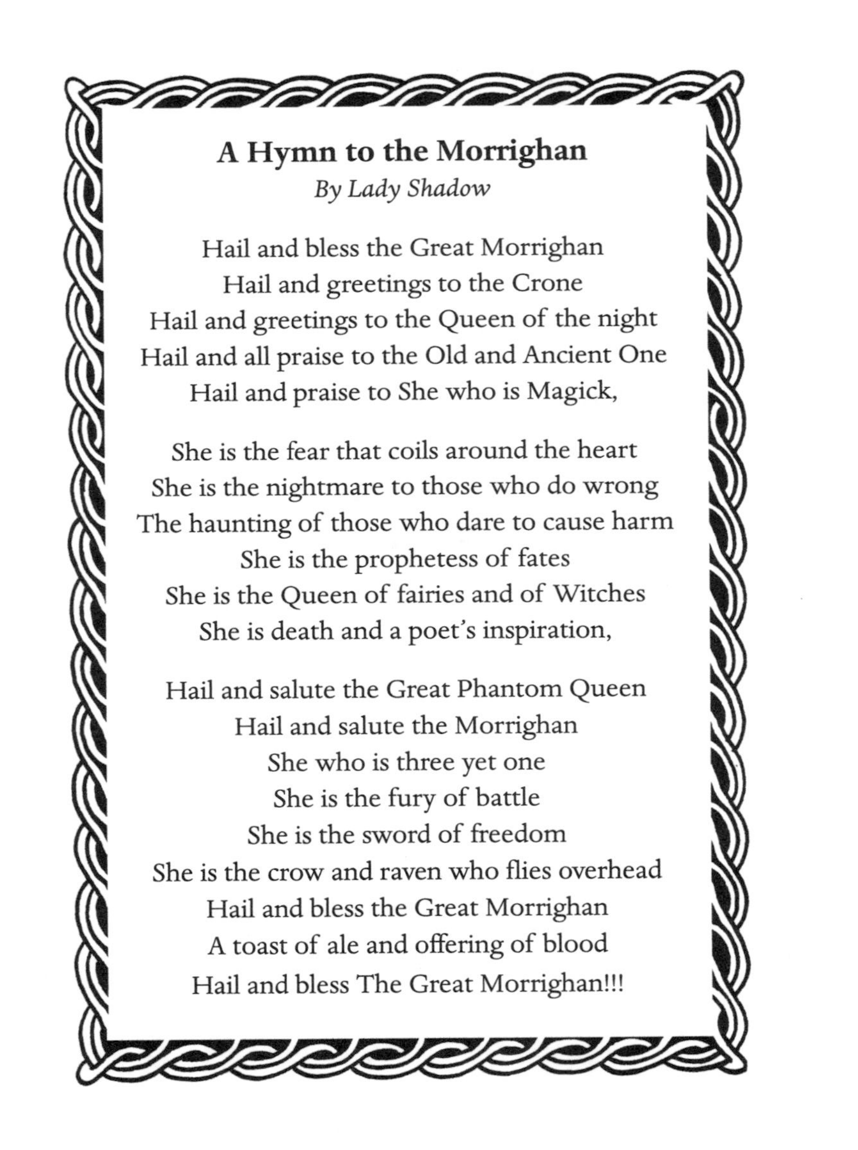

A Hymn to the Morrighan

By Lady Shadow

Hail and bless the Great Morrighan
Hail and greetings to the Crone
Hail and greetings to the Queen of the night
Hail and all praise to the Old and Ancient One
Hail and praise to She who is Magick,

She is the fear that coils around the heart
She is the nightmare to those who do wrong
The haunting of those who dare to cause harm
She is the prophetess of fates
She is the Queen of fairies and of Witches
She is death and a poet's inspiration,

Hail and salute the Great Phantom Queen
Hail and salute the Morrighan
She who is three yet one
She is the fury of battle
She is the sword of freedom
She is the crow and raven who flies overhead
Hail and bless the Great Morrighan
A toast of ale and offering of blood
Hail and bless The Great Morrighan!!!

The Morrigan appears both as a single goddess and as a trio of goddesses. The names of these goddesses are used interchangeably, with the understanding that they all refer to the same being. In some cases these women are specifically referred to as the "Three Morrigans" or "Morígna," making their divine status obvious; other times they are simply referred to as sisters. Each of these goddesses embodies a certain aspect of the whole and allows us to explore different facets of a complex divinity.

The names of the three goddesses that form the Morrigan's triple nature change from myth to myth, making it difficult to understand who exactly belongs in this trio. The *Lebor Gabála Érenn* tells us that Macha, Anu, and Badb are the names of the three Morrigans. Sometimes Danu is added to this trinity as well, and sometimes "Morrigu," an older version of the name Morrigan, is listed as an individual within the trinity rather than the title of the collective unit. "Ernmas had three daughters, Badb and Macha and Morrigu, whose name was Anand."[43] This inconsistency may be due to her myths and names evolving and changing through the years, or it may reflect regional distinctions. While Nemain is almost always mentioned as part of the trinity by modern writers, this goddess was a later edition to the trinity and was most likely included with the trio because she is often confused with Badb. Since their names are used interchangeably in some texts, Nemain and Badb may be the same goddess. At the very least, their identities merged together at some point.

When I first began working with the Morrigan, I worked with her as a whole. I knew she was a triple goddess, but there was very little information I could find about

43. MacAlister, *Lebor Gabála Érenn,* verse 62.

these three goddesses other than their names. It wasn't until much later that I really explored her triple nature and worked with each individual goddess. By working with each of her three "selves," I gained a much greater understanding of the Morrigan as a whole and the complexity of her nature. When I first felt the Morrigan's call, my most pressing need was for protection and strength. As a goddess of battle, she aptly supplied both. I knew from experience that she was a deity of inner strength, but I wasn't able to truly see her more abundant nature until I worked with Macha and Anu. Working with Macha, Anu, and Badb individually gave me a greater understanding of a goddess I thought I already understood, adding new depth to my spiritual practice. As a goddess of self-discovery and inner wisdom, the Morrigan stands ever ready to guide us along our life path. As she challenges us to grow and redefine ourselves, it is only fitting that she should make us look deeper into her own nature.

In this section you will learn how to work with each of the goddesses that form the Morrigan, their myths, and how they can aid us in our spiritual and magickal lives. The invocations you will find for each goddess can be used either for a ritual intended to honor that particular aspect of the Morrigan, or for spellwork. Each chapter will begin with a pathworking exercise designed to help you connect to each goddess's energies and then will go into spells related to that goddess's particular areas of expertise.

Pathworkings

Guided meditations, or pathworkings, are an excellent way to explore the Otherworlds and connect with a deity's energies. As with any meditative work, you should find a quiet place where you will not be disturbed before beginning your pathwork. The key is to be comfortable, so your favorite comfy armchair will work just as well as your sacred space. If you are working in a group, choose one person to read the guided meditation to the rest of the participants; if you are working alone, you might wish to record yourself reading the meditation so you can play it back to yourself.

The meditations presented here are based on my own pathwork experiences with each goddess. They are just a starting point—don't worry if your pathwork experience deviates from the ones I have provided. The Morrigan may wish to share something with you that is not within the guided meditation, and your pathworking experiences may take on a life of their own!

I recommend using a notebook to document your impressions and experiences as you work with each goddess. Pathwork experiences are very similar to dreams in that the details of your experience can fade quickly. Writing down your impressions will help you clarify and remember the experience. If any messages were imparted to you, it is important that you write them down. Your journal entries can be as detailed or simple as you like. If you don't enjoy journaling, even a few quick notes about your experiences will come in handy in the long run. Make sure to go back and read your entries every few months—messages you may not have initially understood could take on new meaning.

In each section there is a list of correspondences for each goddess. You may wish to light a candle or use incense that corresponds to the particular goddess you are working with before beginning your pathwork, or you could use the list of correspondences to help create your own rituals.

Begin each pathworking by taking three deep cleansing breaths and visualizing your daily worries and stress draining away from you. Ground and center, then imagine white iridescent energy surrounding and filling you.

3

MEETING MACHA

Macha, who diffused all excellences ...
the sun of womankind.

—*Edward Gwynn,* The Metrical Dindshenchas

You are on a vast green plain. In the distance you can see lush rolling hills. It is a beautiful summer day, and the sensation of the warm sunlight on your skin exhilarates you. You inhale a deep breath of the clean fresh air and take a few moments to explore your surroundings. After a few minutes, you notice a strange drumming sound. You stop, listening intently to the sound, and you realize you can feel the vibration under your feet. Its rhythm reminds you of a heartbeat, and it's as if you can feel the pulse and flow of the Earth Mother's life force. Then the source of the sound appears. Over the crest of a hill, a herd of wild horses emerges, their powerful legs drumming against the ground in rhythmic time.

As the herd veers in your direction, you see that their leader is a beautiful Red Mare. The Mare's coppery red coat glistens like a flame in the brilliant sunlight. The Mare leads the herd past the hills and, as they come closer to you, the vibrations under your feet intensify. The herd circles around you in a flurry of tossing manes and pounding hooves. As they circle you, you feel all of life's problems shatter and vanish. Nothing can withstand the strength and power of the herd.

The herd slowly changes course, following the Mare onward across the plain. You call after them, not wanting them to leave. They continue on and you run after them. Slowly you find yourself changing. Your hands grow longer, your fingers merge to become hooves, and you now inhabit the shape of a horse. Faster and faster you run, amazed at the strength in your legs. You are moving so quickly, it almost feels as if you are flying. You quickly catch up to the herd and they happily welcome you to their ranks.

You and the herd follow the Red Mare, enjoying the exhilarating speed and power your new form possesses. Ahead you notice a mound and recognize it as a faery fort, a place where the Sidhe are said to live. The Mare leads the herd closer and soon you are close enough to notice stones along the mound's base with spiral designs carved into them. The Mare leads the herd in a long spiraling path around the mound and up to its summit. Here the herd finally rests. While the others graze, you find yourself returning to human form. You feel compelled to find the Mare, and you walk among the horses, only to find she has vanished. In her place stands a tall woman with flowing red hair. She smiles at you, and you know that you are in the presence of the horse goddess Macha. A bronze sword hangs at her side and the sunlight seems to intensify in her presence.

"I am the heartbeat of the land. It is I who establishes the eternal rhythms and patterns of life. As I sustain the bounty of the earth, so too do I sustain and enrich the soul. I am the plentiful mother. Fierce as any force of nature, when provoked I protect and sustain all life. I am the Queen from which sovereignty can never be taken, only granted. To know me is to revel in your own sovereignty and inner strength and to accept the abundance I grant. Would you learn my mysteries?"

You answer and she nods and smiles, pleased with your response. After a few moments, Macha leads you through the heard. "The horse, like the raven, can move easily between the worlds, their strength and protection are boundless. Choose one of my herd to be your guide in the Otherworlds."

You walk among the herd until you find the mare or stallion that you feel most connected to. Note any details about your horse—coloring, markings and so on. When you are ready, tell Macha which horse you have chosen.

"No matter where you are in the Otherworlds, she or he will be able to find you."

Effortlessly you swing onto your horse's back.

"Go now and remember my strength is always with you. I am the sunlight on your face, the fertile soil beneath your feet, the passion within your heart."

You bid Macha farewell and your horse takes off down the mound. You close your eyes to feel the wind and sun. The vision fades, and you find yourself back in your body.

Don't forget to call on your horse guide the next time you visit the Otherworlds!

Macha (MA-ka) connects us to the rich, fertile power of the earth and the vibrant power of the sun. She is both a sun goddess and a goddess of the land; in her darker aspects, she becomes a queen of battle, championing her right to sovereignty and rulership. While not a triple goddess herself, Macha appears in three distinct roles: as a goddess, as a warrior queen, and as a faery woman. All three women are regarded as the same person within the mythological cycle, each acting as a separate incarnation of Macha's personality.

Macha's name means "field" or "plain," connecting her to the land and its abundance. In the *Lebor Gabála Érenn,* she is described as "Macha, greatness of wealth,"[44] emphasizing her bountiful nature. Several places bear her name, including Emain Macha, the mythical capital of Ulster, and Ard Macha (The Heights of Macha). In her incarnation as a goddess, Macha was the wife of the god Nemed. When the Túatha Dé Danann came to Ireland, Nemed cleared several plains and named one for Macha. When she gazed upon the plain, she had a vision of the destruction that would be caused by the *Táin* and died of a broken heart. She was buried on Ard Macha, now the modern-day city of Armagh. Although the goddess Macha dies in this story, her death is not permanent.

Macha's other incarnations are both connected to Emain Macha, the capital of Ulster, and how it came to be named after the goddess. In the first version of the myth, Macha appears as the mortal queen Macha Mong Ruad or "Macha of the Red Tresses." She was the daughter of King Aed Ruad, who ruled Ireland along with two other kings, Dithorba and Cimbaeth. Each king ruled for an allotted seven-year cycle in order to maintain peace in the land. This arrangement worked until Aed drowned. (As the Morrigan is also a river goddess and has several connections to water, the manner of his death may indicate that Aed was an unworthy ruler and his drowning was a way for the goddess to remove him as king.) As Aed's only heir, Macha attempts to take her rightful place as queen when it is Aed's turn to rule, but Dithorba and Cimbaeth refuse to let a woman rule alongside them. Enraged, Macha promptly goes to war with both kings and defeats them. She asserts her right to sovereignty over the land and, in this case, takes it by force.

After Macha had ruled for seven years (the original allotment of time her father and the other two kings had agreed on), Dithorba's sons came to court and

44. MacAlister, *Lebor Gabála Érenn,* verse 64.

demanded that she hand over the kingship to one of them. She refused them, saying: "Not by favor did I obtain it... but by force in the battlefield."[45]

Dithorba's sons raise an army and attack the queen. Once again, Macha goes to war to defend her sovereignty. Unable to defeat her, Dithorba's sons flee. After much searching, Macha finds them hiding in the woods of Connaught. She appears to them disguised as an old leper, and they unwittingly invite her to share their meal. Despite her appearance, the sons find themselves lusting after her and she subsequently leads each of them into the woods to lie with her. One by one she binds them so they can't speak or move, then returns to Ulster with the men in chains. Instead of killing the men, she forces them to build the fort Emain Macha in her honor. The manner in which she instructs the men to build the fort hints at her divine nature. Macha takes off her broach and makes an outline on the ground to show them the dimensions to which her fort should be built: "Thus was the outline of the fort described by the woman, when she was sitting she took her pin from her garment to measure around her with her pin."[46] The reference to Macha's gigantic stature indicates her extraordinary nature. (We saw a similarly reference to gigantic stature when the Morrigan mates with the Dagda with one foot on either side of the river Unius, an impossibly long stretch for a normal-sized person.)

In Macha's third incarnation, she is depicted as a faery woman who marries the widowed farmer Crunnchu. Macha appears at his doorstep one day and immediately begins seeing to the task of putting Crunnchu's house and life back into proper order. She does all the household chores, then shares Crunnchu's bed. Crunnchu's fields and herds prosper in Macha's presence and she becomes pregnant with twins—all signs of her fertile nature.

Before Crunnchu left to go to a fair, Macha made him promise not to boast about her to anyone. Macha remained at their home and Crunnchu left with the intentions of keeping his promise. Once at the fair, Crunnchu naturally forgets his promise and boasts that his wife can run faster than the king of Ulster's horses. The king overhears Crunnchu and imprisons the farmer. Intending to humiliate Crunnchu, the king then has Macha brought before him and orders her to race his horses in order to save her husband's life. Heavily pregnant, Macha appeals to the king and the men of Ulster to wait until she gave birth before making her run the race, crying "Help

45. Meyer, "The Wooing of Emer," *Archaeological Review*, p. 152.

46. Stokes, *Sanas Chormaic*, p. 63.

me! For a mother bore each one of you!"[47] Her pleas are ignored and she is forced to race the king's horses. She wins the race, afterward falling to the ground and giving birth to twins, thus the name Emain Macha, or the "Twins of Macha." With her last breath, she curses Ulster's men for nine generations to feel the pain of childbirth whenever their strength was most needed: "From this hour, the ignominy that you have inflicted upon me will rebound to the shame of each of you. When a time of oppression falls upon you, each one of you will be overcome with weakness, as the weakness of a woman in childbirth, and this will remain upon you for five days and four nights to the ninth generation."[48]

As we saw in chapter 2, this curse plays a major role in the *Táin,* incapacitating the men of Ulster while Maeve's army attacks. Interestingly the hero Cúchulain, the only man in Ulster immune to her curse, had a horse named Liath Macha or the "Grey of Macha." The horse was believed to be a gift from Macha and mysteriously rose out of the pool Linn Liaith, making it a creature of the Otherworlds.

Macha was also connected to crows, specifically the royston-crow or hooded crow. In this form she was believed to fly over battlefields and instigate fighting. Both of her totems, the crow and horse, reflect her dual functions as a goddess of fertile abundance and of death. The crow is traditionally linked to death and prophecy—two attributes Macha displays in her multiple incarnations. Macha possesses an uncanny ability to return from the dead as well as the ability to foresee future events. As the warrior-queen Macha Mong Ruad, she is a goddess of battle, dispensing death to her enemies. As the faery woman, Macha's connection to the horse reflects her ability to bring about abundance. Horses were symbols of fertility and wealth, which her presence brings to Crunnchu's land. Horses plowed fields, connecting them to the wealth of the land, and were used in warfare, connecting them to the cycle of death. The Liath Macha, Cúchulain's horse and a gift from Macha, was said to be the "king of horses," and, like the namesake, it was fierce in battle, killing fifty men with its teeth and thirty with each of its hooves while attempting to protect his fallen master.

As a goddess of the sun, Macha's golden rays bring fertility and new life to the land. She is described in the *Dindshenchas* as "Macha, who diffused all excellences ... the sun of womankind," and "her two names, not seldom heard in the west, were bright

47. Condren, *The Serpent and the Goddess,* p. 31.

48. Cross and Slover, *Ancient Irish Tales,* pp. 208–10.

Grian and pure Macha."[49] Here Macha is both connected to the sun and is equated with another sun goddess, Grian. Her association with horses, a solar animal, reaffirms this connection. The Celts linked horses with wealth, fertility, and the sun, as did many other cultures. The Greek sun god Apollo's chariot was pulled across the sky by a set of fiery horses, as was the chariot of the Hindu sun god Surya. While we tend to think of the sun representing the masculine and the moon the feminine, the Celts saw the sun as neither an absolutely male nor female force, and there are several male and female sun gods in the Celtic pantheon (however, the majority of them are female). The connection between the horse goddess and the sun can also be found in Macha's counterpart, the Welsh Rhiannon, a horse goddess who was clothed in "golden" silks, representing the rays of the sun.

Macha was also associated with the severed heads of battle, which *Cormac's Glossary,* an early Irish glossary containing the etymologies and meanings of outdated words, refers to as the "Masts of Macha" or "Macha's Acorn Crop." "Mesrad Machae, the mast of Macha, the heads of men who have been slaughtered."[50] The Celts believed that a person's soul resided in the head, and the severed heads of enemies were often displayed on war chariots. This corresponds to the Morrigan's role as a harvester of souls, and taking the heads of fallen warriors would have been a symbolic act of collecting souls in order to bring them to the Otherworld. *Masts* could also refer to acorns and other nuts. Wild acorns were used to feed pigs, and ancient people gathered them as a food source for themselves as well. As a reference to actual acorns, *masts* refers to sustenance and the goddess of the land providing for her people.

As a goddess of fertility and the sun, call on Macha's energies to bring abundance into your life. When you need the strength to conquer a difficult task, call upon her warrior-queen aspect. If you feel drained by life's challenges, take a few minutes to go outside and stand in the sunlight. See Macha's fiery and energizing power filling your body until you glow like the unstoppable sun goddess Macha! Macha is a goddess of justice, especially in regard to crimes committed against women, and she can be a powerful ally to women who have been abused. Due to her powers of prophecy, she is also an excellent goddess to invoke when doing any kind of divination.

---

49. Gwynn, *The Metrical Dindshenchas,* p. 127.
50. Stokes, *Three Irish Glossaries,* p. xxxv.

Honoring Macha

There are many ways to honor Macha and welcome her energies into your life. As a goddess of the land, reaffirming your connection to the earth is a great place to start. Spend time outdoors, go hiking, plant a garden. If you live in a city or aren't physically able to go hiking, buy a plant and bring nature to you!

Another way to connect to Macha is through her totem animal, the horse. Horses are amazing creatures and you need only watch the exquisite beauty and grace of these animals firsthand to understand why our ancestors saw them as divine. Horses are also incredibly intuitive. As a child I took several years of riding lessons and eventually worked in a barn to pay for my lessons. One of my instructors at the barn was interested in the occult, specifically animal communication. One day we did an experiment to see how receptive the horse I rode was to telepathic communication. I didn't use reins, didn't give the horse any direction, I just sat on the horse's back and visualized what I wanted her to do. It worked! We got the horse to stop, trot, and even do a figure eight with nothing more than visualization. It was amazing! If you can't spend time with actual horses, spend a day watching horse movies. *The Black Stallion, Black Beauty, Into the West, The Horse Whisperer,* and *Seabiscuit* are just a few examples.

Since she is a horse goddess, grain would be an appropriate offering for Macha. Horses are also sometimes given dark ale to give their coats a healthy shine, making a pint of Guinness or any dark beer an excellent offering to this goddess.

Macha Correspondences

Color: red, dark brown
Herbs: vervain, oats, coltsfoot
Stones/Gems: garnet, clear quartz, citrine
Moon Phase: full moon, waxing moon
Sun Phase: midday, summer, harvest festivals
Animal Totem: horse, crow

Macha Invocation

The following invocation can be used with or without casting a circle. If you are calling on Macha's aid for a specific task, casting a circle may be appropriate. Otherwise you may simply want to light a candle (red or dark earthy brown would be a good choice) to draw on her strength and wisdom. Given that she is a goddess of prophecy and foresight, it would also be appropriate to call on her during divination.

Macha, Faery Queen
Swift-footed Mare
Come, Macha, come!

Sharp spear, ready for battle
Abundance of field and plain
Come, Macha, come!

Great Seeress
Prophetic visions you grant
Come, Macha, come!

You clear away the old
And bring balance to life
Come, Macha, come!

Macha, your presence I invoke
Come, Macha, come!
Come, Macha, come!
Come, Macha, COME!

Calling Upon the Horse Goddesses

The next invocation calls upon the three horse goddesses of the Celts, who share similar attributes. I usually use this invocation at the Autumn Equinox, a time of the year when I feel the most drawn to the powers of the horse goddess. No matter what deity I plan on invoking on the equinox, somehow I always feel drawn to one or all of these goddesses. All three of these horse goddesses are connected to the fertility of the land, and any harvest festival would be an appropriate time to honor them. A full Autumn Equinox ritual that invokes Macha can be found in Part Four of this book. Call upon the horse goddesses for prosperity, swift action, protection, and fertility.

Epona, Macha, Rhiannon
White Mare, Dark Raven, Mighty Queen
Swiftly moving
Hoofbeats drumming on the ground

Epona, Macha, Rhiannon
White Mare, Dark Raven, Mighty Queen
The sharp spear, the field ripe with wheat
The sun's golden rays upon your mighty crown

Epona, Macha, Rhiannon
White Mare, Dark Raven, Mighty Queen
Abundance, Movement, Sovereignty
Your gifts grant to me

Epona, Macha, Rhiannon
White Mare, Dark Raven, Mighty Queen
You keep the balance
Light and dark
Life and death

Epona, Macha, Rhiannon
White Mare, Dark Raven, Mighty Queen
Swift as wind, flashing hooves
Wild, uncatchable, untamed
I honor you, Mare Mothers!

Epona, Macha, Rhiannon
White Mare, Dark Raven, Mighty Queen
Hail and be welcome!

Macha's Spell for Abundance

You Will Need:

1 green or gold candle
Honey
Oats
1 dollar bill
Macha Sun Oil (see page 64)

Carve what kind of abundance you want to attract—a new job, success in business, etc.—on the candle's side. (You can use a pin, a crystal point, or any other sharp object.) Next hold the candle between your hands and visualize your life filled with abundance. See the image traveling from your mind's eye down your arms and into the candle. Concentrate on the image for a few more minutes, then anoint the candle with the honey, starting from the wick and going to the base of the candle. (When drawing something toward you, anoint a candle from wick to base; for banishing, anoint from base to wick, symbolically sending something away from you.) Sprinkle the oats on a plate and gently roll the candle in the oats, which will stick to the honey.

Go to your sacred space. Before you begin, take a few moments to connect to the earth. Imagine your feet changing into roots that sink deep into the living soil. Consider the abundance the earth provides you with—the food you eat and the clothes you wear—all are products of the earth's bounty. When you are ready, light the candle, saying:

Macha, Sun of womanhood
Macha of the golden fields
Macha of the sun-lit plain
Richness in wealth and stores
Your abundance I invoke!

Hold the dollar bill in your hand and concentrate on your goal. See your life filled with the abundance of the earth. Fold the bill three times and dab it with a few drops of Macha Sun Oil, saying:

My wealth and success grows and grows
Mighty Macha, make it so!

Place the folded bill under the candle and let the candle completely burn out. If you cannot do this safely, burn the candle for a few minutes every day until it has burned out. Carry the dollar bill in your wallet until the spell has manifested. Sprinkle any remaining oats outside as an offering to Macha.

Macha's Masts

You Will Need:

1 acorn or other nut

1 fine-tipped permanent marker

This spell comes with a bit of backstory. After invoking Macha during an Autumn Equinox ritual one year, I found myself being bombarded with her masts. Acorns were everywhere. The trees surrounding our house scatter acorns across the lawn and every year they are quickly gathered up by the local squirrels. That year, however, acorns covered the lawn in a carpet of brown, smashed acorns covered the driveway with a layer of brown mash, and I tripped more than once over the nuts as I walked to my car. The number of acorns in our yard became absurd and I kept looking up into the oak branches above, wondering how many more would fall and where all the squirrels were.

During my equinox ritual, I had asked Macha to bring me prosperity. Bills had been piling up and I had been taking on all the overtime I could, leaving me drained and exhausted. In her not-so-subtle way, Macha was reminding me that the universe was full of abundance, and I had to be open to the abundance that was already around me and draw it into my life. Instead I had been concentrating my thoughts on all the bills I had to pay and thinking I'd never have enough money. By concentrating on the negatives in my life (let's face it, when you have a lot of bills to pay it's hard not to get caught up in negativity), I was unconsciously drawing more negativity to me. I'd pay one bill and another would appear in its place. As soon as I consciously opened myself to receiving the abundance of the universe, things began to change. When I got a bill, I would say out loud "I am open to the abundance of the universe. I will have enough money to meet all of my needs." Once I began doing this, my financial situation began improving. Money began coming from unexpected places and I was offered a better-paying job. And the acorns vanished too. It was as if all the squirrels finally realized there was a veritable buffet sitting on my lawn.

Whenever I see acorns, I think of Macha's lesson. The universe is filled with enough abundance to fulfill all of our needs—all we have to do is consciously manifest it within our lives. It's not enough to cast a prosperity spell and then remain in a negative state of mind about your finances. Our thoughts influence our spellwork and the type of energy we attract into our lives. We have to be open to receiving the result of our spellwork. If you don't think you deserve what you are asking for or keep thinking that you'll never get it, your desire won't manifest no matter how many spells you cast.

Acorns are seeds, holding the promise of new life, yet they also provide sustenance and food for many animals. They are a symbol of new life, growth, and fertility. To manifest a desired goal, use the marker to draw a symbol that represents what you want to manifest in your life on the acorn. Don't be too elaborate; the symbol should be simple and concise. If you can't find an acorn, you can use another type of nut in its place. When you are done drawing the symbol, hold the acorn in your hand and concentrate on what you want to manifest. See the flesh of the acorn absorbing the image and say:

I plant the seeds of magick
In Macha's name manifest!

Bury the acorn somewhere on your property.

Macha's Shield Spell

You Will Need:

Incense charcoal

Angelica root

Patchouli

1 crow feather (you may use a synthetic feather, found in craft stores)

4 small mirrors, 1 inch across or smaller (these can be found in most craft stores)

1 black sharpie

9 hazelnuts or acorns

Gardening trowel

In this spell you will call upon Macha to protect your home from negative energies and people. Before invoking Macha's protection, it is important to cleanse the home of any negative emotions and energies. Light the charcoal and burn some of the angelica and patchouli on it. If you cannot burn incense, put a pinch of the herbal mixture in the corners of each room. Go from room to room in a sunwise direction, using the feather to smudge the four corners of each room with the incense.

When you are done, return to your sacred space. You will not need to cast a circle for this spell, as you will be moving around your home and bringing some items outside. Bring your materials into your sacred space and invoke Macha, saying:

Macha
Blood Red Queen
Your masts adorn the battlefield
Your sword clears the plain
Warrior Queen
Mother of Victory
Spread your mantle of protection over this home
Raise your sword in defense of those who dwell here
Macha, your protection I invoke!

Pass the mirrors and hazelnuts through the incense while saying:

In Macha's name, you are blessed!

Starting at the edge of the non-reflective side of each mirror, write Macha's name in permanent marker nine times, each time moving closer to the center to create a spiral. In the center draw the Ogham for rowan, *luis* ᚂ, which is also a symbol for protection. Also draw the Ogham on the hazelnuts.

Moving outside, carry the incense in a sunwise direction around your home or along the borders of your property. When you are done, use the trowel to dig four small holes, one each in the eastern, western, northern, and southern corners of your property. (If you aren't able to dig where you live, use pots of dirt or creative visualization.) Place a mirror in each hole, with the reflective side facing away from your home. Behind the mirror, place one hazelnut and sprinkle some of the patchouli and angelica root over them before covering with dirt. Visualize the mirror reflecting and banishing all evil and negativity coming from that direction while saying:

Macha's shield protects me from all harm coming
from the east/west/south/north
I welcome only positive energies to this place
None shall pass the boundary Macha has marked!

Next return to your sacred space and visualize Macha's protection extending in all directions, sending all evil away from your dwelling and leaving only happiness and balance. When you are done, say:

Under Macha's watch full eye
My home is safe and protected
So mote it be!

Don't forget to leave an offering to Macha. This can be additional incense or milk or wine poured on the ground outside.

Macha Sun Oil

You Will Need:
Sunflower oil
1 part orange peel
2 parts honeysuckle flowers
6 cloves (whole)
1 part eyebright
Cheesecloth
Small glass bottle
1 citrine stone, small enough to fit in the bottle

Use Macha Sun Oil to call upon Macha and the sun's energies. Base oils like sunflower and canola oil work best for making magickal oils. (Olive oil can be used, but its scent will overpower that of the herbs.) The easiest way to make magickal oil is to use a slow cooker. Simply place all the ingredients into the slow cooker (excluding the cheesecloth, citrine stone, and glass bottle, of course) and let them simmer on low heat for four to eight hours. Strain the result through cheesecloth to remove the herbs and any remaining particles. If you don't have a slow cooker, heat the oil in a sauce pan on low heat. Add the herbs and simmer for fifteen to twenty minutes. Strain the oil through the cheesecloth until there are no remaining particles. Pour the oil into the glass bottle.

Next, rinse the stone so there are no particles remaining on it and place it in the bottle. On the next sunny day, place the bottle outside in direct sunlight or in a windowsill where it can bask in the afternoon sun for a few hours.

Use this oil to dress candles or anoint yourself with a few drops before Macha rituals or meditations. To call on Macha's abundant nature, write what you wish to manifest on a piece a paper. Fold the paper and put it in a clear glass bottle and fill it with Macha Sun Oil. Leave the bottle on a windowsill where it can bask in the light of the sun.

Macha Herbal Blend

You Will Need:
Oats
Dried apple peel
Vervain
Coltsfoot
Mullein
Honeysuckle flowers
Eyebright
Jasmine flowers

Herbal blends can be used as incense, put on candles to invoke the goddess's energies, or left as offerings. In a bowl, mix equal parts of the herbs listed above while chanting Macha's name.

If you can't find natural oats at your local health food store, instant oatmeal like Quaker Oats can be substituted. Dried apple or apple peel can also be found in some health food stores. If your local store does not sell them, thinly slice an apple and place the pieces on tin foil; bake on low heat in your oven until the pieces are dried. Then break apart the slices into smaller pieces.

Meeting Badb

The Red Badb will thank them for the battle-combat.

—*J. Fraser,* The First Battle of Moytura

In your mind's eye, you look down at your hands and find that the lines and shape have become less distinct, slowly changing into silky black wings. You feel the rest of your body shrinking, changing bit by bit into the body of a raven. You test your new wings with a few hesitant flaps, then launch into the sky.

Below you can see gently rolling hills and lush rivers covering the land. As you are taking in the scenery, something catches your eye and you circle downward to investigate and land on a bare tree branch. Smoke rises from the small valley, and you watch as men and women fight one another. As you watch them, you realize the sunlight reflecting off the warriors' swords was what caught your eye from above.

One of the warriors falls and after a few moments, you see a strange silver mist forming over the body. You watch as the crystalline mist forms into a translucent version of the lifeless warrior on the ground, and you know this is the warrior's spirit. Reverting back into the silver mists, the spirit warrior rises above the battlefield. Quickly you take flight, following alongside the spirit and making spiraling circles around it. The light that pulses from within the mist fascinates you; you feel compelled to follow it. You rise higher and higher until the world seems to shift and change. It was midday just a moment ago, but now the sky has changed to the muted grey of twilight and you can't quite tell if it is dawn or dusk. Below, the battlefield is gone. You fly with the spirit until you notice a large mound below you. The spirit sees the mound too and begins to descend.

Once on the ground, the warrior returns to his or her human shape and you land on the spirit's shoulder, which is surprisingly solid and warm. The warrior approaches the mound's base and you notice the mound has a doorway carved into its side that is lined with large stones carved with intricate spirals.

The warrior passes the stone threshold and you are in a long, dimly lit tunnel. The warrior continues deeper into the faery mound and it seems like a very long time before the tunnel widens and you enter a large hallowed hall at the very heart of the hill. You hear the sound of boiling water before you see the large black cauldron in the center of the hall. An old woman stands just behind it, whispering to the churning waters. The Crone sees you both and motions for the warrior to approach.

The woman, although old and bent, has a kindly face, and when she smiles at you, you feel completely at ease in her presence. You somehow know she is Badb, of the Morrigan.

"Death is only a new beginning; you have made this journey many times before and will make it again. If you wish, you may wait here in the Otherworlds and rest for a time, or you may return immediately to the earthly plane. The choice is yours."

The spirit considers for a moment, then decides to return. Badb nods and turns her attention back to the cauldron, her outstretched hands making a circling motion over the waters. As she does this, the liquid begins to swirl like a tiny whirlpool, reminding you of the spirals carved into the mound's entrance.

Smiling, the warrior turns to you and thanks you for escorting him or her on the journey. Badb extends her hand and you flutter across to her as the spirit enters the cauldron. The fallen warrior glows brightly for a moment then vanishes.

Badb points to the now-still waters. In the reflective surface, you see a woman in labor. At the midwife's urging, she gives a final push and a tiny baby enters the world. As the midwife presents the child to the mother, you recognize the warrior's soul in the newborn's body.

"Remember, little one," Badb says to you, "nothing in the universe remains stagnant; everything is constantly changing, moving around the wheel of life. Without death, there can be no rebirth. I am the deathblow and the midwife of the soul. It is to I you will come at this life's end, and it is through me that you shall be reborn."

The figure of the woman and the mound begin to fade and you feel your wings changing back to fingers and arms. Slowly you change back into yourself. As the scene fades to black, you find yourself back in your human body.

Badb (BAH-v) calls to us from the misty battlefields of legend. Disguised as a hooded crow, her shrill cries heralded doom for warriors. She is the banshee, a battle fury, and a prophetess. As the gentle Crone, she guides souls to the Otherworlds, to rest and rebirth. With one foot in the mortal realm and the other firmly in the realm of spirits, she holds the gift of prophecy and prophetic speech.

Badb's name means "crow" or "one who boils." Battlefields were once referred to as the "land of Badb" and one of her other names was *Cath Badb* (or Badb Catha), which meant "battle crow." The second translation of Badb's name, "one who boils," refers to the Otherworldly cauldron she presided over. The cauldron is symbolic of the womb and is connected to rebirth; there are several cauldrons in Celtic mythology that could reanimate fallen warriors. As a goddess of death, Badb facilitated the rebirth of souls who passed into the Otherworlds. While the cauldron connects her to rebirth, the Celts also believed the world would end when Badb's cauldron boiled over, its contents spilling across the earth and destroying all life.

According to *Cormac's Glossary,* Badb was the wife of the war god Neit, of whom little is known except for his name. In *The Book of Leinster,* Neit was also the husband of the goddess Nemain, leading some to believe that Nemain and Badb may be the same goddess: "Neit son of Indu, and his two wives, Badb and Neamin."[51] "Badb" was also used as a general term referring to a battle fury, leading some historians to believe that Nemain is this goddess's proper name, while Badb is only a title.

Badb is specifically connected to the "hooded" or "scald" crow, a member of the Corvidae family of birds. This crow has a dark-grey chest with black wings, head, and tail feathers, giving it the appearance of wearing a hood. In the form of a crow, Badb flew over battlefields inspiring battle frenzy, causing confusion, and striking fear into her enemies. When she was not watching over warriors as a crow, she wandered across battlefields in the shape of a wolf. Badb's connection to both these animals (and the Morrigan's connection to them in general) is most likely because both animals could be found scavenging for food on battlefields. By consuming the flesh of fallen warriors, these animals were symbolically ingesting the warriors' essence. Gathering souls in animal form, Badb would then bring them to the Otherworlds and to eventual rebirth.

Badb has several connections to prophecy. She appears as the Washer at the Ford, a phantom who washed the blood-soaked clothes of those who would soon die in

51. MacAlister, *Lebor Gabála Érenn,* verse 64.

battle, and she appeared in dreams to warn kings and queens of future events. In the *Tochmarc Ferbe,* a story that dates back to the tenth century, Badb appeared to both Queen Maeve and the Ulster King Conchobar predicting death and warning against disaster. She tells Maeve that her son will be killed by Conchobar's men and rallies the queen to take up arms. When Badb appears in King Conchobar's dream, she predicts the conflict of the *Táin* several years before the raid began, perhaps giving the king a chance to avoid the devastating war.

Both Conchobar and Maeve describe Badb as a young woman, a "white lady, fair with brilliancy."[52] Similarly in *The Destruction of Da Choca's Hostel,* a story composed sometime around the ninth century, Badb is described as "pale" and "red mouthed." In later myths this pale appearance may have contributed to her transformation into a phantom. Both white and red were associated with the Otherworld, and white was specifically connected to death and mourning. Faery hounds and other animals from the Faery Realm are often described as being white with red ears, similar to when the Morrigan appears as a red-eared heifer to distract Cúchulain. While we in the West connect black to mourning and death today, white remained the color of mourning up until the time of Henry the VIII, who wore white when mourning Ann Boleyn; there is also a portrait of Mary Queen of Scots wearing white while mourning her husband's death. During medieval times, white represented the purity of the soul and the mourner's hope for the soul's entrance into heaven.[53] Since Badb often appears lamenting future deaths, white seems like a fitting color for her.

As the Washer at the Ford, Badb reveals herself to those destined to die in battle. Cúchulain encounters Badb in this form while traveling with a Druid, who warns the hero the washerwoman is an omen predicting his death: "They saw a young girl, thin and white-skinned and having yellow hair, washing and ever washing, and wringing out clothing that was stained crimson red, and she crying and keening all the time… 'Do you see what it is that young girl is doing? It is your red clothes she is washing, and crying as she washes, because she knows you are going to your death …'"[54] This phantom death messenger eventually evolved into the banshee, whose mournful wails herald a death in the family she watches over. As the banshee, Badb's association with war is lost, but her primary role of prophecy and as a conveyer of souls to the afterlife remained in later folklore.

52. Leahy, *The Courtship of Ferb,* p. 78.
53. Gardener, *The Meaning of Witchcraft,* p. 148.
54. Gregory, *Cuchulain of Muirthemne,* p. 336.

The Washer at the Ford was also believed to have appeared to actual historical kings on the battlefield. At the battle of Corcomroe Abbey in 1317, Badb was said to have appeared to Donnchadh O'Brian, warning him of his coming death.[55]

In the story of *The Destruction of Da Derga's Hostel,* Badb appears to King Conaire, who broke all but one of his geasa through a series of strange events. Badb appeared at his door as a hideous hag and asked for his hospitality. His remaining geis was to not admit a single female into his house after sunset. Conaire reluctantly allows her to enter, breaking his final geis. Badb prophesied the king's death; by morning Conaire was dead. Prior to her encounter with the king, she also appeared as a ghostly specter on the hostel's roof. In this story, Badb seems to have a part in making her prophecy a reality rather than simply predicting future events.

While we would presume this phantom death messenger would appear as a Crone, the aspect of the Morrigan most associated with death (the Washer at the Ford) appears in Celtic legends as both a young Maiden and an old Crone. Badb, while often considered the Crone aspect of the Morrigan, appears several times as a beautiful young woman, such as when she appears in Queen Maeve's dream and when she appears to Cúchulain as the young woman washing his bloody armor. When Badb appears to those who have broken a geis or have participated in some type of wrongdoing, she appears as a hag; to the brave warriors she favors, she appears young and beautiful. Appearing as both young and old signifies the close connection between her Maiden aspect and the Crone. While the Crone rules over death, she also oversees rebirth and the regeneration of life, over which the Maiden rules, forming an endless cycle.

While Anu and Macha have firm connections to the land, Badb is closely connected to the element of water. As a death messenger, she washes the clothes of warriors in rivers, tends the waters of the Otherworldly cauldron of rebirth, and destroys the world with the cauldron's boiling waters. Water was a mysterious force to the Celts. Rivers were borders between this world and the Otherworlds. The mythical islands inhabited by the Fae and the Túatha Dé Danann were believed to be hidden under the sea or under lakes. Offerings to the gods were thrown into rivers and holy wells to ensure their entrance into the Otherworlds. Water from holy wells sprang forth from deep within the earth, connecting them to the Underworld and the realm of the ancestors. The island of Inis Badbbha (known today as Boa Island) in northern

---

55. Rankine and D'Este, *The Guises of the Morrigan,* p. 110.

Ireland was named after Badb. The small island is home to several carved stone figures and an early Christian graveyard that may have been built on the site of an earlier Pagan burial ground. Badb's connection to water ties her to both the Underworld and the realm of rebirth and life. She is fluid, moving between the worlds, changing all she touches into new life.

Honoring Badb

Badb is both the Maiden and the Crone. She speaks to us of death and destruction, yet also guides us toward healing and rebirth. Call on Badb for protection, learning about past lives, releasing negative habits and emotions, communicating with the dead, and divination.

As a Crone and goddess of the Otherworlds, the best time to work with Badb's energies is during the new or waning moon. Avalon (which means Isle of Apples) was the Celtic land of the dead, and apples were buried in the ground as an offering to those who had passed on, making them appropriate offerings to Badb. Apple cider can be used as a substitute for wine for rituals involving this goddess. Dark-red wine, symbolizing the blood of death and birth, would also be an appropriate offering to Badb. Her season is winter and late fall.

Badb Correspondences

Color: white, red, dark blue
Herbs: juniper, holly, Solomon's seal
Stones/Gems: onyx, jet
Moon Phase: new moon, waning moon
Sun Phase: dusk, winter, fall
Animal Totem: crow, wolf

Badb Invocation

Battle fury
Feathered Goddess
Warrior, Crone
Badb!

Chooser of the slain
Ferrier of souls
Badb!

Cauldron keeper
Fate weaver
Crow Goddess, come!
Badb, Badb, Badb!

Badb's Protection Powder

This powder can be used in protection spells and a pinch can be sprinkled in the corners of a room to purify the area and for protection.

2 tbsp. frankincense
1 tbsp. sea salt
1½ tsp. dragon's blood resin
1 tbsp. angelica
½ tbsp. Solomon's seal
½ tbsp. juniper berries
1 tbsp. lavender

Mix all the ingredients in a bowl while chanting Badb's name. If you are asking for protection for a particular person, visualize Badb's black wings enfolding that person in a protective embrace.

Hit the Road Jack Powder

This is an excellent powder that can be used in any kind of banishing spell.

3 tbsp. slippery elm root (ground)
1 tbsp. black pepper
2 tbsp. cayenne pepper
1 tbsp. chili pepper
½ tbsp. salt
1 tbsp. garlic powder

Badb's Banishing Spell

You Will Need:
Patchouli incense
1 small bottle or jar
Pen and paper
Vinegar
A few drops of urine
1 black feather
1 black candle
Hit the Road Jack Powder (see page 73)

Light the incense and pass the bottle, paper, and vinegar through the smoke. Write down the name of the person who is bothering you. Hold the paper in your hands and visualize the paper and the person merging and become one. Take as much time as you need to do this—the stronger your visualization, the more effective the spell will be. When you are ready, say the following three times:

Though you were separate
now you are one (name)

Place the paper and Hit the Road Jack powder into the bottle. Next add the vinegar and a small amount of your own urine. (Just a few drops will do. This sounds a little yuck,y but it works! Animals use their urine to mark their territory and tell other animals to stay away.) Visualize the problem person being trapped in the bottle, unable to speak or act against you, their negative energy and actions trapped in the bottle where they can no longer bother you. Seal the bottle, then circle it with the feather counterclockwise, saying:

Swoop low Raven Mother
Nightmare fury
Battle Crow
Fix your eye upon __________
Bind his/her evil this night
No more shall he/she __________
In Badb's name, so mote it be!

Using the black candle, drip wax on the bottle cap—or around the cork, depending on what kind of bottle you are using—so that the bottle is completely sealed. When you are done, hold your hands over the bottle, saying:

Nightmare fury
Battle Crow
As I will make it so!

Put more incense on the burner as an offering to Badb. Bury the bottle somewhere off of your property.

Badb's Cauldron Blessing

Because of Badb's connection to the cauldron, I often use a small cauldron during rituals and spellwork dedicated to her. A cauldron can be filled with water and used for scrying or it can hold a spell candle. You may want to use a specific cauldron only for working with Badb. Use the following ritual to call on Badb to bless your cauldron:

You Will Need:
Cauldron
1 red candle
Small dish of water
Small dish of salt or soil
Frankincense incense
1 black feather

Place the cauldron in the center of the altar. Arrange the candle, water, salt, and incense around the cauldron to represent the elements. The incense should be placed in the east, the candle the south, the dish of water in the west, and the dish of salt or soil in the north.

Light the incense, using the feather to waft the smoke over the cauldron, saying:

Powers of air, breath of life
bring inspiration to my work

Light the candle. Drip three drops of wax into the cauldron. If your cauldron is not easily cleaned, pass the cauldron over the candle's flame instead, saying:

Powers of fire, passion, and will
empower my magick

Use your fingers to sprinkle a few drops of water into the cauldron.

Powers of water, bring wisdom and second sight

Sprinkle a pinch of salt or soil into the cauldron, saying:

Powers of earth, growth, and manifestation,
give form and shape to my work

Raise the cauldron over the altar saying:

Here is the cauldron of Badb
Blessed by fire, water, earth, and air
Vessel of creation and transformation
Give life and form to my magick
In Badb's name, be blessed
So be it!

Badb's Healing Spell

Use this spell to cleanse yourself of negative emotions. It is especially useful for those who have been victims of abuse or have experienced a traumatic event in their lives.

You Will Need:
Sage smudge stick
Large cauldron or bowl
Spring or filtered water
Wine

You will need a large bowl or cauldron, since you will be pouring or washing water over yourself. You could also do this spell in your bathroom and use the shower instead of the bowl of water.

If you decide to use the shower or bathtub, bless your bathroom prior to the ritual by burning sage and smudging each of the room's corners.

Go to your sacred space and light the sage smudge stick. Perform a self-blessing by wafting the smoke over yourself, starting at your crown and ending at your feet. Hold your hands over the bowl of water. Visualize pure crystalline energy flowing into the water, then say:

Badb of the healing waters
Who washes away the sorrows of the soul
And tends the cauldron of rebirth
I place my sorrows before you
Wash my spirit clean of _________

Carefully cup some water with your hands and wash the water over your face, arms, legs, and body. Visualize Badb standing before you, pouring the water over you, and see your sorrows washing away. Take as much time as you need. When you feel fully cleansed, say:

I am cleansed
I am free
In Badb's name, so mote it be!

Hold the cup of wine above the altar, saying:

Lady of the Cauldron
Lady of the healing waters
I honor you!

Take a sip of wine, then pour the rest either into a libation bowl or on the ground outside after the ritual. Pour the water from the bowl outside as far away from your home as possible or into a moving body of water.

Badb's Cauldron Spell

Use the following spell to banish stress of negativity from your life:

You Will Need:
Pen and paper
Vodka or brandy
1 cauldron
Matches

Write down on a piece of paper what you wish to banish. Hold the paper in your hands, imagining the thing you wish to banish becoming one with the paper.

Pour about half a cup of vodka or brandy into the cauldron and light it with a match. Be sure to place the cauldron on a plate or non-flammable surface, as it may get very warm.

Drop the paper into the flames, saying:

Badb of the cauldron
Mother of creation and destruction
Clear away ________
And bring better things in its place

Scatter the ashes outside. Poured some brandy on the ground as an offering to Badb.

Badb's Scrying Mirror

A scrying mirror can be made out of several things. It can be something as simple as the reflective surface of water in a cauldron, a crystal, or an actual mirror. When invoking Badb for divination, I prefer to use a cauldron because of her connection to that particular tool, but a mirror can also be used. To make a traditional scrying mirror, buy a picture frame and remove the glass. Coat one side of the glass with black spray paint. Once dry put it back in the frame with the painted surface facing to the back.

You Will Need:
Mugwort
A bowl of water
A small wash cloth
Scrying mirror
Sage incense

Before scrying, place the mugwort in a bowl of hot water and let it steep for a few minutes. Use a cloth to wash the surface of the mirror with the mugwort-infused water, consecrating and cleansing any negative energies from it.

When you are ready to begin scrying, light the sage incense and move the mirror through the smoke. Pass your hand over the mirror three times in a clockwise motion, saying:

Badb
Lift your Veil
That the past, present, and future
I may see
So mote it be!

You may see images in the mirror itself, or you may see images in your mind's eye. Relax your eyes; don't try to stare or blink too much. When you are done, pass your hands over the mirror three times in a counterclockwise motion. Thank Badb for her aid.

5

Meeting Anu

It is well that she nursed the Gods.

—*Whitley Stokes,* Three Irish Glossaries

You find yourself standing on a vast expanse of lush green land. Apple trees laden with ripe fruit grow on the gently rolling hills. You walk among the trees for a while until you notice a large mound at the edge of the grove. It looks perfectly symmetrical and as you look closer, you see a spiraling path carved around the mound, wrapping around it like a great coiled snake. You realize this must be an ancient earth work—a faery fort and an entrance to the Otherworlds.

You feel compelled to follow the serpentine path and so begin walking along it. The path spirals gently upward and although you are rising quite high, the journey isn't tiring. Now you hear a far-off sound. The higher you climb, the louder the sound becomes. It is the steady rhythmic sound of drumming, reminding you of a heartbeat. For a moment you place a hand over your own heart, feeling its steady rhythm, then you continue upward, drawn by the distant drumming. Soon the drumming becomes even louder, and you feel the vibration in the soles of your feet. As you turn along a bend in the path, you become aware of a cavernlike opening on the side of the hill. You are not far from the summit, but somehow you know the source of the drumming is within the cavern, and you step inside.

The cavern is large enough for you to stand upright comfortably. A passageway leads deeper into the hill, and you follow the sound of the drumming deeper and deeper within the earth. Along the tunnel's walls are hundreds of glistening crystals. You reach out to touch one, and as your fingers graze its surface, a faint glow emanates from the crystals, like distant starlight, lighting your way.

As you travel deeper into the passageway, you notice there is another melody emanating from the earth. The melody is part of the drumming sound, behind and within it, and you aren't sure why you didn't notice it before. It sounds like a woman singing. The passageway ends, and you are now in a large crystal cavern deep within the hill. At its center is a woman singing over a large, richly adorned cauldron. Now having found the source of the sound, you realize it is emanating from both the woman and the cauldron, reverberating outward from the depths of the earth.

The woman's long hair spills down her shoulders in chestnut waves. She wears a long dress the same green color as the grass growing on the hill. Her eyes are the color of the rich soil and they hold your gaze as she looks up, and you know you are in presence of the Great Mother goddess Anu. She motions for you to approach, and you step closer to the cauldron. The cauldron is larger than you first thought, standing as high as your waist and large enough for a man to fit within it. It is made of a dark-grey metal and you see intricate knotwork and carvings etched onto its surface. The metal vibrates. As you put your hand on its rim, you feel a pulsing vibration issuing from it.

"I am the song, the heartbeat, that unites all life," Anu says, her voice rich and sweet like honey. "I establish the rhythms and cycles of life. Mine are the mysteries of the dark soil, the ground beneath your feet. Without me there is no stability, no sustenance. I am within everything that is green and growing. I am within all life, and shall ever remain so."

Anu holds out her hand, palm upward, over the cauldron. In her palm is a small apple seed. "Mine are the mysteries of the earth and growth, knowing there is a time for renewal and a time for decay for all things. And that neither state is permanent. All life is in constant motion, moved ever onward by the drumbeat of life. Would you learn these mysteries?"

You answer affirmatively. Anu smiles and places the seed in your hand. "Drop it into the cauldron," she tells you, and you do so. You hear the tiniest of pings as it hits the metal at the bottom of the cauldron. The drumming sound intensifies, and you can feel waves of sound wash over you. A green sprout raises its head from the bottom of the cauldron. As you watch, it grows larger and larger, changing from a small sapling to an adult tree. The tree's roots climb up and out of the cauldron, burrowing into the ground around you. Soon the tree's branches are heavy with ripe apples.

Anu moves closer to you. She takes your hand and places it on the tree's bark. You close your eyes and become the tree, feeling its roots deep within the earth and the pulse of energies emanating from the soil and moving with the tree. You feel the tree's branches reaching upward, uniting the powers of earth and sky.

"All things grow and change in their own time. Be as the tree, deeply rooted in the earth, yet ever reaching toward the heavens. In winter the tree may lose its leaves and sleep for a time, but the tree knows spring will always come again and bring new beginnings and growth."

You embrace Anu, feeling warmth and love radiating from her and filling your soul. The vision fades, and you find yourself back in your body.

Anu (AN-new) does not simply rule over the land; she *is* the land. Her breasts are the gently rolling hills, the plains her belly, and the crops and harvest the bounty of her womb. She is the Great Mother, a goddess of fertility, and the earth. She is the mother of the gods.

Anu (also spelled Anann, Ana, and Anand) is often omitted as one of the three Morrigans in favor of Nemain, but it is clear that Nemain was not one of the original goddesses in this trinity. In the *Lebor Gabála Érenn*, Anu is clearly listed as the sister of Badb and Macha. "Badb and Macha and Anand, of whom are the Paps of Anu in Luachar, were the three daughters of Ernmas the she-farmer."[56] A few stanzas later we are told, "Ernmas had other daughters, Badb and Macha and Morrigu, whose name was Anand."[57] Here Anu's name is used interchangeably with Morrigu, leaving little doubt as to her connection to the trinity. Nemain's only association with the Morrigan comes from the *Táin*, where we are told Nemain and Badb are the same goddess. It is obvious that Nemain was a later addition to the trinity, and was more or less used as an alternative name for Badb, making Macha, Badb, and Anu a more accurate representation of the Morrigan's three faces.

Anu's name means "plenty" or "wealth," and she is primarily concerned with the fertility of the land, crops, cattle, and livestock in general. Her worship was centered in the province of Munster. One medieval manuscript even refers to Ireland as Iath nAnann, or the "Land of Anu," suggesting her status to be that of a Mother Goddess.[58] In *Cormac's Glossary,* she is described as the mother of the gods, and that "It was well she nursed the Gods."[59] In County Kerry, the Paps of Anu, two hills that resemble breasts, are named after her.

Unfortunately none of Anu's myths have survived through the ages. All we really know about her comes from her brief mention in *Cormac's Glossary* and her connection to the twin hills in County Kerry. It seems apparent that she is an earth

56. MacAlister, *Lebor Gabála Érenn,* verse 62.
57. Ibid., verse 64.
58. McColman and Hinds, *Magic of the Celtic Gods and Goddesses,* p. 43.
59. Stokes, *Three Irish Glossaries,* p. xxxiii.

goddess—the meaning of her name and her association with features of the land confirm as much. Her role as the mother of the Celtic gods, a role usually assigned to Danu, is less clear. Nineteenth-century writers argued that Danu and Anu were in fact the same goddess, and furthermore that Danu's name was derived from Anu. Like Anu, Danu's stories were also lost to time, making it impossible for us to know if they had similar myths. While it is possible that these goddesses merged at some point, they most likely began as separate goddesses. Both are connected to fertility, yet their abundant natures are expressed very differently. Danu was a river goddess, and it is through this element that she bestows fertility to the land. Anu, on the other hand, is primarily connected to the land itself, and her abundance manifests from the soil. The *Coir Anman*, a medieval text that deals with the origins of certain names, describes Anu as the tutelary goddess of Munster, where the Paps of Anu are located. Since Cormac was from Munster, it would make sense for him to list the earth goddess he was most familiar with as the mother of the gods in his glossaries. If this is the case, Anu may have started as a local earth goddess and evolved into a more universal mother goddess over time.[60]

Although we know little about Anu, her energies and powers are just as strong and accessible today as they were in ancient times. Experiencing her energies through ritual or meditation can help us learn what has been lost to time. Through her we see the Morrigan as the mother of the gods, a bestower of fertility and plenty. When working with Anu, try to become more aware of the natural world around you. Spend time outdoors or gardening. If you live in a city, visit a park. No matter where you are, Anu is always there in the earth beneath your feet, an ever-present mother and bestower of plenty.

Honoring Anu

Anu's colors are deep forest green and the dark brown of rich, turned soil. Her seasons are spring and summer. In modern Paganism, Anu is usually considered a goddess of the full moon, and that would be an appropriate time to honor her. Moonstones and apples are also appropriate offerings to this goddess.

Rituals to Anu are best performed outdoors. If it's winter or if you live in a city, bring plants into your ritual area to help you connect to Anu's earthy energies. If you can't have real plants, fake flowers can be used as well. These are sold at most craft

60. Hutton, *The Pagan Religions of the Ancient British Isles*, p. 153.

stores, are easy to store, and don't require watering or any attention. I have a decorative ivy vine that I use when I cannot work outside. The vine is long enough to completely circle my ritual area, and while it may not be a real plant, it's the symbolism that is important.

Anu Correspondences

Color: green, earth tones
Herbs: apples, mugwort
Stones/Gems: amethyst, moonstone, emeralds, clear quarts
Moon Phase: new moon, waking moon, full moon
Sun Phase: dawn, midday
Animal Totem: cattle

Anu Invocation

Anu
Mother of all, who nourishes and sustains

Anu
You who are the dark and fertile soil
The riches and abundance of the earth

Anu
Fertile womb
Flowing breasts

Anu
Deep-rooted one
From whom all life and riches flow

Anu
Great Mother of Gods and men
We are all in your care
Hail mother Anu!

Danu, Anu Invocation

While Danu and Anu began as separate goddesses, the two have become so entwined that they are often considered the same goddess. The following invocation calls upon both of these Great Mothers and honors each one's attributes.

Wisdom of water
Abundance of earth
Danu, Anu

The swiftly flowing river
The dark bountiful earth
Danu, Anu

Earth Mothers
Of the gently rolling hills
And the river's depths
Danu, Anu

Sweetness of summer
A cup very full
Danu, Anu

A shield raised in protection
The ocean's deep roar
Danu, Anu

Wisdom of water
Abundance of earth
Danu, Anu

Flame within the water
Spark of creation
Danu, Anu

Most bountiful Mothers of water and earth
Come now and be welcome
Teach to us the mysteries of abundance and birth!

Anu Herbal Blend

This blend can be used as incense, rolled on candles, or used as an offering to Anu. To make your own dried apples, cut your favorite type of apple into thin slices and place on a baking sheet. Bake the apples on low heat for an hour or until they are hard. You may also use apple chips, which you can find in the health food aisle in most grocery stores. Adding a pinch of soil to the blend brings the energies of the land around you to the mixture. (Soil from your own property works best.) This is an excellent blend to use in any type of earth magick.

You Will Need:
1 pinch of soil
2 tbsp. dried apple chips (crushed)
2 tbsp. pennyroyal
3 tbsp. mugwort
1½ tbsp. Irish moss
1 pinch of dragon's blood resin

Anu's Spell for Abundance

You Will Need:
1 bowl
2 cups of soil from your property
Anu Herbal Blend (previous)
Pen and paper
1 small jar

Mix the soil with the herbal blend in the bowl. About a handful of Anu's Herbal Blend will do. On the piece of paper write what kind of abundance you wish to manifest in as much detail as you can. It could be a new job or a successful business venture. Hold the paper in your hands and visualize your goal. When it is clear in your mind, put the paper in the jar and cover it with the soil and herbal mixture. Seal the jar and hold your hands over it, saying:

Deep-rooted Anu
Goddess who nourishes and sustains the earth

Mother of all life
Bring your bounty forth!

Bury the jar on your property.

Anu Ritual Cider

This tasty cider can be served on Sabbats or Esbats and can be used instead of wine for any rituals invoking Anu.

You Will Need:
1 gallon apple cider
½ tbsp. nutmeg
3 cinnamon sticks
6 cloves
2 apples
1 orange
1½ cups dark rum

Place the apple cider in a large pot and bring to a simmer, then add the nutmeg, cinnamon sticks, and cloves. Cut the apples and orange in half. Using a knife, carve Anu's name into the flesh of the apple pieces. (You may wish to use the Celtic Ogham or another magickal alphabet of your choice to do this.) Put the apple and orange halves into the pot. Simmer covered for one hour, remove the apple halves and cinnamon sticks and strain, then add the dark rum.

Anu Full Moon Apple Spell

You Will Need:
Pen and paper
Knife or athame
1 green candle
Cauldron
1 cinnamon stick
Green ribbon
2 apples
Cider or wine

Apples were both a symbol of the sustenance of the earth and were connected to the Celtic Otherworlds. At Samhain, apples were buried as "food" for the dead, connecting the apple to both life and death, much like the Morrigan.

Cast the circle and call the quarters. Invoke Anu, saying:

Anu, Mother of the Gods
Queen of Avalon
Bringer of life, death, and rebirth
All life is within your care
Goddess of the moon and earth
Bestower of life
I ask of you a boon this night

On the piece of paper, write down in as much detail as possible what you want to manifest. Hold the paper in your hands, visualizing what you want. Using the athame, carve on the candle what you want to manifest or a symbol you have chosen to represent your goal. Hold the candle between your hands for several moments, visualizing what you want and seeing energy flowing from your hands and into the candle. Place the candle in the cauldron and light it. Tie the folded piece of paper to the cinnamon stick with the green ribbon, and place it in the cauldron, saying:

Prosperity and abundance
In Anu's cauldron does grow
That the riches of the earth I may know
I am blessed with _________

Place the apples on the altar and circle them clockwise with your wand or athame. Cut the apples in half. Carve the appropriate symbol or phrase representing what you want to manifest into the flesh of the apples. Place one halved apple at each quarter, saying:

Avalon's bounty, sovereign's power
Abundance and prosperity comes
from the east/west/south/north

Pour some of the cider into the cauldron or libation bowl, then raise it above the altar, saying:

Anu, I give you honor!

When you are ready, close the quarters and open the circle. Bury the halved apples or leave them outside for the wildlife to eat, as an offering to the elements and Anu.

Anu Grounding Spell

As an earth goddess, Anu is an excellent goddess to work with to keep yourself grounded. For this spell you will be charging a bag with the earth's energy. Often we can feel "spaced out" after doing psychic work or astral travel. To help ground and center after any kind of psychic work, hold the bag you will be creating and concentrate on the earth's energies.

You Will Need:
1 piece of hematite or a stone from your property
Small piece of moss
1 small green or brown bag
Anu Incense (see page 92)

Place the stone and piece of moss in a brown or green bag. Burn Anu Incense and pass the bag through the smoke. Hold the bag in your hands and concentrate on the earth's energies. See yourself rooted in the earth, your feet sinking into the ground like a tree's roots, keeping you connected to the earth and the material plane. When you are ready, say:

Anu, mother whose spirit lives in the land
Deep-rooted one
Strong and enduring as the stones of the earth
Bring me closer to your realm
Though my spirit may fly
I remain grounded in the earth

Hold your bag whenever you feel the need to be grounded or connected to the earth's energies.

Anu Earth Magick Spell

For this spell you will be calling on Anu and the element of earth to manifest your desired goal. This spell is useful for bringing material things your way, such as money to pay bills, a new job, a new house, or anything that has to do with the earthly and material realm.

You Will Need:
Anu Incense (see page 92)
1 small bowl
1 cup of soil
Athame

Light the incense and pass the bowl through the smoke. Fill the bowl with the soil (preferably from your property). When you are ready, hold your hands over the bowl, saying:

I am one with Anu
Mother of the land
Whose body is the green and fertile hills
Whose blood flows through the rivers
Whose bones are the stones of the earth
The power of earth flows through me
I am one with the body of the Goddess
I am one with the spirit of the earth
I am one with Anu!

Using your finger or your athame, draw a symbol that represents what you wish to manifest into the soil. Hold the image of your desired goal in your mind's eye. When the image is clear in your mind, see it flowing into the soil, moving from the realm of unmanifested energy to the physical realm to become real.

When you are done, sprinkle the soil outside on your property. During winter when the soil is frozen (or if you live in a city), you can substitute a dish of salt for the soil. Draw the symbol in the salt and leave it on your altar for three days. As salt is not good for your flower beds, don't deposit it outside.

Anu Incense

1 small pinch of soil
3 tbsp. mugwort
2 tbsp. Irish moss

6

The Trinity & Additional Connections

Badb and Macha and Anand, of whom are the Paps of Anu in Luachar, were the three daughters of Ernmas the she-farmer.

—*R. A. S. MacAlister,* Lebor Gabála Érenn

While Anu, Macha, and Badb are the Morrigan's most recognizable faces, they are not her only incarnations in the Celtic pantheon. As we have already discussed, Nemain's association with Badb has linked her to the Morrigan's myths. The Welsh goddess Modron bears a striking resemblance to the Irish Morrigan. Modron's myths were assimilated into the stories of King Arthur, and she eventually became the legendary Morgan le Fay. Making her home on a hill not far from the Paps of Anu, the Munster Faery Queen Áine gives us insight into the Morrigan's Maiden aspect. The Celtic Great Mother Danu, said to be the Morrigan's other name as well as her foster mother, shows us the Morrigan's possible origins.

Each of these goddesses gives us a new perspective and greater insight into the Morrigan's role in the Celtic pantheon and our lives. As with Anu, Macha, and Badb, you will find pathworking exercises, rituals, spells, and lore for each of the goddesses in this section.

Combining the Three Faces of the Morrigan

Now that we have met the three goddesses that form the Morrigan's triple nature, it is time to meet her in a more unified form. Use the following invocations and spells to experience an integrated version of the Morrigan.

The Morrigan's Trinity Invocation

You Will Need:
1 white candle
1 red candle
1 black candle
Cauldron or triskele

Place the white, red, and black candles (each representing one of the three Morrigans) around the triskele or cauldron. The triskele is a Celtic symbol representing the Triple Goddess. There are many versions of this symbol, and you can use whichever one appeals the most to you or make a copy of one of the triskeles here. If using the triskele, place a candle over each spiral.

While saying the following chant, make a circular motion over the candles with your hand or wand. You could also use a black feather if you wish.

Anu, Macha, Badb
The three in one
Anu, Macha, Badb
I call thee Morrigan, come!

Light the white candle.

Anu
Wisdom of the deep and fertile earth
I call thee Morrigan, come!

Light the red candle.

Macha
Mare Mother
Warrior-Queen
Sword ready for battle
I call thee Morrigan, come!

Light the black candle.

Badb
Cauldron Mother
Life and death are in your keeping
I call thee Morrigan, come!

Triple Goddess
Of sovereignty's power
I call thee Morrigan, come!

Cúchulain's bane
Dagda's wife
Nine braids in your hair
I call thee Morrigan, come!

Faery Queen
Prophecy your natural tongue
I call thee Morrigan, come!

Lady of Avalon
Mistress of fate
I call thee Morrigan, come!

Shape-shifter Goddess
Raven of Battle
I call thee Morrigan, come!

Anu, Macha, Badb
I call thee Morrigan, come!

Anu, Macha, Badb
I call thee Morrigan, come!

Anu, Macha, Badb
I call thee Morrigan, come!

Meeting the Trinity Spell

The following is a simple ritual designed to welcome the Morrigan's energies into your life and help you connect to her. You can make it as simple or elaborate as you wish. It is not necessary to cast a circle, although you can do so if you wish.

You Will Need:
Athame or knife
1 dark-red candle
Dragon's blood oil
2 parts juniper berries
2 parts mugwort
2 parts vervain
1 part dragon's blood resin

Using a knife or your athame, carve the Morrigan's name into the wax of the candle. You may wish to do this using the Celtic Ogham or a magickal alphabet of your choice. Anoint the candle with the oil. Mix the herbs, berries, and resin together on a plate. When they are evenly mixed, roll the oiled candle in the herbs. Sprinkle any remaining herbs around the base of the candle.

Sit in your sacred space and light the candle, saying:

Morrigan
You who are Maiden, Mother, and Crone
Triple Goddess of creation and destruction
Earth Mother, River Goddess, and Dark Crone
Mistress of Magick and change
Shape-shifting goddess of transformation
Lover and mate of the Dagda
Warrior most bold
I honor you and seek your wisdom
Morrigan, I call to you
In all your faces and guises, I welcome you!

The next part of the ritual is a guided meditation. You may wish to read through it beforehand and run through it by memory, or you may wish to record it and listen to it during the ritual. If you are working with a group, choose one person to read the meditation to the rest of the participants.

Sit in a comfortable position and take three deep cleansing breaths. Visualize crystalline white light surrounding you …

You find yourself walking along a winding path. The road doesn't seem to go in any particular course, weaving back and forth in several different directions. The longer you walk, the more lost you feel. Somewhere above you hear the fluttering of wings. Circling in the air is a raven. Her black eyes regard you curiously before she flies off. You step off the path to follow it.

Soon you find yourself in front of a large grass-covered burial mound. At the base of the mound is a small entranceway leading deep into the earth. Three large stones decorated with spirals and Celtic Ogham symbols hold the entryway open. The raven circles the mound, then lands on one of the stone pillars. Slowly you walk up to the passageway and trace the spirals with your fingers. You know this is an entranceway to the Otherworld, a place to honor the ancestors who rest within the hill. Inspired, you decide to leave an offering, only you realize you haven't brought anything with you to offer. After a moment you decide what to do. Taking the small knife that hangs on your belt, you cut a lock of your own hair and place it at the entranceway. The greatest thing you can offer is yourself—that your actions, thoughts, and deeds might honor the ancestors and the mysteries this place represents. You take a moment to think about how this is a place of transitions and consider the changes you wish to make in your own life. Looking up at the raven, who still regards you with its black eyes, you think of the wild raven goddess Morrigan, who ruled over life, death, and change of any kind. She is the goddess who cared for the souls of the dead, including those buried within the mound before you, and inspired the great deeds of heroes.

The raven calls out and you look up just in time to watch the bird flutter off the stone, transforming midair into a woman before reaching the ground.

Her hair is the same black color as the raven's feathers, with a small streak of white on one side. She stands a little taller than you, and even under the purple and red robes she wears, you can see her body is lean and muscular. You can't quite tell how old she is; she seems young and ancient at the same time, and there is an ageless feeling to her presence. Unable to turn away from her gaze, you watch as her face and features change from those of a young maid to a woman of middle years, vibrate and regal, then to an elder, brimming with secret knowledge. Even her clothes change—one moment she wears dark armor, trimmed with black feathers, then a richly embroidered gown of fiery red and deep forest green, then dark purple-black robes.

"I am all things; I was with you when you first drew breath and will be with you when you breathe your last. I am the Maiden, the Mother, and the Crone. My face is both loving and harsh. I create as easily as I destroy. Though many fear me, my love is unending for all things. Men and women have sought my strength not only for battle but for inner wisdom and strength, to learn the mysteries of the earth and the art of prophecy."

She smiles at you and holds out her hand. You take it, feeling a surge of power flow through you. "I offer you the knowledge of self. For learning my divine nature is to delve into the depths of the soul and emerge reborn, a sword forged and tempered in my fire, enfolded in my boundless strength. Will you learn from me, my child?"

You give her your answer. She smiles, pleased with your response. Between one breath and the next she turns, changing back into a raven and taking to the air. A single black feather falls soundlessly into your outstretched hand, and you know the Morrigan will always be at your side, filling you with her strength, ready to teach you her mysteries and guide you through life's battles.

The scene fades and you find yourself back in your body.

Extinguish the candle and thank the Morrigan. Light the candle whenever you wish to connect to the Morrigan's energies.

Meeting Nemain

Neman appears as the confounder of armies, so that friendly bands, bereft of their senses by her, slaughter one another.

—*W. Y. Evans-Wentz,*
The Fairy-Faith in Celtic Countries

You find yourself standing at the edge of a great plain. At first nothing seems to be amiss, but as you look closer, you see signs that this place was the site of a fierce battle. Tentatively you take a few steps farther onto the plain and take in your surroundings. Pieces of armor, broken arrows, and discarded shields all lie scattered across the grass. Somewhere overhead you hear the hoarse cries of a crow. The cries sound like they are coming closer, and you look up to see a crow flying overhead.

The bird lands at your feet and, to your amazement, begins to change into a beautiful young woman. She is dressed like a warrior, with armor the same color as the crow's feathers, a sword in one hand and a shield in the other. Her long hair is the purest black and her eyes are a deep brown, almost black. She smiles warmly at you and you feel at ease and unafraid.

"I am Nemain. While many fear me, I protect my chosen warriors. To you I will be a source of protection, strength, and encouragement. We all face many battles in life, this is only one; know I shall be at your side guiding you toward victory through all of life's battles. You need only call and my strength shall be yours."

Nemain approaches you. Leaning forward, she breathes lightly on your forehead, and you feel her protection flow over you and fill your spirit. Nemain hands you her sword and shield. As you look down, you see the rest of her armor is now on you as well. When you look up, the goddess has vanished.

In your new armor you explore the battlefield with more confidence. You do not see anyone else on the plain nor do you see any bodies from the battle that was fought here, but you do feel as if invisible eyes are watching your every move. Before long you hear a shout behind you. You turn to see an enormous warrior racing toward you, sword raised. Immediately you realize this is no ordinary warrior—although you can see his armor, there is no face behind the helmet he wears, invisible fingers grip the sword he points at you, and you know it is a phantom, a physical manifestation of a problem or situation you are currently dealing with in your life.

You confidently raise your shield and block the warrior's blow. Up close the warrior is gigantic and towers over you. He thrusts his enormous sword at you, but you parry the blow with your own sword then thrust at the phantom's side. Your sword connects, but there is no blood; instead, as you lunge and hack, the warrior begins to shrink. As the phantom becomes smaller and smaller, you feel as though a great weight is being lifted from your shoulders. Overhead you can hear Nemain in her crow form encouraging you, and you feel a surge of strength rise up from within. The power of Nemain fills the core of your being.

Now the phantom stands before you only a few feet tall, weak and shattered. His sword drops to the ground. Holding the sword of Nemain in both hands, you sever the phantom's head with a single blow, sending an empty helmet crashing to the ground. The rest of the armor falls to the ground as well, and all the phantom's armor begins to fade away as if it never had existed.

The crow swoops down from the sky and lands on your shoulder, wings spread, heralding your victory with its harsh cackling cries. Victorious, you raise your hands and let out a loud triumphant battle cry. As you call out, the last traces of the phantom warrior vanish into nothingness.

While modern authors include Nemain (NEE-vuhn) as one of the three Morrigans, she is not one of the original goddesses in this trinity. Nemain's only connection to the trio can be found in the *Táin*, where she is equated to Badb. The *Lebor Gabála Érenn*, which lists the lineages of the Túatha Dé Danann, clearly lists Macha, Badb, and Anu as the three goddesses that form the Morrigan. Nemain (also spelled Neman or Nemhain) is listed as having a very different genealogy, being the daughter of the god Elcmar, not the goddess Ernmas (who is the mother of the Morrigan's other sisters, Badb and Macha).

Nemain's connection to the Morrigan comes to us through the goddess Badb. Badb was a battle fury like Nemain, and the two goddesses shared a husband. According to *Cormac's Glossary*, Badb and Nemain were the two wives of the war god Neit.

In the *Táin,* however, the lines between these two goddesses blur and their names are used interchangeably, "Nemain, which is Badb."[61] Since the name Badb was used both as a proper name for the goddess and as a title for a battle fury, it is possible that Nemain was another name for the same goddess or at the very least was conflated with Badb at some point in time.

Nemain's name means "venomous" or "frenzy" and is related to the old Irish root *nem*, which means "to deal out," and to *nemi,* which means "poison." Nemain has been equated by some authors to the Greek Nemesis, another battle fury. She is known for her battle cry, which in the *Táin* kills one hundred of Maeve's men. "Then Cuchulain arose... and sent out the hero's shout from his throat, so the fiends and goblins and sprites of the glen and demons of the air wave answer for the fearfulness of the shout that he lifted on high, until Nemain, which is Badb, brought confusion on the host... that an hundred warriors of them fell dead that night of fright and of heartbreak."[62]

Nemain's shrieks, like Badb's, connect her with the banshee of later folklore, although Nemain's cry causes death rather than predicts it. Both in the *Cogadh re Gallaibh (The War of the Irish with the Foreigners),* a medieval manuscript chronicling the Irish's conflict with the Vikings, and in the *Annals of Lough Ce,* Nemain was said to have appeared during a battle in which King Brian Boru won a victory against the Viking invaders. During the battle Nemain flew above the heads of the warriors, shrieking and striking fear into the Vikings.[63] Similarly in the *Táin* she is equated to a "demon of the air."

Like Badb, Nemain is connected to prophecy: "Nemain of prophetic stanzas."[64] This is mostly likely due to her association with Badb, as she is never specifically mentioned as predicting any events.

It is also possible that Nemain is related to Nemetona, the Celtic goddess of sacred groves. Besides the similarity in the two names, there are several inscriptions found in Britain and Gaul pairing Nemetona with the war god Mars and on other occasions Mercury, both being gods the Romans might have equated to Neit.

Like Badb, Nemain is a goddess of battle and victory. While she is deadly and fearsome to her enemies, she is a protector to those she chooses as her champions. In our modern lives, she is a goddess of life's battles, pushing us onward to defeat our own

61. Dunn, *The Ancient Irish Epic Tale Táin Bó Cúailnge,* ch.17.
62. Ibid., ch.17.
63. Rankine and D'Este, *The Guises of the Morrigan,* pp. 40–41.
64. Epstein, *War Goddess,* p. 61.

personal demons. As the "venomous" goddess of destruction, she helps us to overcome the obstacles blocking us from achieving our goals, destroying all that is stagnant and no longer useful in our lives.

Honoring Nemain

I personally feel that Nemain and Badb were originally separate goddesses whose identities merged over time. It is obvious she was not originally one of the three daughters of Ernmas, but she can still be a powerful ally. As far as working with the Morrigan, Nemain can be viewed as another form of Badb.

Call on Nemain for protection and to overcome obstacles. The best time to honor her is during the new or waxing moon. Since she is connected to the element of air, she can be called upon to stop gossip and reveal the truth about a situation. Also call upon Nemain during divination and when seeking justice. Red wine, whiskey, and raw meat are appropriate offerings to Nemain.

Nemain Correspondences

Color: white, red
Herbs: patchouli, oak
Stones / Gems: onyx, obsidian
Moon Phase: new moon, waxing moon
Sun Phase: dusk
Animal Totem: raven, crow

Nemain Invocation

Phantom Fury
Wrathful and Venomous Queen
Come to me, Nemain!
Over the battlefield echoes the sound of your fearful cries
To some you bring terror and death
To others victory

Phantom Fury
Death's mighty queen
Come to me Nemain!
Spirit of the air and glen
Empowerer of heroes
Chooser of the slain

Phantom Fury, Blood Red Queen
Wrathful and Venomous One
Come to me, Nemain!

Nemain's Wrath Spell

You Will Need:
1 black candle
1 black feather

As a battle fury, Nemain can be called upon for justice and to bring swift resolution to a given situation. Cast a circle, call the quarters, and invoke Nemain. On a black candle, write the situation you wish to resolve. You can use a pencil or pen, or use a pin to carve words in the candle. Light the candle and circle it with the black feather while chanting:

Nemain of the whirlwind and storm
Nemain, fury most dark
Whose cries rend and empower the heart
Daughter of earth and Shadow
I call for your swift justice!

Nemain Herbal Blend

This herbal blend can be used as incense, on candles, or simply as an offering to Nemain.

2 tbsp. patchouli
1½ tbsp. juniper berries
1 tbsp. oak leaves
½ tbsp. Solomon's seal

Meeting Áine

Áine that some said was the daughter of
Manannán, but some said was the Morrigu herself.
—*Lady Gregory,* Gods and Fighting Men

You find yourself standing on a carpet of lush green grass. Although it is dusk, the air is pleasantly warm and the trees and shrubs around you are in full bloom. Summer is at its peak and everything is green and growing. A few yards away from you is a large grass-covered hill. As you watch, a spark of light flickers on the hilltop and then two large balefires catch fire and come to life. You can't see who lit the fires; the hilltop appears deserted. Curious, you walk along the hill's base to get a better view.

As you move around the hill, a rustling sound catches your attention from the bushes just ahead of you. Three slender figures emerge from the greenery. Their lithe forms move with an Otherworldly grace and their skin seems to give off a slight glow. You know immediately that they are faeries. When you look closely at their garments, although beautiful and well-tailored, they are made from leaves and pieces of the woodlands, sewn together to resemble patterned fabric. They smile at you and ask why you have come to the sacred hill. You tell them you are trying to see who lit the balefires.

"This is Cnoc Áine, the Hill of Áine, and the fires have been lit for the midsummer festivities, of course!" Giggling, they ask if you wish to accompany them to the celebration. You say yes, and one of the faeries takes you by the hand.

As the fairies guide you up the hill and you come closer to the summit, you hear a whole host of voices, some singing, some laughing, and the sound of a drum accompanied by the shrill notes of a flute fills the night air. When you reach the top, you find it filled with Faery Folk. They dance in a loose circle and you feel your blood stir and your pulse quicken as you listen to the Otherworldly music; you are eager to join in the revelries. One of your guides pulls you toward a large group of Sidhe and soon you have a faery hand in each of your own and you are spiraling around the balefires. Somewhere ahead you can just make out a tall woman dressed in yellow and red silks leading the dance. She glows brighter than the others, as if a halo of fire surrounds her. In the circle she is a fiery sun that the rest of the dancers spin and move around like planets caught in her orbit.

Beneath your feet you feel as if the earth is drumming out its own tune and soon you feel flushed as energy flows up from the earth, filling you and the other dancers. As the dancing and music reach their peak, some of the dancers begin to break off from the circle and pass between the balefires. Your faery guide tells you they are passing between the fires to receive a blessing.

Slowly each dancer passes between the bales. Finally it is your turn, and you approach the fires. The fires reach high above your head, their flames dancing to the beat of the drum. You begin to walk between the bales only to find a woman now stands between them blocking the way. It is the same woman who led the faery procession. She glows like the sun fallen to earth, the yellow, red, and orange silks looking like flickering flames as she walks toward you. Her hair is a loose tumble of golden curls, her eyes the fathomless blue-grey of the sea. While there is a sense of command about her, there is also a playfulness in the way her lips curve up to smile at you. There is no doubt in your mind that you are standing before the sun goddess Áine, whom the hill you stand on is named after.

"I am both the sun and the inner fires that dance within your soul. I am pleasure and joy and love. And I am the vengeance of a woman wronged. I revel in the pleasure and joy life has to offer. To honor these things is to honor me, for I am the fire of passion, the caress of a lover, the flash of inspiration to the bard, the moment of ecstasy that sets all life into motion. I am a force of creation and, like the fires of the sun, I can bring fertility to the sun-kissed fields or burn them away in my wake.

"Fire can be harmful or serve as a source of illumination and nourishing warmth. We all touch one another's lives for good or ill, and whether you allow your inner fires to burn bright and bring good things to yourself and those around you or you let your emotions and passions burn out of control will be your choice. It is I who guard inner illumination. If you would burn away the lies and illusions of your life, step through my fire and be renewed."

She gestures to the fires. After a moment you step between the balefires, the flames' warmth kissing your skin. You feel the cleansing power of fire flow through you, reawakening in you passions and dreams that you have let lie dormant and thought were extinguished. When you open your eyes, you find yourself alone on the hill. The fires still blaze behind you, and you can barely hear the beat of a drum off in the distance. You know now that the Fae you met at the base of the hill must have brought you into Faery. Feeling cleansed and renewed, you whisper your thanks to Áine and the faery host.

Áine (pronounced AWN-yah) is the Irish goddess of love, fertility, cattle, and the sun. Her worship was centered primarily in the southern province of Munster. Her name means "brightness," "pleasure," or "melody." Like so many Celtic goddesses,

Áine became a Faery Queen after her worship died out, and she eventually became known as a Leanan Sidhe, or Faery Lover, because of her habit of taking mortal men to her bed. According to *The Book of Leinster,* Áine was the daughter of Eoghanach, the Faery King of Munster, while other sources name her as either the wife or daughter of the sea god Manannán mac Lir.

At first glance this goddess seems to have nothing to do with the Morrigan. After all, she is never mentioned as one of the three Morrigans in any early Irish texts, yet the famous Irish folklorist Lady Gregory tells us that Áine "was the Morrigu herself."[65]

If Áine is "the Morrigu herself," as Gregory says, then more specifically she is the goddess Anu, the mysterious earth goddess so little is known about. Most likely Áine was a later version or a regional variation of Anu. Bearing similar names, both goddesses' worship was centered in the province of Munster and both were connected to the fertility of the land. Cnoc Áine, a mound sacred to Áine, stands only a few miles from the breastlike hills that form the Paps of Anu. Other similarities may have existed, but unfortunately none of Anu's myths have survived through the ages and we can only guess what other traits these two goddesses may have shared.

Because she is a sun goddess, the Summer Solstice (when the sun reaches its peak of power) was especially sacred to Áine. There is no evidence that the Celts saw the sun as solely a masculine force. While there were sun gods like Belenos and Lugh, the majority of Celtic sun divinities were female. Bonfires were lit on Cnoc Áine at midsummer, and torches were carried down the hill in a procession and were waved over fields and livestock to bless them with Áine's fertile power. According to local legend, the procession did not take place one midsummer due to a local man's funeral. That night torches were seen atop Cnoc Áine, and it was believed to be the Faery Folk led by Áine herself. It is for this reason she was known as Áine O' the Wisps, "wisps" referring to the ghostly faery torchlights seen on the hill.[66]

Áine's sister Gráinne (pronounced GRAWN-yah) was another sun goddess and has a similar hill dedicated to her, Cnoc Greine, which stands a few miles away from Cnoc Áine. It is believed that Áine ruled over the bright half of the year while Gráinne ruled over the dark half. According to the *Dindshenchas,* Gráinne was another name for the goddess Macha. If this is true, it connects Áine to the Morrigan not only through her possible connection to Anu but through her connection to Gráinne/ Macha as well.

---

65. Gregory, *Gods and Fighting Men,* p. 82.
66. Rolleston, *Celtic Myths and Legends,* p. 128.

Áine was also a goddess of healing: "those that did cures by herbs said she had power over the whole body."[67] She was said to rule over the life-spark that flowed through all living things. This life-spark was believed to flow through the body, making a complete circuit every twenty-four hours. Surgery or any medical treatment involving cutting a patient was banned on the three days after the festival of Lughnasadh, which were considered sacred to Áine. The belief was that the life-spark would escape through any cuts made in the patient during these three days, causing their death. Áine is also connected to Tobar-Na-Áine, the Well of Áine, whose waters were credited with healing and restorative powers. Most likely many of the wells dedicated to the Christian Saint Anne were originally wells sacred to Áine.

While Áine is never mentioned with horses in any of her surviving myths, she is called the Lair Derg, or Red Mare, which would indicate she was also a horse goddess. Since the horse was a solar animal and Áine was a sun goddess, it is understandable that a connection between the two would have been made. Her connection to the sun and horses is also reminiscent of Macha, who was both a horse goddess and a goddess of the sun.

Like the Morrigan, Áine had a large sexual appetite and enjoyed taking mortal lovers. Although seen as a goddess of love, the love Áine rules over is the lusty sort that has little to do with monogamy or marriage vows. Áine exudes fiery passion and unrepressed sexuality at its rawest and most natural level. Áine was also said to have given the meadowsweet, an herb traditionally used in love spells, its scent. One of Áine's lovers was Finn mac Cool, a leader of the warriors of the Red Branch. Although she was contented with Finn, their affair was short lived. Áine had foolishly made a vow never to sleep with a grey-haired man. Jealous of Áine's happiness, her sister, Miluchrach, used her magick to make Finn's hair turn grey. Áine kept her vow and was forced to give up her lover.

Another of Áine's lovers was Gerald, the Earl of Desmond. In one story Gerald happened upon Áine when she was washing in a river and instantly fell in love with her. He stole her cloak and refused to return it unless she consented to marry him. In another version he throws the cloak over her and abducts her. Like the Morrigan and Dagda, Áine and Gerald meet and unite by a river. Áine promised to wed Gerald so long as he vowed never to be surprised by anything their children might do. Gerald agreed but later broke his promise after seeing their son magically change his height,

67. Gregory, *Gods and Fighting Men,* p. 86.

shrinking so he could fit inside a bottle. With his promise broken, Áine and their son turned into birds and flew away to Lough Gur, a lake near Cnoc Áine. Áine was said to be seen combing her hair along the shores of Lough Gur and on days when the waters of the lake were calm, one could see Áine's castle that was hidden at the bottom of the lake.

Áine was also connected to the yew, a tree traditionally associated with death, showing another parallel to the Morrigan. She is not simply a goddess of love and pleasure, but is also connected to the darker cycles of death and change. In local legends Áine was identified with the banshee, a faery also associated with the Morrigan, and a being connected to the cycles of death. She is described as a "wailing woman" in the eulogy of a member of the Fitzgerald family, who claimed her as an ancestress. "Áine from her closely bid nest did awake, the woman of wailing from Gur's voicy lake."[68] Here Áine acts as both a banshee and a kind of ancestral guardian. In the nineteenth century she is depicted combing her hair on the shores of her lake, Lough Gur, giving her another parallel to the banshee who is sometimes described as combing her long ghostly hair while she laments. When the famous bard Thomas O'Connellan died at the castle of Lough Gur, Áine was said to have stood on a rock and keened as the funeral procession passed the castle.

Although not a goddess of battle, the Eoghanacht tribe asked for her aid in taking over *Druim Choilchoille,* or the "Hill of the Hazelwood," which was later known as Cnoc Áine. Áine promised them victory only if they would name the hill after her, which they did.

Áine's connection to the Faery Folk mirrors the Morrigan's role as Queen of the Sidhe. In some stories Áine is a Faery Queen, and in others she is a mortal woman tricked into becoming one of the faeries. These myths most likely evolved with the coming of Christianity and became a way of demoting Áine to a less-than-divine stature. Besides being a Faery Queen, Áine is one of the Leanan Sidhe, a kind of faery lover who drained men of their life force. Like the Morrigan, her exuberant libido becomes something dangerous and out of control in the eyes of the new religion, to the point of making her physically dangerous to men.

Áine was also a goddess of inspiration. She carried a harp, and it was believed that the stone on top of Cnoc Áine could bestow inspiration on those she favored or madness on the unworthy. Swans, her totem animal, are also connected to music and

---

68. Evans-Wentz, *The Fairy-Faith in Celtic Countries,* p. 81.

inspiration, bringing to mind one of the translations of Áine's name: "melody." Áine could shape-shift into the bird and sometimes wore a cloak made from swan feathers. Swans were sacred to bards, and their feathers and skin were used to create ceremonial cloaks called *tugen*.

In Áine we see the Morrigan's face as the Maiden, the youthful and exuberant lover who enjoys all of life's pleasures while still maintaining a connection to the earth and the realms of the Otherworlds. As goddess of the sun, she brings the gifts of healing and fertility. As the faery lover, she not only ignites love's spark but soothes those who have been betrayed—as she herself was betrayed by those she loved—or those who have lost loved ones through the deceit and jealousy of others. Through Áine we can also strengthen our connection to Anu, giving her a more defined presence than the little information that folklore has left us.

Honoring Áine

A simple way to honor Áine is to light a red or gold candle. Because she is a goddess of the sun and midsummer, fire is especially sacred to her. As one of the queens of the Faery Folk, Áine would enjoy offerings that are traditionally given to the faeries—such as milk or honey. Áine also teaches us to embrace our inner fires. Take a day to celebrate your own creativity or anything you feel passionate about. As one of the translations of her name is "melody," playing music that inspires you would be appropriate. Call on Áine for inspiration, healing, abundance, and any spell that relates to love. As she had a less-than-perfect love life, Áine is an ideal goddess to call upon to heal a broken heart.

Áine Correspondences

Color: red, gold
Herbs: meadowsweet, yew
Stones/Gems: garnet, rose quarts
Moon Phase: full moon
Sun Phase: noon, midsummer
Animal Totem: horse, swan

Áine Invocation

Queen of Elphame
Keeper of life's spark
Faery Lover
Summer's Bright Queen
Goddess of sunlight
And love's sweet melody
Healer, lover, poet, enchantress
Áine, stir the fires within
Ignite within me your passion
Bestow upon me your inspiration
Fill me with your fiery spirit!

Áine's Spell for Inspiration

Jasmine is considered the herb of poets and brings inspiration with its sweet scent. Mixed with meadowsweet, which Áine was said to have given its scent, it draws on Áine as a goddess of inspiration.

You Will Need:
1 cup of jasmine tea
Jasmine flowers
Meadowsweet
Incense charcoal

Before you begin you will need to brew a cup of jasmine tea. Place the tea on your altar and put equal parts jasmine flowers and meadowsweet on the incense burner. Hold the cup above the altar, visualizing Áine's creative power flowing down into the cup. When you are ready, say:

Mistress of the faery hill
Inspiration's cup for me now fill!

Drink the tea, visualizing Áine's creativity flowing through you.

Áine Water

Áine Water can be used to raise the positive vibrations in a room, for general blessings, and to anoint candles for rituals invoking Áine. Only bottled water or water collected from a sacred place should be used. If you are using water gathered from a well or river, filter it through the cheesecloth to remove any particles before using it.

You Will Need:
1 glass bowl
Fresh meadowsweet flowers
Cheesecloth
1 dark glass bottle for storage

Pour three cups of water into a large glass bowl and cover the entire surface of the water with the meadowsweet flowers. Take the bowl outside and raise it in the air, visualizing Áine's blessings flowing from the sunlight and into the water. Leave the bowl outside in the sun for at least three hours. When the meadowsweet looks slightly wilted, it is ready to be brought back inside. Throw away the meadowsweet flowers and strain the water through the cheesecloth to remove any particles. Store in a dark glass bottle. To give the water a longer shelf life, add seven drops of one-hundred-proof alcohol per cup of water.

Áine Faery Round Spell

This is a general spell that calls on Áine's power. It can be chanted over a candle while you circle it with either your hand or your wand. A friend of mine uses this spell quite effectively by writing what she wishes to manifest on a piece of paper. She then lights a candle and slowly circles her sacred space in a sunwise direction while saying the chant, much like walking a labyrinth in meditation. Then she burns the piece of paper. Regardless of how you use the following chant, it can easily be worked into any sort of spellwork.

Round and round the faery mound
Áine sings, feet drumming on the ground

Mistress of life's vital fire
Bring to me all I desire

Round and round the faery mound
Áine sings, feet drumming on the ground

Mistress of heat and fire
Bring to me my heart's desire

Round and round the faery mound
Áine sings, feet drumming on the ground

Mistress of the faery hill
Of Will O' Wisps and sacred fire
Bring to me what I desire

Sensuous, swan-like
Leanan Sidhe
Bring what I ask, now to me!

Meeting Modron

Modron resides in each one of us and in all aspects of nature. She is the deep well of knowledge, the hidden core of wisdom.

—*Michelle Skye,* Goddess Alive

You are walking along a dirt path. It is a warm day and the sun's rays leave you feeling warm and content as you walk along the road. As you continue on the path, two ravens appear in the sky above you. You look up as they call to you in their harsh cackling voices. One is the purest white, and the other the deep black of a starless night sky. The ravens circle around you once more, then fly off into the woods that line either side of the path. Curious, you follow the crows' flight. Once in the woods you can hear the sound of rushing water nearby. There is another sound too—a low humming, as if someone is singing by the river bank. You stop to listen, but you only catch a word or two—the rest of the song is drowned out by the sound of the rushing water.

Determined to find the source of the singing, you follow the sound deeper into the woods until the trees open to a river bank. You make your way through the large grey and black boulders that litter the river bank, following the sound of the singing. Soon you come upon a woman standing at the river's edge. She stands with one foot in the rushing water and the other firmly on the sandy shore. Beside her on the bank is a large bronze cauldron, filled to the brim with dirty linens. The two ravens are perched on a nearby boulder. They appear to be watching the woman as she works, and they call out their greetings as you approach.

Even with her brown hair tied in a loose bun behind her head and the sleeves of her purple and burgundy dress rolled up so as not to get in the way of her washing, the woman holds herself as regally and with as much grace as a queen in her throne room.

She tells you the ravens must have brought you here to help her with her work, and she points at the birds perched on the nearby boulder. As if they can understand her words, they call out with their harsh crackling voices. Smiling, she tells you that she will reward you if you help her with her labor.

Agreeing to help, you lift a mud-stained sheet from the cauldron and bring it to the water's edge. The woman holds one side of the sheet and you hold the other, and together you rinse it in the chilly river water. Slowly the mud washes away, carried downstream by the quickly moving waters, leaving the sheet clean and white. Holding the now-clean sheet up from the water, the woman moves her hand across the fabric and it warms to her touch, drying instantly.

"Water is a powerful force; it is the lifeblood of the earth. Without it there can be no life, no sustenance; crops could not grow, the earth would be thirsty and dry. It is water, the rushing rivers, that are at the heart of the earth's fertile power. Water can both nurture and heal; it cleanses and washes away the clutter we create in our lives and spirits. It cleanses, it heals, and it sustains. From the water in your blood, flowing through your veins, to the mother ocean, water moves and perpetuates all life."

As the woman speaks, you become more aware of the water rushing past you and swirling around your feet, its pulse and flow, and you feel similar rivers flowing through your body and in your veins.

You continue your work, going quickly through the pile of linens, and with each piece you feel lighter, as if a weight is being lifted from you and washed away by the river water. When the last piece is clean, you feel like you are glowing, cleansed of the worries and doubts that have littered your mundane life. The woman looks at you, a pleased smile on her face, and you realize this is no ordinary washerwoman you have encountered, but Modron the Welsh Mother Goddess and patroness of rivers and the sacred power of water.

"We clutter the fabric of our life with so many things. Sometimes it is stained with negativity and our daily worries. If we do not cleanse and release our negativity and fears, they become a burden, weighing heavily on our spirits.

"Mine is the power of change. I move like the water, endlessly changing, circling, becoming and unbecoming. My waters nourish and wash away that which is no longer necessary. I am both the fruitful mother and lonely phantom washer who brings release and transformation. I am the cycle of nature, endlessly turning; my mystery is accepting change, for change when willingly sought need not be a painful transition."

Modron reaches behind her and holds up a golden chalice richly engraved with spirals and wave like designs. Within in is the clearest water you have ever seen—it sparkles like liquid moonlight in the chalice.

"Drink deep of my waters and embrace the transformation I offer." You take the chalice in your hands and drink the cool liquid, feeling Modron's power flow through you, filling your body, mind, and spirit.

Modron was the Morrigan's counterpart in Welsh mythology. She was the Welsh Mother Goddess and a goddess of fertility. While Modron's name is often translated as "the mother," in a singular sense, the Venerable Bede (a Christian cleric from the eighth century) translated it as "the mothers," plural, indicating she may have been a triple goddess at one time.[69] It is believed that she was derived from the Gaulish Matrona, whom the Marne river in France was named after. Matrona's name meant "great mother," and she possesses attributes similar to Modron.

What remains of her myths can be found in the *Trioedd Ynys Prydein* or *Welsh Triads,* and she is also mentioned several times in conjunction with her son, Mabon, in the *Mabinogion.* The *Trioedd Ynys Prydein* is a collection of triadic sayings regarding events, places, and characters found in the *Mabinogion,* and it dates back to the thirteenth century. It is believed that these triads were used by bards in order to learn large amounts of traditional lore. Modron does not make an appearance in the *Mabinogion,* but she is mentioned several times as the mother of the god Mabon, reaffirming her

69. Skye, *Goddess Alive,* p. 139.

importance as a mother figure. Unfortunately, the *Mabinogion* suffered from a great deal of editing and alterations through the centuries, and the divine nature of the gods mentioned in the text are harder to unearth than their Irish cousins. While the gods of Túatha Dé Danann diminished in size and importance to become the kings and queens of the Faery Folk, their Welsh counterparts became mortal kings and queens, blurring history and myth together. While it is clear that some characters were once Welsh gods, other characters—such as King Urien, who was said to be Modron's husband—were actual historical figures.

The Welsh Triads tell us there was a certain river ford in Denbighshire where dogs would go to bark. No one knew what the dogs were barking at until King Urien went to the ford to investigate. There he found a woman washing in the river. Instantly taken with the woman, he made love to her then and there by the ford. Sound familiar? Except for Urien being a mortal man rather than a god, this story is identical to the Morrigan's union with Dagda at the ford of the river Unius. While Urien is mortal, he is a king and is responsible for the welfare of the land and the people he rules, similar to Dagda's role as the Irish All-Father and god of fertility and plenty.

After their union, Modron tells Urien that she is the daughter of Avallach, the king of Annwfn (also known as Avalon and the Welsh version of the Otherworlds), making her one of the Faery Folk. She had been under a curse to wash at the river ford until she conceived a son by a Christian. (Here we can see the heavy Christian influence in the text. In the original unaltered version, their union would most likely have been part of a seasonal rite meant to bring prosperity to the land.) Modron instructs Urien to return in a year to receive the child they had conceived together. When Urien returned, he found not one child but two children, a twin boy and girl, named Owain and Morfudd. The twin children represent Modron's fertile nature as a Mother Goddess, and we can find a parallel in the myths that surround the goddess Macha, who gave birth to twins after being forced to race the king of Ulster's horses. The number of children both goddesses bear are symbols of their fertility. Two may not seem like a bountiful number of children by today's standards, but if the Celts had the knowledge we have today and access to modern fertility drugs, these goddesses would probably have given birth to sextuplets or octuplets.

While Modron's washing does not herald a death or any other catastrophe, she does bear a striking resemblance to the Irish Washer at the Ford. Like the Morrigan, Modron is connected to rivers and bodies of water. Her myths seem to have evolved in a different direction than the Morrigan's and her role remained that of a Mother goddess and a goddess of fertility rather than of war, again giving us insight into the Morrigan's original function.

As mentioned earlier, the *Mabigonion* sometimes blurs Welsh deities with historical figures. There was a historical King Urien who ruled northern England during the sixth century. Whether the mortal king is the same one mentioned in this story or the historical king was simply named after the king in the story is unclear. In later Arthurian legends, Urien is said to be the husband of Morgan le Fay, who is a further evolution of Modron and the Morrigan within Celtic lore. Owain, the twin son Modron bears to Urien, was said to be the son of Morgan le Fay in the later Arthurian tales, meaning that Modron, the Morrigan, and Morgan le Fay are one and the same. Owain was also given a flock of ravens, a gift from his mother, adding yet another link to our Irish raven goddess.

As for Morgan le Fay, she is sometimes described as the half-sister of the legendary King Arthur. In Sir Thomas Malory's versions of the Arthurian saga, *Le Morte d' Arthur,* she is the king's half-sister and a sorceress who uses her powers to thwart her brother and eventually tries to remove him from the throne. In this version she also has an incestuous relationship with Arthur, from which her son Mordred was born. This incestuous relationship may hint at her original role as a goddess, as marrying and bearing children with siblings and parents is commonplace in the lineages of the gods and goddesses of many cultures. In the Morrigan's case, she is both the daughter of Delbaeth and the mother of his children. Many of the characters in the *Mabinogion* were once Welsh gods, possibly even Arthur; thus a union between the two, as a goddess and a god, would not have been out of place. Once these two become a mortal king and queen, their incestuous relationship becomes a perversion, illustrating Morgan le Fay's evil nature.

In Geoffrey of Monmouth's 1150 CE *Vita Merlini,* Morgan is a healer and one of nine sisters that lived on the Isle of Avalon. This version seems closer to Modron's mythology, since she was also connected to Avalon. The nine sisters mentioned in the *Vita Merlini* point to Modron being a many-faced goddess, with each sister representing one of her aspects. This Morgan escorts a dying Arthur to the Isle of Avalon, where she promises to heal the king so he may one day return to the mortal world.

In the fourteenth-century poem *Sir Gawain and the Green Knight,* Morgan le Fay is specifically called a "Goddess," hinting at her divine origins.

"So 'Morgan the Goddess'
She accordingly became;
The proudest she can oppress
And to her purpose tame—"[70]

Unlike Malory's version of Arthurian lore, Morgan le Fay here acts as Arthur's adversary, sending the Green Knight to Arthur's court to test the worthiness of his knights, not unlike the Morrigan testing Cúchulain's worthiness in the *Táin*.

As with the Morrigan, Morgan le Fay had three incarnations in Arthurian lore, manifesting as Arthur's three half-sisters: Morgan, Elaine, and Morgause. In earlier works Morgause was called Anna, possibly connecting her to the goddess Anu.[71]

In later years, Modron may have evolved into the Christian Saint Madron (also called Saint Madurn). Saint Madron is associated with a well in Cornwall known for its healing properties. Nothing is known about this saint other than his association with the healing well and that he was from Cornwall, leading many to believe he is a masculinized version of the goddess Modron. As a river goddess, a sacred well or spring would have been an ideal holy place for this goddess. The lack of knowledge about Madron and the similarity between the saint's name and the goddess's name all point to Modron's assimilation into Christianity.

HONORING MODRON

As a river goddess, rivers and other bodies of water are especially sacred to Modron. Offerings to her can be thrown into running water (so long as the offering is not harmful to the environment) or left alongside a body of water. If you do not live near a body of water, you can call upon Modron's energies by simply running some water over your hands in the kitchen or bathroom while silently asking for her blessing.

Modron Correspondences

Color: blue, green
Herbs: mugwort, vervain
Stones/Gems: clear quartz, stones found in river beds
Moon Phase: full moon
Sun Phase: midday, summer
Animal Totem: raven

70. Stone, *Sir Gawain and the Green Knight*, p. 112.
71. Moorman, *The Works of the Gawain-Poet*, p. 291.

Modron Invocation

Modron
Divine Mother of the life-giving waters
Great Mother of All
Weaving magick
Singing spells
Enchantress and healer of the faery isle
Morgan le Fay, full of guile
Matrona, triple one of mystery and power
Modron, River Goddess
To us let your blessings flow!

Modron's Water Divination Spell

You Will Need:
Modron Incense (see page 119)
A dark-colored bowl or cauldron
Filtered water

In your sacred space, light the incense and pass the cauldron or bowl through the smoke. Pour the water into the cauldron, then take a few moments to ground and center. When you are ready, say:

Modron, daughter of Avalon
Mother of the Gods
Lady of the mists
Part the Veil that I may see
What is and what shall be

Imagine you stand before a sacred well. Modron stands on the other side of the well waiting for you. You ask your questions, and she passes her hand over the well waters and tells you to look into the waters.

Open your eyes and gaze into the water in your cauldron. Your gaze should be relaxed, and it is perfectly okay to blink. You may see images in the water or you may see images in your mind's eye. When you feel your question has been answered, thank Modron and pour the water on the ground outside.

Modron Incense

½ tbsp. heather
1½ tbsp. mugwort
2 tbsp. sandalwood

Meeting Danu

Danu rolls in the midst of never-ceasing currents
flowing without a rest forever onward.
—*T. H. Ralph,* The Rig-Veda

You are walking through a vast expanse of darkness. The echo of your footfalls is the only sound in the dark. Although you can feel a pathway below your feet, you cannot see the path you walk upon, or anything else for that matter, giving you the odd sensation of walking in midair. The darkness around you doesn't feel empty, as you would have expected; instead it feels heavy with potential, as if the darkness was waiting for something to animate it. Now you know you are in the Void between worlds, where all things have their beginnings. On impulse you reach out your hand and draw some of the dark formless energy to you. You watch as it changes shape in your hand, then dissolves like mist back into the vast darkness around you.

You continue along the path for a time until you become aware of the sound of running water somewhere in the distance. Soon you see an iridescent shimmer gliding alongside the path. Energy from the vast expanse around you seems to be accumulating farther ahead and is being filtered into a river of glistening energy. Instinctively you know this focused energy is flowing into the material world to form the atoms, plants, animals, and matter of the physical plane. Curious, you follow the river, eager to find its source.

After following the river for a time, you see a spark of light in the darkness. It seems terribly bright compared to the pitch black that surrounds you. As the light grows, you find yourself standing at the river's source, which is a small well. The well is a simple stone structure, its only decoration a string of unfamiliar symbols etched along its rim. Standing over the well is a woman, her hand raised, stirring the air just above the well waters. The waters mirror her movement, spiraling within the well, as if they were a part of her. She wears long green robes with golden spirals embroidered along the sleeves and neck. Her brilliant green eyes remind you of the color of new leaves, and her golden hair is the color of honey or wheat. She looks up from the well and smiles at you.

"Mine are the waters of the womb, tears shed in joy and sadness, the healing waters that wash away the old and bring new beginnings. I am the mother of the world, my essence flows

in the waters of all rivers, in the ebb and flow of the sea. Many are my names. I am Danu, the River Mother, the Great Mother of Gods and Men, the Divine Waters of Heaven that birthed life out of darkness."

She motions for you to drink from the well, and you scoop up a handful of the water and put it to your lips. A thousand different tastes and sensations flow through you, as if you were tasting life itself. It leaves you feeling invigorated.

"To drink of my waters is to drink of the endless potential of the universe, to become all things and for all things to become you." As she speaks, Danu's form shimmers and melts into the waters, sending a fine spray of water against your face. Before you can react, you find that you too are dissolving and becoming part of the waters. You flow through the well, into the river of life, feeling the waters of Danu change and bring form to whatever they touch, creating the world and all existence. As you flow through the Void, you lose all sense of yourself, becoming one with the element of creation and the creatrix of all life. You feel all life, every shinning atom, within and without you, linked by the simmering divine waters of Danu.

Danu's name (DANN-oo) is derived from the Celtic root *dan,* which means "knowledge." She is a goddess of rivers and fertility, and the mother of the Celtic gods. Her name is remembered in the Túatha Dé Danann (which literally means "Children of the goddess Danu") and in the names of several rivers in Europe, most notably the Danube. She was the mother of the Good God Dagda. She was also associated with craftsmanship and smithcraft. The three smith gods Brian, Iucharba, and Iuchar were known as the Tri De Danand, or the "Three Gods of Danu." In the *Lebor Gabála Érenn,* the smiths are said to be the sons of Danu; but in one version of the text, they are called sons of the Morrigan, leading some to believe the Morrigan is a darker aspect of Danu.

The Morrigan and Danu are linked both directly and indirectly several times. Nineteenth-century writers equated Danu with Anu, claiming they were the same goddess. In *The Book of Lecan,* we are told that the Túatha Dé Danann were named after the Morrigan's "other name," which was Danu: "The Morrigan ... and it is from her other name Danu the Paps of Ana in Luchair are named, as well as the Túatha Dé Danann."[72] Ravens, the Morrigan's totem animal, were used to represent the Túatha Dé Danann in *The First Battle of Moytura.* Before the battle, one of the Fir Bolg kings

72. MacAlister, *Lebor Gabála Érenn,* 188; Redaction 3.

had a prophetic dream in which a flock of black birds attacked his men. In the battle, the wing of the finest of the birds was cut off. The king's Druid interprets the birds to be the Túatha Dé Danann and the bird who lost its wing to be their leader, Nuada, who later had his arm cut off in battle. If Danu did not have some connection to the Morrigan it would seem unlikely that the Túatha Dé Danann would be described as a flock of black birds, a totem animal that has no real connection to Danu. In *The First Battle of Moytura,* Danu is listed as one of the Morrigans, while in other passages Danu is mentioned as the Morrigan's foster mother: "We will go with you, said the women, that is, Badb, Macha, Morrigan and Danu."[73] In *Cormac's Glossary,* Anu, one of the three Morrigans, is referred to as the mother of the gods, a title usually given to Danu. The number of times their names are used interchangeably makes it clear there was some connection between the two goddesses.

Unfortunately, as with many other Celtic gods, Danu's myths and stories have been lost to us. We know the Celtic gods can trace their ancestry back to her and that she was the wife of the god Bile. Bile was a god of the dead who escorted souls to the Otherworld. This is reminiscent of Nemain and Badb's pairing with Neit, the god of war and death. Like the mating of the Morrigan with Dagda, Danu and Bile represent the joining of life and death.

Besides Danu's numerous children, her fertile nature is expressed through her connection to rivers and the element of water. It is no surprise that there are so many Celtic river goddesses. To the Celts, water represented the life force and possessed cleansing and healing powers. Rivers nourished the land, fertilized crops, and sustained livestock. Rivers and bodies of water were entrances to the Otherworlds, and offerings to the gods were ceremonially deposited into rivers. Swords, jewelry, and small figurines representing those seeking cures from their ailments have been found in river beds throughout the areas inhabited by the Celts. Placing offerings into rivers was a way to transport that offering into the Otherworlds. Wells and springs were often dedicated to a particular goddess, and offerings were left to the goddess of a particular well in a similar fashion. These practices survive today in the form of wishing wells and throwing pennies into fountains.

Danu also makes an appearance in the Hindu religion, where she is again honored as a primordial mother goddess and goddess of rivers, supporting her origins as a Proto-Indo-European goddess. In Sanskrit her name means "waters of heaven."

---

73. Epstein, *War Goddess,* p. 78.

She was the mother of the serpent Vrtra, whose body formed seven rivers when he was slain. Similarly the Morrigan's son Méche had serpents in his three hearts and was thrown in a river after being slain. In the Welsh tradition, Danu became known as Don, who was also seen as a river goddess and had several rivers names after her in England, Scotland, and Russia. She was also the ancestress of the Children of Don (the Welsh equivalent of the Túatha Dé Danann), who warred with the Children of Llyr for control of Britain.

Honoring Danu

Honor Danu by cultivating your own innate creativity. I feel the most attuned to her creative power when painting or doing other projects where I can make something meaningful or beautiful out of nothing. The power of creation is vast; we can channel our creative energies into art, our careers, creating a business ... the possibilities are endless. As a goddess of the primordial waters, Danu can be honored by going to the beach or visiting a natural body of water near your home. There are many organizations dedicated to keeping our rivers and lakes clean, and you may want to donate your time to one of these organizations. Keeping a small fountain in your home or near your altar is also a wonderful way to honor Danu. Bottled or filtered water can be poured on the ground as an offering to Danu.

Danu Correspondences

Color: blue, green, white
Herbs: heather, Irish moss, lotus
Stones/Gems: moonstone, clear quarts
Moon Phase: waking moon, full moon
Sun Phase: dawn, midday
Animal Totem: none

Danu Invocation

Danu
Wellspring of life
Ever-flowing one
River mother
Eternal, primordial one
From whom all life springs
Your waters flow through us

Blood to blood, spirit to spirit
Encircle us in your loving embrace
Danu, Goddess of the Divine Waters
Mother of Gods and mortal men
Let your blessings flow forth!

Danu's Blessings Spell

You Will Need:
1 chalice
1 cup of milk
1 tbsp. honey
Cauldron or libation bowl

Invoke Danu at your altar. Hold the chalice of milk above the altar while visualizing Danu's blessings flowing into the liquid as a pure white light. When you are ready, say:

Danu of the cauldron of life and rebirth
Pour your blessings out upon me and mine!

Mix a tablespoon of honey into the milk, stirring it in a clockwise motion. As you stir the liquid, repeat what it is you want to draw into your life, such as "prosperity," "healing," etc.

When you are ready, pour some of the honeyed milk into your cauldron or libation bowl. Take the rest outside and sprinkle the liquid around your property, moving in a clockwise direction. Pour any remaining liquid on the ground.

The Waters of Danu

It is important to make sure the water you are using doesn't have any impurities, or you will not be able to store it for very long. Bottled water or filtered water is ideal. If you plan to store the water longer than a few weeks, add a few drops of alcohol to the mixture as a preservative.

You Will Need:
Danu Incense (see page 125)
1 large glass bowl
Bottled or filtered water
1 clear quartz crystal
1 dark bottle

During a full moon, take your materials outside, preferably somewhere the moonlight can shine on the surface of the bowl. Light the incense and pass the bowl through the smoke. Hold the bowl up in the moonlight, saying:

Blessed is the Holy Well
The womb of the Goddess
Essence of creation
That brings forth life

Pour the water into it, saying:

Blessed be the water
Blood of Danu
From which I was created and shall one day return
Water of life and creation be blessed
Danu, Waters from Heaven
Goddess of the sacred waters
Bless this mixture with your divine essence

Place the crystal in the bowl. Raise the bowl, letting the moonlight wash over the waters. Visualize Danu standing before you. She holds her hands over the bowl, and her blessings flow into the waters. Leave the bowl in the moonlight for an hour, then pour the water into the bottle. Use the water for self-blessings or to cleanse an area of negative vibrations.

Danu Herbal Blend

This herbal blend can be used as an offering to Danu or rolled on candles when invoking Danu.

1 tbsp. heather
1 tbsp. Irish moss
1 tbsp. mugwort
1½ tbsp. lemon balm
2 tbsp. jasmine flowers

Danu Incense

3 tbsp. myrrh
1 tbsp. Irish moss
½ tbsp. heather
1 tbsp. jasmine flowers

Part Three
The Faces of the Morrigan

The Dark Goddess, or Dark Mother, embodies the energy we need to become whole ... Depending on the circumstance, she appears as a fearsome old crone or a youthful, radiant beauty ... Only when we have reached self-knowledge... does she reveal her radiant face.

—Willow Ragan,
Wisdom on Black Wings

The Morrigan Speaks

By Stephanie Woodfield

Your first and last breath belong to Me
I who am the embodiment
Of destruction and creation
Who revels in the chaos of change

It is only I who can navigate you
Through the ruins of your soul
So, you call me the Dark Mother
The Raven of War
And I am, and I am not
For I am ever and only Myself
Beyond the definitions of humanity

If I destroy, it is only to create anew
From the ashes of the old
I am the fertile darkness
Deep within the soul

I am the forge that tempers the Will
I am the rage that empowers
I am the soul that will not suffer
Or endure injustice
I am the strength that emerges
From the darkness of self-doubt
Self-knowledge attained from loss
So drink in My Darkness
And discover the beauty within
And learn the wisdom that only I can teach

The *Vita Merlini* tells us the Isle of Avalon was inhabited by nine sisters, of whom Morgan le Fay was the most skilled in every magickal art. I have often wondered about the significance of these women. Who were these sisters? Morgan le Fay is the only recognizable figure among them. The names of the other eight sisters do not appear in any other surviving mythology, and all we know about them are their names and their relation to Morgan le Fay. Were these nine women originally mortal Priestesses remembered later in Geoffrey of Monmouth's retelling of the Arthurian saga as mythical figures? Or were these sisters really aspects of a single goddess, like other sacred groupings of women, such as the muses or the seven sisters or the fates? Were they the personification of Morgan le Fay's complex personality, and thus of the Morrigan's?

Whether or not the Morrigan was ever seen as a ninefold goddess and only later remembered as a group of mortal Priestesses is debatable, but she does appear to us in a multitude of guises. Like any true shape-shifter, the Morrigan has many faces and her role in our lives changes as we ourselves change. The goddesses that make up her triple nature—Anu, Macha, and Badb—shed light on the Morrigan's origins and bring to light her role in the Celtic mythological cycle. But the ever-elusive Morrigan is more than the sum of her parts. Throughout her myths the Morrigan's complex nature manifests in nine distinct guises. In her brighter aspects, she is the alluring Faery Queen, a goddess of sexuality, a fertile earth goddess, a goddess of sovereignty bestowing on kings the power to rule, and the mistress of magick weaving spells. In her darker guises, we see her as a goddess of shape-shifting, the queen of battle, the seeress uttering prophecies of victory, and the Washer at the Ford, guarding the death of heroes.

Together the Morrigan's shifting guises form a ninefold path of transformation and healing. Each of her faces can lead us to a deeper understanding of ourselves, guide us toward self-healing, and give us the strength to face our fears and self-made illusions. Each of her nine guises brings her image into sharper clarity, shedding light on a complete figure that mirrors the fullness of life and the full scope of the Divine Feminine.

In Part Three, we will explore the mysteries and lessons of each of the Morrigan's nine guises, how they relate to her myths, and how to harness their power within our lives. As with the previous section where we met the main facets of the Morrigan, each chapter opens with a pathworking exercise to help you connect to the powers of each guise as well as rituals, chants, and spellwork for each aspect of the Morrigan. There is no particular order for working with these guises. I suggest that you read through each of them and pick one to work with for a set amount of time, whether that be the next few weeks, a moon cycle, or longer. Remember to document your experiences in your journal.

No matter what form she appears in, the Morrigan stands ready to teach each of us to embrace her transformative power, to harness our inner strength, and to peer into our own darkness in order to make ourselves whole.

7

Shape-Shifter

The Dagda's wife found her; the shape-shifting goddess.

—*Edward Gwynn,* The Metrical Dindshenchas

You find yourself on a hill overlooking a meadow filled with lush green grass. You hear the soft bellows of cattle below as they graze and enjoy the afternoon sun. You take a few moments to watch them and then sit down on the grass to enjoy the warm sun yourself. Soon you begin to doze. Just before you close your eyes and fall asleep, you hear the flutter of wings. You sit up just in time to see a woman with dark hair and flowing purple robes fasten a rope around one of the bulls and lead him away. You call after her, telling her to stop, but she pays you no heed. Moving incredibly quickly, she and the bull disappear down a path cut through the woods surrounding the meadow. Determined not to have one of your cattle stolen, you quickly run down the hill and follow.

The forest path winds through the ancient trees for several miles, and although you can see the woman and the bull not far ahead of you, you never seem any closer to catching them no matter how fast you run. They remain fixed on the horizon, never any closer or farther away.

Eventually you come to a wide river. It flows by too quickly for you to ford the icy waters without being swept away. You watch as the woman and bull fade away in the distance on the other side of the river. Feeling defeated you sit down along the shore, uncertain of what to do. After a short time a woman appears from the woods. It is not the cow thief, but a young woman dressed in green with fiery red hair. She smiles at you and asks what is wrong, and you tell her about the stolen bull and the mysterious woman.

"Well then you shall just have to get across this river," she says. You tell her you cannot swim across and she nods. "Yes, but if you were a bird, you could fly across. But you are far

too burdened to glide upon the air. Give me something from the pack you carry and I will teach you how to change into the shape of a raven."

You had forgotten about the heavy pack you have been carrying. You took it with you when you left the meadow to chase the woman, but can't quite remember why you brought it along. You open it and give the woman something from the pack. Instantly you feel lighter and more at peace. The woman thanks you and hands you a single black feather in return. As soon as you touch the feather, you feel yourself begin to change. Arms become glossy black wings, feet become claws, and soon you find yourself standing along the shore in the body of a raven. You launch into the air, flying high above the rushing water, and land on the opposite shore with ease. As soon as you touch the ground, your body returns to normal.

In the distance you can still see the bull and the woman and so you continue your pursuit. Again you seem unable to get any closer to catching them. You run and run, but they remain beyond your reach. Finally you stop, unable to run any longer.

It is not too long before you see the red-haired woman again. She waves to you and asks you what is wrong. You tell her again how you cannot catch the mysterious cow thief. She nods and says, "If you only could run with the vigor and speed of a horse, surely you will catch this thief. Give me something from your bag and I will show you how to become the swiftest of horses." You do as she asks and again feel lighter, your pack nearly empty. She hands you a leather bridle, and you begin to change as soon as you touch it.

You feel yourself growing taller and stronger; the muscles in your arms and legs urge you to run. You look down to see your limbs replaced by long legs that end in hooves. As a horse you find the strength and will to continue onward. You follow the dark-haired woman and the stolen bull for a long time, traveling many miles, until the landscape begins to change. The forest gives way to open fields and they in turn change into rolling mountains, covered in ancient trees.

After countless miles you feel yourself changing back and again you are in your own body. Again you feel as if you failed—you are no closer to the woman than you were when you started. Just when you are about to turn back and give up, you realize that you are not alone. The red-haired woman appears from behind one of the ancient pines and comes to sit beside you. "If only you were a wolf, sure-footed and silent. You could sneak up on that woman and she would never hear you coming. If you give me what remains in your pack, I will show you how to become a wolf." You agree and hand her the entire pack and instantly feel lighter, freed from a great burden you hadn't realized you had been carrying.

The woman hands you a sharp canine tooth, and you feel yourself changing once more. This time your skin becomes fur and your hands become padded and clawed. As the stealthy wolf, you follow after the stolen bull, this time hiding among the trees and hills, completely silent as you stalk your prey. And this time you do come closer to the woman. Closer and closer you creep, staying invisible among the forest until you are only a few feet away from your goal.

The woman stops, as if sensing your approach. Ahead of her is the large mouth of a cave, and you know she intends to lead the bull there. Now is your chance. You emerge from the trees and the woman turns toward you. Again you return to your own body and demand she return the bull. She smiles, saying, "What you seek was never stolen." Confused, you notice the bull is nowhere to be seen. Did the woman really take it?

"If I had not tricked you, how else would I have made you follow me so far? I may at times seem a villain or an adversary, but if I did not challenge you to change, how would you grow? But always know I help you along the way." And now you realize the red-haired woman and the woman standing before you are the same being. "Shape-shifting requires that we transform within and without. To release that which holds us back and deters us from our path to transform that which burdens us into power and strength. Shape-shifting will not only strengthen your connection with the natural realm, but your connection with the inner realms as well. It is upon these inner realms that the greatest shape-shifting occurs."

The woman steps closer to you. "Remember, the power of transformation is within you." Then she places her hand on your shoulder and you feel her power flow through you, and into the very depth of your being. The scene fades and you find yourself back in your body.

Throughout her myths, the Morrigan is always shifting and changing. She transforms from a woman to an animal, from a fertile Earth Mother to a bringer of death. Her ability to shape-shift plays a pivotal role in both her personality and her function in the Celtic pantheon. Her abilities and guises change to match the situation at hand and emphasize her multiple spiritual functions.

There are two types of shape-shifting found in Celtic mythology: The first and most common is the transformation from human to animal shape. The Celts believed in *transmigration,* or the soul's ability to return as either an animal or human in the next life. In the Celtic mind, humanity and the animal kingdom were intimately connected. This interconnection with nature was reflected in their gods, who took the forms of the animals they revered, blurring the distinction between the animal and human realms. By transforming into their totem animal, the deity added that animal's power to their own. Interestingly the Morrigan usually isn't recognized in her human form at all. In every instance that she appears to Cúchulain in human form, the hero fails to recognize her. It is not until she transforms into a raven that he knows who she is. While other Celtic gods could take animal form, they were not necessarily referred to as shape-shifters, yet the Morrigan's ability to change shape is emphasized. In the *Dindshenchas* she is specifically referred to as "the shape-shifting goddess"—it is not until several verses later that her name is given, as if the description of her abilities was enough to identify her. The Morrigan's shape-shifting is not limited to human and animal form. As Morgan le Fay, she transformed herself and her companions into standing stones, illustrating the Celtic belief that all living things—human, animal, and even the land itself—possessed a spirit. The Morrigan shifts back and forth between these with ease.

The second type of shape-shifting involves the transformation from young Maiden to Crone, which reflects the dual roles many Celtic goddesses filled. Mother and Crone traits blur in the myths of many Celtic goddesses, not just the Morrigan's, where they act as both bountiful Mothers and death Crones leading souls to rest in the Otherworlds. Professor Ann Ross tells us that "duality is then at the basis of all Celtic thought; everything had for them a double meaning; many of their artistic forms are meant to be seen in two different ways; and also to possess a duality of significance—naturalistic and symbolic. In the literary motif of Goddess into hag this trait is very obvious."[74] While the Morrigan seems to favor shape-shifting into animals, when she does make an appearance in human form, she often shifts from Maiden to Crone, depending on the actions of the hero in the tale. If the hero scorns the beautiful Maiden, he is certain to feel her wrath as the Crone. After Cúchulain insults the Morrigan's lovely youthful face, she shows him her darker side, hindering his endeavors and finally appearing to him as a hag when she forces him to eat the roasted flesh of a dog, breaking his geis and causing his death. As Macha she is the fertile sovereign of the land, but when challenged by the sons of Dithorba, she pursues them disguised as an old woman. Appearing both young and old at the same time, the Morrigan's face and abilities change depending on the circumstance at hand, reminding us that part of her nature remains hidden beneath her appearance.

The Morrigan's transformative powers are not limited to changing her own form. In the *Dindshenchas* she transforms Odras into a river. Here her shape-shifting can be seen as a function of the goddess of death. Reintegrating Odras's mortal

---

74. Ross, "The Divine Hag of the Pagan Celts," *The Witch Figure*, p. 147.

body into the earth is a symbolic death. Instead of her physical body returning to the earth through decay, her death comes in the form of a magickal transformation. Her transformation occurs near the entrance of the Cave of Cruachan, a known entrance to the Otherworlds, which Odras's spirit presumably passes through after her transformation. Here shape-shifting becomes symbolic of the soul's transition from life to death.

While we think of shape-shifting as a physical transformation, actual shape-shifting is less about a physical transformation than an inner one. Shape-shifting is about shifting energies, your own or those around you, to effect change. In a way, we are performing shape-shifting every time we use magick. Magick is the art of shaping energy to manifest a desired result. Shape-shifting is no different, only the changes we are manifesting are on that of the inner landscape. The shape-shifting we will be exploring involves connecting to the essence of animal allies. By connecting to the animal world, we can strengthen our link to nature and the earth's natural rhythms and cycles that our animal cousins are so attuned to. We will explore the wisdom of the animals associated with the Morrigan as well as other animal allies in the Celtic tradition. Since the Celts viewed all things in nature, including trees and plants, as have their own spirits, we will also learn to connect to the transformative and healing energies of the plant realm.

In her guise as the goddess of shape-shifting, the Morrigan blurs the lines between human and animal, drawing her power and personality from both. When the Morrigan appears to us as the shape-shifter, it signals a time of transformation. She challenges us to reshape our lives, to strengthen our connection to the realms of nature and to discover that we are a part of the natural world, rather than separate or above it.

Celtic Animal Allies

We usually think of totems or animal allies in relation to the traditions of the Native Americans, but animals have always played a significant role in human religion and spirituality worldwide. In Norse shamanism, totem animals are referred to as *fetches;* to the Aztecs they were the *nagual*; in Witchcraft they are sometimes referred to as *familiars,* although the term can also refer to a living animal the Witch is working with.[75]

---

75. Penczak, *The Temple of Shamanic Witchcraft,* p. 160.

In the Celtic mind, animals acted as a link between the mundane world and the divine one, facilitating communication with the Otherworlds. The remains of ravens and horses, both believed to travel between the worlds, have been found in Celtic graves and burial sites. Animal images predominate Celtic manuscripts and metal work. Stylized images of cattle, sheep, and horses served as handles to cauldrons and cook wear. Images of bears and boars were frequently used to adorn swords, scabbards, and armor. These images evoked the qualities of the animals they depicted. The image of a cow on a cauldron wasn't just art; it evoked the wealth and sustenance that animal represented. The image of a boar on a sword evoked the ferocity of the boar in the warrior who wielded it in battle.

Animals also acted as ancestral spirits. Several Celtic clans claimed ancestry from animals, such as the Catti (Cat-People) from Scotland, the Kintyre (Horse-People), the Taurisci (Bull Folk), and the Branovices (Raven Folk).[76] Other families displayed their animal totems in family crests.

Each of us has a personal animal ally, whether we are aware of their presence or not. Our animal allies act as spiritual guides, protectors, and teachers within this lifetime. We may work with other animals along our life journey, but there will always be one animal in particular that we resonate with most and whose energies complement our own. When people first begin working with animal allies, they automatically assume their favorite animal will be their totem, but this is very rarely the case. My favorite animal is the horse. I've been horse crazy since I was a kid and begged my parents for horseback riding lessons. They relented, but when they couldn't afford it any longer, I worked in a local barn mucking out stalls to pay for my lessons. So naturally when I first started working with animal allies, I assumed the horse would be my totem. This was not the case! The animal that began appearing in my dreams and was making itself known to me was the hawk. The more I ignored the connection, the more impatient the hawk became with me. I noticed hawks more frequently when I went hiking, and on one hike, a hawk followed me for an entire two-hour trek through the woods. I had noticed the bird circling above me a few times, then I began spotting it landing in the trees several yards ahead of me on the hiking trail. As I came closer, the bird would fly several yards ahead and perch on another branch, always staying within sight. At the time I thought I had somehow managed to follow the bird. A little unnerved by the situation and the scenes from Hitchcock's *The Birds* that

76. Matthews and Matthews, *Taliesin*, p. 154.

were going through my mind, I started to walk back to where I parked my car, intentionally taking a route away from where the bird was perched. Alas, the bird followed me for the two-mile return to the road. I zig-zagged, I back-tracked, I tried everything I could think of to lose the bird, but it just kept following me. After that day, I got the hint and began working with the hawk through meditation and ritual and have never regretted it. As much as I love horses, the hawk's energies complement my own and are a better fit.

Animal allies will usually appear to you within dreams (especially if your animal ally is not native to where you live) or during meditations. Sometimes they may make themselves known to you even before you consciously choose to work with the animal realm. Also pay attention to the animals you encounter in the mundane world. If the animal chooses to reveal itself in the physical world, you will know if the encounter is legitimate (rather than mere chance) by the animal's behavior or—as with my experiences with the hawk and crow—the frequency with which you encounter it.

There is also no rule that says you have to have only one power animal; you may eventually find yourself working with several. These other animals may be related to the energies of your patron deities or may enter your life to help you deal with specific situations. When I began working with the Morrigan, the crow and raven also became my allies, making their presence known both in the mundane world and in dreams along with my hawk ally.

Animal allies can be called upon during magick, as guides through the Otherworlds, or to practice the art of shape-shifting. But more importantly, working with the animal realm will help you sense the interconnectedness of all living things. While human beings like to think of themselves as a step apart from the animal kingdom and our egos want us to believe we are superior, there is a vast amount of wisdom to be gained from the animals who share this planet. All we need to do is listen.

Exercise 1: Animal Ally Shape-Shifting

Practicing the art of shape-shifting will help you deepen your connection with your animal ally and harness that animal's specific energies and characteristics for a given task, whether it be magickal or mundane.

Go to your sacred space. If you prefer to work outside, cleanse and bless the area in which you will be working. (Casting a circle is not necessary unless you plan on doing a spell or ritual that will involve calling on the animal's energies and aid.) Having a statue or picture of the animal you wish to work with would be ideal, even if it's just a printout from your computer. There is a list of Celtic animal allies at the end of this section—you can incorporate the accompanying chants into your shape-shifting exercises if you wish. For this exercise we will be connecting to the energy of the raven, the Morrigan's favorite totem. The raven is a messenger of the gods that rules over magick, protection, and divination.

Sit in your sacred space, take three deep breaths, and visualize white light moving from your feet slowly up to the crown of your head, cleansing and filling your spirit. As the light passes over your body, all your tension drains away, until you are fully relaxed ...

You find yourself in a clearing. Tall pines surround the open area, and sunlight streams through the branches to warm your skin. Somewhere above you hear a raven calling out. The bird circles above then lands on the grass a few feet in front of you. Its black feathers have a radiant sheen to them in the afternoon sunlight, reflecting purple and blue. The raven cocks its head to the side and looks at you with curious black eyes.

Suddenly you find yourself changing. You watch as the outline of your shadow blurs and shifts. Fingers turn into black feathers, your face elongates, and a beak emerges. You find yourself shrinking, and soon you are no longer looking down at the raven on the ground.

You become aware of laughter. The sound is not quite audible, and you realize you are hearing the sound in your mind. It is the raven. Your surprise at your transformation amuses him. You take a few minutes to speak mind to mind with the raven, finding him to be just as sentient as yourself. When you are done speaking with him, he launches into the air and you follow, enjoying the feeling of the wind under your feathers.

When you are ready to end the journey, return to the meadow and visualize yourself returning to your normal form.

With practice you will become more familiar with the energies you experience when shape-shifting and will be able to call on that energy whenever you want, whether that be in your mundane or magickal life. Perhaps you might call upon the tiger to exude confidence during a job interview or you want to connect to the raven during a divination session—the possibilities are endless. Simply imagine yourself in the form of that animal to connect to that animal's energies. Once you are familiar with an animal's energies, you can do this in your mind within seconds and will not require an Otherworld journey.

Exercise 2: Connecting with the Plant World

Shape-shifting is not limited to the animal world. Connecting to the plant realm can help us learn the magickal uses of plants and enhance our awareness of earth's natural rhythms and energies. The ground beneath our feet holds a vast amount of power, and connecting to the green and growing things on your property or those in the wild can help you attune to and draw upon those earthy energies.

We have become so disconnected from the planet that many people have trouble listening to the subtle voices of plants, so we'll begin by connecting to the earth. For the next three days go outside and stand with your feet slightly apart. Feel your feet and legs becoming one with the ground, being made of the same material as the surface beneath you. Let your awareness spread out past your body, becoming one with the spirits of the land around you. Visualize energy moving up through the ground and into you, rising from your feet to your crown then flowing down your body and back into the ground. Visualize this energy looping through you several times.

When you are ready to end the exercise, see your feet becoming separate from the ground and allow your inner awareness to return to your body. Each day try to expand your awareness of the earth around you; with practice you will begin receiving impressions from the land. When I first began doing this exercise in my backyard, I kept getting the strangest sensation of being bound with ropes. I didn't feel threatened, just uncomfortable. At first I couldn't understand the connection between this odd feeling and the land around me, but it continued to happen every time I connected to the earthy energies in my yard. Several days later I realized that one of the trees in my yard had a thick vine of poison ivy growing around its trunk. The vine was three inches thick and looked very much like a thick rope wrapping around the tree. If the vine had been left alone, it would have strangled the tree, killing it. Once I hacked off the vine, I no longer felt the strange smothering sensation when I connected to the land. It was like the tree was saying "Hey get this thing off me, will ya?" the whole time. You can do this exercise in your backyard, your local park, or any place where nature grows freely. Make sure to record any impressions you receive in your journal.

After you have practiced connecting to the energies of the earth in general, choose a plant you wish to work with. It can be a plant you come across on a hike or a potted flower or herb purchased from a garden center. Sit next to the plant, visualizing your essence flowing into the plant and its energies merging with your own. Feel the plant's leaves, stems, and flowers becoming part of you. Express your interest in working with the plant and your willingness to learn from it. Plants communicate in feelings and visual impressions, and you may receive a feeling or simply a sense of knowing. If you wish to harvest part of the plant, ask for its permission first and always remember to leave something in return, even if it's a simple offering of a little bottled water.

Exercise 3: Invisibility

Learning to shift our personal energies can also help us learn the art of invisibility. Invisibility is about blending with the energies of your surroundings; you will not literally become invisible but instead will avoid notice.

Pick a wall in your home and stand with your back against it. Visualize your aura becoming the same color as the wall. If you have wallpaper, see your aura taking on the same pattern until you cannot see where the wall ends and your body begins. Practice the same visualization while moving through a room, seeing your aura melting into the energies surrounding you.

This can be a useful skill if you are alone at night and feel threatened. I used to work for a company that had an office in a bad part of town, and a few employees had been mugged in the parking lot. Unfortunately, I didn't always work with another person at night, leaving me without another employee to accompany me to my car. When that happened I used this technique, seeing myself blending into the parking lot, invisible to any onlookers, while I walked to my car.

Animal Allies Connected to the Morrigan

The following are the animal allies the Morrigan is the most connected to. Working with the Morrigan's animal allies can help strengthen our connection to her, and give us a deeper understanding of the primal power she holds sway over.

Raven

Aspect: Morrigan in general / Badb / Nemain
Element: Air

The Raven is connected to magick, prophecy, and the Underworld. Ravens are highly intelligent, having the largest brain of any bird species, and are highly mischievous. In the wild ravens live ten to fifteen years, although ravens in captivity have lived up to the age of forty. Larger than their crow cousins, ravens have a four-foot wingspan and are roughly the size of a hawk. Wild ravens will work together in groups and are very territorial. Ravens play the wise tricksters in many myths, and wild ravens enjoy playing tricks and mimicking the sounds they hear. Ravens in Olympic National Park in Washington State have been reported to mimic the sounds of the auto flush urinals in the park's bathrooms and the call used by park personnel during avalanche-simulation trainings.

Ravens are opportunistic omnivores, eating anything they can scavenge and would have been found on ancient battlefields scavenging for meat. Since the Celts believed that eating something meant you were taking in its spirit, ravens were believed to carry the souls of the dead to the Otherworld.

Ravens have been considered the messengers of the gods in several different cultures. In Norse mythology, Odin had two ravens that brought him news. They were originally white until they brought the god bad news and he turned their feathers black. For good or ill, the raven's news will always be truthful. The Celtic Bran, his sister Branwen, and the sun god Lugh were all associated with ravens. Ravens warned Lugh of the approach of the Fomorians, again fulfilling the role of a messenger.

In Native American lore, the raven created the earth by dropping a stone into the primordial ocean. The stone expanded to make the continents. Raven was also credited with putting the sun in the sky, turning his white feathers black in the process.

Ravens are connected to prophecy and can aid in divination. The raven is linked to the realm of spirits as a divine messenger and is associated with magick and the mysteries of death. Several of the raven's myths revolve around the bird's feathers changing from white to black, hinting at inner transformation. The raven is also connected with the sun, both in Native American and Celtic legends, making the raven a bird of spiritual illumination. The raven was the totem of Lugh, the Celtic sun god; as we have already seen, the Morrigan is a sun goddess when she appears as Macha and Áine.

Chant:
Dark one of magick and trickery
Messenger of the Gods
Children of the Morrigan
Between the worlds easily you pass
Noble Raven
Your wisdom and mysteries I would know.

Crow

Aspect: Morrigan in general/Badb/Nemain/Macha
Element: Air

Crows are spiritual messengers and are connected with death, the Void, and creation. They are part of the Corvidae family, along with magpies and ravens. Crows are omnivores, often scavenging for food and eating carrion. Like their raven cousins, crows are highly intelligent. In Israel, wild hooded crows have been seen using bread crumbs as bait for fishing. In cities crows are known to drop nuts in streets and wait for cars to crush and open them. Wild crows have been known to use twigs and grass stems to retrieve food. Crows are very territorial but will work together in groups with other crows. To establish a pecking order, they do a type of mid-air jousting with one another.

Crows are connected with prophecy, and in Scottish folklore there were twenty-seven different types of crow calls with meanings varying from good luck to death to the arrival of visitors. The hooded crow in particular is sacred to Badb and Macha. Crows and ravens were seen on the battlefields, which were called the "land of Badb," to scavenge for meat. By eating the flesh of the dead, they symbolically gathered the spirits of fallen warriors.

Chant:
Carrion eater
Cunning trickster
Noble messenger
Who brings new life from the Void
And knows the mysteries of creation and destruction
Birth, creation, life, death
All are one to the crow.

Cattle

Aspect: Morrigan in general / Macha / Áine / Anu
Element: Earth

Cattle were not only work animals but provided meat, hides, and milk. The number of cattle a person owned was a direct indication of their wealth and social status. The early Irish unit of exchange was a *séd,* which was the equivalent to one milch (milk) cow.[77] In Celtic folklore the cow was connected to fertility and abundance. According to legend, all the cattle of Ireland descend from three magickal cows that emerged from the sea on the festival of Beltane. They were called Bó Finne (White Cow), Bó Rua (Red Cow), and Bó Dubh (Black Cow), the traditional colors associated with the Triple Goddess. Each cow went in a different direction—the red to the north, the black to the south, and the white to the center of Ireland—and gave birth to twin calves, and it was these calves that all Irish cattle descended from. Another legend speaks of the Great Glas, a white cow that could ceaselessly produce milk. The Glas was able to fill a bucket of any size with her sweet milk. A farmer tried to drain the Glas with a sieve and was turned to stone for his greed. The Glas was said to graze in the sky, in what is known today as the Milky Way.

The Morrigan often appears with cattle or in the shape of the animal. She transformed into a heifer as part of her magickal attack on Cúchulain. In the *Tain Bó Regamna,* Cúchulain encounters her leading a cow through Ulster. She steals one

77. Ellis, *The Ancient World of the Celts,* p. 107.

of Odras's cattle, and in the form of a raven she warns the magickal Brown Bull of Maeve's approaching army. The cow connects the Morrigan to fertility and the wealth of the land.

Call on the cow to connect to the Triple Goddess in her guise as the abundant Earth Mother. The cow teaches us that there is enough prosperity and wealth in the universe for everyone, so long as we are not greedy and don't attempt to drain the Great Glas.

Chant:
Gentle cow
Crescent horns pointing toward the moon
Mother and nurturer
Bó Finne, Bó Rua, Bó Dubh
Great Glas
Your abundance, your fertile power
Flows over the land
Bless me with your kindness, with your loving and giving nature.

Wolf

Aspect: Badb
Element: Earth

The Celtic name for wolf meant "wild dog," and Celts were known to crossbreed wolves with their domesticated dogs. Wolf teeth were worn as ornaments and charms. King Cormac was reared by a she-wolf and was often accompanied by a pack of wolves.

There is a common misconception that wolves are large, dangerous animals. In reality, wolves are about the same size as the average dog, standing about the same height as a German shepherd. While groups of wolves can take down large prey such as deer or elk, the majority of the wolf's diet is small prey, which includes rabbits and rodents.

In the wild, wolves and ravens are often seen together. Ravens are known to follow wolves in order to scavenge meat from their next kill, and ravens will also eat wolf scat for nourishment.

When the Morrigan attacked Cúchulain on the battlefield, she appeared as a grey-red wolf. Badb was also said to appear on battlefields in the shape of a wolf. In connection to the dark goddess, the wolf, like the hound, became a guardian of the Underworld. Wolves were also known to scavenge for food on battlefields. By consuming the flesh of the dead, they took on the warrior's essence and were believed to ferry the spirits of the dead to the Otherworlds.

Call on the wolf as a guide during meditation and for protection.

Chant:
Children of Badb
Sleek grey wolf
Cunning hunter
Fierce protector
Brother/Sister Wolf
Guide and guard me on my journey.

Horse

Aspect: Macha / Áine
Element: Earth and Fire

Like cattle, horses were symbols of wealth and social status to the Celts. They were essential for travel, war, and farming. Horses acted as messengers between the worlds and were believe to carry the souls of the dead to the Otherworlds. Horses have been found in burial pits along with dogs and ravens—all animals believed to be able to move between the worlds. The horse is also a solar animal, pulling the chariots of the Greek sun god Apollo and the Hindu sun god Surya, and is also connected to fertility. (This is especially true for stallions.) The horse carries us through all the phases of our lives. It pulled the chariot of the sun through the sky, symbolizing the horse's link to creation and birth. In the mundane world, they helped humanity farm and travel; at life's end, they carried the spirits of the dead into the Otherworlds.

The horse is the Morrigan's totem in her guise as Macha and Áine, both goddesses connected to the sun. Macha's connection to the horse is the most obvious, having been forced to race the king of Ulster's horses as a result of her husband's boastfulness. In Macha's story the horse is a symbol of freeing oneself of burdens. Macha is burdened with the physical demands of racing the king's horses while pregnant. After winning the race she dies, symbolically returning to the Otherworlds free of her task. One of Áine's names was *Lair Derg,* or Red Mare, suggesting a strong connection to the animal. Like the Morrigan, the horse rules over the entire life cycle, from birth to death. As a solar symbol, the horse embodies strength and can teach us to free ourselves of life's burdens.

Chant:
Red Mare
Swift and uncatchable
Who draws the chariot of the sun and moves between the worlds
Noble Horse
Lend to me your strength and grace
Guide me on life's journey.

Eel

Aspect: Morrigan in general
Element: Water

Eels are part of the fish family, with the largest, the giant moray eel, growing up to twelve feet long. Only the Anguillidae family of eels live in fresh water, although they return to the sea to spawn. Eels are adept at camouflage, burrowing in the sand and mud at the bottom of streams or hiding in holes. They primarily hunt at night and have sharp teeth and powerful jaws that allow them to eat larger prey. According to Celtic legend, the eel can grow legs and walk on land and return to it serpentine form when in water. The two faery pig keepers who eventually became the two bulls fought over in the *Táin* transformed into eels as part of their magickal contest.

As an eel, the Morrigan coiled around the hero Cúchulain's legs, hindering him when battling in a stream. The eel is connected to the Morrigan as a goddess of rivers and the sea. As a creature connected with the element of water, the eel rules over change and the shadowy side of our emotions. Like the Morrigan, the eel is a shape-shifter, embodying the ability to change and adapt to a given situation. As an animal skilled in camouflage, the eel can teach us to uncover hidden truths and ferret out lies and illusions.

Chant:
Serpentine One
Hidden secrets you uncover
Shape-shifting, changing, mysteries unraveling
Eel, help me to uncover the knowledge I seek.

Additional Celtic Animal Allies

Bear: Although bears were not indigenous to Britain or Ireland, the continental Celts were familiar with the bear and honored the bear goddess Artio. King Arthur's name is derived from *Art,* the Celtic word for bear. Call on the bear to connect to the primal power of the earth, sovereignty, intuition, and protection.

Cat: Several Scottish tribes held the cat as their totem animal. The Kati, a Pictish tribe, were named after the cat. The fourteenth-century *Yellow Book of Lecan* describes warriors wearing the skins of wild cats, in the same manner warriors wore boar and bear skins, to call on the animal's protection and ferocity. The Cath Sith, giant faery cats, were called upon to see the future. Call on the cat for divination and independence.

Crane: In Celtic mythology the crane was associated with the moon and the Crone. Three cranes were said to guard the entrance to the Celtic Underworld. Similarly the god Midhir had three cranes that guarded his castle—the cranes of Denial, Despair, and Churlishness—who could prevent unwanted travelers from entering his home. Manannán mac Lir had a magickal "crane-bag" made out of crane skin. The crane is also connected to the Ogham, the Celtic tree alphabet. Some sources credit its creation to the observation of wild cranes and the patterns their long legs made.

Deer: Present on nearly every continent on the planet, the deer shows an ability to adapt and thrive in unfamiliar habitats. Hinds (female red deer) were called "faery cattle" and were believed to be milked by the Faery Folk. White hinds were especially sacred and appear in numerous Celtic stories to lead heroes to meet their destiny or to great adventure; its white color clearly marks it as a creature of the Otherworld. Deer have especially acute hearing and eyesight designed to spot movement from a distance. This farsightedness has also connected the deer to divination and seeing into the future or past, thus the term *hindsight.* Both the gods Cernunnos and Herne wore deer antlers, a sign of their connection to the animals and woodland realm. Since the deer's antlers are right behind its eyes, the horns worn by these gods may signify a heightened sense of sight, both in this realm and for seeing into the Otherworlds.[78] Call on the deer for clear-sightedness, adventure, and divination.

78. Andrews, *Animal Speak,* p. 262.

Dog: The dog is known for its devotion and loyalty. Dogs have acted as protectors and companions for humans since our earliest ancestors domesticated wild dogs in order to protect themselves and their herds. In the Celtic tradition, the dog is a powerful guardian and guide. The sun god Lugh had a magickal dog that was invincible in battle. Heroes and kings incorporated the dog (Cú) into their names, such as the hero Cúchulainn (Hound of Culann), who accidently killed Culann's watchdog and vowed to take the dog's place as a guardian of Culann's household. The British kings Cúnobelinn (Dog of Beli) and Cúnoglasus (Tawny Dog) both had the dog incorporated in their names, symbolically adding the animal's traits to themselves. Dogs also guarded the gateways to the Underworld and were depicted on grave markers, at crossroads, and beside Underworld goddesses such as the Greek Hecate. Celtic myths often describe dogs running into the sea or other bodies of water, which were known entrances to the Celtic Otherworlds. Mad dogs were said to gather at Cnoc Áine, after which they ran into the sea, again describing their ability to travel between the worlds. The Black Dog, a phantom hound who appeared before a person's death, acting like the death-messenger banshee, further connected the dog to the Underworld. Call on the dog for protection and as a guide between the worlds.

Eagle: The eagle is connected to both the sun and the stormy forces of thunder and lightning. Eagles were sacred to the Celtic god Taranus, a god of thunder and lightning, and to the Roman Jupiter, who shared similar traits with Taranus. In Gaelic the eagle is called Suil-na-Greine, or "Eye of the Sun," and was one of the oldest animals. Llew, the Welsh version of the Irish sun god Lugh, was transformed into an eagle until his foster father Gwyddyon changed him back into a man. Working with the eagle can awaken spiritual illumination, enabling us to soar to new heights.

Fox: The fox is adept at concealing itself. Its ability to move swiftly has associated it with invisibility, and its habit of stealing chickens and other livestock ties it to trickery and cunning. Call on the fox to learn invisibility and to uncover secrets.

Hare: Hares were sacred and were associated with fertility, luck, and the moon. Hares were also used for divination. According to the Roman historian Cassius Dio, Queen Boadicea used a hare to predict the outcome of battle. She would release the hare from the folds of her dress, and if the hare ran in a certain direction it was taken as an auspicious sign. Hares were sacred to Andraste, a goddess of battle and victory, and to Cailleach, a Crone goddess of winter. In Ulster, hare hunting was referred to as "Chasing the Cailleach." The hare's connection to both goddesses of death and fertility is a prime example of the interconnection the Celts saw between life, death, and rebirth.

Hawk: The hawk's excellent eyesight makes it a bird of visions, awakening the abilities of foresight and prophecy in those who work with this animal. The hawk of Achill was one of the oldest animals in Celtic legend. It plucked out the eye of the salmon of wisdom, symbolically gaining his wisdom. As one of the oldest Celtic animals, the hawk represents a far-reaching memory and the hunt for spiritual knowledge. Hawks kill their prey by piercing the animal's vital organs with their talons, and the hawk can teach us how to take hold of our dreams and champion our hunt for spiritual wisdom. Hawks were messengers between the worlds, and seeing a hawk can indicate that messages or information is coming your way.

Otter: Otters were sacred the sea god Manannán mac Lir. Otter skins were considered to be magickal, granting healing and protection. Cerridwen turned into an otter to pursue Taliesin when he turned into a fish. The otter's playful nature teaches us to relax and enjoy life.

Pig: Sows are connected to fertility and regeneration, while the boar is connected to ferocity and vigor. There are many Celtic stories concerning pigs that continually regenerate after being eaten, bestowing on their owners a neverending supply of food. If the pig was not providing an endless feast, it was granting endless inspiration. The White Boar of Marvan granted its owner poetic and musical inspiration. The goddess Brigid owned a similar boar called Orc Triath that also granted inspiration. Images of boars decorated swords and helmets, giving the warriors who wore them the boar's ferocity. A magickal boar named Formael was said to be able to kill fifty armed men in a single day, linking the boar with prowess in battle. The hero Culhwch had to defeat two magickal boars as part of thirty-nine impossible tasks he was given in order to win Olwen's hand in marriage. Call on the pig for strength, leadership, fertility, and inspiration.

Salmon: The salmon was said to be one of the oldest animals. Swimming in the Well of Segais (Well of Wisdom), it ate the hazelnuts that fell from the nine hazel tress that grew around the well. It was believed that anyone who ate the salmon would gain its vast wisdom.

Swan: The swan's graceful body has associated this bird with beauty, love, and femininity in general. There are several tales of faery maids and goddesses who transform into swans. The goddess Áine had a cloak of swan feathers and could shape-shift into the bird. In the *Dream of Oenghus,* the Celtic god of love Oenghus (another name for Angus Mac Og) dreams about a beautiful maiden. When Oenghus woke he immediately sought her out, eventually learning that the maid transformed every other year into a swan along with one hundred and fifty-one of her maids in waiting. The maiden's father promised Oenghus her hand so long as he could identify her from among the other swans. Luckily for Oenghus she wore a golden chain around her neck while all her maids wore silver, and he easily identified his love. Faery birds and goddesses are often identified by the gold or silver chains worn around their necks or used to tether multiple birds together, marking their otherworldly nature. Swans were also connected to music, being sacred to Áine, who could grant inspiration or madness; the Greek Apollo, the patron of music; and Sarasvati, the Hindu goddess of wisdom and music. Celtic bards wore cloaks decorated with swan feathers. "Swan song" referred to the last or greatest work of a bard, since it was believed that the mute swan was silent all of it life until the moment before its death, when it sang a single beautiful song.

Shape-Shifting Spell

You Will Need:

Dragon's blood oil
1 small can of modeling or quick-drying clay
1 candle

Inscribe on the candle what you wish to manifest. Anoint the candle with dragon's blood oil or another oil appropriate to the situation. Light the candle in your sacred space.

Roll the clay in your hands for a few minutes while visualizing the situation you wish to transform and the clay becoming one. When you can hold your visualization clearly in your mind, chant:

Morrigan
Shape-shifting Goddess
Crow, then woman and back again
Your form fluid like water

Ever-changing, forming, reforming
Essence without boundaries
Grant the change I ask of you
Morrigan, bring change
Renew, reform, rearrange
Morrigan, bring change!

Shape the clay into a symbol representing what you want to manifest. If it's prosperity, you might create a dollar sign; if it's protection, a spear or shield. As you continue to shape the symbol, chant the following as many times as you wish. Three, six, or nine times would be best.

Renew, reform, rearrange!

Let the candle burn out. Let the clay symbol dry overnight on your altar, then carry the symbol with you. Bury it when your desire has manifested.

Animal Magick Ritual

At some point you may wish to cast a circle while connecting to your animal allies, to practice shape-shifting or to call on the Morrigan in her shape-shifting aspect to bring about change in your life. The following ritual calls upon the elemental animals most associated with the Morrigan.

Cast your circle in whatever manner you choose. Light the incense, carrying it around the circle in a clockwise motion, stopping at each cardinal direction. Return the incense to your altar. If you wish, call upon your personal totem or guide to aid you. Call the quarters as you face each direction, saying:

East:
Crow women
Raven Queen
Regal swan
Feathers upon your crown
Come now on black wings

Come now, shape-shifter Goddess
Bring to this rite the power of air!

South:
Red Mare
Lair Derg
Liath Macha
Weeping crimson tears
Guiding the war chariots of heroes
and the chariot of the sun across the sky
Come now, shape-shifter Goddess
Bring to this rite the power of fire!

West:
Serpentine eel
Guarding the hidden Well of Wisdom
You who walk between the worlds
Come now, shape-shifter Goddess
Bring to this rite the power of water!

North:
Grey-red wolf
Red-eared heifer
Keepers of earth, wealth and strength of the clan
Hunter and hunted
Come now, shape-shifter Goddess
Bring to this rite the power of earth!

Return to the altar and hold your arms upward in an invoking position, saying:

Raven mother
She-wolf
Red-eared heifer
Serpentine eel
Morrigu
Shape-shifter Goddess
Cúchulain's bane
Morrigan, I call your name

Fluid as water, swift as air
You shift and change
Essence without boundaries
Ever-changing, ever reforming
Hail, Crow Goddess
Dark one of transformation and change
Whisper to me your mysteries
Teach me how to shift and change!

Proceed with your planned spellwork or meditation. When you are ready to end the ritual, go to each quarter, saying:

Depart in peace, guardians of the east/south/west/north
Element of air/fire/water/earth
Blessed be!

Open the circle.

Morrigan Shape-Shifting Invocation

Raven mother
She-wolf
Red-eared heifer
Serpentine eel
Morrigu
Shape-shifter Goddess
Fluid as water, swift as air
You shift and change
Hail, Goddess of transformation!

Shape-Shifter Incense

2 tbsp. cedar
½ tbsp. Irish moss
1 tbsp. lemongrass
½ tbsp. sage

8

Faery Queen

We could lose our way in this mist, wander off into the realms of faery and never return at all to this world . . .

—Marion Zimmer Bradley, The Mists of Avalon

You find yourself walking along a dirt road. On either side of the road is a thickly wooded forest. The world is submerged in twilight, and you are unsure if it is dawn or dusk. You walk along the path for a while until you become aware of a presence at your side. Although you thought you were alone, an old woman is walking on the path beside you, leading a plump red-brown cow. The woman wears a dark cloak, and long strands of white hair escape from the hood of her cloak. The cow looks up at you with friendly black eyes, and you pat its head. The woman smiles, and you ask her where she is going. She tells you that she is traveling to the faery mound not far down the path and asks if you wish to join her. You accept, and the three of you continue down the path until the trees begin to thin and a large mound covered in lush green grass appears.

When you come to the base of the mound, the woman walks up to the edge of the hillside and passes her hands back and forth over the grassy slope. Where there was grass a moment ago is now a wooden door in the hillside. The door is richly carved with Celtic knots, with a seven-pointed star prominently carved in the center of the door.

"This is the entrance to the Faery Realm, the Land of the Sidhe and home of the Faery Folk. It can be a place both dark and bright, just as the Sidhe can be both benevolent and dangerous. But if you enter with an open heart, Faery can be a place of learning and magick." The woman knocks three times on the door, and it swings open on its own. She motions for you to step through and you do, with the faery woman following close behind.

Surprisingly you find yourself not in a tunnel or hollowed-out hill but standing in a vast wooded area. Although you traveled past woods on the road to the faery mound, the trees here can only be described as ancient; their trunks are so large it would take several people with their arms outstretched to circle them. Even the air smells fresher here. After taking a few moments to absorb your surroundings, you turn to look back at the faery woman. She stands alone now; you aren't quite sure where the cow went. She pulls off her cloak and you find she is no longer an old woman. Her hair is a fiery red and catches the sunlight, making it look like a thousand tiny flames. She wears a long green gown, and you can't quite tell if the leaves and vines on the fabric are real or embroidered. She extends her hand to you, and you realize it was the Morrigan in her guise as the Faery Queen who escorted you to the Land of the Sidhe.

"The doorway to Faery is now open to you. Whenever you wish to enter Faery, all you need do is see yourself at the door you have passed through today."

You take her hand and she leads you through the maze of trees. Soon you come to a small grove. At the grove's center is a small stone altar. Colorful flowers dot the boundaries of the circle, but the one thing you haven't seen yet are faeries. You ask the Morrigan why this is, and she laughs. Then the Morrigan kisses you on the forehead, and your vision blurs for a second. When your vision clears you find that there are several faeries in the grove smiling mischievously at you—they've been there the whole time, you just couldn't see them.

"As you explore the Faery Realm you will need a guide, one who will steer you away from faery mischief and toward greater wisdom, a Faery Fetch." She turns toward the Sidhe gathered around the grove. "Who here will be a friend and companion, a bridge between worlds to one who seeks the wisdom of the Sidhe?"

After a few moments one of the faeries comes forward. Take a moment to speak with him or her. When you are ready, the scene fades and you know the next time you enter the Land of the Sidhe your Faery Fetch will be there to guide you on your journey.

In the final invasion of Ireland, the Sons of Mil—the mystical ancestors of the Irish people—claimed the island from the Túatha Dé Danann. The Túatha Dé Danann retired peacefully into the faery hills and mounds, becoming the invisible inhabitants of Ireland and leaving the visible realm to mortal men. The Sons of Mil could not defeat them, only banish them. Like the Sons of Mil, Christianity could not completely eradicate the belief in the old gods or the Faery Folk from the Irish people. The old gods and the Sidhe diminished in importance under the new religion but were not completely forgotten. Some of the Celtic gods were assimilated into the new religion as saints; others whose personalities were not compatible with sainthood were reduced to mere faery kings and queens. The Túatha Dé Danann, once the title of the Irish gods, became a generic name for the Faery Folk. Burial mounds, rivers, wells, and lakes—all places once held sacred to the gods—became entrances into the Faery Realm instead of the realm of the gods. The Faery Folk also changed, becoming fallen angels or the souls of the damned.

The Morrigan's sexual nature and ferocity in battle certainly didn't have any of the Christian monks clamoring to make her a saint, and so she became one of the faeries. It is in this transition from goddess to faery woman that many of the negative stereotypes associated with the Morrigan originate. As one of the Faery Folk, her divinity became hidden, and her sexuality and power over death and prophecy morphed into something dangerous.

As Queen of the Faeries, the Morrigan became associated with a wide range of faery beings, from Breton water sprites to the infamous sorceress Morgan le Fay. As a faery she retained her connection to magick, death, and sexuality. Days that were sacred to Morrigan the goddess became associated with Morrigan the faery. According to Irish folklore, the Morrigan led her faery court across the land each year on the night of Samhain, the same festival originally honoring the goddess's union with Dagda.[79]

One of the translations of *Morrigan* is "Sea-born" or "Sea-Queen," and it is no surprise that she is associated with sea faeries. Morgans or mari-morgans were Breton sea sprites, similar to mermaids, that lured sailors to their deaths. Their singing was irresistible, drawing sailors to the source of the sweet melody; unfortunately the enamored sailor died as soon as the Morgan touched him. This left the faery's passions unfulfilled and condemned the sailor's soul to eternally wander the seas. The tale of the mari-morgans warned against giving in to passion and sexual desires, something deemed sinful by the Church. Like most of the Morrigan's faery counterparts, their sexuality became something dangerous.

Another faery associated with the Morrigan is the banshee or Bean Sidhe, which means "faery woman" or "woman of the mound." The banshee was a later version of the Washer at the Ford, both being spectral death messengers. The Scottish version of the banshee, the Bean Nighe, meant "little washer at the ford." The banshee

---

79. Rankine and D'Este, *The Guises of the Morrigan*, p. 66.

attached itself to a particular family and would keen for family members who were about to die. The banshee's sorrowful wails are reminiscent of Nemain's battle cry (although Nemain's voice did not predict death but caused it). The banshee's cries came in sets of threes, a number associated with the Morrigan. Some families had several banshees, and the number of banshees who cried for a family member reflected how good of a person they were. "When several keen together it foretells the death of someone very great or holy."[80]

The banshee was particularly associated with noble families, and some folklore claims they would not cry for anyone who was not of noble blood. Some noble families even had a particular banshee, known by name. Aiobhill was the banshee of the Dalcassians of North Munster, and the McCarthys of South Munster had a banshee named Cliodna.[81]

As Áine, the Morrigan was the Faery Queen of Munster. Originally a sun goddess, Áine evolved into a Faery Queen with an appetite for mortal men. Áine was considered a Leanan Sidhe, a type of faery who seduced men and drained their vital life force, eventually killing them. Like the mari-morgans, Áine's sexual nature was viewed as dangerous, even deadly. Cnoc Áine, the hill sacred to Áine, was thought to be an entrance to the Faery Realm, and there have been numerous faery sightings around the hill, especially on Midsummer, a day that was sacred to Áine.

The Morrigan's connection to the Faery Realm does not begin with her evolution into a Faery Queen. As a goddess, she is connected to a faery conflict that eventually caused the cattle theft in the *Táin*. The two bulls Maeve was determined to own were actually two reincarnated faeries. These faeries were once swine herders for the faery kings of Munster and Connacht. The two men were friends, but the kings they served were enemies, and eventually the herders turned against one another. Attempting to prove one had greater magickal power than the other, they shape-shifted into various forms, including birds, stags, and water creatures. When they transformed into worms, one was swallowed by a cow that belonged to Dáire mac Fiachna and the other was eaten by a cow that belonged to Maeve. The cows gave birth to the two bulls (the reincarnations of the swine herders) that *Táin* was fought over. At the end of the story, these two renewed their fighting and tore each other apart. David Rankine and Sorita D'Este comment, "By creating the situation where the two could fight again (as bulls) the Morrigan brings an unresolved fairy feud into the mortal realm,

80. Briggs, *A Dictionary of Fairies*, p. 14.
81. Franklin, *The Illustrated Encyclopedia of Fairies*, p. 22.

which also has the added benefit of a huge amount of slaughter to keep her more bloody-thirsty side happy."[82]

Morgan le Fay

The Morrigan's most well-known connection to the Faery Realm is through Morgan le Fay of Arthurian legend. Morgan le Fay evolved from the Morrigan's Welsh counterpart, the goddess Modron. Both were married to King Urien and both were mistresses of the Isle of Avalon. As Morgan le Fay, the Morrigan comes full circle, evolving from goddess to faery to mortal woman throughout the span of Celtic folklore and literature.

The best-known versions of the Arthurian saga are Sir Thomas Malory's *Le Morte d' Arthur* and Geoffrey of Monmouth's *Vita Merlini,* both of which were drawn from multiple sources, accounting for a number of variations between the two and for their differing views concerning Morgan le Fay. In *Vita Merlini* Morgan was a healer and one of nine sisters who dwelled on the island of Avalon. In this version Morgan was seen as a benevolent force, using her powers to aid the king. Like the Faery Folk, she lives not in this realm, but in the Otherworlds on the Isle of Avalon. She seems more connected to the Faery Realm than the mortal one, and no mention of her familial relationship to Arthur is given.

In Malory's version, we see Morgan as a mortal woman, Arthur's half-sister. Here Morgan is portrayed as a villain and Arthur's constant rival. Morgan's seductive nature, a trait often associated with faery women, appears in her incestuous relationship with her brother. In some versions Morgan le Fay seduces Arthur and bears him a son; in others it is his other half-sister Morgause who seduces him. Morgan also attempts to dethrone Arthur and replace him with her young lover, Accolon. Like the ancient goddess of the land, Morgan holds the right to dispose of the king if she feels he is no longer upholding his vows to her or the land. She becomes a figure akin to the faery Leanan Sidhe or the Breton mari-morgans in that her sexuality becomes something dangerous. While as a goddess her sexuality would have been linked to sovereignty and the ability to bestow the right of rulership on kings, her true nature becomes twisted as a faery woman or a mortal in touch with the Faery Realm. What was once sacred to the goddess becomes a menacing aspect of her personality; she retains her power, but its significance—its sacredness—is lost.

---

82. Rankine and D'Este, *The Guises of the Morrigan,* p. 66.

In *Sir Gawain and the Green Knight,* Morgan le Fay sends the Green Knight to Arthur's court to test the courage of his knights. The Green Knight specifically calls Morgan le Fay a goddess, making her divine nature obvious. "So Morgan the Goddess, She accordingly became."[83] Although she is treated as a faery woman in the story, she still retains the title of Goddess. The Green Knight, whom she commands, may in fact be another denizen of the Faery Realm. The Green Knight is described as having not only green clothes and armor, but green skin and hair, reminiscent of the Green Man from earlier Celtic myths.

In Danish legend Morgan le Fay (here Morgue le Faye) brought the hero Ogier the Dane to the Isle of Avalon, as she did her brother Arthur, to sleep until his country needed him again. It was also believed that Morgan le Fay was the mother of Oberon, the king of the faeries.

In her guise as Faery Queen, the Morrigan can help us navigate the Otherworlds and call upon the magick of the Faery Realm. As Morgan le Fay, she tests the worth of kings and heroes, teaching us to learn our own self-worth. As the Bean Sidhe, she rules over prophecy, challenging us to draw on our psychic nature. And as the marimorgan and Leanan Sidhe, she rules over sexuality and fertility, encouraging us to honor the temple of our bodies and embrace our creativity. Despite her diminished status, she retains the roles and powers of a goddess. When the Morrigan appears to us as the Faery Queen, it marks a time of magick and an opportunity to draw on the wisdom of the Otherworlds.

The Faery Folk

Faeries are present in the myths and folklore of every culture around the world, and the Celtic tradition is especially rich with stories of faery encounters. Believing faeries were easily insulted, the Celts referred to them by a number of "polite" names such as the Good Folk, the Kind Ones, the Gentry, and the Fair Folk. Despite these titles, they were blamed for all sorts of mischief. Faeries were believed to live "under hill" in sacred mounds and earthen works. These mounds were called Sidhe (pronounced shee), and this eventually became the generic Celtic term for the Faery Folk, meaning "the people of the mounds." Other names for faeries include Sith, Fae, and Twlwwyth Tegs.

83. Stone, *Sir Gawain and the Green Knight,* p. 11.

The images of tiny Tinker Bell–like faeries that most of us are familiar with became popular during the Victorian era and do not reflect how the Celts saw the Fae. Faeries in Celtic lore were the same size as humans and even occasionally intermarried with humans, creating half-faery/half-human offspring. Faeries ranged from hauntingly beautiful to hideously ugly, beneficial to downright dangerous.

Faeries are often confused with nature spirits or elementals. While faeries may work with elementals, they are not the same class of beings. Elementals are solely composed of the energies of a single element and work only with that elemental realm, while nature spirits are the spirits of a certain place—a forest, a river, and so on. Nature spirits do not move beyond the area they inhabit, and some Witches believe they are made up of several different elementals. Faeries can work with any element and, like humans, have individual personalities, customs, social laws, and taboos, which is not so of elementals or nature spirits.

Another misconception is that faeries are the diminished gods of the Túatha Dé Danann. As Christianity took hold in Ireland, the worship of the old gods waned, and it was believed that the Túatha Dé Danann departed into the faery mounds, becoming the Sidhe. While it is true that the Túatha Dé Danann were later equated to faeries, there is a clear distinction between the gods and the Faery Folk in Celtic lore. The Pagan Celts saw the Fae and the gods as separate races of beings. In the eyes of Christianity, turning the old gods into the faeries was a way to discourage their worship. Even after Christianity became the dominant religion in Celtic countries, the belief in the Faery Folk remained strong. The Church was unable to eradicate its followers' belief in the faeries, and so used fear to discourage contact with them, deeming faeries to be fallen angles or souls denied entrance into heaven.

So if the faeries are not the gods of the Túatha Dé Danann and are not fallen angels or damned spirits as Christianity claims, what are they? Faeries live on a plane of existence that overlaps our own. The Faery Realm is one of the many planes of existence that make up the Otherworlds. These planes of existence are similar to the pages of a book, each vibrating at a different frequency, separate from one another yet intrinsically interconnected. Events on this plane influence the other realms and vice versa. Faeries can pass easily between this world and their own, to work with nature or with Witches and other humans. The Faery Realm is connected to our own realm, just as our physical plane is connected to the divine realms. So technically the Faery Realm and the divine realm are all around you, in your home, your office, your car—you just have to look hard enough to find them! Traditional entrances to the Faery Realm are in river banks, under hills, and through sacred mounds. Certain times of the year also have heightened faery activity, such as the dates of the eight Pagan Sabbats, especially Midsummer, Beltane, and Samhain, when they are believed to troop across the land.

Like humans, faeries have individual personalities and temperaments. Thankfully most are willing to work with humans to the benefit of both races, but some beings of the Faery Realm may have no desire to work with humans. When working with the Fae, we must remember that they do not have the same customs or sense of humor as we do. Faeries are notoriously sensitive; it is important to always be polite to any faery being you encounter. Faeries also love mischief, and many of their pranks may be aimed in your direction. Faery pranks are never mean-spirited. Faeries simply like to have fun, and sometimes we need to learn to laugh along with them, even if the joke is on us. If treated with respect, faeries can be powerful magickal allies and spiritual guides. When working with faeries, either as co-magicians or as guides to the Otherworlds, remember you should never order a faery to do anything; they have to choose to work with you and should be treated as equals.

There are several different subgroups of faeries ranging in size, shape, and temperance. While all these beings are considered part of the Faery Realm, what we consider to be faeries encompasses several different races of beings. At the end of this section, you will find a list of several faeries of Celtic origins. This list is by no means complete, but it will give you a good place to start. Dozens of books have been written about the different types of faeries. If you want to learn more about faery lore, Edain McCoy's *A Witch's Guide to Faery Folk* and many of the books found in the bibliography are excellent resources.

All faeries work closely with nature and so spending time outdoors, gardening, or simply taking time to admire the beauty of the natural world are all good first steps to connect to the Faery Realm. Faeries like statues and art that depict themselves, and purchasing a faery statue and placing it on your altar or hanging a painting that depicts faerie beings will attract their attention and pique their interest. As you begin working with the faeries, you may find certain faery beings attaching themselves to your home and you for a certain period of time. Some will act as guides through a certain period in your life, while others will work with you for longer periods of time.

Once you have opened the doorway to the Faery Realm and built a relationship with its inhabitants, it is important to maintain that relationship. You cannot start working with the faeries then stop when you get bored. If you create a faery altar and leave offerings on a regular basis and then suddenly stop, don't be surprised if the faeries make their displeasure known and you become the target of faery mischief. What is important is that you remain consistent with your dedication to working with the faeries.

Exercise 1: Creating a Faery Altar

The first step to working with the faeries is to invite their presence into your life. An easy way to do this is to create a faery altar, a sacred space were you can honor and connect to the Faery Realm. An altar can be a table, a flat stone, a tree stump, or even the top of your dresser. Your faery altar will act as a bridge between you and the Faery Realm. It is a place to meditate, make magick, and communicate with the Fae. Offerings of milk and butter were traditionally left for the faeries to attract their attention and engender their good will, so you may also wish to purchase an offering dish for your faery altar. When leaving offerings on your faery altar, hold the offering in your hands and fill it with your goodwill toward the Good Folk and your wish to work with them. Traditional offerings include milk, butter, honey, grain, and bread. Anything sweet like sugar and chocolate will also work. Mead and sweet wines would also be appropriate offerings.

You may also wish to place ritual tools that you have set aside specifically for faery magick on your altar. Traditionally the Faery Folk do not like iron, so avoid putting any items that contain iron on your altar. Decorate you altar with images of faeries and nature. A variety of faery statues are available on the market, and most craft stores sell fake vines and flowers that can be used for decorations.

If you have a garden on your property, you may wish to make an outdoor faery altar. An outdoor altar does not have to be elaborate. My outdoor faery altar is a piece of flagstone I purchased from a garden shop. Plant herbs you plan to use in faery magick around your outdoor altar to imbue them with the energy of the faeries.

Once you have created your altar, light incense that reminds you of the faeries and waft the smoke over the altar, saying:

I bless this altar in the name of Sidhe
That it may be a place to weave faery magick
And honor the Fair Folk
So be it!

Take a few minutes to silently welcome the faeries and concentrate on your willingness to work with and learn from them.

Exercise 2: Creating the Faery Star

The septagram, or seven-pointed star, is a symbol used both by Pagans who follow the Faery Faith and by those who work with the Faery Realm in general. When used in faery magick, it can be a bridge between you and the Faery Realm. It has also been called the Mystical Star, the Faery Star, and the Elven Star. The septagram has been used to represent the seven planets, the seven alchemical metals, and the seven days of the week, but it most commonly is used to represent the seven directions (east, south, west, north, above, below, and center). The septagram can help align us with the Faery Realm and connect with the energies of the faeries and nature.

For this exercise you will be making your own faery star. The faery star can be used during spells and rituals to represent your connection to the Faery Realm, or it can be placed in your home to welcome the faeries. Your star can be as simple or complicated as you wish. You may want to make a larger copy of the one pictured above and cut out the star or paint one on a wooden disc, which you can find in most craft stores. It can be painted on wind chimes, and placed in your garden to entice the faeries. What matters is that by creating your faery star, you are consciously seeking to work with the Faery Realm, and in doing so you are inviting the faeries into your life.

To bless your faery star, go to your sacred space or outside where you feel the most connected to the faeries, light the incense of your choice, and pass the star through the smoke three times. Anoint the star with Faery Oil (see page 171), saying:

I bless this Faery star
Symbol of the Faery Realm
And my connection to the Fae
In the name of the Morrigan
Queen of the Sidhe
I bless and consecrate thee as a tool of positive magick
So mote it be!

Hold the star in your hand and spend a few minutes concentrating on your interest in working with the Faery Realm. Mentally welcome the faeries into your life. When you are ready, hold your hands over the star and say:

I open myself to the Faery Realm
And welcome the Fae to this place
Friends and allies in magick
Hail and welcome be!

Place your faery star on your altar when doing faery magick or when you wish to connect with the Faery Folk.

Celtic Faeries

Ballybogs: *Ireland.* Also known as peat faeries or bogles. These faeries guard swamps and bogs. They are small and brown and are usually covered in mud.

Bean Sidhe: *Ireland.* A faery washerwoman who evolved into the banshee. The Bean Sidhe watches over a specific family and her fearful cry foretold a death in the family. Her appearance varies from an old woman to a young maid, and she is usually seen washing clothes in rivers or combing her beautiful hair along the shores of lakes.

Bean tighes: *Ireland.* The bean tighe is a faery housekeeper. They attach themselves to a house and do chores or mend things. They like children and are attracted to homes with children. They are usually seen as small and wizened. If you keep your home too neat, giving them nothing to do, they will leave!

Boggarts: *Ireland/Britain.* Boggarts will take up residence in households with the intent of causing mischief. They like to make things disappear and turn milk sour.

If a family moves, the boggarts may follow them to their new home to continue to torment them. They are squat and hairy in appearance.

Brownies: *Wales*. Also called bwca or bodach. These faeries are small and either have brown skin or wear brown clothes. They usually live in houses and come out at night to fix things. These are the faeries that are in the fairytale "The Elves and the Shoemaker."

Clouricauns: *Ireland*. A faery who lives in wine cellars and enjoyed drinking wine or any other alcohol that is handy. They are similar to leprechauns.

Coblynaus: *Wales*. These faeries live in mines and in general are small and ugly. They will help miners by tapping on the walls where rich deposits of metals can be found.

Cu Sith: *Scotland*. Also known as Black Angus or the Black Dog. A faery dog, whose appearance usually foretells ill fortune or someone's death.

Geancanach: *Ireland/Scotland*. Small pixie-like beings with large eyes and wings. They guard hearths and firesides. Like brownies, they are the most active at night.

Gruagach: *Scotland*. A faery who watches over cattle. An offering of milk was left for the gruagach every night, otherwise the cows would produce sour milk or no milk at all.

Kelpies: *Scotland/Ireland*. A water faery who usually takes the form of a horse, although sometimes it appears as a beautiful young woman and lures its victims to rivers and ponds to drown them. A kelpie can be identified by its mane, which is always dripping wet.

Knockers: *Cornwall*. Mine faeries who are usually friendly to humans. They knock where rich veins of metal and ore can be found.

Leanan Sidhe: *Ireland*. A faery woman who grants the gift of inspiration to those she favors. The Leanan Sidhe drains the life force of her lovers, who live short but brilliant lives. She is sometimes referred to as the Faery Sweetheart or Faery Lover.

Leprechauns: *Ireland*. A faery who enjoys practical jokes, usually solitary and guards a pot of gold. They are great tricksters and if a mortal does happen to find their gold, they can usually trick them into giving it back. They dress in greens and brown and are excellent at making shoes.

Merrows: *Ireland/Scotland.* The equivalent of mermaids and mermen, they are human from the waist up and have the body of a fish from the waist down. Female merrows were very beautiful, but the men were very ugly in appearance, which may be why female merrows have a habit of seducing human men. The merrows had webbed fingers and could exchange their fish tales for human legs for a time. They were known to intermarry with humans, although the urge to return to the sea was usually too great to resist permanently. The merrows had special red caps called *cohuleen druith* that allowed them to go beneath the waves. If their hat was stolen, they were trapped on land and could not return to the sea.

Morgans: *Wales/Brittany.* Also called mari-morgans. Similar to sirens, these sea faeries lured men and women to their deaths with their ethereal beauty and enchanting voices.

Muryans: *Cornwall.* These faeries are as small as ants, and in fact their name means "ant." Every time they change shape, they grow smaller and eventually become so small they disappear altogether.

Oakmen: *Britain.* Faeries who live in oak trees and groves. They guard the animals living near their oaks but do not like contact with humans. They wear toadstool caps and look similar to dwarves. The saying "faery folk are in old oaks" refers to these faeries.

Phooka: *Ireland/Scotland.* Also called pooka, pwca, or puka. The phooka is a mischievous shape-shifting faery. The phooka's favorite form is a sleek black horse that lures the unsuspecting to get on his back and take a ride, which will usually end with the rider being thrown into a bramble bush. Although mischievous, the phooka is known to give advice and divert those they like from harm. They are generally benevolent.

Red caps: *Britain/Scotland.* These faeries like to live in castles and ruins that have a violent history. They look similar in appearance to brownies but wear red caps that have been dyed red from the blood of passersby that they have hit with stones.

Selkies: *Scotland.* Selkies appear as seals but can shed their seal skins and take human from. Men who fell in love with selkie women would steal their seal skins to prevent them from returning to the sea. They would live happily for a time, but the selkie never gave up looking for her skin. If the selkie found her skin, she was unable to resist the urge to return to the sea.

Sidhe: *Ireland.* Meaning "the people of the mounds," *Sidhe* became a generic term for the Faery Folk. The Sidhe usually refers to the human-sized faeries who make their homes in the sacred mounds and faery forts that fill the landscape of Celtic countries.

Trows: *Orkney, Shetland Islands.* Also called trowes, these faeries are similar to trolls and are short and ugly. They live in caves or on hillsides and are fond of music. Sometimes they abduct musicians or lure them to their dens. Sunlight turns the trow into stone.

Simple Faery Spell

This is a simple spell to invoke the aid of the Faery Realm. You will need a candle in a color that corresponds to your desired goal—green for wealth, red for passion and love, etc. Inscribe what you wish to manifest on the candle and anoint it with Faery Oil (see page 171) from wick to base to draw something to you, or from base to wick to banish something. Place the candle in front of your faery star. Light the candle, saying:

Morrigan, faery woman
Morrigan, Queen of the Sidhe
Morrigan, sea maid, and banshee
Sidhe of earth and air, water, and fire
Raise my magick higher and higher
Bring life and form to my desire!
(State what it is you wish to manifest)
In the name of the Morrigan and the Sidhe
As I will so shall it be!

If you cannot use candles, an alternative version would be to use a knife to write on a stick of butter what you wish to manifest (faeries were often accused of stealing milk and butter in folklore and both are good offerings to the Faery Folk). Bury the stick of butter on your property.

Morrigan Faery Rite

You can use the following ritual to call upon the faeries to aid you in spellwork or pathworking. This ritual can be done indoors, but ideally it should be done outside.

You Will Need:
Wand
Athame
Faery star
A small bowl of milk mixed with honey
Apple cider or mead
1 candle to represent the faeries
1 candle to represent the Morrigan

Cast the circle using your wand, saying:

In the name of the Morrigan
Queen of the Sidhe
This circle is cast and sealed
So mote it be!

Return to the altar. Light the central candle that represents the Sidhe, while saying:

I welcome the Sidhe to this rite
Old Ones, skilled in the art of magick
Wise to the ways of nature
Share your wisdom here with me.

Take a few moments to mentally welcome the Faery Folk. Concentrate on your desire to work with them and the friendship you wish to form with them. When you are ready, go to the directions and say:

Hail to the Fae of the East
Spirits of Air
Keepers of inspiration and creativity
I welcome you to this faery rite!

Hail to the Fae of the South
Spirits of Fire
Keepers of passion
Flame that consumes and creates
I welcome you to this faery rite!

Hail to the Fae of the West
Spirits of Water
Hallowed and deep
Keepers of emotion and healing
I welcome you to this faery rite!

Hail to the Fae of the North
Spirits of Earth
Keepers of abundance and growth
I welcome you to this faery rite!

Return to the altar and light the candle you are using to represent the Morrigan, saying:

Hail Great Queen of the Túatha Dé Danann
Morrigan, Faery Queen
Morgan le Fay, Faery Enchantress
Goddess of magick and the Sidhe
Lady of Avalon
Keeper of the Mysteries
Lend your strength and magick to this faery rite!
Hail and welcome, Morrigan!

Proceed with any spellwork or pathwork that you have planned. When you are ready, put the chalice of mead on the faery star, circling it with the wand three times before holding it above the altar. Say:

I honor you, Morrigan
Faery Queen of the Túatha Dé Danann
And leave this offering in thanks for your presence here.

Pour some of the mead into the libation bowl; if you are doing your rite outside, pour it on the ground near the altar. Put the dish of milk and honey on the faery star, circling it with the wand three times while saying:

I leave this offering for the Fae
For sharing their wisdom
and magick here with me this day/night.

When you are ready to close the quarters, go to each direction, saying:

Sidhe of the east/south/west/north
I thank you for joining this faery rite
Depart in peace, with my thanks and blessings
Hail and farewell!

When you are ready to end the rite, cut the circle with your wand, saying:

This circle of faery magick is now open, but never broken!

Faery Oil

Use this oil to anoint yourself during faery rituals or on candles used for faery magick. To make this magickal oil you will need 3/4 cup of base oils (sunflower and canola oil work well). Add the appropriate amounts of essential oils to the base oil and mix until thoroughly blended. Place a moonstone or clear quartz in the container you are storing the oil in.

10 drops gardenia essential oil
6 drops lavender essential oil
6 drops violet essential oil
10 drops rose essential oil
6 drops jasmine essential oil
1 moonstone or clear quartz

Morgan le Fay Faery Herbal Blend

Use this blend as an incense or roll on candles when invoking Morgan le Fay or when working with the Faery Realm.

1 tbsp. Irish moss
4 tbsp. lavender
2 tbsp. violet
2 tbsp. rose
2 tbsp. witch hazel flowers

Faery Morrigan Invocation

Use the following invocation to call upon the Morrigan in her guise as Queen of the Faeries:

Morrigan, Queen of the Sidhe
From the faery mound
From the hidden glen
From the hallows of the earth
From beyond the ninth wave
Great Queen of the Túatha Dé Danann
My spirit calls to thee
Morrigan, enchantress
Morrigan, Lady of Avalon
Morrigan of the faeries
Come and weave your magick here with me!

Sea Morgan's Bath Salt

You Will Need:
1 cup epsom salts
1 cup sea salt
½ cup baking soda
10 drops lavender essential oil
10 drops rose essential oil
5 drops patchouli essential oil
Handful of lavender flowers

Morgans or mari-morgans are seas sprites similar to mermaids. Call upon the morgans and the cleansing power of water when using these bath salts. Say the following chant as you are mixing all the ingredients in a large bowl:

Morgans of the sea
Wild and free
Bring your blessings unto me
Healing, strength,
Balance, and harmony
So mote it be!

Store the mixture in a glass jar until needed. Repeat the chant while pouring the bath salt into your bathtub. While bathing, visualize all negative energies draining away from you and flowing down the drain. Thank the sea sprites when you are done.

9
Earth Mother

The land is the source of both sovereignty and fertility and it is in the service of sovereignty that sometimes the spirit of the warrior must be invoked.

—*Carl McColman & Kathryn Hinds,*
Magic of the Celtic Gods and Goddesses

You find yourself in an open field. Ahead of you a small green hill rises from the surrounding landscape. You can hear the low lowing of cattle as they graze from the nearby fields. One animal looks up from its meal and watches you with curious dark eyes. As you approach the hill you see that there is a small opening at the base, with a large flat stone lying across the top of the opening. This is the Cave of Cruachan, an entrance to the Otherworlds and the home of the Morrigan. The entrance is small; you have to get on your hands and knees as you pass through the opening, leaving the world of light behind you. After a few feet, the cave opens into a larger cavern and you can stand upright again. It is pitch black in the cave and you put a hand on the stone walls to help find your way in the dark as you walk into its depths. You wish you had brought a torch, but while you would like some light, the darkness has a soothing quality to it, like you are floating in the dark cavern of your mother's womb, and you almost think you can hear a rhythmic sound emanating from the darkness, like your mother's steady heartbeat. Finally you come to the end of the cave. You feel just a little disappointed—the Cave of Cruachan is supposed to be an entrance to the Otherworlds and you had hoped to find that other doorway leading deeper into the hill. Instead the stone you touch with your hands stands firm and unmovable. But even as that thought flows through your mind, the hand that was touching stone only a moment ago now rests on warm flesh. Quickly you remove your hand from the rock wall and watch as a woman emerges from the rock face as if moving through water. Her fiery red hair glows like a halo of flames, and the cave becomes illuminated in soft golden light. In the new light you can see the woman clearly. She is a woman ripe with power and nude. You can see her breasts are full and her belly is rounded and slightly swollen, showing the beginnings of pregnancy. Her skin is painted red with ... blood, paint, clay? You are uncertain, but whatever the paint is made from, you can see symbols and spirals painted on her body with it. She reminds you of the Red Goddess who gave birth to Queen Maeve in this very cave, who could be another face of the Morrigan.

"You have descended into the womb of the earth, a place to both shed that which is old and stagnant and create anew. It is a place of healing and rebirth and of the deaths we experience a thousand fold in life—the death of one phase to birth another, the transition from childhood to adult, from innocence to enlightenment. Why have you come here?"

You answer that you have come here for healing and to shed the negative energies of the past.

"These things you wish to be rid of, place them upon the stone and soil. Let the earth reshape and reform them into better things." She touches the ground with a painted red hand, and you kneel down and do the same, placing your palm against the floor of the cave. All the things you wish to release you see flowing through your body and into the ground, flowing deeper and deeper into the earth and into the dark rich soil, where they disintegrate and reform into positive energy, just as the soil would break down a fallen tree or dead animal into rich nutrient soil. You rise and the Red Woman seems pleased with you.

The woman holds up a beautiful carved chalice and offers it to you. You take the cup in your hands and, as you do, you see in your mind's eye what the cave truly is: the Cauldron of the Otherworlds. The image of cave and cauldron merge in a strange moment of double vision, and you realize the woman is offering you the sacred and cleansing waters of the Otherworldly Cauldron. You take a sip, then drain the cup's contents, the intoxicating liquid filling both your body and spirit with healing light. The woman smiles at you. You return the cup to her.

"You have tasted of the waters of the great cauldron of life, death, and rebirth. Remember it is of the earth you were born, it is of her bounty you are sustained in life, and it is to her dark soil that you will one day return. The power of earth is not only in her generous bounty but in her ability to transform and regenerate. You see it yearly in her changing faces ... the decay of fall and the barrenness of winter transforms and gives way to the new growth of spring and the fruitfulness of summer. The bodies of that which has died break down and refertilize the soil. Nothing is wasted. All things that no longer have a use become transformed into new usefulness. I create, I destroy, and I remake anew. Draw on my power and you too will be transformed and will bring your desires into being."

The Red Woman steps back into the shadows of the cave. You hear her whisper, "Create, destroy, remake, transformation in my wake," before she fades completely back into the darkness and the stone of the earth.

You silently thank the Earth Mother for her wisdom and healing, then turn back toward the cave's entrance. As you emerge out into the sunny meadow, you feel cleansed and restored.

The Morrigan's mythology is rich with symbols linking her to fertility and the land. Like other ancient goddesses of the land, the Celts named hills and features of the land after her, keeping the tradition of seeing the land and the Great Goddess as one and the same being. Her sexual nature linked her with fertility and abundance; her connection to cattle and horses, with wealth and sustenance. Over time—and through Church influence—the Morrigan's image and functions changed. Thus the goddess of the land became demoted to a "bloodthirsty" goddess of war, her original function stripped away. The very fact that there is so much emphasis on the Morrigan's bloody nature enhances rather than disguises her importance in Irish mythology prior to the monks' heavy-handed editing. If she hadn't filled an important role in these myths, there would not have been any reason to debase her image. When we look past the goddess of war, we find that the Morrigan's original function was not that of a goddess of battle but a goddess of the land and sovereignty.

The first hint to the Morrigan's original function as an earth goddess comes from her mother, the goddess Ernmas. The powers and abilities of the Celtic gods were often reflected in their children. In a way, the children of a deity were an extension of the deity, becoming a different aspect of the parent god or goddess. Like their mother, all of Ernmas's other children show an affinity for the earth and fertility, making it likely that the Morrigan would share a similar connection. Ernmas's name means "She-Farmer," and she was a goddess of fertility and agriculture, referred to on occasion as a Witch. Her abundant nature was reflected in the numerous children she bore: two sets of female triplets (one being the Morrigan) and five sons. Ernmas's other set of triplets (Eriu, Banba, and Fotl) were Irish goddesses of sovereignty who all gave their names to the land. Eriu is still the Gaelic name for Ireland, Banba was a goddess of the Slieve Mish Mountains, and Fotla's name literally means "a sod of earth." Similarly, Macha's name translates to "field" or "plain," and Anu is specifically mentioned along with the hills that bear her name. Given the connection that all

Ernmas's other children have for the land, it is likely that the Morrigan would share similar attributes.

For a goddess commonly associated with war, the Morrigan is linked to a surprising number of landmarks and earth works. According to W. M. Hennessy, "the name of the Morrigan enters not a little into the composition of Irish topographical names."[84] In County Meath a few miles away from Newgrange, there are a pair of hills called the Dá Chich na Morrigna (the Two Breasts of the Morrigan). There is a district in County Louth called Gort na Morrigna (the Morrigan's Field), reminiscent of the meaning of Macha's name, "field." Mur na Morrigna (Mound of the Morrigan) is an earth work found in the Boyne Valley. The Bed of the Couple, a depression in the land beside the river Unius, marks the spot where the Morrigan mated with Dagda. Lios Baidbhe (Badb's Fort), a ruin in County Kerry, was believed to be the home of Badb. Emain Macha, the ancient capital of Ulster, was named after the Morrigan in her guise as Macha. Armagh, a city two miles away from Emain Macha, was once called Ard Macha, or the Heights of Macha.

According to the *Dindshenchas,* the Morrigan's home was in the Cave of Cruachan (also called Oweynagat). It is from here that the Morrigan flies forth to take part in the conflict in the *Táin,* and it is through it that she leads the cow she steals from Odras into the Otherworlds. The cave sits near Rathcrogan in County Roscommon, which contains over seventy archeological sites (primarily mounds and hill forts) and was once the royal seat of power for the kings and queens of Connacht. The Cave of Cruachan was believed to be a doorway to the Otherworlds, especially on the night of Samhain. In *The Adventures of Nera,* the hero Nera tells Maeve's court how he entered the land of the Sidhe through this cave on Samhain. There is also a story about three wolves (totem animals of the Morrigan) who emerged from this cave to steal from the surrounding farms. The wolves also had the ability to shape-shift into three beautiful women, an ability shared by the Morrigan. Another tale tells of a faery woman dressed in fine silk and carrying two spears who emerged from the Cave of Cruachan every Samhain to steal nine of the best cows from every herd. That certainly sounds like the cattle-raiding Morrigan!

Crochan Crogderg, whom the cave of Cruachan was named after, was a handmaiden of the goddess Étain and mother of Queen Maeve. Supposedly she gave birth to the infamous queen within the cave. Interestingly, Crochan Crogderg is described

84. Hennessy, "The Ancient Irish Goddess of War," *Revue Celtique*, p. 32.

as having red skin and hair, a description also given to the Morrigan when Cúchulain attempts to foil her cattle raiding, possibly indicating that she and the Morrigan are the same being. It is unclear whether Crochan Crogderg was a goddess or mortal heroine; as with Maeve, the lines between goddess and mortal woman are blurred. Crochan Crogderg means "blood-red cup" or "cauldron," and Maeve means "intoxicating one." Here Crochan Crogderg represents the Otherworldly cauldron and Maeve is its intoxicating brew. While hills like the Paps of Anu were the breast of the goddess of the land, caves like the Cave of Cruachan represented her life-giving womb. Entering a cave was a symbolic death—one was entering the Underworld and re-emerged into the world above symbolically reborn. This cave was also said to house Dagda's famous cauldron after it was removed from Tara.

In more recent times, the Cave of Cruachan has been called the Hell-Mouth Gate of Ireland. The Pagan Celts had no concept of Hell or the devil, so this name is a reflection of how the early Christians viewed the ideology of the Pagans. To them, Hell and the Celtic Otherworlds were one and the same, thus the cave, once a doorway to the Otherworld realm of the gods and Sidhe, became a doorway to the Christian Hell.

In County Tipperary there is a *fulachtas* (burnt mound) called Fulacht na Mór Ríoghna, or the Cooking Pit of the Mórrígan. Fulachtas can be found throughout Ireland, England, and Scotland. They are low, horseshoe-shaped mounds with a depression in the center accompanied by heat-shattered stones and charcoal-enriched soil. It is uncertain exactly what purpose they served, but it is generally believed that they were used as outdoor cooking areas. They were constructed in the mid to late Bronze Age, and there are over 4,500 such sites in Ireland alone. One of the magickal items the Morrigan possessed was a cooking spit. This spit held three types of food on it: a piece of raw meat, a piece of dressed meat, and butter. A cooking spit seems like a fitting tool for the Morrigan, who delights in poking and prodding us into action, forcing us to face our fears and preventing us from remaining stagnant.

Gerald of Wales, a medieval clergyman and chronicler, linked Morgan le Fay with Glastonbury Tor and the surrounding land in his version of the Arthurian saga. As in Geoffrey of Monmouth's version, Morgan ruled over an island, which Gerald names as Glastonbury. He also names her as the ruler and matron of the area. Despite her diminished status, this sounds very much like the description of a local tutelary goddess. Even when she was no longer worshipped as a goddess, her connection to the land remained.

Besides her connection to the land, the Morrigan also draws her fertile nature from rivers and bodies of water. Many of the Celtic mother goddesses were river deities—Danu, the mother of the Celtic gods, is the best example. Water held a mystical quality, emerging from deep within the body of the earth to feed wells and springs, and was closely connected to fertility and healing. Rivers fertilized crops and sustained both the human inhabitants of the land and their livestock. Water was the fertilizing element that made the land abundant. When the Morrigan mated with Dagda, it was astride a river. She distracted Cúchulain in the form of an eel as he waded across a river during his battle with Loch. When she offered her love to Cúchulain, it was at a river ford. Even the Morrigan's magick revolved around water. When fighting the Fir Bolgs, she summoned a magickal rain that resembled blood. When the Morrigan comes across Odras sleeping in the woods, she sings spells over her, turning her into a pool of water.

Corryvreckan, a whirlpool in the Inner Hebrides, was sometimes called the Morrigan's Cauldron. The island of Inis Badbbha in northern Ireland was named after the goddess Badb.

The Morrigan's association with cattle in her mythology is another clue to her role as a goddess of the land. Other than the raven, the animal the Morrigan most commonly appears with is the cow. Lady Augusta Gregory, a nineteenth-century collector of folklore, commented that the Morrigan "was much given to meddling with cattle."[85] While Gregory fails to take this thought further, the Morrigan's association with cattle is a significant connection to the land and its fertility. Cattle were often linked with river goddesses, their nourishing milk equated to the life-giving waters that fertilized the land. Celtic society relied heavily on cattle, sheep, and other livestock. They were not only a source of food, but a measure of wealth. The Celtic obsession with cattle created over one hundred Gaelic words relating to the animal, and dowries, rents, and bard fees could all be paid in cattle. Besides normal cattle, the Celts believed that faery cattle lived under the sea and ate seaweed, only rarely walking on dry land.

The Morrigan's connection to horses also links her to fertility and the land. Horses, like cattle, were symbols of wealth and were prized for their use in war, agriculture, and travel. As a solar animal, horses were particularly connected to fertility. As the horse goddess Macha, the Morrigan made her mortal husband's fields

85. Gregory, *Gods and Fighting Men*, p. 85.

prosperous; she gives birth to twins after racing the king's horses, again showing her fertile nature with the number of children she bears, much like her mother Ernmas.

As the fertile river goddess and abundant sovereign of the land, the Morrigan displays both the ability to create prosperity and the strength to defend it. Like all the ancient Earth Mothers, she can destroy and create with impunity—she both nurtures and culls her creations.

Redefining the Mother

Of the Great Goddess's three faces, we are generally the most comfortable with the Mother. All of us came from a mother and have experienced a mother figure, biological or otherwise, in our lives. As we progress on our path, we learn to claim the wild Maiden and delve into the darker mysteries of the Crone, but do we really understand the Mother?

As patriarchal culture took hold in Ireland, women were stripped of the right to own property and act as religious leaders. The only role that could not be taken from them was the biological one, the ability to bear children. Our modern concept of the Mother has been watered down to only encompass fertility and childbearing. But is this what defines the Mother? Is her function limited only to fertility and reproduction? Is she only a nurturer?

The Morrigan is almost never mentioned as a Mother goddess. She is a goddess of sex and fertility, but we seem only comfortable giving her power over the act of conception but not the resulting motherhood. The Morrigan is clearly an earth goddess, so her connection to fertility should associate her with the Mother aspect of the goddess, yet we often see her only as a Crone.

The problem we have with seeing figures like the Morrigan as fertile Earth Mothers comes from our own cultural concepts of motherhood. In our modern culture, mother figures, divine or otherwise, are expected to be fertile, nurturing people who dispense unending love. This all-nurturing concept of femininity is not how the Pagans of the past viewed the divine Mother. Earth goddesses were not only goddesses of the land but the personification of both the creative and the destructive forces of nature. This is true not only of the Celts but of other pantheons as well. Gaia, the ultimate mother figure in Greek mythology, is praised in the Orphic hymns as the "All-Fertile, All-Destroying Gaia ... Mother of all,"[86] showing she controlled not only

---

86. Stewart, "Orphic Hymn to Gaia," *Sybilline Order.*

creation but destruction. Unfortunately, positive mother figures that display both nurturing and destructive aspects have become unfamiliar in our society. Women in the culture the Morrigan originated from were allowed to participate in warfare and fill leadership roles. In the Celtic mind, participating in warfare did not make a woman any less feminine or motherly. Taking into consideration that a Celtic woman who owned land was *expected* to participate in warfare (or send a kinsman in her stead) if her land or tribe was threatened, it is easy to see how the image of a goddess of battle and a goddess of the land might merge. The Morrigan's involvement in battle and warfare is a protective act, fulfilling her role as a tutelary goddess by defending the land and its people.

To understand Mother figures like the Morrigan, we must shed our preconceived ideas about the Mother. Many of us still hold on to unhealthy ideals regarding the role of motherhood. Mothers in today's culture are expected to give totally of themselves and often forget to turn their nurturing energies toward themselves.

The ancient goddess of the land was a balanced figure. She may seem harsh at times to the modern seeker, but she is no less a mother. She embodied the ability to create; she is the Creatrix, the sovereign goddess who protects her children; she is a woman at the height of her power, her nurturing and creative energies bestowed on others or withheld to nourish her inner self. She both created life and took it away. In spiritual matters she both nurtured and disciplined when necessary, just as the Morrigan both aids and hinders the hero Cúchulain.

Exercise 1: Defining the Mother

The first step to redefining and reclaiming the Mother is to create a list of what you feel defines the Great Goddess in her aspect as the Mother. So grab a pen and paper and go to your sacred space. Take a few minutes to relax, light your favorite incense, and take a few deep cleansing breaths. Concentrate on the Mother. Who is she? Are there any images or memories that come to mind? Any positive or negative experiences from your childhood or from your own experiences as a mother/parent that define who the Mother is for you? Write whatever comes to mind: emotions, experiences, maybe a quote that resonates with you. Your list could be bullet points, paragraphs, whatever feels rights.

When you feel you are finished, take some time to examine what you have written and why each thing appears on your list. Hold on to this list, as you will be using it for the following ritual.

Reconnecting to the Mother Ritual

You Will Need:

1 red candle

List you created from Exercise 1

Go to your sacred space. You do not have to cast a circle, but you can do so if you wish. Take three deep breaths and visualize your feet changing into roots and anchoring themselves into the earth, the Ultimate Mother figure who supports all life on this planet. When you are ready, light the red candle, saying:

I open myself to the Goddess in
Her aspect as the Mother
Divine Creatrix
You who are present within all acts of creation
Mother of creativity and inspiration
Lady of Protection
Divine Queen of Sovereignty
Fertile Earth Mother
From whom all life flows
And to whom we all shall someday return
I reaffirm my connection to the Divine Mother
And all that she embodies
I am open to her wisdom and mysteries
The Divine Mother is _________

Pick some of the descriptions from the list you have created. There may have been some negative images or experiences that surfaced on your list. To fully embrace the Mother, you may wish to release these experiences and the feelings attached to them. You can go about this in several ways—again, do whatever feels right for you. You may wish to take a pair of scissors and cut out the negative parts from the list you created, or you might copy them onto a separate piece of paper and burn them during the ritual. Since water is an element closely related to the Mother, representing nourishment and the womb, you may want to take a bowl of water and submerge the paper in it, letting what you have written dissolve; by doing this you are "washing" them away. When the ritual is finished, pour the water (or ashes if you burned anything) outside, away from your property, saying:

I release these negative experiences
I recognize the lessons I have gained from them
But shall no longer allow them to influence my life.
I release my negativity
In the name of the Mother of all things.
So mote it be!

When you are ready to end the ritual, extinguish the candle, saying:

Whenever I light this candle I will be one with the
Divine Creative principle of the Universe
So be it!

Leave an offering in your libation bowl or outside for the Great Mother. For the next three days, go to your sacred space and relight the candle, taking a few minutes to meditate and connect with the Mother. Record your impressions in your journal.

The Hidden Mothers: Learning to Connect to the Earth

The Celtic goddess of the land was a sovereign, a fertile mother, and sometimes (like the Morrigan) a goddess of battle and death. She encompassed all of life. But the Celts did not see this Mother as existing apart from the world. She *was* the world. It is evident they saw the land as the living body of the Great Goddess in the names they left upon the land. Hills became breasts, like the Paps of Anu; cairns erected on top of these hills added to the illusion, forming nipples. Tom Cowan calls these Celtic earth goddesses the Hidden Mothers, writing that they "are hidden in the land. Perhaps it would be better to say that they are hiding in the land, preserving it, keeping it fertile, bringing forth life. They are invisible beings ... All Goddesses are like this. They are hidden, in the land. In the birthing of children. In the eyes of lovers, in the battle cries that scream across war-torn lands, in the final breath of the dying. In the first new shoots of grass in springtime. The Mothers are always present, even when they are invisible."[87]

When I go hiking I search for the goddess of the land, for the Hidden Mother. It is not hard to imagine the curves of a woman's body in the hills and mountains in the shadow of the Appalachian mountains. A green hill can be a breast or a round belly full of potential; a valley, a curvaceous waistline. No matter where you live, you just might see the Hidden Mother who resides within the earth if you look hard enough. She surrounds us, in the air we breathe, in the ground beneath our feet, in the water we drink. When I see the goddess of the land, I feel like a child within her mother's womb, surrounded by the Mother's flesh, given life and sustenance from her body. Existing within her, as a part of her. At first we only see trees, earth, and grass. The goddess of the land is invisible, but she is always there; we just have to look past the physical to the spirit beneath, where she is waiting for us to acknowledge her.

Over the next few days, take some time each day to find the Hidden Mother. Maybe you see the graceful form of a woman in the curve of a tree trunk or the gentle rise of a hill or her persevering spirit in a blade of grass growing in the cracks of a city street. Go hiking or spend some time in your local park. The more you look for her, the more she will speak to you.

If you can spend time outdoors, find a comfortable place to sit or lie down. See your body becoming part of the landscape; grass and moss covering your skin, rocks becoming your bones, etc. Feel your energies merging with the land beneath you. You may wish to take a small stone or other natural material from the land and try the same visualization in your home, learning to draw on the earth's energies no matter where you are.

Exercise 2: Morrigan Staff

The staff is a tool of authority that grounds us and connects us to the earth. It can be a doorway between the worlds. The staff represents the World Tree or Tree of Life that connects the three worlds: Underworld, Middleworld, and realm of the gods. Trees were viewed as living beings, their wood endowed with magickal properties. The

87. Cowan, *Yearning for the Wind,* pp. 43–46.

letters of the Celtic Ogham were named after trees. In Celtic myths, trees were the ancestors of humankind and were seen as doorways to the Otherworlds. Their roots went deep into the earth, connecting them to the Underworld; their branches reached skyward toward the realm of the gods. Oaks were particularly sacred. The Celtic word for oak was *daur,* which is the origin for *door*, reflecting the belief that trees were doorways between the worlds.

Staffs can be used like large wands to cast circles and to help you ground and connect to the earth's energies. They can also be used during shamanic journeys to represent the Tree of Life and the three worlds.

The staff we will be creating will be a tool to connect you to both the vast energies of the earth and the Morrigan in her aspect as an Earth Mother. The Morrigan's staff can be as simple or elaborate as you wish. For connecting to earth energies, it would be preferable to make a staff from natural materials. Consider what you wish to use the staff for before adding too much decoration. Do you plan to use this staff primarily outdoors or indoors? I have several staffs that I use for different purposes. I have one that I only use when hiking, which has less decoration (a simple leather strap and a falcon feather I received on a hike), but it is sturdier than my other staffs and the wood has been treated to make it waterproof. Although my hiking staff is simplistic, it has been very useful on my outdoor adventures, and I have used it to connect to the earth's energies and to cast a circle for a spontaneous outdoors ritual.

I found the staff I use for rituals involving the Morrigan while hiking along the Appalachian trail. As soon as I saw it, I simply knew it was my staff. I had found a crow feather during the beginning of my hike and I only noticed the branch when I turned to look at a crow that was calling out not far from the path. It was taller than my other staffs, reminding me of the Morrigan's power and authority. The staff was perfectly straight except for a small area toward the bottom, where the wood curves in a "U" shape, as if it had grown around something before returning to its straight shape. This bend in the wood reminds me that life's path isn't always straight. Life throws the unexpected in our way and leads us in unexpected directions, but ultimately gives us a chance to grow.

I suggest finding the wood for your staff from nature, but if you live in a city or just don't like hiking, a wooden dowel from the hardware store will do. If you do plan to use your staff outside more often than not, I suggest you purchase a wood sealer to make your staff waterproof. If finding your staff in nature, bring along a tree field guide so you can identify the species of tree your staff belongs to. Decorate the staff in any way you wish—carving your name in Ogham letters into the staff, attaching black feathers, or adding crystals all work well.

Morrigan Staff Blessing

You Will Need:

Staff
Sage stick
Fireproof bowl or burner
Dragon's blood oil

Once you have decorated your staff, bring it to an outdoor place where you will not be disturbed. Pick a place where you feel most attuned to the earth's energies. Burn sage and pass the staff through the smoke, saying:

I banish all negative energies from this staff
that it may be a tool of positive magick

Stand with the staff in your power hand (whichever hand you write with). Raise the staff up toward the sky to honor the realm of the gods, then hold it at chest level to honor the Middleworld or physical realm, then tap the staff on the ground to honor the Underworld. Visualize the bottom of the staff sprouting roots that dig deep into the earth; from the top of the staff, branches reach skyward. See a golden light spiraling up from the ground and filling the staff to where your hand holds it at its center. Now see a spiral of light flowing from the sky down into the top of the staff to where your hand holds the staff's center.

I bless this staff in the name of the Morrigan
Symbol of my connection to the wisdom
and strength of the earth, and the three worlds

Anoint the staff at the top, middle, and bottom with the dragon's blood oil, sealing the blessing. Leave an offering outside—milk or bird seed would be appropriate. Use your staff during earth magick and rituals involving the Morrigan.

Calling on the Earth Mothers

The following are invocations and chants to call upon the power of the Morrigan in her guise as a tutelary earth goddess, as well as spells to draw on that same power. Besides the Morrigan herself, there are invocations for her mother, Ernmas, and the Morrigan's Welsh counterpart, Modron, who was the Welsh mother of the gods. Also included is an invocation for Maeve, who is closely connected to the Morrigan in the stories of the *Táin*. If we choose to see her mother (the Red Woman or Crochan Crogderg) as another face of the Morrigan, then Maeve may be a daughter of the Morrigan. In the *Táin,* Maeve represents the land's sovereignty, a role of an earth goddess. Her many husbands and large sexual appetite reflect her fertile nature.

The power of the Earth Mother is rooted in abundance and the transformative powers of the earth. All of these goddesses embody the powerful energies of the earth and can help us transform our lives, bringing to it the earth's bounty. Remember to thank the Earth Mothers for their aid; if you wish to leave offerings to these goddesses, milk, honey, fresh flowers, nuts, or anything that comes from or reminds you of the natural world would be appropriate.

Ernmas Invocation

Ernmas
She-farmer
Witch of the Túatha Dé Danann
Whose daughters each in turn gave their names to the land
Mother of the fields and ripening crops
Source of enchantments

Weaving spells, changing fates
I call upon your fertile bounty
I call upon the mighty power of the earth
Come to me, O noble Ernmas!

Earth Mother Invocation

Use this invocation to call upon the Morrigan in her guise as an Earth Mother. You will need a pinch of soil from your own property (you can substitute salt for the soil) and a small dish of water, both of which will be sprinkled into the cauldron. Place the cauldron on your altar or in your sacred space. When you are ready, say:

Mother of the land
Whose bones are the stones of the earth
(Sprinkle the soil into the cauldron)
Whose blood flows in the rivers and oceans
(Sprinkle a few drops of water in the cauldron)
Whose breasts are the hills and mounds of the Sidhe
Morrigan
Earth Mother who shapes the land
Morrigan
Whose body is the earth that sustains me
Morrigan
Mistress of fertility and creation
By your blood and bone
By earth and sea
Come now to me!

Modron Invocation

Hail Modron
Mighty Queen
Mother of the Gods
Enchantress, and healer of the faery isle
Goddess of the healing waters
let your blessings flow upon me!

Maeve Invocation

Maeve
Intoxicating, insatiable one
Daughter of red-skinned Crochan Crogderg
Bold warrior
Fair-haired Wolf Queen, proud in posture
I drink deep of your honey-sweet spirit
Let your fiery power and mine be one!

Earth Mother Protection Spell

This spell can be used to protect a child or other family member, especially if they are traveling or going on a trip.

You Will Need:
1 piece of paper
1 brown candle

Write the person's name on a piece of paper and draw an arc over the name, representing the mantle of the Morrigan's protection. On the brown candle carve the person's name and "safe travels," "protection," or whatever is appropriate for the situation. Place the candle on top of the paper. Visualize an impenetrable bubble of clear crystalline energy surrounding the person in question, protecting them from all harm. Light the candle, saying:

Morrigan, Goddess of the land
Protectress of your children
Guide and guard _________
Protect him/her from all harm
Lady of the shield and plow
Upon _________ place your protection and blessings

Earth Mother Prosperity Bag

You Will Need:

1 tiger's eye stone
1 part basil
1 part ginger
1 part orange peel
7 apple seeds
Pinch of ground cinnamon
1 green bag

Place the stone, herbs, and seeds in a bowl and mix the contents with a finger in a clockwise motion, saying:

Morrigan
Goddess of the Land and Sea
Prosperity and riches come now to me
As I will so mote it be!

Place the herbs and stone in the green bag and hold it in your hands while visualizing success and wealth coming into your life. Be specific. If you want a raise, see yourself looking at your increased paycheck. If you want to have enough money to pay off your bills, see yourself writing out those checks and mailing them. Carry the bag with you until your desire has manifested, then sprinkle the contents outside and bury the bag.

Earth Mother Incense

Use this incense to call on any of the Celtic earth goddesses and to welcome their energy into your life.

2 tbsp. cedar
½ tbsp. mugwort
1 tbsp. lemon grass
9 drops of apple oil (or dried apple blossoms if you can't find the oil)
½ tbsp. basil
½ tbsp. ginger

Connecting to the River Goddess

While the earth is the body of the Great Goddess, the rivers, lakes, and waters that flow across the land are her blood. In the Celtic mind, the element of water was closely linked with the fertility of the earth, and many river goddesses double as fertile earth goddesses. The earth could not be fertile without the waters of the river goddess. Modron—the Welsh mother of the gods and the Welsh equivalent of the Morrigan—was cursed to wash laundry in a river until being rescued by King Urien, linking her to the element of water. Danu, the Irish mother of the gods, was also a river goddess. Her later merger with Anu gave her power over both water and earth. The Morrigan also has numerous links to water. She mates with Dagda by the river Unius, she courts Cúchulain at a river ford and also hinders him in the form of an eel when he fights in a river. In Arthurian legends, Morgan le Fay brings the wounded Arthur to the Isle of Avalon to heal from his wounds. As a river goddess, the Morrigan holds the power of healing, transformation, and fertility.

Water is naturally in motion, flowing and transforming. Like the Morrigan, it is a natural shape-shifter, changing from liquid to solid, from water to ice or into gas, becoming part of the air. Naturally, water magick is about transformation. As water can transform and change from solid to liquid to gas, so too can we use it in magick to change our circumstances, freeze a problem person in their tracks, or wash away pain and grief. As Morgan le Fay brought Arthur to the watery shores of Avalon for healing, so too can we be healed through the magickal water of the Otherworlds.

Waters of Avalon

The Morrigan is connected to the mystic island of Avalon, a place of healing and rest. Apples, the fruit this isle gets its name from, were also connected to healing, immortality, and well-being, thus the saying "an apple a day keeps the doctor away."

This mixture can be used to promote healing and positive energies. Use the water in healing spells or during rituals invoking the Morrigan and Morgan le Fay, or sprinkle it around a room or ritual space to purify the area.

You Will Need:
1 glass bowl
Filtered or spring water
1 apple
9 apple seeds
1 cup lavender
Cheesecloth
Bottle or vial for storage

Go to your sacred space. If you wish to cast a circle and call the quarters, do so. Place the bowl in the center of the altar and pour the water into the bowl, saying:

I pour the sacred waters of Avalon
Isle of healing and rest
Home of the Sidhe and honored dead

Cut the apple in half, revealing the pentagram within. Place three slices of the apple in the water (thinly sliced pieces work best). Place the apple seeds in the water, along with the lavender. Trace the Ogham for apple and healing, *quert* ᚊ, over the water. You could also carve *quert* into the apple slices you placed in the water. Hold your hands over the water, saying:

Morrigan, Queen of Avalon
Lady of magick and healing
Bless this water with your healing touch

See the Morrigan stepping forth from the mist-shrouded isle to stand in front of the bowl. She places her hands over the bowl, her healing powers and the healing energy of Avalon flowing from her hands and into the water.

Thank the Morrigan and close the circle. Leave the mixture in a sunny place where it will not be disturbed for a few hours. Strain the water through the cheesecloth to remove the apple and herbs, and store in a dark glass bottle.

Frozen in Place Ice Spell

On a piece of paper, write a problem or name of the person you wish to neutralize. Hold the paper in your hands and visualize the problem or person becoming one with the paper. Fold the paper and put it in a small metal bowl (you can use an ice tray instead of a bowl, but you will need a tiny piece of paper!). Pour filtered or spring water over the paper and put it in the freezer. Visualize the problem or person covered in ice. He / she / it stands frozen in place, unable to act against you or do you any harm. For added strength, add slippery elm (banishing) and angelica (harmonious energies) to the water before freezing. You can also make a tea from the herbs and freeze the tea rather than adding whole herbs.

Melt Away Ice Spell

This spell can be used to defuse anger and hurt feelings. Water rules over emotions and can help us to keep them balanced. For this spell you will need an ice cube and a metal bowl. If you wish to use herbs, freeze lavender with the water you are using to make the ice cube, or make a tea from the herb and freeze the tea.

Place the ice cube in a bowl and hold your hands over it, visualizing the ice cube and your negative feelings or anger becoming one with the ice. Visualize these feelings melting away as the ice begins to melt. This spell works especially well if you have just gotten into a fight with someone and feelings on both sides are bruised. You could also visualize the fight and see the scene melting away, and any emotional turmoil melting away and being healed for both parties. Leave the ice in the bowl to melt. For fast action, place the ice cube in a pot on the stove. I've even used this spell at my office by putting the ice cube in a bowl and putting it in the microwave in the break room.

Creating a Wishing Well

Holy wells and springs were considered places of healing to the Celts. They left offerings in the sacred waters and tied ribbons on the surrounding trees. The tradition of throwing pennies into water fountains is a modern carryover from this ancient tradition. You may not live near a body of water, but you can still call on the sacred power of water from right inside your home.

Most garden shops or home décor stores carry small fountains that can be set up inside your home. These small fountains are an excellent tool for meditations and for connecting to the element of water.

For cleansing and to clear your aura of negative vibrations, sit comfortably by the fountain and visualize crystalline healing waters flowing over you, filling you with clear healing light. Continue until you feel cleansed.

To manifest a wish, use a permanent marker to draw a symbol of what you desire on a penny (a dollar sign for prosperity, a heart for love, etc.). Hold the penny in your hand and visualize your desire manifesting. When the image is clear in your mind, drop the penny into the fountain.

10

Goddess of Sovereignty

She is the clan leader, ruler of her domain. She utilizes power with grace, and reveals the unseen aspect of growth and change ...

—Elizabeth Davis and Carol Leonard,
The Women's Wheel of Life

You find yourself in a forest. Sunlight streams through the trees, sending splashes of golden light to the ground. As you take in your surroundings, you hear the sound of wing beats above your head and look up in time to see a crow fly overhead. The crow calls out, its harsh voice imploring you to follow it deeper into the forest. You do so. After a while you come to what appears to be the mouth of a large cave. The crow lands on the top of the moss-covered opening and tilts its black head to one side to look down at you. It seems pleased that you have followed it here. The cave entrance is overgrown with vegetation, but as you examine it more closely you realize it is not a cave at all. You trace spiraling symbols carved into the stone and realize it was once the entrance to a massive building that now lies in ruins. On impulse you decide to step through the opening. On the other side you find yourself in a vast hall, brightly lit from torches hanging on the walls. On this side of the entrance the hall looks to be newly built! The spiraling designs you saw outside are carved along the walls on either side of you and your footsteps are softened on richly embroidered rugs that extend down the long hall to a dais, where a woman sits upon a large stone throne.

You did not notice her at first, but now you see she has been watching you very closely. The woman appears to be in her middle years, neither old nor young, but somewhere in between. She wears a finely made dress of the deepest blue, with a long purple mantle draped over her shoulders. Her posture exudes command and royalty, and you can see a thin golden circlet on her head. The throne she sits upon seems to be connected to the floor, as if it was carved from the rock of the earth and the hall was built around it. You can almost feel the deep hum of power flowing up from the earth beneath you, moving through the throne and into the woman. Beside the dais you see a basket of ripe wheat and another of freshly picked apples, harvest offerings left to the woman seated upon the throne.

You approach the dais, bowing before the woman, knowing you have encountered the Queen, the Goddess of Sovereignty. She smiles, pleased at your show of respect. "I am the Sovereign Queen, she who holds the mantle of her power securely upon her shoulders; I am the regal one, crowned with my own self-knowledge, and none can deny my power. My wisdom is the knowledge of self. I am the fullness of power, tempered by the forge of experience. Every warrior, every king and lord, every man and woman who has come seeking me has been humbled at the foot of my throne, for I am True Sovereignty. I am true power, she who holds sway over creation and destruction."

You notice now she holds a sword on her lap, a hand resting gently on the hilt. "The unworthy do not pass by my gaze unscathed." She motions for you to stand and you rise, meeting her gaze, unable to look away. "Do you seek to claim Sovereignty?" You answer her in the affirmative, and she smiles. For a moment you feel disoriented. You feel yourself shifting and changing, the Queen's power flowing through you, becoming part of you. You close your eyes to concentrate on the strength and power flowing through you. When you open them again you find you are sitting upon the throne, wearing the robes of the Queen, the sword of swift action sitting across your lap and the harvest of wheat and apple—symbols of the knowledge harvested through experience—at either side of your throne.

You take a few moments to savor the Queen's power, then the scene begins to fade and you find yourself back in your body.

As the Great Queen, the Morrigan is a goddess of sovereignty, both over the land and over the self. She personifies inner strength and power, the regal queen who anoints and sanctifies mortal kings and holds power over the land as well as the animals and people who live upon it. To modern women she represents a fourth face to the Great Goddess, reflecting maturity and the wisdom of experience.

For the Celts, true kingship required the king to be ritually linked to the land by entering a sacred marriage with the goddess. The power of sovereignty was not shared; instead it was conveyed from the goddess to the king, who acted as her representative. So close was the bond between the king and the land that he could not be disfigured in any way, lest his blemish be transferred to the land. We can see this in the *Lebor Gabála Érenn* when Nuada, the original leader of the Túatha Dé Danann, was forced to relinquish his kingship when his hand was cut off in battle.

This marriage between goddess and king, land and ruler, was not necessarily permanent. If the king no longer acted to the benefit of the land or was too old or disfigured, the goddess could leave the marriage and anoint a more suitable leader.

For this reason sovereign goddesses are usually linked to love triangles involving an older king and a younger man who eventually takes his place. This love triangle is present in several Celtic myths, and remnants of this theme can be found in Arthurian legend with the relationship between Guinevere, Arthur, and Lancelot. As with Guinevere, many sovereign goddesses were portrayed as lustful and wanton women in later myths. As Christianity influenced these ancient stories, the goddesses of sovereignty diminished into mortal queens. A powerful woman in control of her sexual nature did not appeal to Christian morals. As women's sexuality became the property of their husbands, so too did a goddess's right to choose her sexual partners change, becoming distorted into the image of a sinful woman.

The Morrigan's sexual nature is often seen as a negative aspect of her personality. She sleeps with many men, both gods and mortals, and is often seen as wanton and spiteful, as when she hinders Cúchulain in battle because he refuses to sleep with her. As a goddess of sovereignty, the Morrigan maintains the right to choose her sexual partners, bestowing those she favors with true kingship. When we see the Morrigan in this light, her sexual nature is no longer fierce and uncontrolled but holds a deeper purpose. Refusing her advances becomes a refusal to acknowledge her power. When the Túatha Dé Danann attempted to overthrow the Fomorians, it was not until the Dagda's sexual union with the Morrigan that their victory was assured. As one of the kings of the Túatha Dé Danann, Dagda's union with the goddess of the earth ensured the Túatha Dé Danann's sovereignty over the land and established them as the rightful rulers of Ireland.

In many Celtic stories, the goddess of the land appears to the would-be king disguised as a hag in order to test the man's worthiness. The story of *Niall of the Nine Hostages* is a prime example of the sovereign goddess's test. Niall and his two brothers were cooking in the woods and became thirsty. They search for water and come across a well that was guarded by an ugly old woman. The woman refuses to give the men water unless they kiss her. Niall's brothers refuse, but Niall accepts. After he kisses the hag, she transforms into a beautiful young woman. When Niall asks her name, she answers "I am Sovereignty." Here shape-shifting is employed not only to test Niall but also to represent the cycles of the land, both fruitful (summer/youth) and barren (winter/old age). Niall must accept the land as it is: both fruitful and barren, beautiful and dangerous.

These same themes play out in Cúchulain's interaction with the Morrigan in the *Táin*. Cúchulain is not a king, but as a champion of Ulster, Cúchulain acts in much the same way a king would by protecting the land. By refusing to have sex with the Morrigan, he refuses to acknowledge the power of the goddess who personifies the land. Fueled by his ego, he believes he does not need her favor to win his battles. After rejecting her offer of a sacred union and thereby her conferred sovereignty, she wounds Cúchulain in battle. Here her shape-shifting happens in reverse. First she appears as the Maiden then as the Crone after being rejected. Cúchulain's ability to wound her in return suggests a connection between the two. The belief that whatever happened to the king also befell the land is clearly seen here. Each wound the Morrigan inflicts on Cúchulain is equally dealt to her. Each wounds the other three times, showing that whatever happens to one will happen to the other. After his battle with Loch, Cúchulain is inflicted with terrible thirst and meets the Morrigan disguised as a hag leading a three-teated cow. He blesses her for each drink he takes from the cow, thus healing her wounds. Again the cow is another hint to the hag's identity as a sovereign goddess connected to the land, as is her shape-shifting from Maiden to Crone, which parallels Niall's story. After unintentionally healing her, Morrigan finally aids Cúchulain, killing a portion of Maeve's army with her fearful screams. Healing the Morrigan seems to be the hero's belated acceptance of her sovereignty.

In the event that a king proved himself to be unworthy, a goddess of the land would take quick and decisive action against him. The Morrigan does not put up with troublemakers, especially those who do not recognize or who misuse her power. As Macha Mong Ruad (Macha of the Red Tresses), she appears as a mortal queen, daughter of Aed Ruad, who ruled along with two other kings, each ruling for an allotted number of years. When Aed Ruad died, the other two kings refused to allow Macha to take her turn ruling in her father's stead. With her right as a sovereign challenged, she makes war with the other kings and defeats them. When the sons of the defeated kings come to Macha demanding their right to rule, she does not grant it to them. Here she is both able to bestow kingship and refuse it to the unworthy. The sons attempt to steal the kingship by force and a war ensues. What is interesting is the manner in which Macha defeats the men and forces them to serve her. After being beaten on the battlefield, they flee. Disguised as an old woman, Macha goes to the woods of Connaught where they are hiding. Despite her appearance, all five sons become sexually attracted to her. Each man goes off into the woods with her. After lying with Macha, the men become magically bound and can neither speak nor move. The use of a sexual union to both confer and remove power marks Macha as a goddess of sovereignty.

Similarly in *The Destruction of Da Derga's Hostel* Badb brings about King Conaire's death after he proves unworthy to rule. Having broken a number of his geasa, Badb forces him to break his final taboo, which leads to his death. Badb appears at the king's door as an ugly old woman. Conaire refuses to admit her into the hostel since his last remaining geis was to never admit a single woman into his home after sunset. She mocks him for his lack of hospitality, and he eventually allows her to enter. Having broken this final taboo, Conaire is killed the next day. Similarly the Morrigan tricks Cúchulain into breaking his geis by eating dog flesh, shortly after which the hero dies in battle.

In Arthurian myths Morgan le Fay attempts to overthrow Arthur in order to make her lover, Accolon, king in his place. Here the goddess is replacing an unworthy king and enters into a sacred marriage with a younger, more fit ruler. Usually this struggle is between an older man and a younger one, the older representing the waning half of the year and decline and the young man representing the light half of the year and renewed growth and fertility. Since the king's well-being was reflected by the land, this struggle represents the cycles of nature and the turn of the seasons, which the goddess presides over. She chooses to mate with the younger king to renew the land and bring to it a new cycle of fertility.

Before making the Cave of Cruachan her home, the Morrigan was said to dwell at Tara. Tara was Ireland's sacred center and the royal seat of power for the high kings. Kings were inaugurated on the hill of Tara where the Lia Fáil, one of the four treasures of the Túatha Dé Danann, stood. Also known as the Stone of Destiny, the Lia Fáil was said to cry out when the rightful king touched it. As a Great Queen and goddess of sovereignty, this seems like a fitting home for the Morrigan.

While today the Morrigan no longer dethrones wayward kings, she can teach us to assert our own sovereignty. To her champions she can confer the power to overcome obstacles and learn to become true leaders.

Self-Sovereignty & the Fourfold Goddess

In modern times the Morrigan's role in our lives has shifted from rulership over the land to ruling our own self-sovereignty. She is the Great Queen who personifies inner strength and power. To the Pagans of the past, the earth goddess and sovereign queen were one and the same. But today the sovereign queen has been divorced from our concept of the Divine, a result of patriarchy stripping away the power and rights of females and perverting the stories about women of power into tales of sexually wanton women. Thankfully modern women are beginning to reconnect to this aspect of the Great Goddess and are beginning to explore her full potential. Some Pagans are even adding the Queen to the archetype of the Triple Goddess, creating a fourfold model of female divinity.

My first encounter with the Queen was at a Pagan festival in upstate New York. Several of us began talking about sovereignty, and how we were honoring our own inner sovereignty. One woman was going through a divorce and spoke about how the power of the sovereign archetype had given her the bravery to leave an abusive situation. We all shared stories, and after a while decided to do a spontaneous ritual honoring this aspect of the Great Goddess. We cast a circle and called the elements; then one of the women whom we had just met at the festival began invoking the Goddess. "We invoke you Maiden, Mother, Queen, and Crone ..."

That part caught my attention. Queen? I had been a Witch for several years, and had never heard anyone talk about a fourth face to the Goddess. Still, I had always felt that something was missing from the Mother aspect of the Goddess. I saw the Mother as a figure like the Empress in the tarot, stately and regal, both bearing children and holding sway over creation and her own personal power, blending the power of sovereignty and creation together. I had never imagined that others were seeking out a new aspect of the Goddess, embodying the traits I had thought were missing from the Mother. Fascinated, I asked the woman about her invocation after our ritual. She told me she began to embrace the Queen when she turned forty. Her kids were grown up and out of the house, and she had gone back to school to finish a degree, something she had neglected to do when she was younger in order to be a stay-at-home mom. She didn't feel like she identified with the Mother during this new phase of her life, but she didn't feel quite like a Crone either, and from that realization she discovered the Queen.

The Maiden, Mother, Crone archetype was formed in a time when human life expectancy was much shorter. Women are living much longer now, the average life span being seventy-five, while only a few centuries ago it was less than half that, creating a gap between the Mother and Crone phase in a woman's life. The Triple Goddess is often compared to the three phases of the moon, but as Barbara Ardinger tells us in her article about the Queen, the moon actually has four phases. "We like to think that the moon has three phases ... these are said to correspond to the maiden, mother, and crone. But the moon clearly has four phases: Waxing, Full, Waning, and dark. The new moon is actually the very beginning of the Waxing phase. Keeping our thinking symmetrical, if we see only three lunar phases, we also like to allot only three phases to a woman's life. But these days life is a lot more complicated than that."[88]

While the threefold Goddess is the most common multiple divinity we find in mythology and archeology, the Goddess does appear elsewhere in other multiple forms. There are nine muses, twenty-seven Valkyries, and even double goddesses such as Demeter and Persephone, who act as mother and daughter while they are really two aspects of the same goddess. The Triple Goddess is only one of many ways the Great Goddess expresses her divine nature to us. Paganism is not dogmatic, and we should feel free to explore all the many ways the Goddess shows herself to us, whether that be as a triple, fourfold, or ninefold divinity. While the Triple Goddess is a fundamental archetype of modern Paganism, I think there is room for the Queen. The Queen's power can be just as potent in our lives whether you see her as a fourth face to the Goddess or simply as another archetype to be explored. That being said, let's learn who exactly the Queen is.

In *The Women's Wheel of Life,* Elizabeth Davis and Carol Leonard call the Queen the "Matron" and describe her as a leader who is secure in herself. Davis and Leonard also name her as the phase in a woman's life between Mother and Crone, although they name thirteen total archetypes in a woman's life rather than four.

> *She is us, when childbearing urges begin to wane, when careers are well established and a sense of mastery comes upon us. She is the clan leader, ruler of her domain. She utilizes power with grace, and reveals the unseen aspect of growth and change ... in this stage women manifest their queenly essences and natural leadership abilities. Why then, is the Matriarch historically absent from the Goddess trinity? In terms of our life cycles, a longer lifespan and later onset of menopause have combined to open wide the window between childbearing and old age.*[89]

---

88. Ardinger, "Why We Need to Claim the Queen," *SageWoman Magazine,* Issue 74.
89. Davis and Leonard, *The Woman's Wheel Life,* pp. 4, 5.

The Queen is firmly centered in her image of self, honoring her own self-worth and taking responsibility for her own decisions and dreams. She rules over her own fate and destiny, not allowing others to rule over her. She is the sovereign of her life, the forger of her own destiny. She has earned authority and respect by overcoming life's obstacles. She is the embodiment of strength and grace under fire. If we keep with the triple Goddess model and associate her with the moon, she rules over the waning moon, a time of shedding the old and of renewal. The fourfold model also corresponds to the four seasons (interestingly, the Celts only recognized three seasons), where she ruled over autumn and the harvest, whether that be a harvest of crops or of life's wisdom. It also fits nicely with the four directions and elements, where she rules over the west and the element of water.

In a time when women are beginning to reconnect to the Great Goddess's full potential, the Queen beckons us to explore our inner sovereignty and challenges our perspective of Divinity. Just as with the Maiden, Mother, and Crone, we can access the power of the Queen no matter our age or what phase of life we are currently in. Women of all ages can benefit from harnessing their inner strength and reclaiming their sovereignty. Whether you need to access the Queen to further your career, heal your self-esteem, or take the first steps to rebuild your life, she is a potent archetype for the modern woman.

Exercise 1: Oath of Sovereignty

Prior to performing the next ritual, you will need to write what I call an Oath of Sovereignty. When sovereigns are crowned, they usually recite a vow to their people or nation. Your vow is not to a country, but to both yourself and the Great Goddess. It can be as long or short as you wish and should express what you wish to gain from the Queen phase of your life or from the Queen archetype in general. Don't worry about being poetic; your oath doesn't have to contain flowery words, it just has to resonate with you and with what you wish to accomplish by claiming sovereignty over your life. Perhaps it is a vow to honor your inner sovereignty, a vow to take care of your own needs rather than ignore them, or a vow to begin a new venture in a new part of your life. Whatever your vow, it should be in your own words and should not be made lightly.

Claiming Sovereignty Ritual

The following ritual can be used as an initiation for a woman entering the Queen phase of life or for a woman of any age who wants to cultivate her inner sovereignty, as you will be crowning yourself as a sovereign. Connecting to the Queen of sovereignty is not limited to women; men can and should learn to connect to the Queen aspect of the Goddess. A torc can be substituted for a crown for men connecting to this archetype. Torcs were braided neck rings worn as a symbol of office by the Celts. Women may choose to use a torc as well, since it is documented that both male and female leaders wore them. Since my path is primarily Celtic, I chose to use a torc because it reminded me of the ancient queens of Celtic mythology. Use whichever you feel the most comfortable with, but a crown or tiara would also be very good choices.

As the Queen demands authority and command, I prefer to use a sword during the ritual involving the Queen, but you can also use a wand or athame if you prefer or have limited space to work in.

You will need the Oath of Sovereignty you created in the previous exercise. Prior to the ritual you should take some time to meditate or do pathwork to connect to the Queen. If you wish to do pathwork during the ritual, record the planned pathwork ahead of time; if working with a group, choose one of the participants to lead the pathwork. The best time to perform this ritual is during the waning moon, the phase associated with the Queen.

You Will Need:

Athame or sword
1 blue candle
Great Queen Incense (see page 211)
A crown or torc
Dragon's blood oil
Goblet of wine
Oath of Sovereignty

Cast the circle with your sword or wand. As you call each quarter, visualize the Maiden, Mother, Queen, and Crone emerging from each of the four directions. The Maiden stands with the wind blowing through her loose hair, the sound of birds singing behind her; the Mother stands wreathed in a mantle of fire, belly round with the promise of new life; the Queen stands upon the surface of a river, offering the cup of wisdom; the Crone stands amid a snowy forest, a twisted staff in her hand. Feel the power of each aspect of the Goddess and their element flowing into the circle and through you.

East:
Maiden most fair, who rules the power of air
Keeper of creativity and inspiration
I call upon you to witness this rite of sovereignty!

South:
Mother who rules over the power of fire
Creative forces of sun and flame, courage and passion
I call upon you to witness this rite of sovereignty!

West:
Sovereign Queen, who rules over the power of water
Regal one of power, wisdom gained through experience
Mistress of sea, river, and stream
I call upon you to witness this rite of sovereignty!

North:
Crone, old one of winter, stone and ice
Who rules over the power of earth
Keeper of the Underworld, death and rebirth
I call upon you to witness this rite of sovereignty!

Light the blue candle representing the Queen. With your sword or athame, draw an invoking pentagram over the candle, saying:

Maiden, Mother, Sovereign, Crone
Fourfold Lady of Power
Initiator and maker of Kings and Queens
Goddess of the Land

Noble one of sovereignty
Regal one at the fullness of power
Your wisdom, the knowledge of self
Great Queen, I honor and welcome you here!

Light the incense and pass the crown or torc through its smoke. Anoint it with the dragon's blood oil then hold it above the altar, saying:

Morrigan, Goddess of Sovereignty
Great Queen who grants rulership to Kings and Queens
I bless this crown/torc in your name
Symbol of my inner sovereignty, of self-mastery
that I may shape my life, my body, and destiny.

Place the torc around your neck; if using a crown, place it on your head. Circle the wine three times with the sword/athame. Raise it above the altar, saying:

I honor you, Morrigan
You who are the Maiden, Mother, Sovereign, and Crone
With this offering I seal my vow to you, forever.

Take a sip of the wine then pour the rest into your offering bowl or on the ground outside once the ritual is over.

Take some time for pathworking or simply a few minutes to commune with the Queen. Recite your Oath of Sovereignty. When you are ready, close the quarters, saying:

East:
I thank the Maiden and the powers of air
Depart in peace, with my thanks and blessings.

South:
I thank the Mother and the powers of fire
Depart in peace, with my thanks and blessings.

West:
I thank the Queen and the powers of water
Depart in peace, with my thanks and blessings.

North:
I thank the Crone and the powers of earth
Depart in peace, with my thanks and blessings.

Close the circle. Place your torc or crown in a safe place where it will not be disturbed. Wear it when invoking the Queen during rituals or when you need to replenish your personal power.

Fourfold Goddess Moon Ritual

This ritual can be used during any phase of the moon to draw upon the fourfold Goddess and the moon's power.

You Will Need:
1 moonstone
Small bowl of water
4 white candles
Wand or athame

Prior to the ritual, place the moonstone in the bowl of water, letting it soak for at least an hour. If possible, place the bowl outside in the light of the moon. This moon water can be bottled and stored for use in later rituals and can be used to bless and cleanse an area or object.

Place the four white candles (or an image that represents the fourfold Goddess) on the center of the altar. As you cast a circle, visualize the light of the moon filling your wand and a silvery white light emanating from it to form the circle's boundaries while saying:

In the name of the Maiden, Mother, Queen, and Crone
I cast this circle of moonlight
In the name of the fourfold Goddess, this circle is sealed!

Go to the altar. Using your fingers, sprinkle the moon water around the circle.

In the name of the ever-changing Lady of the Moon
I bless this sacred place

If you wish, perform a self-blessing by anointing yourself with the moon water. When you are ready, go to each quarter, saying:

East:
From the East I call upon the Goddess of the Waxing Moon
Lovely Maiden who rules over the powers of air
Keeper of new beginnings and renewal
Hail beloved Maiden!

South:
From the South I call upon the Goddess of the Full Moon
Mother of all creation, ripe with fiery potential
Her growing belly mirrored in the full and radiant moon
Hail luminous Mother!

West:
From the West I call upon the Goddess of the Waning Moon
Lady of sovereignty, noble and regal Queen
Keeper of wisdom and the realm of water
Hail sovereign Queen!

North:
From the North I call upon the Goddess of the New Moon
Shadowy Crone, lady of winter, stone and ice
Keeper of the Underworld and the realm of earth
Hail dark Crone!

Go to the altar. Invoke the Goddess by saying:

Fourfold Lady of power
Bright Maiden
(Light the first candle.)
Fruitful Mother
(Light the second candle.)
Regal Queen
(Light the third candle.)
Dark Crone
(Light the forth candle.)
You mirror the fullness of a woman's life

Like the moon you shift and change
Ever moving, ever learning
Waxing and waning
As you shed the old and no longer useful
And spin and shape your dreams and desires
You wear many faces
As the Maiden you are Blodeuwedd and Áine
As the radiant Mother you are Anu and Brigid
As the Great Queen you are the Morrigan and Rhiannon
As the wise Crone you appear as Cerridwen, Badb, and others
Tonight I welcome you in all your many faces and guises
Hail most radiant Goddess of the moon!

Do any planned spellwork or pathworking. When you have finished, extinguish the candles and thank the Goddess. Close the quarters by saying:

East:
Depart in peace, Lady of the Waxing Moon and powers of air.

South:
Depart in peace, Lady of the Full Moon and powers of fire.

West:
Depart in peace, Lady of the Waning Moon and powers of water.

North:
Depart in peace, Lady of the New Moon and powers of earth.

Open the circle.

Great Queen Invocation

Use the following invocation to call upon the Morrigan as the Great Queen and Lady of Sovereignty. Call upon this aspect of the Morrigan when you feel the need for inner strength, when facing a difficult situation, or when beginning a new phase in life.

Hear me, O Morrigu
You who once dwelled at Tara
Keeper and sovereign of the land
Mistress of all she surveys
Noble, regal Queen
Macha marking the boundaries of your realm with a broach
Anu, Goddess of the land, maker of kings
Badb, shadowy Queen of the Otherworlds
Together you are the Great Queen
Teach me to rule myself
Power within and without, to mirror your own
Fill the body of this your daughter/son and Priest/ess
Let us be one this day, O Goddess of Sovereignty!

Great Queen Incense

3 tbsp. dragon's blood resin
2 tbsp. myrrh
2 tbsp. rose petals
1 tbsp. amber resin

Symbols of the Great Queen

We are familiar with the symbols of the Triple Goddess, but what are the symbols of the Queen? Here are a few symbols I use to represent the Queen aspect of the four-fold Goddess. As there are no traditional symbols for this aspect of the Goddess, feel free to add to this list as you work and connect with the Queen aspect.

Autumn leaves: As the Queen's season is autumn, orange and red leaves make excellent decoration to use for an altar dedicated to the Queen or during rituals invoking her. For spells involving the Queen, you can write your petitions on an autumn leaf.

Broach: In Macha's myths she traces the boundaries of the fort Emain Macha with her broach. Through this magickal act she is claiming the boundaries of her world and affirming her power to rule her domain. Wearing a broach, especially one with a Celtic design, is a wonderful way to invoke Macha's energies and can be used to symbolize your own queenly power.

Crown: As a symbol of rulership, this a natural symbol for the Queen. And as the Morrigan is the Great Queen, it is a fitting symbol for her in the guise of the goddess of sovereignty.

Purple: Purple is the color of royalty and ideal for representing the Queen.

Scepter/staff/wand: There is a long tradition of scepters adorned with royal insignia being used to represent a sovereign's authority to rule. Scepters were originally staffs that were eventually shortened to resemble wands, making the wand or staff the ideal ritual tool to represent the Queen. Since the Morrigan is connected to the hazel, a staff made from hazel wood would be an appropriate tool to connect to the Morrigan in her aspect as the goddess of sovereignty.

Torc: The Celtic equivalent of a crown, the torc is also an excellent symbol of royalty and the Morrigan as the Great Queen.

Waning Moon: Falling in between the full moon (Mother) and new moon (Crone), this phase of the moon is sacred to the Queen. A waning moon can be carved onto tools or candles to represent this aspect of the Goddess.

11
Seeress

I have fled in the shape of a raven of prophetic speech.

—John Matthews and Caitlin Matthews, Taliesin: The Last Celtic Shaman

You find yourself standing on a sandy shore, ocean waves crashing against the beach and swirling around your feet. You watch the waves for a few minutes and notice that there is a small wooden boat gliding across the water. As the small craft comes closer, you see it is richly carved with many weaving knots and its bow is carved into the head of a dragon. A woman with raven hair stands in the boat. Her robes of green and blue match the color of the ocean water. She holds a branch that shines as if it is made of silver, with nine red apples hanging from it. You watch as she moves the branch from side to side and the boat seems to follow her motions. Soon the boat floats only a few feet from where you stand on the shore. Curious, you ask the woman where she is from. She smiles and says, "I come from a country where there is nothing but truth, where nothing grows old or withers away. I am from the Land of the Young, which lies beyond the Ninth Wave, and I will take you there if you wish."

You realize this is the seaborn Morrigan, goddess of the sea, rivers, and sacred waters, lady of the Isle of Avalon. After a moment's hesitation, you agree to accompany her and wade out into the water. You take the woman's arm and she pulls you up into the little boat. With a quick motion of the branch, the boat begins to gain speed as it heads out toward the open sea. The farther out the boat sails, the stronger the waves grow, and the little craft rises and falls as the foaming waves pass by trying to reach the shore that is steadily disappearing into the distance. You count as the waves pass. One, two, three ... the shore is almost completely out of sight ... four, five, six ... only the blue-green of the ocean water and the white foam of the cresting waves fill your vision ... seven, eight, nine ...

As the boat passes over the ninth wave, the woman waves the silver branch in a long arching motion through the air. Although you were sure there was nothing on the horizon a moment ago, you now see a mist-shrouded island not far off. The mist rises to reveal a shore with green rolling hills. As the wind blows, you catch the scent of sweet ripe apples.

"Avalon, Apple Isle, the Fortunate Isle. The Land of the Young has many names. It is as distant as the stars or as close as your our own heart, but we are always connected to it. The wisdom of the Otherworlds flows through all of the worlds and each of us, if we are willing to listen."

After a few moments the boat glides to the green shore and you and the woman step out, the sea gently swirling around your feet as you wade through the water and onto the isle. The woman places a hand on your shoulder and leads you through a maze of wild apple trees. It seems like a long time before you hear the sound of rushing water—not ocean water, but the sound of a stream. A well comes into view a moment later. It is low to the ground, its grey stones etched with spiral designs. Water rushes over the stones, overflowing from the well. As the well water spills over the edge, it divides into five separate streams. You also notice there are nine hazel trees growing around the well. As you look up at the trees, a hazelnut falls from a branch and splashes into the well. A fish appears and quickly eats the nut before vanishing back into the depths of the well.

"All who live drink from these five rivers. They are the earthly senses." She scoops up a handful of water from one of the streams and lets it flow through her hands, "Sight, sound, touch, taste, and scent... all that make up our earthly experiences. All who live drink from these rivers, but only the People of Vision drink from both the rivers and the Well of Wisdom."

She points toward the grey well with its flowing water. "The flesh is not just of the flesh, spirit lives within and behind it, as the Otherworlds exist alongside and beyond the earthly plane. All things must move through the realm of spirit before they can manifest upon the physical plane. To drink from the rivers and the well is to see through to the Otherworlds and the realm of spirits, to see that the past, present, and future exist all at once." The woman holds out a chalice and offers it to you. "If you are willing, drink and the gift of the Seer will be yours."

You take the chalice and dip it into the first river. As you drink, the world seems brighter and your vision sharper. You dip it into the second stream, and as you drink the cold water your hearing becomes clearer and the wind passing through the trees sounds like a soft melody. As you drink from each stream, your senses seem more alive than they have ever been. Finally you come to the well. You dip the chalice into the pool and let the sweet water fall on your tongue. As the water flows down your throat, you feel as if a veil has been lifted from the worlds. You look down into the waters of the well and images appear on the mirrored surface of the water. You stand at the well for a time watching the images, asking questions that bring new images into focus on the water's surface.

When you are ready, the Morrigan takes your hand and brings you back to the shores of the Fortunate Isle, and you sail back across the waves, knowing that your sight and all your senses can reach into the Otherworlds whenever you seek their wisdom.

If the Morrigan wasn't prophesying the future in her myths, she was shaping the fates of those she favored or those who had earned her wrath. She could foresee victory or doom and make either fate come to pass. She appeared in dreams and foretold wars and death. As the Washer at the Ford, she appeared to warriors who would soon fall in battle. In all her myths, prophecy and seership are always present.

Women in general were considered to have the ability to see the future in ancient times, and there are many female seers in Celtic mythology, ranging from mortal women to faeries and goddesses. The Roman historian Tacitus describes this belief among the Celts in his historic accounts: "There is, in their opinion, something sacred in the female sex, and even the power of foreseeing future events. Their advice is, therefore, always heard; they are deemed oracular."[90]

Of the three Morrigans, Badb is the most closely connected to prophecy and predicting the future. She appears to kings and queens in dreams, foretells the fates of gods, and appears as the Washer in the Ford, warning her favorite warriors that they would soon fall in battle. Her most well-known prophecy was delivered after the Túatha Dé Danann defeated the Fomorians. Here Badb is specifically mentioned as the sister who delivers the prophecy. "And Badb, the sister of the Morrigan prophesied . . ."[91] The Christian monks who wrote down the older mythology interpreted this vision as a prediction of Armageddon, while modern critics claim it predicted the Irish potato famine.

In *The Destruction of Da Derga's Hostel,* Badb appeared to King Conaire, who asked her, not realizing it was Badb, if she could foretell the future. She answers him by prophesying the king's death. "Truly I see for thee . . . that neither fell nor flesh of thine shall escape from the place into which thou has come, save what the birds will

90. Tacitus, *The History Germania and Agricola,* p. 317.
91. Gray, "The Second Battle of Mag Tuired," verse 166.

bear in their claws."[92] In another story Badb appears to both Queen Maeve and the King Conchobar of Ulster in their dreams. She predicts the devastation of Ulster by the *Táin* and tells Conchobar he will accomplish great deeds in the future. When Badb appears to Maeve, she predicts the death of the queen's son in battle and rallies Maeve to go to war to avenge him. "O Maev[e], why lie you in sleep? ... If you be skilled in prophecy, it should be time for you to arise."[93]

Before his final battle, Cúchulain is warned of his impending death when he encounters Badb as the Washer at the Ford. Again Badb's prophecies revolve around predicting battle and death, a function she retains in later folklore as the banshee, whose mournful cries heralded a death in the family she watched over.

While Badb is the most connected to prophecy, Macha and Nemain also possess the ability to predict the future. When Macha gazed across the plain her husband had named for her, she foresaw the destruction the *Táin* would unleash upon the land. The vision was so vivid that she died of a broken heart. In her incarnation as a faery woman, Macha warns her mortal husband not to boast about her abilities. He forgets her warning, and her husband's boasting leads to her death. Although it is not specifically stated that she foresaw these events, her warning implies that she had some foreknowledge.

Nemain's connection to prophecy is vague. In the *Lebor Gabála Érenn* she is described as a seer, "Nemain of prophetic stanzas,"[94] although she is never mentioned using this ability in any of her myths. Her description as a prophetess may be due to her connection with Badb. Since Badb and Nemain's names were often used interchangeably, their abilities may have been conflated as well.

The manner in which the Morrigan deals out her prophecies implies more than simply seeing the future. She manipulates fate to her liking. Victory for both mortals like Cúchulain and the gods of the Túatha Dé Danann was often the direct result of the goddess's intervention. After mating with Dagda, she predicts victory for the Túatha Dé Danann and vows to fight alongside them. Her prophecy of victory seems less about predicting the future than creating the outcome she desires. Dagda earned her favor through their union; as a goddess of fate, she makes certain he wins the battle, sealing the fate of the Fomorians. Similarly, after Cúchulain blesses her when disguised as a hag, she kills part of Maeve's army for him. When Cúchulain

92. Stokes, "The Destruction of Dá Derga's Hostel," p. 59.
93. Leahy, *The Courtship of Ferb*, p. 77.
94. Epstein, *War Goddess*, p. 61.

encounters the Morrigan in the *Táin Bo Regamna* and accuses her of stealing one of Ulster's cows, she predicts the hero's death, measuring the time he has remaining in life with the age of the calf the cow was carrying. "'It is at the guarding of thy death that I am; and I shall be,' said she ... 'It is up to that time that thou art in life, so long as the calf which is in this cow's body is a yearling.'"[95] Again her prophecy is more of a decree, a punishment for slighting her, than a prediction. Perhaps if Cúchulain had not offended her, Maeve would never have stolen that magickal bull and Cúchulain might have lived to see an old age. Her choice of words, "the guarding of thy death" insinuates that she can choose the time of the hero's demise, either allowing him to fall in battle or granting him victory, leaving his death for another day. As in her other myths, she acts as both a prophetess and a goddess of fate, both foreseeing and decreeing the fates of heroes.

The Morrigan is frequently described as a poet and identifies herself as such to Cúchulain in the *Tain Bo Regamna.* Poets or bards were believed to possess the ability to foresee the future.

For the Morrigan, prophecy and fate go hand in hand. She both predicts and creates the future, taking fate into her own hands. She is both a seer and a weaver of destinies. As the Seeress, the Morrigan can help us to peer into the mysteries of the past, present, and future in order to seek our own truths and weave the threads of our own fates.

Divination

Anyone can learn divination. Why? Because everyone is naturally psychic. Most people have simply learned to tune out this part of their nature, believing such phenomena to be mere coincidence or delusion. Have you ever heard the phone ring and simply knew who was calling? (And, no, I don't mean caller ID.) Have you ever dreamed about running into an old friend, then bump into them the next day? While some prefer to call these things coincidences, these are all examples of psychic phenomena that everyone has experienced. While some people may be more sensitive to psychic impressions than others, it is something we all possess. When we learn to open ourselves to our intuitive nature, we unlock the door to the vast wisdom of the universe.

The art of divination has been practiced in every culture and religion around the world. From the Chinese I Ching to the ever-popular Tarot, divination has been

95. Leahy, *Heroic Romances of Ireland,* p. 375.

employed for centuries to discern everything from the outcome of battles to the fate of one's love life. Today more than ever there is a great deal of interest in divination. There are literally hundreds of themed Tarot decks available for purchase. With the popularity of the Tarot, other divination systems such as the Norse Runes and Celtic Ogham are also seeing renewed interest.

I had already been reading Tarot cards for myself and others for several years before I began working with the Morrigan. When I began incorporating the Morrigan's energies into my life, I found myself relying more and more on my intuitive nature, not just in my readings but in other parts of my life as well. My readings became more intense when I called on her energies and began having vivid prophetic dreams.

As a goddess of prophecy and second sight, the Morrigan's energies can help enhance any type of divination work. While we will be discussing a Celtic form of divination in this section, there is no reason why you must use a Celtic method of divination when working with the Morrigan. If using the Norse Runes or a deck of Tarot cards works the best for you, go ahead! The Morrigan will be happy to work with you in any endeavor of divination regardless of the tool. Whether you are new to the art of divination or have been practicing for years, the Morrigan can help develop and strengthen your intuitive nature.

Asking the Right Questions

When working with any divination system, asking the right question is of utmost importance. Asking specific questions and setting a time frame that you are asking about will result in readings that are more accurate. For example instead of asking "Will I have a successful career?" which is very open-ended and can refer to two months from now or two years from now, asking "How will my career progress in the next three months?" would give a more accurate reading. I prefer to do readings for a time period of six months or less. Reading for any time period past six months will not always yield accurate information. The future is not set in stone—it is fluid and will change based on the choices you make. In readings for time periods longer than six months, there are simply too many choices you can make now that will alter the outcome of the reading.

THE OGHAM

The Celtic Ogham, also known as the Tree Alphabet, consists of twenty-five letters created by a combination of bisecting lines. Each letter corresponds to a sacred tree or plant, with the exception of *koad* and *mor,* which were later additions to the alphabet and are not connected to specific trees. Much of what we know about the corresponding meanings of the Ogham comes from the twelfth-century *Book of Ballymote* and three lists, or "word Oghams," that survived within other manuscripts; these are the *Word Ogham of Morainn mac Moin*, the *Word Ogham of Cuchulain,* and the *Word Ogham of Óengus*. Ogma, the Celtic god of wisdom and eloquence, was credited with the alphabet's invention. Historically the Ogham is thought to have been created sometime between the first and third centuries CE, although some scholars believe it is older.

We know from Caesar's accounts that the Druid tradition was purely oral, which begs the question: why would the Druids need an alphabet? There is no historical evidence that the Ogham was ever used to write books, and with the Druids' taboo against committing spiritual knowledge to paper, it seems unlikely this was ever a function of the Ogham. Ogham inscriptions have been found throughout Ireland and England to mark graves and land boundaries, so we know this was part of their function. Others have suggested that the Ogham was used by the Druids as a secret form of communication, since the symbols could easily be replicated by putting a certain number of fingers across an arm or leg. Whether the Ogham was used as a means of conversing in secret is unknown, but literary sources do point to the Ogham's use in magick and divination, and it is this application we will be exploring. In the story *The Wooing of Étain* there is a description of a Druid using the Ogham to divine a person's location: "He made three wands of yew and upon the wands he wrote an Ogham, and by his keys of poetic wisdom that he had and by the Ogham, it was revealed to him that Étain was in the fairy mound of Bri Leith."[96]

There are several readymade Ogham sets available on the market, but I suggest making your own set. To create your own Ogham, you will need twenty-five sticks of equal length; these can be dowels purchased from a craft store or natural wood gathered from outside and sanded. The letters of the Ogham can be carved or painted onto the wood. You could also use a wood-burning tool to carve the letters. Since several letters of the Ogham can be confused with one another, you may want to write the name of each tree on your sticks as well. While most Ogham sets are carved onto wood, I have also used a set painted on flat stones with great success. Some people prefer to have sets made from the wood of each of the trees the Ogham letters represent, but a set made from a single wood will work just as well. There is no right or wrong method for how you should create your Ogham set—go with what feels right to you.

---

96. Leahy, *Heroic Romances of Ireland,* p. 21.

Place your Ogham sticks in a small bag or pouch so they will not be disturbed by others when they are not in use. Your Ogham set should be ritually cleansed and blessed before you begin using it.

If you are more comfortable with a Tarot-style divination system, there are several Tarot-style Ogham sets available with both the Ogham letters and pictures of the trees they represent printed on cards. The Ogham can also be used in conjunction with the Tarot. To do this, draw your Tarot cards in your chosen spread. Then draw your Ogham sticks in the same order, placing each Ogham on top of the corresponding card. The Ogham you draw will clarify and add additional insight into the meaning of its corresponding Tarot card in the reading.

A complete list of the Oghams and their meanings can be found in the next section. I suggest you become familiar with the meanings of each Ogham and research the individual trees they represent before using the Oghams for divination. The more you know about each symbol, the more in-depth your divinations will become.

The Ogham can also be used during magick to write on candles, decorate magickal tools, or write magickal petitions. When writing on a candle, begin by carving a straight line along the length of the candle. Ogham letters were written from bottom to top, so begin carving the appropriate strokes at the base of the candle and work your way toward the wick.

Basic Ogham Reading

You will need a cloth or flat surface for your reading. A square of any fabric will do. Spread out your cloth and draw nine Oghams from your bag. Shuffle or roll them around in your hands while concentrating on your question, then toss them onto the cloth. Any letters that fall face down should be returned to your bag. If all the Oghams are face down, return them to the bag and start over.

The Oghams that fall the farthest from you represent the future; those closest to you represent the past or the current situation. The meanings of any Oghams that touch or overlap are related to one another. Also note if any Oghams appear upside down or reversed, as they will have different meanings.

Some people prefer to throw all twenty-five Ogham staves in a reading, but these readings can become more complicated. If you are new to the Ogham, begin with the basic nine-stave reading until you are comfortable with this form of divination.

Tarot-Style Ogham Spread

If you are more comfortable with a Tarot-style reading, you can use the below spread with the Ogham. You could use any Tarot spread with the Ogham, but the smaller spreads work the best since there are only twenty-five Oghams versus the Tarot's seventy-eight cards.

(1) The past.
(2) The present.
(3) The future.
(4) The overall outcome of the situation.

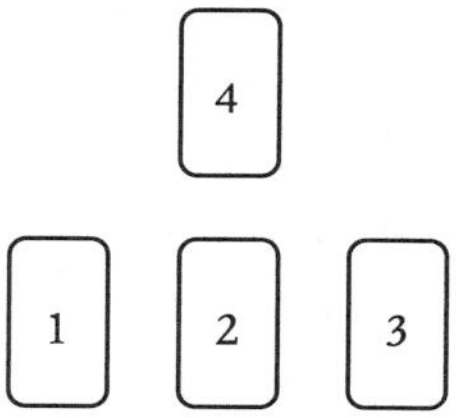

4

1 2 3

THE OGHAM LETTERS EXPLAINED

Beith/*B*/*Birch*

ᚁ

Divinatory Meaning: New beginnings, a fresh start. Renewal and birth.

Reverse Meaning: Let go of the past or you will remain stagnant.

Tree Lore: One of the first trees to flower in spring, the birch has been linked with renewal, banishing evil spirits, and protecting children. The first message written in the Ogham alphabet was *beith*, warning the sun god Lugh of his wife's abduction, and it has been associated with the sun and light ever since. Birch was also traditionally used in Witch's brooms.

Magickal Uses: New endeavors, rituals invoking Lugh.

Luis/*L*/*Rowan*

ᚂ

Divinatory Meaning: Protection, being shielded from harm.

Reverse Meaning: Vulnerability to danger or negative influences, strengthen your defenses.

Tree Lore: Rowan is known for its protective qualities. This Ogham has been described as the "friend" or "strength" of cattle, referring to its magickal use in protecting cattle and preventing evil spirits and the Faery Folk from souring their milk. Rowan was planted near homes, churches, and sacred sites for its protective qualities and to ward against evil spirits. A sprig of rowan tied three times with red thread was thought to break spells. Connected with the sun and sun deities, rowan is particularly sacred to the goddesses Brigid and Brigantia. Brigid carried rowan arrows that could ignite into flames at will.

Magickal Uses: Protection magick.

Fearn/*F*/*Alder*

Divinatory Meaning: Good counsel and guidance. Receiving spiritual guidance. Intuition. Wisdom from the Otherworlds, inspiration.

Reverse Meaning: Ignoring good advice, not listening to your intuition.

Tree Lore: A tree that loves water, the alder is often found growing near rivers. After shedding its leaves, its black cones remain on the branches. These cones or "heads" may be why the tree was linked to Bran the Blessed, whose head continued to speak and encourage his companions after being beheaded in battle. The wood was also used as supports in bridge construction and houses, and was used to make shields. In *The Battle of the Trees,* Bran's followers wore sprigs of alder as a sign of their allegiance.

Magickal Uses: Seeking wisdom from the Otherworlds.

Saille/*S*/*Willow*

Divinatory Meaning: Intuition, psychic flashes, the influence of the moon, secrets revealed.

Reverse Meaning: Being overwhelmed, the need to control your emotions. Emotional upheaval.

Tree Lore: The botanical name for this tree, *Salix,* comes from the Celtic word *Sal,* meaning "near" and *lis* meaning "water," referring to the willow's love of growing in marshes and along riverbanks. The Celts left offerings to the gods in rivers and other bodies of water. Rivers were seen as doorways where one could enter the Otherworlds and communicate with the gods. In the *Word Ogham of Morainn mac Moin,* the phrase "hue of the not living" is connected to this Ogham, referring to *saille*'s connection to the spirit realm, rather than to death.

Magickal Uses: Psychic work, enhancing your psychic senses, moon rituals.

Nuin/*N*/*Ash*

Divinatory Meaning: Transformation and change is possible. Magick and shape-shifting.

Reverse Meaning: Not taking control of your circumstances, feeling powerless.

Tree Lore: Ash was sacred to the magician-god Gwyddyon. It was used to make spears and arrows, urging us to take control of our lives instead of standing by and letting outside circumstances control us. Both the spear and arrow are reminiscent of the wand, signifying the use of magick to instigate change and transformation. Ogham wands were originally made of ash, and the root word of *nuin, nin,* means "letters." Three of the five sacred trees of Ireland were ashes. In Norse mythology, Ygdrassil, the World Tree, was an ash.

Magickal Uses: Transformation magick, creating change in one's life.

Huath/*H/Hawthorn*

Divinatory Meaning: Challenges, obstacles obstructing a goal. Complications concerning love.

Reverse Meaning: Trying to take the easy way out. Obstacles cannot be ignored, they must be dealt with.

Tree Lore: A faery tree, hawthorns were used as maypoles and the flowers were worn by brides to bring happiness in a union. Hawthorn torches were carried in wedding processions to honor the Roman goddess Cardea, to whom the tree was sacred, although it was believed that she would only bless the marriage if the groom had made appropriate sacrifices in her honor. Olwen, the Celtic goddess of spring, was the daughter of the giant Yspaddadden Pencawr, whose name means "Giant Hawthorn." Wherever she walked, white flowers sprang from the ground, reminiscent of the white blooms of the hawthorn. When the hero Culhwch fell in love with her, he was given several impossible tasks to complete before he could wed Olwen, linking the hawthorn with love, fertility, and overcoming obstacles.

Magickal Uses: Calling on the Faery Folk, overcoming obstacles.

Duir/*D/Oak*

Divinatory Meaning: Strength and endurance, strong foundations, new doorways opening.

Reverse Meaning: Misusing strength, weakness.

Tree Lore: With a lifespan of up to seven hundred years or more, the oak is one of the longest-living trees in the Northern Hemisphere. Oaks are deep-rooted and resilient. Their acorns were once used as a food source, linking it with prosperity and plenty. Oaks were sacred to Dagda, the All-Father of the Celts, a god of plenty and fertility. Dagda had a harp named *Dur-da-Bla* (The Oak of Two Blossoms). The tree was also sacred to Taranus, god of lightning and storms, since it has a tendency to be struck by lightning, and charred and blackened oaks are a testimony to the oak's qualities of endurance.

Magickal Uses: Money magick, prosperity, seeking wisdom.

Tinne/*T/Holly*

Divinatory Meaning: Challenges and trials. Being under attack. Take action to defend yourself.

Reverse Meaning: Running from life's challenges. Attempting to circumvent a problem rather than face it.

Tree Lore: The oak and the holly are closely related—the two trees are next to one another in the Ogham sequence and relate to the yearly battle between the Holly King and the Oak King, who battle to rule their respective halves of the year. While the Oak King rules the waxing half of the year, the Holly King rules the dark waning half, which reaches its zenith on the Winter Solstice. The holly's evergreen leaves represented immortality and its red berries mean fertility. In *Sir Gawain and the Green Knight*, the Green Knight comes to Arthur's court to challenge his knights during their midwinter feast, wearing a crown of holly and bearing a holly club, illustrating both the holly's connection to the winter festival and to standing up to challenges. *Tinne* means "fire," reminding us of the sacred fires lit on the Winter Solstice, when the sun king is reborn. Charcoal made from holly was used by smiths to create swords, and holly was one of the three woods used to build chariot wheels.

Magickal Uses: Protection magick.

Coll/*C, K/Hazel*

Divinatory Meaning: Ancestral wisdom, inspiration, a state of enlightenment.

Reverse Meaning: Ignorance, disillusionment.

Tree Lore: Known as the "food of the gods," hazelnuts served as a food source for the ancient Celts. The Otherworldly well of wisdom was surrounded by nine hazel trees. Their nuts fell into the well and were eaten by the salmon who lived there. It was believed that anyone who ate the salmon of wisdom was gifted with great knowledge. This passing on of knowledge, from tree to salmon to man, can indicate a period of learning. When *coll* appears in a reading, wisdom may be passed down during a time of apprenticeship, or it could indicate ancestral wisdom. Wands made from hazel were used in magick to manifest wishes and desires and such wands were known as "Wishing Rods." As the ninth Ogham, it is linked to creative energies and Goddess energy.

Magickal Uses: Manifesting wishes and desires, seeking wisdom.

Quert/*Q*/*Apple*

Divinatory Meaning: Regeneration and healing.

Reverse Meaning: Needing to take time to rest and regenerate your strength.

Tree Lore: Apples in Celtic lore granted healing and immortality. Avalon, the island where Morgan le Fay brings Arthur to heal from his wounds, was part of the Celtic Otherworlds where the souls of the dead went before returning to life. Apples were left at Samhain as food for the dead. In the tale of *Oidheadh Clainne Tuireann* (The Fate of the Children of Tuireann), the god Lugh describes the magickal "golden apples of the sun," which tasted of honey and were able to heal any sickness or bestow immortality to those who ate them.

Magickal Uses: Healing, honoring the ancestors.

Muin/*M*/*Vine*

Divinatory Meaning: Harvest. The successful completion of a project. Celebrations.

Reverse Meaning: Indulging in excess, intoxication.

Tree Lore: It is unclear whether *muin* refers to the grapevine, which was introduced to the British Isles during the Bronze Age, or, as some modern scholars suggest, the blackberry or mulberry. The *Book of Ballymote* tells us *muin* was used to make mead, which can be distilled using blackberries. Regardless of which type of vine it refers to, the vine is linked to harvest and the brewing of alcoholic beverages. Here the process of fermentation, of grapes/berries to wine, is symbolic of the soul's transformation.

Magickal Uses: Prosperity magick, bringing a goal to fruition.

Gort/*G*/*Ivy*

Divinatory Meaning: Breaking down barriers, perseverance and persistence.

Reverse Meaning: Feeling constricted, restrictions, ruthlessness.

Tree Lore: Ivy is a very tenacious plant. It uses its fellow plants and trees to support itself, climbing tree trunks to reach the sunlight. Unfortunately, its strong hold on its neighbors usually leads to the deaths of the trees it climbs. A reversed ivy stave warns us to learn to let go. Reversed, it can also indicate others are restricting our lives or that others are attempting to control us. Ivy is also associated with protection. The hero Fin mac Cumhail took shelter from harm in an ivy-covered tree. Ivy was also sacred to the goddess of the moon and is worn for fidelity in love and to bring luck.

Magickal Uses: Luck, overcoming obstacles.

Ngetal/*NG*/*Broom*

Divinatory Meaning: Healing, sweeping away negative energies.

Reverse Meaning: Illness and disease, the need for healing.

Tree Lore: Broom was traditionally used for the handles of Witches' brooms and is used to banish negative energy. Broom's yellow flowers make it a solar plant, connecting it to the sun and regeneration. Broom's healing qualities can help us sweep away both emotional and physical illness. Reversed, *ngetal* can also indicate emotional imbalance and depression rather than a physical illness.

Magickal Uses: Emotional balance, cleansing rituals, banishing negativity.

Straif/*ST, SS, Z*/*Blackthorn*

Divinatory Meaning: Division, conflict, the need to establish healthy boundaries between yourself and others.

Reverse Meaning: Allowing yourself to be open for attack, emotionally or physically.

Tree Lore: *Straif* is related to the word *strife*, connecting this Ogham to conflicts. Blackthorn was traditionally used for hedgerows, to keep out both unwanted humans and unwanted spirits. In spring it has white blossoms, but its most predominant feature is its thorns, connecting the blackthorn to swords, spears, and other piecing objects. Blackthorn wood was also used to make cudgels, further connecting it to warfare and conflict. The berries or sloes the blackthorn produces are a rich source of vitamin C and were used as a remedy for inflammation. Its leaves were used to clear toxins and excess fluid out of the body. While *straif* does symbolize a conflict or your path being blocked, the blackthorn can also teach us how to "detoxify" the situation if we listen to its wisdom.

Magickal Uses: Establishing boundaries.

Ruis/*R*/*Elder*

Divinatory Meaning: Knowledge gained from experience. Moving forward, shedding old habits. Transformation, the end of one cycle and beginning of a new one.

Reverse Meaning: Regrets, holding on to the past.

Tree Lore: *Ruis* is derived from *ruise* or *reudh,* which both mean "red," relating to the way the tree "bleeds" sap when cut. Witches were thought to be able to transform into elder trees, possibly because the tree bled as if it were human. It was used in British burial rites to represent the transformation of the spirit as it passed from life to death. Standing under an elder on midsummer was believed to allow one to see the Faery Folk and it was believed that faeries live inside the tree.

Magickal Uses: Faery magick, transformation.

Ailm/*A*/*Pine or Fir*

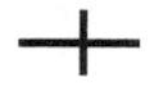

Divinatory Meaning: Initiations, birth and death, beginning of a new phase in life. Foresight and farsightedness. A clear view of a situation.

Reverse Meaning: Not seeing a situation clearly, blindness, or inability to see the truth.

Tree Lore: *Ailm* is "the loudest of groans" according the *Word of Ogham of Morainn mac Moin.* The tree's wood makes a "groaning" sound when it bends and sways in the wind; hence the association. Some have connected this groaning to the cries of child birth, signaling you are embarking on a new phase in life or a time of initiation. Both the pine and fir are evergreens and are known for the great heights to which they can grow, connecting *ailm* with clear sight, farseeing, and insight. The Scots Pine, which was very prevalent in the lands occupied by the Celts, can live up to 600 years and can grow to 120 feet or higher in good conditions. The bark of the Scots Pine is red, and the tree's resin was used to line beer barrels, seal wooden boats, and in the wax used for official seals. The bloodlike color of its resin connects it to birth and the life force. Firs were also sacred to the goddess Diana, who ruled over childbirth, and to Druantia, the Gaulish goddess of fir trees. During the Winter Solstice, pine needles were burned for purification and to encourage the sun's return. Yule logs were made from pine wood, the tree's evergreen leaves symbolic of immortality and rebirth.

Magickal Uses: Purification magick, clear sight, divination.

Ohn/*O*/*Gorse*

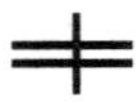

Divinatory Meaning: Sexuality, passion. Love, relationships.

Reverse Meaning: Lack of passion in a relationship, career, or project.

Tree Lore: Gorse, also called furze, is an evergreen shrub known for its fragrant yellow flowers. Its connection to sexuality and passion comes from its links to fire and the sun. There is also an old folk saying that "When gorse is in bloom, kissing is in season." Gorse grows in sunny areas and its seed pods burst in the heat of the sun, releasing thousands of seeds. Gorse was used for fuel. Farmers would burn away the gorse's old stems and encourage new growth, so their livestock could graze on the plant. Gorse was also associated with dawn and springtime. The gorse's yellow flowers are loved by bees, and it can alternately symbolize the collection of knowledge and receiving important information.

Magickal Uses: Love magick, invoking sun gods and goddesses. Gathering information, uncovering the truth.

Ur/*U, W*/*Heather*

Divinatory Meaning: Healing, creating a sacred balance. Love, fertility.

Reverse Meaning: Being out of balance. This imbalance could be a physical one or can signify an emotional or spiritual imbalance.

Tree Lore: Heather is a low-growing perennial shrub commonly found in moors. It provides food and nesting material for birds and was used to make brooms, weave baskets, and thatch roofs. Heather is considered a plant of healing and is thus associated with maintaining a sacred balance in our emotional, physical, and spiritual selves. It is also associated with fire, as heather is used as fuel, making it a solar plant. White heather is said to bring good luck, especially in one's love life, and was put in bridal headdresses. Lovers would lie together in beds of heather. While both heather and gorse are associated with love, gorse represents sexuality and lust, while heather represents the emotional aspects of love and can represent a love of life. If *ur* is drawn in regard to a relationship, it signals a deep emotional connection. Heather was also used to distill wine, and both the plant and the alcoholic beverages made from it were sacred to the Breton goddess Uroica.

Magickal Uses: Healing and love spells, fertility.

Eadha/*E/White Poplar or Aspen*

Divinatory Meaning: Overcoming doubt and fear. Overcoming obstacles, inner guidance.

Reverse Meaning: Being paralyzed by doubts and fears.

Tree Lore: Aspens have extensive root systems and grow to be sixty to eighty feet in height. They are one of the most widely distributed trees in North America. Aspen bark was used as a tonic to cure heartburn and weakness, and its leaves were used to treat inflammation and arthritis. *Eadha* is associated with "trembling" or "quivering." The leaves of the poplar and aspen appear to tremble in the wind, connecting *eadha* to fear. The wind moving through the aspen's leaves also sounds like whispering, making it an oracular tree. It is thought that one can hear messages from the gods when listening to its whispers. The North American Blackfoot tribe used aspen to make whistles. The aspen's tough, shock-absorbing wood was used for shields, and this Ogham can help us shield and repel our fears and doubts. Wreaths of aspen leaves have been found in burial sites, and the Greek hero Heracles wore a wreath of aspen when he made a journey to Hades, the Greek land of the dead, connecting the tree to the Underworld and the realm of the ancestors. The top part of the aspen leaf is said to be dark because it was scorched by the fires of Hades; the bottom of the leaf absorbed the hero's sweat and consequently turned a silver color.

Magickal Uses: Banishing negative emotions. Honoring the dead.

Ioho/*I, J, Y/Yew*

Divinatory Meaning: Death and rebirth, a time of transitions and change.

Reverse Meaning: Grief, inability to accept change.

Tree Lore: The yew is slow growing but extremely long lived. The Fortingall Yew in Perthshire Scotland is estimated to be between two and five thousand years old! The yew is generally associated with death. Its wood is strong and flexible and was used to make longbows, a particularly deadly weapon in medieval warfare, and both its seeds and its leaves are poisonous. The Celtic chieftain Catuvolcus killed himself with a poison made from the yew rather than submit to Rome. The tree is also commonly planted in graveyards. As the tree ages, the trunk eventually becomes hollow. These hollow areas are seen as gateways or entrances to the Otherworlds. The yew's branches grow into the soil, taking the place of the old hollowed-out trunk, an act symbolic of reincarnation.

Magickal Uses: Transformation magick, honoring the ancestors, summoning spirits.

Koad/*Ch, Kh, Ea*/*Grove*

Divinatory Meaning: Attaining knowledge, unity, secret wisdom.

Reverse Meaning: You can't "see the forest for the trees." Not looking at the big picture.

Tree Lore: *Koad* represents the grove and therefore all the trees in the Ogham. It is symbolic of spiritual knowledge and wisdom coming together. All things come together in the grove. It can also represent the eight Pagan festivals.

Magickal Uses: Attaining balance, working with seasonal energies.

Oir/*th, oi*/*Spindle*

Divinatory Meaning: Sudden insight, enlightenment. Purification, initiations, blessings.

Reverse Meaning: Difficulty completing a task. Leaving work half finished.

Tree Lore: The spindle tree has been used to make pegs, spindles, bobbins, and knitting needles. It is a small tree with white flowers and red fruit. The fruit is a powerful insecticide and the bark is used to make red and yellow dyes. It is a hardy tree that can grow in any kind of soil.

Magickal Uses: To gain deeper insight into a situation. Inspiration.

Uilleand/*P, Pe, Ui/Honeysuckle*

Divinatory Meaning: Happiness, reaching out to attain one's desires.

Reverse Meaning: Depression, denying yourself happiness.

Tree Lore: The honeysuckle is a shrub with vines that have a tendency to wrap around neighboring trees and plants. If grown by the home, it was said to bring wealth and prosperity. The vines are used in love spells. Breaking off a flowering branch of honeysuckle and bringing it into one's home was said to bring about a wedding. The honeysuckle has sweet-smelling flowers, and its name comes from the sweet taste of its nectar. The berries of the plant are toxic.

Magickal Uses: Love spells.

Phagos/*Ph, Io/Beech*

Divinatory Meaning: Examining the past to understand the present. Guidance from the past.

Reverse Meaning: Repeating past mistakes.

Tree Lore: The beech can grow up to 120 feet and has low branches with glossy leaves. Beech nuts were used as a food source, and the oil from the nuts was used to make soap and used in cooking. Beech forests were used in Europe for grazing pigs, who ate the tree's nuts. The tree's hard wood has been used to make furniture and hand tools. The bark and leaves were used to cure skin aliments and scabs.

Magickal Uses: Seeking wisdom from the ancestors.

Mor/*Ax, X, Xi/The Sea*

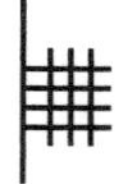

Divinatory Meaning: Travel, life's journey, feminine energy.

Reverse Meaning: Letting your emotions take control of you.

Tree Lore: *Mor*, like *koad*, is a later addition to the Ogham and refers to the sea. The sea represents the moon and femininity in general. The sea is also linked to travel, and on a spiritual level it is symbolic of life's journey.

Magickal Uses: Any spellwork calling on the sea's energies or sea gods and goddesses.

Divination Tool Blessing Ritual

Whether you have purchased your divination tool or have made your own, you should bless and consecrate it before beginning any divination work. If you are reading for others, your tools may retain some unwanted energies and you may want to re-bless your divination tools on a regular basis.

The best time to perform this ritual is at Samhain, a traditional time to bless divination tools; otherwise it should be performed during the new moon.

You Will Need:
2 tsp. sage
2 tsp. patchouli
2 tsp. mugwort
Incense charcoal
Fireproof bowl or incense burner

Mix the sage, patchouli, and mugwort in a bowl. Light the incense charcoal and sprinkle some of the herbs on it. Pass your divination tool through the smoke three, six, or nine times, until you feel all negative vibrations have been purged from the object. See a white cleansing light filling the tool, then say:

In the name of the Morrigan
I bless these (cards, Ogham, Runes, etc.)
and banish all negative energies from them

Place the tool on your altar and sprinkle the remaining herbs in a circle around it. Using your hand or wand, circle it saying:

Washerwoman at the river's ford
Phantom Queen of prophecy and second sight
Ravens upon your shoulder
Whispering to you their secrets
Morrigan, keeper of prophecy and fate
Fill these _________ with your power

Guide my hand, open my sight
That the past, present, and future I may clearly see
In the Morrigan's name
So mote it be!

Leave the tool on the altar overnight, then store it in a safe place where it will not be disturbed.

Bird Augury

The Druids used several forms of divination which included astrology, the Ogham, observing weather patterns, and observing the behavior of animals. When Queen Boadicea led her revolt against Rome, she released a hare (an animal sacred to the battle goddess Andraste) on the battlefield in order to predict the battle's outcome by the animal's movements.

Birds in particular were believed to be especially prophetic. Bird augury was not unique to the Celtic world and was also practiced by the Greeks and Romans. In Greece this practice was called ornithomancy, and there are several historical references to its use in classical works such as in *The Iliad* and *The Odyssey*. The type of bird, the direction it flew, how high it flew, and whether or not it sung while in the air were all factors in predicting future events. The Romans had a special branch of priests dedicated to this form of divination. These priests would sit in tents on hilltops and offer libations of wine to Jupiter, the lord of the skies, prior to interpreting the actions of passing birds.

The Celts considered the raven a bird of omens and a messenger from the Otherworlds. The Irish proverb "To have a raven's knowledge" referred to someone having the gift of foresight or clairvoyance.[97] In her book *Animals in Celtic Life and Myth*, archeologist Miranda Green tells us that "The concept of ravens as birds of omen is interesting; indeed, they were used by Irish Druids in augury, predicting the future by studying the flight of birds ... The connection between ravens and oracular utterances may have arisen because of the harsh but distinctive 'voice' of the raven, which may have been perceived as resembling human speech. Usually the gift of prophecy is sinister, but in the case of the Irish hero-God Lugh, ravens warn him of the approach of his enemies."[98]

97. Jones, *Power of Raven, Wisdom of Serpent,* p. 127.
98. Green, *Animals in Celtic Life and Myth,* p. 178.

When working with the Morrigan, you may become more aware of the activity of her favorite totems, the raven and crow. These birds may gift you with their feathers and can act in a divinatory role. When I first started working with the Morrigan, I was gifted with several crow feathers. I lived in a fairly rural area of Connecticut but in the several years I had lived there, I had never found crow feathers before. After I dedicated myself to the Morrigan, I seemed to find feathers everywhere. They appeared on my car and outside the office building where I worked. I placed several feathers on the Morrigan's altar and used others to decorate ritual tools used specifically for rituals where the Morrigan was invoked. Looking back I realize she was trying to get my attention; it was the Morrigan's way of saying "I'm here, you can't ignore me!" Now I find feathers more infrequently, but when I do receive them, they herald important events or times in my life. The type of feather and the position you find it in can reveal the feather's meaning. The numbers in which crows and ravens appear can also be significant, and studying numerology can be useful in deciphering their meaning. A list of numbers and their significance can be found at the end of this section.

As you continue your journey with the Morrigan, be aware of the presence of crows and ravens. Her feathered allies can warn you of danger or simply offer answers to oracular questions. A crow crossing your path to the right or a feather found to your right is a sign of good things to come or a general positive outcome to a question. A crow crossing your path toward the left is a warning to proceed with caution, there's trouble ahead, or a general negative outcome in regard to a question.

While I was driving home one day, a crow swooped down over my car. For a terrifying moment I thought the bird would hit the windshield; it just appeared out of nowhere like a feathered kamikaze, hell-bent on dive-bombing my car. But only the tips of the bird's wings brushed against the windshield, and the crow flew off just as quickly as it had appeared. I immediately slowed down, taking the crow's appearance as a warning. The roads in my area of Connecticut are winding and narrow and the crow appeared right before I went around a particularly narrow turn. A car had stalled in the middle of the road just around the curve and the driver was frantically trying to move the car to the shoulder so no one would hit it. I wasn't speeding, but since the car was hidden from view, I wouldn't have had enough time to slow down and may have hit the car or, even worse, the driver.

If you have a specific question you wish to ask the Morrigan, sit in front of your altar and visualize the Morrigan standing in front of you. Ask her your question; you may get an immediate response, but if not, ask her to answer your question through her raven and crow children. Watch for any crow or raven activity during the next three days and you will receive your answer. This is a very open-ended type of divination, but it works. The trick is to believe she will send you an answer; if you aren't expecting one, it simply won't come. A variation of this technique would be to ask your question while holding a crow feather (or a black feather from the craft store), then let it fall to the ground. If the feather falls to the right, it is a positive or "yes" response; if it falls to the left, it is a negative or "no" response.

Raven Oracle Invocation

Use this invocation to call on the prophetic powers of the raven, or when using raven feathers in divination work.

Raven, bird of omens and prophetic speech
Children of the Morrigan
Messengers of the Gods
Your knowledge and wisdom I do seek

Morrigan Seeress Invocation

Use this invocation when calling upon the Morrigan as a goddess of prophecy, during divination work, or to strengthen your psychic senses.

Hail Morrigan
Poet and prophetess
Keening banshee
Goddess of vision
Mistress of Fate
Your gaze pierces the Veil
Seeing into all realms
The past and present and things yet to be
Come to me, O Mighty Seeress
Grant me vision and second sight
Part the Veil for me this night!

Divination Chant

You can use the following chant before any divination to call on the Morrigan's energies. Say the affirmation while visualizing yourself becoming one with the all-seeing Morrigan.

Morrigan
Goddess of prophecy and might
Guide my hand
Grant me Second Sight

Morrigan Divination Ritual

By Fae Asterope

You Will Need:

Mugwort

Rosemary

1 white, 1 red, 1 black candle (represents each aspect of the Triple Goddess)

White sage

An obsidian sphere (or any other scrying tool)

Cloth or paper towel

An offering to the Morrigan (red meat, menstrual blood, red wine, apples, or pomegranates)

Mix the mugwort and rosemary in spring water, then consecrate it for the purpose of cleaning and empowering your scrying tool. Cast your circle. Light the candles, then light a little bit of white sage to clear the energy of the area. Run your scrying tool through the white sage smoke.

Dip a cloth or paper towel into your mugwort potion, and cleanse / wipe off your scrying tool with it. Make sure your intention is to cleanse and purify your scrying tool and to prepare it for psychic use. When you are finished, hold both hands over your scrying tool. Visualize energy going from your hands into your scrying tool, then from your scrying tool back into your hands. Connect with it. Then recite this invocation:

I invoke you, Morrigan, for this Psychic Charm
To be forewarned is to be forearmed
Goddess Morrigan, please come to me
Open my third eye, allow me to see
The past, present, future, whatever shall be
Please give me clarity, shed some light
Help me to lift the Veil tonight!

Proceed to scry. Gaze into your scrying tool and allow the images or words to form. When you have finished, thank the Morrigan for assisting you with your divination. Give her the offering. Remember to ground. You may do so by sitting on the floor, with your palms on the floor. Release any excess energy into the earth. When you are done, give thanks and close the circle.

Numerology

Numerology can be incorporated into any form of divination. For numbers larger than nine, add each of the individual digits together to add up to a single digit. For example, the number 14 would add 1+4 to equal 5.

One: new beginnings, initiation, the sun, masculine energy

Two: partnership, balance, duality, choices and decisions, the moon, feminine energy

Three: magick, growth, creativity, the Triple Goddess

Four: stability and foundations, grounding, rest, elemental energies

Five: travel, motion, change, the pentacle

Six: enlightenment, harmony, generosity

Seven: esoteric knowledge, thought, consciousness, good luck, the chakras

Eight: success and wealth, infinity, completion of cycles

Nine: completion, accomplishment, wisdom, the Ninefold Goddess

Morrigan Dream Pillow

The Morrigan rules over the shadowy realm of dreams. She appeared to kings and queens through this medium to dispense her warnings and prophecies. Although most people do not immediately associate foreseeing the future or divination with dream work, the two have always been linked for me. The females on my mother's side of the family are known for having dreams about future events or have received warnings from deceased family members in dreams. As a child I would have prophetic dreams, and I incorporated dream work into my magickal practices when I began practicing the Craft. When you are asleep, your spirit body naturally travels to the astral plane and visits the Otherworlds, making this the easiest time for the gods, spirits, or ancestors to relay information to you.

Cut out two pieces of fabric (purple or blue fabric would be ideal) to the desired size and sew three of the four sides together. Turn the pillow inside out, so the stitches you just made are on the inside and will not show. Fill one-third of the pillow with fiberfill/batting (available in most craft stores). In a bowl, mix the following together:

3 parts mugwort
1 part meadowsweet
1 part catnip
3 apple seeds
9 drops apple oil

Add the mixture to the pillow, then add any additional batting to fully fill the pillow. Sew the remaining side of the pillow closed and add any decorations you wish. Bring the pillow to your sacred space. Take a moment to think about what you wish to accomplish. Do you want to communicate with an ancestor through dream work, or receive the answer to a question? When you are ready, chant:

Queen of Phantoms, bringer of dreams
Ruler of shadowed realms, riding the dark winds of night
Pierce the Veil and grant me second sight!

Sleep with the pillow for the next three nights or until you receive your answer.

12
Queen of Battle

You float upon a blood red wave,
Of swords and spears and knives.
Your voice inspires fear and dread
That you'll cut short our lives.
—*Isaac Bonewits,* Hymn to the Morrigan

You find yourself standing upon a vast plain. To either side you see tattered banners and ruined armor strewn across the grass, the remnants of long-ago battles. You can hear the harsh cries of a raven, and you look up to see the bird circling overhead. It circles above you then flies farther into the plain and out of sight. You decide to follow it and begin to walk in the same direction.

Soon you see someone standing on the rise ahead. It is a woman, clad in bronze-colored armor, holding a short double-edged sword. She doesn't move toward you or make any indication that she sees you. Slowly you approach the warrior. You can't continue on without passing her. When you are only a few feet away from her, she raises her sword. "You cannot pass this way until you prove you possess the traits of a true warrior. Mine is the test of bravery. Will you meet my challenge?"

You answer in the affirmative. Almost immediately she swings her sword in a great arching motion. You know if you show fear—if you flinch, or make any movement—the sword will cut through you. You have no weapons, you cannot strike back. For a moment a crippling sense of terror runs through you. In the air above, the raven reappears and you hear it calling out. The sound fills you with an inner calm and all your fear evaporates. The blade stops just a moment before it touches your neck, held motionless in the air by the warrior. She holds the sword there for a moment, then lowers it.

She smiles, pleased at your show of bravery. "You have passed the trial of bravery. You may pass this way with my blessings."

Instead of sheathing her sword, she holds it in both hands and offers it to you. You reach out to grasp the hilt and raise the sword. Its hilt is covered in intricate Celtic knots, and a soft glow seems to emanate from the metal of the blade. As you lift the sword, the warrior woman vanishes.

The raven calls out one last time from above and again flies farther across the plain. You continue to follow its flight. You pass more remnants of ancient battles: banners torn to shreds by long-dead enemies, broken swords, and rusted shields litter the ground.

Soon you come to a stream. It cuts across the plain in either direction blocking your path. Not far away you see a wooden bridge. The bridge appears to be the only way across the river. As you approach the bridge you see that a man is standing in front of it, blocking the way across. He wears dark armor the color of rich plowed earth and holds a large circular shield with an intricate spiraling pattern. He raises his sword as you approach.

"Only a true warrior may pass here. Unless you meet my challenge, you may not pass this way." He swings his sword in your direction and you move to the side and out of his reach before it can cut you. You raise the sword the first warrior gave you and meet the man's challenge. You exchange several blows, but the warrior seems undaunted. No matter how much of your strength you put behind your blows, he stands unmoved as if made of stone. Soon you begin to tire; your sword feels heavy and clumsy in your hands. Just when you think the warrior is unbeatable and you consider giving up, the raven appears overhead once again. It calls out and immediately fills you with an Otherworldly strength. Your sword no longer feels heavy, and your muscles no longer ache. You feel unstoppable. You raise your sword, and this time your blows make the warrior step back, losing ground. You make one final exchange, and the force of your blow against his sword makes him lose his footing and he falls to the ground. He holds up his hands in surrender and smiles at you. "You have passed the trial of strength. Pass with my blessing." He kneels and offers you his shield. You take it, and the warrior man vanishes.

With the shield on one arm and the sword in the other, you cross the river. You see the raven flying yet farther across the plain and follow it. Soon the raven begins to circle a grass-covered mound not far ahead. Standing stones circle the top of the mound, and the raven lands on one of them.

You approach the mound and climb to the standing stones. Once on top of the mound you look for the raven, but it has vanished; in its place stands a woman. Her hair is the black of raven feathers and is set in nine long braids. She wears leather armor that has been dyed black.

The overlapping pieces of leather are shaped like feathers. In her hands she holds a spear. She speaks: "I have been with you since the beginning of your journey, and I will be with you at its end. I have watched over you, and I have lent you my strength. I am the strength within, the instinct to survive and the will to overcome adversity. I am the glimmer of hope that shines in your darkest hour. I am the Warrior, the Queen of Battle who whispers to you to continue onward, to overcome all that would conquer your spirit.

"You have defeated my champions, and you have proven you possess the traits of a warrior. But to truly be one of my warriors, I require from you a sacrifice. It is not only outside forces that the warrior confronts. Truly it is the shadows and demons within that assault and weaken us. Sacrifice the darkness within you to me—your demons, your anger, your pain. All that lays siege to your spirit, this is the sacrifice, the tribute, I demand of my warriors!"

With her words you hear something approaching, making its way up the mound. You turn from the woman to see shadowy figures advancing on the stone circle. Some seem to be made of smoke and shadow, others have mist-shrouded faces. You recognize them as the manifestation of all that holds you back in your life—dark emotions, past hurts, and self-made illusions that you have not released or confronted. Suddenly you feel afraid and unprepared to face these demons. Then you feel the Morrigan place her hands on your shoulders, and her strength and calm radiate through the heat of that touch and fill you. "Know I am always with you," she whispers, and you know it is true. The Queen of Battle will always be at your side.

You close your eyes and take a moment to drink in the feeling of the Morrigan's strength and power. When you open your eyes, you look down to find that you are wearing the same black armor she had been wearing. Confident, you raise both your sword and your shield and meet the first attacker, easily cutting through shadow and mist, destroying the phantom. You meet each attack and soon you stand alone on the mound, your inner darkness defeated. You feel lighter, as if a great burden has been released from your spirit. Victorious, you raise the sword high above your head and let out a fierce battle cry, as the strength of the Queen of Battle radiates and flows through you.

It is difficult for us to understand the role war played in Celtic society. We live in a world where we do not have to worry about our food being stolen by people in the neighboring town; the battlefields our armed forces fight and die on are often far away, leaving us with the illusion that the violence of war is something distant, only to be seen on TV. More often than not, modern warfare is motivated by political agendas, but to the ancient Celts, war was an aspect of everyday life and survival.

Today the violence and aggression we associate with war is seen as part of the masculine realm. While Celtic women participated in warfare and could be warriors, modern women are only beginning to be allowed to fight alongside men in defense of their country. The warfare we are familiar with is primarily a male world, and when we think of deities associated with battle, male figures like Mars or Ares come to mind. But the Celts were distinctly lacking in male gods of war. Celtic war deities were female, and war in the Celtic world had a distinctly feminine side to it.

Celtic myth tells us that war was invented by two sisters, Ain and Iaine (pronounced Awn and Ea-AWN-ah). In order to ensure no other family could lay claim to their land, the sisters married their own brothers and invented warfare to forcibly take the rest of Ireland for their family. Ain and Iaine represent the goddess of sovereignty, who was the very land itself. Only those who wedded them—who were dedicated to both the goddess and the land they represented—could hold any claim to the land. By inventing war, Ain and Iaine show they both hold sovereignty over the land and have the means to defend it. Thus sovereignty and war became linked. War itself was about survival and defending one's land, family, and livelihood (cattle and other livestock) from harm. The primary type of warfare the Celts participated in was cattle raiding. Cattle ensured food and wealth for the tribe and were linked to the goddess of sovereignty. The great Irish epic the *Táin* is not fought over a political dispute; it is fought over a bull that represented Queen Maeve's continued sovereignty over her land. Maeve herself is a goddess of both sovereignty and of war. Like Ain and Iaine (and Maeve), the Morrigan is both a sovereign over the land and a goddess of war *par excellence*.

The Morrigan appears in Celtic mythology wherever there is battle and strife. As a goddess of war, the Celts called upon her to grant them victory in battle. She struck fear into the hearts of the weak and granted strength and valor to the warriors she favored. While the Morrigan is far from a mere goddess of war, battle still plays an intricate role in her personality, as it played a vital role in the culture she originates from. What we must remember about the Morrigan in her guise as the Queen of Battle is that even in her fiercest form, she is no less a mother goddess. She evolved from the mother goddess to the warrior queen out of a cultural need, out of the need to protect what we hold dear, out of the need to bring justice and balance. She asks us what in life is worth fighting for. What do you love enough to go to war for, to risk your life for? As the warrior she goads us, willing or not, toward change. She makes us confront our inner demons and challenges us to overcome life's many battles.

To understand the Morrigan as a goddess of war, we must consider how the Celts defined warfare. War deities reflect the type of warfare their culture participated in, embodying their ideals of honor and glory on the battlefield. War itself varies from culture to culture. The highly organized warfare of the Roman legions bears little resemblance to the somewhat haphazard style of warfare the Celts participated in, nor to our modern-day high-tech approach to war. Irish warfare in particular revolved around cattle raids. A.T. Lucas comments, "Indeed, a review of the numerous references to raids makes it plain that any kind of military action, arising from whatever cause and prosecuted for whatever end, almost certainly involved an attempt by the aggressor to secure a prey of cows from the party attacked, whether as a primary or a secondary objective."[99]

Cattle, seen as the ultimate source of wealth, were used as currency to pay debts and as bride prices. Cattle raids against other clans were a way not only to add to the wealth of the clan through livestock and conquered land, but to establish a leader's prowess on the battlefield. The fact that Celtic warfare revolved around cattle—and ultimately, sovereignty over the land and its wealth—is reflected in their goddess of war. The Morrigan is both connected to sovereignty as an earth goddess and is frequently linked to cattle, whether it be stealing them, herding them, or making it difficult for others to obtain them; all of these are functions that reflect the Celtic cosmology of warfare.

Some modern sources claim that the Morrigan never directly participated in battle, instead watching from afar to lend strength to her favorite warriors. This seems like an attempt to make the Morrigan's character more palatable to a modern audience and is simply not true. Several myths specifically mention her participating in battle and bragging about the prowess she would display in the fray. When the Túatha Dé Danann go to war with the Fomorians, the Morrigan clearly states her intent to fight. When asked what power she will bring to the battle, she replies, "I will be able to kill; I will be able to destroy those who might be subdued."[100] After mating with Dagda, she vows to help the Túatha Dé Danann by killing the Fomorian king, Indech, and that she would take the blood of his heart and use it to bless the warriors

99. Lucas, *Cattle in Ancient Ireland*, p. 125.
100. Gray, "The Second Battle of Mag Tuired," verse 93.

of the Túatha Dé Danann. These hardly seem like comments made by someone intent on watching the battle from afar!

We also find the Morrigan participating in battle in her other guises. Macha waged war to secure rulership over Ireland. Áine turned the tide of battle for her foster father, Eoghanacht, when he was unable to claim from another clan the hill that would later bear Áine's name. Áine vowed to aid him win the battle, with the condition that he name the hill after her in return for her help. Badb flew over the heads of warriors as a crow, encouraging her favorite warriors and striking fear into the hearts of others.

Besides her participation in the many battles of the Túatha Dé Danann, the Morrigan turned the tides of mortal battles and bestowed her favorite warriors with superhuman strength. As a battle fury, the Morrigan could inspire her favorite warriors into *riastradh,* a type of frenzy that made them unconquerable in battle. Riastradh is described as transforming a warrior's muscles and limbs, making them swell with inhuman strength, sometimes transforming the warrior into a giant on the battlefield and causing their eyes to bulge with the force of their frenzy. When Cúchulain entered riastradh, he was able to kill one hundred of Maeve's warriors in a single battle. On the battlefield the Morrigan could inspire courage and frenzy or prey upon the fears of her enemies, sending them running from the field of battle or killing them instantly. As Nemain she killed part of Maeve's army with the fearful sound of her battle cry. As Badb she sent a prophetic dream to Queen Maeve of her son's death at the hands of an enemy. "Raise thyself and avenge thy son ... Thou shalt cruelly cut asunder troops when you awakest, O Maev[e]!"[101] The dream ignited the queen's battle frenzy, and she took up arms to seek revenge for her slain son.

When the battle had ended and battle frenzy had ceased, warriors would leave the battlefield until the next morning, allowing the Morrigan to claim the heads of fallen warriors, also known as "Morrigan's Acorn Crop." For the Celts, the head was the seat of the soul; by collecting heads, the Morrigan symbolically gathered the souls of those who fell in battle, much like the Norse Valkyrie, who gathered the souls of the dead and brought them to Valhalla. Like the Valkyrie, the Morrigan also had a group of female warriors who may have functioned like the Norse gatherers of the slain. The only mention of these women comes from the story of Donn, Son of Midhir, in which the sons of the god Midhir fought three yearly battles with the rest

101. Leahy, *The Courtship of Ferb,* p. 77.

of the Túatha Dé Danann. When asked which of the Danann gods fought against them, Donn named several of the Túatha Dé Danann, including "the children of the Morrigu, the Great Queen, her six-and-twenty women warriors... Those are the chief leaders of the Túatha Dé Danann that come to destroy our hill every year."[102] Unfortunately there are no other surviving references to these twenty-six warrior women, and we can only guess at the function they played alongside the Morrigan. The fact that these warriors are all women, like the Valkyrie, may suggest a parallel between the two. Gathering souls would be a fitting occupation for warrior–hand maidens of the Morrigan.

Unless you are serving in the military, it is unlikely that you will find yourself on an actual battlefield, but that does not mean that the power of the Queen of Battle is no longer needed in modern times. As the Morrigan led Celtic warriors to victory on ancient battlefields, so too can she lead modern seekers to victory over the battles we face throughout life, lending us strength to conquer our fears and inspiring us during our darkest moments. The Queen of Battle stands ready, sword raised high, shield at her side, ready to guide and protect each of us.

Connecting with the Warrior Goddess

The Celtic tradition is rich with images of battle goddesses, mighty queens, and fierce warrior women: Queen Maeve strides boldly across the pages of myth, waging war in order to claim the one object that can ensure her continued sovereignty. The Great Iceni Queen Boadicea's quest for vengeance after the rape of her daughters nearly drove the Romans from the English Isle. The mysterious warrior woman Scáthach trained the mighty Cúchulain in the art of war. The battle goddesses Andraste, Epona, Badb, Macha, and the Morrigan all speak to us with their deeds and unconquerable warrior spirits. The Celtic female, divine or otherwise, was a formidable figure. She could be both a nurturer and a warrior. She could bring life into the world or destroy it when provoked. In a culture that idealized war, these warrior women represented the highest attainment of feminine power. They brought victory in their wake and were the forgers of heroes.

When the religious and social mores of the culture that had once idealized her changed, the warrior goddess's image was altered. While other goddesses could be tamed into more acceptable roles, transforming into saints, the goddesses of war and

102. Gregory, *Gods and Fighting Men*, p. 20.

battle proved impossible to conquer. The only other means the new culture had to deter worship of the ancient warrior goddess was to demonize her. Thus the Morrigan and goddesses like her have been labeled "evil" or "bloodthirsty." Yet her male counterparts (e.g., Dagda, Lugh, and Bran) who participated in battle do not retain a stigma for bloodthirstiness. The simple fact that she is female and a warrior makes the Morrigan dangerous. An independent woman, one who could fight and defend herself, who did not need to rely on a male for protection, went against the weak and diminutive ideal of femininity that the new religion endorsed.

Even today women who aggressively pursue their dreams and desires (whether that be a career or any other goal in life) and stand up for themselves are often labeled as "unfeminine" or are accused of acting like men. We can see this especially in the business world. Women are taught to be passive when instead they should learn to take action. If we are always passive, always nurturing, we allow others to walk all over us. The message our culture is sending women is that strength and power belong to the realm of men and that it is unnatural for women to display these traits. Yet these qualities can be found in warrior goddesses in cultures all around the globe. The Celts saw her in figures like the Morrigan, Maeve, and Andraste; in other cultures she is Kali, Freya, Athena, and Oya.

In her warrior aspect, the Great Goddess is the guardian of personal power, a deep well of strength that exists within each of us; brandishing both sword and shield in defense of herself and others, she refuses to allow others to use her. Like the Queen, the Warrior is an archetype we are only beginning to reclaim. We must look through the prejudice of the past to see not "evil" or "bloodthirsty" women, but instead women of power, goddesses of strength and perseverance, whose mysteries and lessons can fill the modern seeker with the strength and resolve of their unconquerable spirit.

Often the warrior is the very first face we encounter when working with the Morrigan. She is concerned with all forms of conflict and its resolution, and her knack for bringing victory to those who worship her make her a powerful deity to invoke when dealing with life's problems. Following a warrior path has nothing to do with brandishing a sword or joining the military. You can be a pacifist and still follow a warrior path. Modern warriors can be found in the most mundane places: the single mom working two jobs to provide for her family, firefighters, police officers, teachers, social workers, and environmental activists—these are all warriors. People who draw on an inner strength to help themselves and others embody the warrior spirit. Being a warrior requires patience and strength. It challenges us to stand up and be counted, to draw on our inner strength and fight life's battles. The most important wars are not the physical ones.

Maybe the Morrigan will challenge you to fight a "war" against poverty by working to help low-income families. Maybe your "war" will be against animal cruelty and you will feel drawn to donate time at an animal shelter or get involved in your community in any number of ways that can bring about positive change.

Whenever we need the strength and will to engage in life's battles, the Queen of Battle stands ready to lead us to victory. Draw on the strength of the Morrigan to settle conflicts, end an abusive relationship, deal with any kind of legal battles, confront sexual harassment in the work place, or negotiate a raise from your boss. As on the ancient battlefields, the Morrigan will fight beside us, making us her champions. All we need do is to call upon her warrior spirit.

Macha's Lesson on Inner Peace

Although all of the Morrigan's guises display some connection to the warrior, it is Macha's image that strikes me as the quintessential warrior. She is a regal queen and a mother figure connected to fertility and agriculture; her warrior aspect only appears when others seek to harm or steal from her. She does not idly stand by and allow others to take her throne or use her as a doormat. She faces her problems head-on.

When I've encountered Macha in dreams and meditations, she appears in a chariot, spear in hand, her red hair in nine braids spilling down her shoulders. There is an earthiness about her. She looks at you with an easy gaze, grounded and secure in the knowledge of herself, confident in her abilities, whether they be in war or healing. She is absolutely and utterly *herself*. Nothing can shake Macha's confidence. She is the queen of all she surveys, and she knows it.

What strikes me about Macha in her warrior aspect is the calm and inner peace she radiates. You would expect a warrior to have a fierce demeanor and a snarling face, but not Macha. When I asked her why this was, she told me, "You cannot go to battle when you are at war with yourself." And of course she's right. Part of the path of the warrior is finding an inner balance and learning to become centered. We can't face all the stress and challenges life presents to us when we are not at peace with ourselves.

Part of finding inner peace is learning to be present—to be present in the moment and in our bodies and surroundings. Inner chaos and turmoil distracts us, making us forget to see the beauty around and within us. We get so caught up in thinking about things that will happen a day from now or a week from now that we forget to live in the now—to think about the present, to be aware of what is happening and what we are experiencing in this very moment. As a warrior, being present helps us to be aware and centered no matter the situation at hand, allowing us to act when necessary. Try incorporating being present in your daily meditations. Ground and center, then become aware of your body, of every breath and heartbeat, then expand this awareness to your surroundings. Then try doing this when you are outside or at work.

Another aspect of inner peace is release. Too often we hold on to negative emotions, hold grudges, and allow bad habits to influence our lives. As in the pathwork at the beginning of this section, we must sacrifice our personal demons to the Queen of Battle. Holding on to pain and negative emotions ties us to a cycle of negativity. To move past them, we must learn to release the negativity in our lives and welcome positive energies and experiences into our lives instead.

Macha's Spell for Inner Peace

Sometimes finding inner peace requires us to release harmful feelings and habits from our lives. Use this spell to release that which is no longer necessary in your life. Decide beforehand what it is you wish to release and write it on a piece of paper.

For part of the ritual you will need to make an herbal smudge bundle. Unlike smudge sticks that are burnt, the herbs in this bundle will be run along your body, so fresh herbs work the best. Dried herbs will crumble, since you will be dipping them in water, and will not have the same effect. I use catnip for this spell because of its association with love and happiness in general, but you can use any herb that is connected to happiness and cleansing. If you don't grow your own herbs or it is winter and you can't get your hands on anything fresh, you can purchase sage and other fresh herbs in most grocery stores.

You Will Need:
Fresh catnip or other cleansing herbs
String
1 red candle
Fireproof bowl
Bowl of water
Sandalwood incense
Pen and paper
Wine or cider

Take a handful of the herbs and tie them together at the base with the string to create a handle. Leave the top of the smudge loose; since you will be running it over your body, it should be loose and does not need to be tightly bundled together.

Place the red candle and fireproof bowl in the southern quarter of the altar, the bowl of water in the west, the incense in the east, and the herbal smudge in the north.

Cast the circle, then using your sword or athame draw an invoking pentagram in each of the four quarters, saying:

East:
Crow Goddess
Black feathers gliding upon the wind
Swift-footed mare
Untamable, wild, and free
Macha, now hear me
Macha, be near me this day![103]

South:
Macha of the red tresses
Sun of womanhood
Fierce and cunning Queen
Riding upon your chariot, spear in hand
Macha, now hear me
Macha, be near me this day!

---

103. Adapted from an invocation to Bridget by Diana L. Paxton that appeared in *SageWoman* magazine issue #46.

West:
Seeress, Lady of visions and far-reaching sight
Mistress of realms seen and unseen
Between the worlds you walk
Macha, now hear me
Macha, be near me this day!

North:
Lady of the Masts
Of the ripe and fertile plain
Marking the boundaries of your realm in earth and stone
Macha, now hear me
Macha, be near me this day!

Return to the altar, hold your hands in an invoking position, visualize Macha standing in front of you, then say:

Macha of the sovereign's crown
Macha, Seeress of the plain
Macha who cursed the men of Ulster
Great Queen, grant to me a boon of healing
Grant me your strength in the face of adversaries
Grant to me your fearlessness, your unwavering inner peace
That my mind, body, and spirit may move in harmony!

Write down on the piece of paper what you wish to release. Hold the paper in your hands for a few moments, seeing the thing you are banishing filling the paper. Then light the paper in the candle's flame and put it in the fireproof bowl, saying:

Fire burn away all that hinders me,
all (sorrow, darkness, doubt, etc.)
By fire I am cleansed!

Waft some of the incense over yourself, saying:

Air blow away all _________
By air I am cleansed!

Dip the catnip smudge into the bowl of water and run it along your body from head to foot. Chant:

Earth bury all _________
Water wash it away!
By water and earth, I am cleansed and free!

When you are ready to close the ritual, hold the cider or wine above the altar, saying:

In Mach's name, I am cleansed
May her strength and warrior spirit guide and guard me!

Take a sip, then pour some cider into your libation bowl or pour it outside after the ritual. When you are ready, close the quarters and open the circle.

The Warrior's Tools

The primary tools of the warrior are the sword, athame, spear, and shield. You may already be familiar with some of these tools and already use them in your magickal endeavors, but you may wish to have separate tools specifically set aside for rituals invoking the Morrigan in her warrior aspect. Your warrior tools should be stored separately from your other magickal tools, in a place where no one else will touch them.

Depending on what tradition you follow, the sword can represent either the element of fire or air. In warrior rituals, the sword is a symbol of leadership, authority, and protection. There are many decorative swords available on the market, but a basic well-made blade will work just as well if not better for magickal endeavors. When purchasing a sword, you should consider the weapon's weight and size. A claymore, while an impressive weapon, is not very practical if you have a small ritual space, and it may be too heavy to be used easily. If you are not able to own a sword, an athame can be used in its place.

Proper care for your magickal sword is also essential. Regularly oiling or greasing your blade will help prevent rust. (A light coating of WD-40 works nicely.) Also avoid touching the blade with your hands—the oils and salts on your skin can cause pit marks if you do not clean and grease the blade after touching it. Ritual salt will also cause pits, so if your sword or athame comes into contact with water or salt during a ritual, you will want to clean and oil it immediately. Also refrain from keeping your sword in the scabbard for long periods of time. The scabbard can hold humidity and cause the sword to rust. If you do find rust on your blade, mild chemical cleaners such as Nev-R-Dull, which can be purchased in your local hardware or automotive store, can be used to remove it. Leather scabbards or handles should be treated with paste wax to prevent cracks.

The spear represents the element of air, although it is sometimes used to represent fire. Spears were often launched in the air or used like a javelin, so to me air seems like the best element for the spear. The spear represents clear thought, focus, and direct action. The spear is sometimes used in Celtic magick to represent one of the four treasures of the Túatha Dé Danann but otherwise is not a very commonly used ritual tool. A spear can be used like the sword to cast a circle or can be used in place of a staff. Purchasing a spear may be more difficult than buying a sword or athame, which are fairly easy to find. Metal spearheads are more readily available and can be mounted on a wooden dowel from the hardware store. Like the sword, an overly long spear can be difficult to handle during rituals and could potentially knock over candles and other items on your altar. Purchasing a spearhead and mounting it yourself might be ideal, since you can choose the length of the dowel you are placing it on.

The shield is also an essential tool for the warrior. Since one of the warrior's goals is to neutralize harm and protect oneself, you may find yourself using a magickal shield quite often in your work as a warrior. Several websites sell wooden shields that you can paint yourself, or you can cut a piece of plywood into the desired shape and paint it. Decorate your shield with symbols and images that signify your path as a warrior. You may wish to write your warrior name in Ogham or another magickal alphabet on the shield or perhaps the names of warrior goddesses you feel connected to. A pentagram or other symbols of protection would also be appropriate. Smaller shields can be used in spellwork as a type of talisman. These can be made out of cardboard or heavy craft paper and can be placed in the home or carried on your person.

All of your ritual tools should be given a magickal name. This should be chosen prior to blessing and consecrating the weapon. Avoid names with negative connotations like "Death Bringer." Names that remind you of the tool's power, or the element it is connected to, or the name of a famous warrior would be appropriate, such as "Sun Fire" or "Boadicea."

Warrior Dedication Ritual

At some point you may wish to formally dedicate yourself to the path of the warrior. The new moon, a time for new beginnings, would be ideal for this ritual. Prior to the ritual, you should choose a warrior name. During this ritual you will be blessing your warrior tools, a sword and shield in particular. If there are other tools you wish to use, you can bless them in the same manner. You will also need something to symbolize your rank as a warrior: a torc, broach, or decorative belt would be good choices and can be worn during a ritual invoking the warrior goddess.

Before the ritual, you will need to write a warrior's oath. Your oath should state your intent to dedicate yourself as a warrior, name the traits you wish to strive for as a warrior, and outline how you will use your skills as a warrior for the benefit of yourself and others. I have included the oath I used in my dedication ritual so you may use it as a guide to writing your own.

You Will Need:
Sword
Shield
Dragon's blood incense and oil
Wine

Cast the circle with your sword, saying:

I cast this circle in the name of the Morrigan,
Warrioress of the Túatha Dé Danann,
Queen of Battle who dwells between the worlds,
That it may be a place of strength and enlightenment,
Between the realms of gods and men

Stand before the altar with your sword in hand. State your intent to dedicate yourself as a warrior to the Morrigan in these or similar words:

The Goddess has three faces—Maiden, Mother, and Crone
But I see a fourth face among her many faces and guises
The face of the Warrior

She who protects and fights for all of her children
Who fights ignorance and lies with truth and light
She who uses her wisdom along with her sword
Whose shield is her magick and the cunning arts
Today I come to dedicate myself to the Warrior Goddess

Go to each quarter and draw an invoking pentagram with your sword, saying:

From the East I call upon the Morrigu
The three who is one, Queen of Battle, maker of kings
Cunning raven woman, whose battle cry stills the hearts of men
Morrigu, bear witness to my oath
And bring to this circle your warrior spirit!

From the South I call upon Macha
Lady of Battle, the masts of war are your fitting tribute
Macha, bear witness to my oath
And bring to this circle your warrior spirit!

From the West I call upon Badb
Queen of shadowy battlefields
You who stir the cauldron of life, death, and rebirth
Badb, bear witness to my oath
And bring to this circle your warrior spirit!

From the North I call upon Anu
Keeper of the mysteries of the earth
The blood of birth and death spills upon the ground
And fertilizes your dark soil
Anu, bear witness to my oath
And bring to this circle your warrior spirit!

Return to the altar. Hold your arms up in an invoking position, sword in hand, and say:

Dark Morrigan
Terrible Mother, Warrior Goddess
Fierce and uncompromising
You shatter your foes

You drink deep from the well of self-knowledge
Of strength, of wisdom, of power
Dark Morrigan
Chooser of the slain
Your battle cry stills the hearts of men
Raven Mother thirsty for battle
Be here now
Fill this thy Priest/ess with your warrior spirit!

Take a few minutes to feel the Morrigan's presence, then pass the shield through the incense. Anoint it with the dragon's blood oil, saying:

Shield, my protector and ally in magick
In the name of the Morrigan, I name you _________

Bring the shield to each quarter and hold it up, saying:

I am protected from all negativity and harm
coming from the east/south/west/north

Return to the altar, pass the sword through the incense, and anoint the blade and hilt, saying:

Sword, my protector and ally in magick
In the name of the Morrigan, I name you _________

Bring the sword to each quarter and hold it up, saying:

I am protected from all negativity and harm
coming from the east/south/west/north

Return to the altar. Next you will make your vow, dedicating yourself as a warrior to the Morrigan. As I said before, you should write your own vow. Below is the vow I used for my own ritual—use it as a guide for your own vow.

Great Goddess Morrigan, Warrior Queen of the Túatha Dé Danann and the children of the wise. I, _________, *dedicate myself to you as a warrior of the Goddess. I vow to protect myself and others, to harm none and never act in anger. I shall strive to use wisdom and peace above violence and to honor and protect all life and above all the sacred earth, mother of us all. I shall defend my rights and the rights of all Witches so all people may one day live together in harmony and peace. I vow to uphold this sacred vow now and forever. May the Goddess accept my oath and forever guide me upon my path as a peaceful warrior*

Anoint the torc (or whatever you are using as your symbol of rank) with the oil and hold it above the altar, saying:

I bless this _________ in the mane of the Goddess Morrigan
That it may be a symbol of my honor
Rank and obligation as a warrior
May it strengthen and protect me

Put the torc on, then say:

I am _________, warrior of the goddess Morrigan!

Take a few moments to feel the strength and power of the Morrigan fill you, then take the chalice of wine and hold it above the altar, saying:

With this toast I seal my vow!

Pour some of the wine into your libation bowl or pour some outside after the ritual. When you are ready, thank the Morrigan and close the quarters, then close the circle.

Exercise 1: Forging Psychic Armor

Sit in a comfortable position. Take three deep breaths, ground, and center. How you choose to see your armor is up to you. You could see it as medieval chainmail, as dragon scales, or simply as an impenetrable layer of white crystalline energy. Whatever you choose, make sure it is something you can visualize and see clearly in your mind. Concentrate on the image of the armor, feel it on your skin. Know your armor fills you with strength and courage, repelling any unwanted negative energies; nothing can pass through your protective armor. Spend a few minutes each day concentrating on your armor.

Morrigan's Shield Spell

This spell relies on your ability to use visualization. It does not require an actual shield but rather a psychic one.

You Will Need:
Patchouli incense
Crow or black feather
1 red candle
1 clear quartz crystal

Light the incense, using the feather to smudge your body beginning at the crown of your head and moving toward your feet. Light the candle, saying:

I light the flame of the Morrigan
Raven Mother, Phantom Queen
Mistress who rules over Life, Death, and Rebirth
Know you are honored here
Hail and welcome!

Hold the crystal in your hands and take a few moments to feel the Morrigan's presence. Visualize the Morrigan standing in front of you. She tells you to craft a shield. Take a few moments to visualize the shield in front of you. What does it look like, what is it made of, what does it feel like? Hold the image of the shield in your mind and see the crystal mounted somewhere on your shield. When you are ready, you present the shield to the Morrigan. She holds it high over your head and says, "Here is the shield of the Morrigan, and behold that which I put into place is unmovable." As she speaks you feel her strength and power flow through the shield until it shines with a brilliant golden light. Place the crystal on each of your chakras and visualize a shield of brilliant golden light surrounding you. Chant:

Behold the shield of the Morrigan
Unbreakable and impenetrable

The shield of the Morrigan protects me from all harm
I am safe and protected
So be it!

Leave the crystal on the altar overnight. Carry it with you when you feel the need for protection and strength.

Morrigan Warrior Invocation

Black winged phantom shrieking war cries
Carrion raven feasting on the slain
Descend now, corvine Goddess
Full of magick, full of guile
Warrior Queen
Sword lusting for blood
Crow of Battle, you who delight in chaos and strife
Mighty Goddess, bringer of swift justice
Who lays her enemies low
Come now, O Morrigan
Take up my cause
Lead me to victory!

Warrior Queen Incense

2 tbsp. dragon's blood
1 tbsp. basil
1 tbsp. angelica root
1 tbsp. cedar
½ tbsp. ground cinnamon
1 crushed bay leaf

Morrigu Warrior Ritual

The following ritual calls on the power of the Morrigan in her guise as the Queen of Battle and can be used to call on her protective energies, win court cases, or banish a stalker, or for any task that requires the fighting spirit of the warrior goddess.

I have included Nemain in this ritual in place of Anu because of her association with war and battle. Anu may have had warrior attributes, but none have survived in mythology.

You Will Need:
Warrior Queen Incense (see page 260)
Sword
Red wine

Light the Warrior Queen Incense. Cast the circle using your sword. Salute each direction with the sword, saying:

From the East I call upon Nemain
Raven woman, on black wings you circle the battlefield
Your battle cry fills your enemies with terror and fright
Bring to this circle your warrior spirit!

From the South I call upon Macha
Blood-Red Queen who instigates battle
Forger of heroes, warriors, and kings
Bring to this circle your warrior spirit!

From the West I call upon Badb
Washer at the Ford, gathering the spirits of the dead
Queen of shadowy battlefields
You who stir the cauldron's life-giving waters
Bring to this circle your warrior spirit!

From the North I call upon the Morrigan
The three who is one
Queen of Battle who defends the sovereignty of the land
Your dark soil drinks up the blood of the slain
The bodies of the fallen fertilize the land
Bring to this circle your warrior spirit!

As you call each element, visualize each of the goddesses standing before you: Nemain with the wind blowing through her hair, spear in hand; Macha with a halo of sunlight around her, holding a fiery sword; Badb standing alongside a river stirring her cauldron; Morrigan standing in a regal chariot with lush green hills behind her.

Go to the altar. While holding your sword or athame, raise your hands upward in an invoking position, saying:

Hearken round me, Mothers and Warriors of old
Who together form the Morrigu
Lady of battle
Dark Raven Queen
Guide and guard your child this night
Fill me with your warrior spirit!

Do any planned spellwork or pathworking. When you are done, circle the wine with the sword, then hold it above the altar, saying:

I honor the Raven of Battle
Goddess of Life, Death, and Rebirth!

Take a sip of the wine, then put it aside. After the ritual pour the wine on the ground outside as an offering to the Morrigan. When you are ready to end the rite, thank the Morrigan and close the quarters, saying:

Depart in Peace, Warrioress of the east/south/west/north

Open the circle.

Celtic Warrior Ritual

This rite calls on the Celtic warrior goddesses Andraste, Maeve, Scáthach, and the Morrigan. Call upon the warrior goddesses for protection and new beginnings, and to overcome obstacles.

You Will Need:
Sword
Athame or wand
Warrior Queen Incense (see page 260)
Wine

Cast the circle using your sword. Salute each quarter with your sword while saying:

East:
Morrigan
Raven of battle, Warrior Queen
In the form of a raven you fly across the field of battle
Bringing fear to your enemies and victory to your champions
Lady of the whirlwind, spear in hand
Bring to this circle the power of air and your Warrior Spirit!

South:
Maeve
Fiery, intoxicating One
Noble Queen, sensual and strong
Warrior, keen for battle
Bring to this circle the power of fire and your Warrior Spirit!

West:
Scáthach
Shadowy One, forger of heroes
Warrioress upon your mist-shrouded isle
Hearken to the warrior's call
Bring to this circle the power of water and your Warrior Spirit!

North:
Andraste
Invincible One, granter of victory
Bright Lady of battle and the sacred grove
Goddess of fertility and war
Through you all that falls rises anew
Reborn from the womb of the earth
Bring to this circle the power of earth and your Warrior Spirit!

Go to the altar and raise your hands upward in an invoking position while holding your sword. Say:

I call upon the Warrior Goddess
Upon Boadicea, Maeve, Scáthach
Morrigan, Cathubodua, Epona, Andraste
You are the strength within me
The sword point of my will

The shield that guards me
The forge that shapes my spirit
Goddesses of Battle, bringing victory in your wake
Great Queens avenging wrongdoing
Trainer of heroes, spear and sword in hand
In all your names and guises
I call upon your warrior spirit
Guide my actions
Grant to me your protection and lend to me your strength
O Mighty Goddesses of Battle!

Do any planned spellwork or pathworking. When you are ready to close the ritual, take the cup of wine and circle it three times with your athame, saying:

Blood of birth, that brings life and new beginning
Blood of death, that fertilizes the land and brings change
Life and death, change and rebirth
All these belong to the Warrior Goddess
Hail Andraste, hail Maeve,
Hail Scáthach, hail Morrigan!

Drink some of the wine, then pour some into your libation bowl or outside after the ritual. When you are ready to close the ritual, thank the warrior goddesses for their aid, then go to each quarter, saying:

Depart in Peace Warrioress of the east/south/west/north

Open the circle.

13
Phantom Queen

It is at the guarding of thy death that I am;
and I shall be.

—*A. H. Leahy,* Táin Bó Regamna

You feel yourself changing. Your arms transform into velvety black wings, your feet into claws, and you feel yourself shrinking as your body reforms into that of a bird. As a raven you fly over a green valley. Along the valley floor a river weaves a serpentine path across the earth, its water glistening silver in the ebbing sunlight. There is a chill in the air, and although most of the trees are still green, you see patches of yellow, red, and brown leaves marking the approach of winter. Movement by the river's edge attracts your attention. Descending in slow spiraling circles you see a small troop of soldiers marching along the river bank. They wear leather armor over rough woven tunics. Some have metal helmets fashioned in the likenesses of birds and boars. Spears and swords in hand, they walk onward to some unknown battle.

As you perch on a branch overlooking the river, one of the soldiers looks up at you, his expression somber, as if your presence is an ill omen. You ruffle your feathers and squawk at him, and he turns away.

Suddenly the procession stops; the tall man leading the group gasps in surprise, and the others turn to see what is wrong. You tilt your head to the side too, wanting to see what had startled the warrior. An old woman stands knee-deep in the river water. You are certain, as is the warrior, that she was not there a moment ago. The water rushes quickly by her, but she seems unaffected by the strong current. She holds something in her hands, lifting it in and out of the water as if washing it. The leader of the group looks at the woman and turns pale. He asks, "Is that my armor and my sword you are washing, old woman?"

The woman looks up at the man as if she has just noticed him. She lifts a cloak from the water, its pattern stained with blood; in her other hand she raises a sword, red liquid still dripping down the blade despite her attempts to wash it away. "Yes, it is your armor I wash, warrior. If you will but turn back from this course, you will live to see another sunrise and many more afterwards. But if you continue onward, I see only death and blood in your future. Will you heed my warning? There is no dishonor in living and leaving death for another day."

The warrior shakes his head and speaks of the great deeds he will do in the coming battle, and that he is willing to take his chances. The warrior turns and the others follow him, whispering to one another. No one else saw the woman, only their leader, who marches on toward his death.

The woman sighs. Looking up, she beckons to you with a wrinkled hand. You glide down, landing on her boney shoulder. She ruffles the feathers on your neck in an absent sort of way. "I try to warn them," she says confidingly.

Another group of soldiers wanders near the river, and again the washerwoman gives her warning to those who will fall in battle. One or two turn back, but most continue into the valley. The woman carries on her washing until the water turns a bright scarlet. In the distance you can hear the sounds of a great battle—the rattle of chariots, the ringing of metal clashing with metal, and a chorus of battle cries. Soon the sounds fade and the battle is over. The woman looks up from her washing, and between one moment and the next you find yourself and the woman standing much farther upstream, where the battle took place. Many bodies litter the grassy plain. Whoever the victors were, they are long gone, leaving only the dead as a testament to the battle fought here. Overhead other ravens circle the battlefield, preparing to feast on the flesh of the slain.

The washerwoman walks toward the corpses. She leans down over the nearest one, drawing a mark on the warrior's forehead with a damp hand. Then she blows across the warrior's body. When she does this, you see a ghostly image rise as the spirit of the warrior leaves his body behind. The spirit warrior walks to the water's edge. As his feet touch the shore, he vanishes, passing beyond the Veil to the Otherworlds. The river shore itself seems shadowy now, the Veil between the worlds swung slightly ajar to allow the dead entrance to those other lands. This process continues until all those who have fallen have passed through the Veil.

Having gathered the souls of the slain, the washerwoman sighs and gazes upon the battlefield. "Who would care for the dead if not I? Some would see me as unkind, even cruel. But mine is a realm through which you all must pass. Death and change are natural laws none can avoid. Truly do you think you would be better off without me? I am the onward march of time, the endless cycle of the seasons. You think I bring ends, but I am the gatekeeper to new beginnings. Without me the wailing child can never grow to the adult, the seasons would not turn, spring would never follow the winter. Death is only part of my realm, but what you call death, I see only as a transition. Everything is constantly in motion, moving from one form to another, then another, a constant spiral. Death and change are simply my tools; transformation is my goal. You meet my challenges many times over as I midwife you through life's many cycles, leading you toward change." She turns back toward the river, looking past the glittering Veil and into the Otherworlds beyond. Slowly she walks back to the river waters.

"Who would care for the dead if not I?" she asks no one in particular. She lightly ruffles your feathers again, and you can only agree with her. The washerwoman is not unkind, nor can you see the old woman as evil. She is a force, a law of nature. You take to the air, leaving the woman and battlefield behind. The scene fades and you feel yourself returning to your normal shape and body.

As the Phantom Queen, the Morrigan appears to us as the ghostly death messenger, prophesying the death of heroes and kings. She is the sorrowful Washer at the Ford, warning warriors of their coming deaths, and she is the faery banshee keening for those soon to die. The Phantom Queen is the goddess of death and transitions, who rules over the process of change. She destroys us, our egos, our misconceptions and illusions, then puts us back together again, stronger than we were before. Although these figures seem sinister at first glance, it is through the Morrigan's darker aspects that she teaches us inner transformation, destroying our illusions and fears, and challenges us to shed that which is old and no longer useful. The Phantom Queen, the goddess of death, is really the goddess of rebirth in disguise.

The mournful Washer at the Ford is perhaps the Morrigan's most enigmatic guise. The Washer at the Ford appeared in rivers washing the bloody clothes of warriors about to die. This phantom washerwoman appears on some occasions as a young woman and other times as a hag, showing her connection to both death (Crone) and rebirth (Maiden). She usually appears wearing red clothing, although sometimes she wears white—both colors are associated with the Otherworlds and attributed to Badb. Her connection with the color red is most likely due to the nature of the clothing she washes, the blood-stained spoils of dead warriors giving her own red garb a more grotesque connotation. On other occasions she washes the entrails of warriors rather than their clothes, reminiscent of the Morrigan's boast to claim certain organs from a Fomorian king as a spoil of war. The Washer at the Ford was also accredited with the ability to make water run red with blood (probably from washing all those entrails).

In early accounts, the Washer at the Ford was identified as the goddess Badb. When Cúchulain encounters such a washerwoman she is described as "Badb's daughter." When Badb appears as a Maiden rather than a Crone, she is described as the "daughter" of Badb; when she appears as a Crone, she is described simply as Badb. It seems while both are Badb herself, the "daughter" description is added to distinguish her Maiden form from her Crone aspect. In the *Bruiden Da Choca,* Badb appears washing a chariot in a river ford.[104] In both instances she appears as the goddess of death and fate. In these stories her divine nature is not questioned; however, in later folklore, the Washer at the Ford was reduced to either a faery woman or a ghost.

There are several faery washerwomen found in Celtic folklore. Although they vary in appearance, ranging from grotesque to beautiful, their functions remain the same as their divine predecessor. The Bean Nighe was a faery who washed bloody clothes in desolate rivers. Seeing this faery was usually an omen of one's death, although some tales claim the Bean Nighe would grant wishes if she was approached properly. She is described as being ugly, with red webbed feet and large teeth. These phantom women were believed to be the souls of women who died during childbirth and were destined to wash their bloody laundry until the time they would have died of natural causes. The Breton *Les Lavandieres de Nuit* (Laundresses of the Night) were women condemned to wash at rivers and streams as penitence for their sins, which ranged from committing suicide (usually by drowning), infanticide, or having the misfortune of dying unbaptized. These washerwomen would intentionally lure victims to the water's edge, asking for help with their washing, then drown their unsuspecting victims. While *Les Lavandieres de Nuit* were considered faeries, they have evolved into something more akin to ghosts or phantoms.

Although this faery does not wash her laundry in rivers, the Bean Sidhe—better known as the banshee—is another death messenger connected to the Morrigan. Despite its dark image, the banshee was a benevolent faery who watched over certain families. The keening wails of the banshee could be heard before a family member's death. If a person was particularly holy or valorous, more than one banshee would keen for them. These banshees, like the Morrigan, appeared in groups of three. Like

104. Koch, *Celtic Culture,* p. 220.

the Washer at the Ford, the banshee appeared near bodies of water, such as rivers, lakes, and holy wells. *Bean Sidhe* means "Faery Woman," bringing to mind the Morrigan's connection to the Faery Folk. Since the faeries were believed to be the spirits of the dead in Christian times, this phantom faery took the place of the goddess of death, guarding the transition from life to death. The banshee's appearance is almost identical to that of Badb. When Badb appeared to mortals, she took the form of a "pale" woman or "white lady." Similarly the banshee appears as a woman dressed in white (a color the Celts connected with death) and could take the form of a hag or a young woman.

As the Phantom Queen, the Morrigan was believed to visit battlefields at night and reanimate the corpses of slain warriors in a macabre spectral display. Reanimating the fallen warriors is symbolic of their rebirth in the Otherworlds and shows that the Morrigan held sway over life and death, being able to reverse it at will. The Phantom Queen also gathered the bloody heads of warriors. The Morrigan's head hunting may seem gruesome, but the head was the seat of the soul and housed the spirit in Celtic beliefs. The taking of heads becomes symbolic of gathering the spirits of the dead. The Morrigan was not alone in her habit of collecting skulls. Other dark goddesses connected to death, such as the Indian Kali, also made a habit of collecting severed heads.

As a goddess of death, the Morrigan rules over not only physical death but the many transitions and little deaths we experience throughout our lives. Death is only change to the Morrigan, an endless and necessary cycle for growth. Without change the world would be stagnant, yielding no new life or ideas. Without death there can be no rebirth or new life. Learning to understand death is learning to understand change and its necessity to our lives and spiritual growth.

Understanding the Goddess of Death & Transformation

At first glance, this lonely washerwoman seems a figure to be avoided, but once we shed our fears surrounding death and change, the Phantom Queen can be a powerful ally, shattering our misconceptions and self-created delusions. She does not cause death or disaster but warns us of the consequence of our actions and guides us through transition and change. The warriors she forewarns rarely seem to listen to her; perhaps if they had, they would have lived.

If you have ever used a Tarot deck, you may be familiar with a very misunderstood card. The antagonist in the card is usually a shadowy veiled figure, not unlike the Washer at the Ford. Sometimes his face is hidden by dark robes; other times his pale skeletal figure is plain to see. His name is Death, and he always seems to cause a stir when he makes an appearance in a reading. Unfortunately some people take this card at face value, assuming it is an omen of literal death. But the Death card has surprisingly little to do with actual death and everything to do with change. In the Dragon Tarot deck I use for my readings, the Death card has an egg resting to one side, representing rebirth, reminding us that the end of one thing is only the beginning of another. Birth and death are intrinsically connected. Like the Death card, the Washer at the Ford is not a figure to be feared. She represents concepts that we may be uncomfortable with or afraid of, but she is also our guide through our darkest hours, leading us past her waves of destruction and toward renewal.

Americans are very familiar with death, but by most accounts we don't really understand the process of dying or how to grieve. We see death all the time. On the news we hear about mass murders, school shootings, and homicides, and we can see death in gruesome detail in movies and video games. But when it comes to dealing with the aftermath of death, of dealing with loss, we often don't know what to do or how to react. In their book *Death and Dying, Life and Living,* Charles A. Corr, Clyde Nabe, and Donna M. Corr observe that our culture desensitizes us to death but ignores grief and the aftermath of losing a loved one: "What is most remarkable about the typical portrayal of death in these media is that it is usually very unrealistic or fantasized. Those who die are unimportant people or 'bad guys.' Violent fantasies of a very graphic nature are acted out—but suffering, grief and other consequences of this violence and death are mostly noticeable for their absence."[105]

In other cultures we find grief and death handled in a very different manner. In Asia, ancestor altars within the home are commonplace. The dead have a very real presence among the living. The ancestors and beloved dead are given offerings and honored throughout the year. In high school I was lucky enough to witness a *jesa* ceremony at a Korean friend's house. This ceremony is done every year on the anniversary of a loved one's death. A small table in the corner of their living room served as a year-round ancestor altar, with framed pictures of deceased relatives, candles, and incense. Wine and food were placed on the altar, prayers were said, and

105. Corr, Corr, and Nabe, *Death and Dying, Life and Living,* p. 89.

the family held a large dinner afterward. It was early June and we were studying for our finals that night, but I felt like it was October. It reminded me of Samhain nights when I had lit candles to honor the dead, and dumb suppers where the dead feasted alongside the living.

The dead similarly held an honored place in Celtic life. Relatives erected cairns and burial mounds and yearly honored their ancestors on Samhain. The dead were never really gone from this world. Just as the Faery Realm was just a side-step away from our own world, so too was the realm of the Honored Dead. The fact that all the Celtic goddesses of death, the Morrigan included, are equally connected to rebirth reflects the Celtic belief in reincarnation and the continuation of the spirit; and it is through these goddesses that we can see how they viewed the process of death and dying. The Phantom Queen's lesson is this: there is no death, only change. Death is not an end, only the beginning of a new phase. We experience death many times and on so many levels within our lives. The death of our child-selves makes way for the adult-selves. As we grow and change throughout life, we shed the skin of our old selves, growing and reinventing ourselves as we learn life's lessons.

The Phantom Queen teaches us that death is a part of life, and she shows us how to part the Veil to honor those who have passed and how to draw on the wisdom of our ancestors. The Phantom Queen can also teach us to conquer our own self-made phantoms and shadow-selves. She teaches us to emerge from the Underworld, claiming self-knowledge and shedding our illusions and self-doubts.

Exercise 1: Creating an Ancestor Altar

Creating an ancestor altar is a way to honor your relatives and loved ones who have passed on as well as your cultural ancestors. By burning candles, leaving offerings, or simply spending a few minutes quietly reflecting by your ancestor altar, you are sending energy to the spirit realm and fostering a connection between yourself and your ancestors.

Your altar can be as simple or elaborate as you wish. Most ancestor altars are simply a collection of photos on a dresser or small table. Besides pictures or personal items of those who have passed, you may wish to add something that represents your cultural ancestors. Since I am of Irish descent, I have a coin from Ireland and a cloth with Celtic knotwork on my ancestor altar to represent my cultural ancestors. You may also wish to add an offering dish to your altar or an incense burner, depending on what kind of offerings you plan on using.

For those who have recently lost a loved one, an ancestor altar can be a way to gain closure, especially if you did not get a chance to talk to your loved one or say goodbye before they passed. I view my own altar as a "spiritual telephone." If I want advice or simply need to talk to a deceased loved one, I go to my altar and light a white candle to represent the person's spirit. I then visualize the person standing in front of me and just start talking. No ritual circle or chants—I just talk. There is no doubt in my mind that I am being heard. On some occasions an answer may come right away; other times I might see that person in a dream, but a response always comes one way or another.

Building a connection with the ancestors can be a profound and healing experience, allowing us to maintain a connection to those who have gone before, to learn from their wisdom, and to honor those who have shaped our own lives. After you have created your altar, spend time there at least once a week, and remember to document your experiences in your journal.

Ancestor Altar Blessing

You Will Need:

Sage incense
Small bowl
Water
Salt

Prior to using your ancestor altar, the space should be cleansed and blessed. Begin by clearing the altar of all objects. Light the incense and waft the smoke over the altar, saying:

I cleanse and bless this altar in the name of my ancestor
that I may honor the wisdom and sacrifices of those who
have gone before.

Pour about half a cup of water into the bowl and add three pinches of salt. Stir with your finger, then sprinkle the water over the altar, saying:

I cleanse and bless this altar in the name of the beloved dead
That this may be a place to remember and honor
Those who have passed
And that I may learn the wisdom of my ancestors and
Those who have come before me
In the name of the Morrigan,
Lady of the Land of Shadows so be it!

Pass any decorations or objects you wish to place on the altar through the incense before placing them on the altar.

A Candle Ceremony for One Who Has Passed

You Will Need:

Phantom Queen Incense (see page 283)
1 white candle

After a loved one has passed, you can do this simple ceremony to send them loving energy. Light the incense. Place pictures or personal items of the loved one around the altar. Carve the person's name on the candle and light it, saying:

Phantom Queen
Crone of death and transformation
Wrap _________ in your loving embrace
Guide him/her beyond the Veil and to rest and rebirth.

Sit in front of the candle and send loving energy to the person who has passed. If there is something you wish to say to your loved one, do so now. When you are done, extinguish the candle and thank the Morrigan.

Exercise 2: The Dumb Supper

You may already be familiar with the dumb supper as a way to honor the beloved dead on Samhain, but this ritual does not have to be limited to Samhain celebrations. Traditionally the table is set with food and an additional plate is set to represent the departed loved one during a dumb supper. The participants eat in silence, remembering and honoring the spirit who has passed. An updated version of the dumb supper can be held any time of the year to honor one who has passed or to honor and become closer to your ancestors.

Dumb Supper to Honor a Departed Loved One

To honor a specific person who has passed, create a dinner featuring their favorite foods. I prefer to do the supper on the loved one's birthday or the anniversary of their death. The participants should place a white candle in the center of the table to represent the deceased loved one's spirit. Place pictures of the loved one around the candle. An additional plate should also be put on the table in honor of that person. Before serving dinner, light the candle and welcome the person's spirit to the table by saying:

Morrigan, Lady of the Land of Shadows
Open the gates between life and death
*We have gathered here to honor*_________
And invite him/her here to this place
To sit among friends and family for a short while
And to know that he/she is remembered and loved

The participants should eat and reminisce about the person who has passed. This does not have to be a solemn occasion. This should be a celebration of the person's life and should bring a smile to your face as you remember happy moments you spent with this person. If anyone has something specific they wish to impart to the loved one, they may speak directly to the person's spirit. When the supper is over, extinguish the candle, saying:

Morrigan, Lady of the Land of Shadows
Close now the doors between life and death
Depart in peace, _________, with our heartfelt love and blessings

Ancestral Dumb Supper

Dumb suppers do not have to be held in honor of a specific person who has passed. Holding an ancestral dumb supper is a nice way to honor your heritage and your ancestors. Decorate the table with things that remind you of your ancestors. This can get rather interesting if you come from several backgrounds! You could concentrate on one particular part of your background or all of the groups you descend from. Serve traditional foods from your cultural background. Light a white candle to honor your ancestors. While eating dinner, the participants should reminisce about your family's history and the mythology or history of your ancestral culture(s).

Confronting the Shadows of the Past Ritual

In this ritual you will be calling upon the Phantom Queen as a healer to dispel emotional trauma and release the negativity of the past. It can be used after a bad breakup or during a particularly difficult time in your life. It is especially helpful for those healing from domestic abuse or helping victims of rape release feelings of shame and guilt. The Phantom Queen takes our inner darkness and helps us reshape it into something new and positive.

For part of the ritual you will be rinsing your body with water, symbolically cleansing your spirit. You can sprinkle water over yourself with your hands or you may wish to perform the ritual in your bathroom and place the herbs in your bathtub and fully submerge yourself.

You Will Need:
Pen and paper
Rose oil
1 white candle
Small fireproof bowl
Bottled or filtered water
Salt
1 large cauldron or bowl
Comfrey
Chamomile
Milkweed

Before the ritual, write what it is you wish to release on the piece of paper. Be as detailed as possible. (If releasing emotional trauma from a painful time in your life, you could burn something that represents that time, a picture, or some other object that has meaning to you instead of burning the piece of paper.)

Cast the circle, then anoint yourself with the rose oil while saying:

Blessed be my feet that I may walk in balance and harmony
Blessed be the womb/phallus that brings forth life
Blessed be my heart that I may be filled with the
Healing love of the Divine
Blessed be my lips that I may breathe in the essence of the Goddess
Blessed be my eyes that I may see the wisdom of the Goddess

When you are ready, go to each quarter and call the elements.

East:
I call upon the power of air
Winds of knowledge and thought
Cleanse my mind and body of pain
Bring me healing from the east!

South:
I call upon the power of fire
Temper my mind and will
With courage and strength
Bring me healing from the south!

West:
I call upon the power of water
The healing waters of the Ocean
Of holy wells and sacred springs
Wash away all illusions and despair
Bring me healing from the west!

North:
I call upon the power of earth
Fill me with the strength and vitality
Of the green and growing earth
Bring me healing from the north!

Return to the altar, light the white candle, and hold up your arms in an invoking position, saying:

Phantom Queen
Goddess of the Underworld
Who rules over change and rebirth
I have come to face and overcome my shadows
To conquer fear and self-doubt
And to heal the scars of the past
Queen of Shadows
Who dispels illusions and heals the soul
Goddess of the Underworld
Guide me toward healing!

See the Phantom Queen standing before you. Tell her what it is you wish to release. Listen for any advice or encouragement she may give you. See yourself and her becoming one, her powerful essence filling you, cleansing your spirit and lending you her strength.

Close your eyes and think about the negative events or emotions you want to banish. Think about the lessons you have learned from these experiences, and acknowledge that you are ready to let these emotions or events go to begin the healing process. When you are ready, say:

May the lessons I have learned from these experience remain
And their pain be wash away from my spirit

Take the folded paper and tear it a few times, and put the pieces in the fireproof bowl. Breathe lightly on the paper, saying:

By the breath of the Goddess, I banish thee!

With your fingers sprinkle a few drops of water (just a few or the paper will be hard to set on fire) on the paper, saying:

By the blood of the Goddess, I banish thee!

Sprinkle a small pinch of salt over the paper, saying:

By the flesh and bone of the Goddess, I banish thee!

Use the candle to light the paper on fire, saying:

By the will of the Goddess, I banish thee
Be gone!

Take a few deep cleansing breaths, feeling the energy of what you have banished draining away from you. When you are ready, fill the cauldron or large bowl with water. Hold your hands over the bowl, saying:

I bless this water in the name of the Phantom Queen
That it may bring me healing and
Wash away all that hinders my spirit.

Put the herbs in the water. A small amount of each herb will do; if you choose to do this ritual in the bathroom and substitute your bathtub for the cauldron, you can use larger amounts. Stir the water nine times counterclockwise with your finger, saying:

Blood-stained Washerwoman
Old woman of knowledge
Goddess of death and wisdom
Old Crone spinning the tread of fate
Mistress of the Underworld
Keeper of primordial wisdom
Crone
Phantom

Chooser of the Slain
Chase away the shadows within
Destroy illusions and self-doubt
Guide me toward healing and self-knowledge!

Using your hands, gently sprinkle the water over your body. Take as long as you need. You could also dip a small hand towel into the water and use that to wash the water over your body. When you feel fully cleansed, thank the Phantom Queen and close the quarters. Pour the herbs and water on the ground outside.

Morrigan's Renewal Spell

Sometimes life can overwhelm us, and we need to release our stress and negative emotions and recharge ourselves. The Phantom Queen rules over the end of cycles and the beginning of new ones, helps us shed negative emotions, and empowers us to face the difficult situations life throws at us.

You Will Need:
A handful each of patchouli and lavender
1 black pen or marker and paper
1 black candle
1 fireproof bowl

Begin by taking a ritual bath. Add patchouli (for banishing and cleansing) and lavender (for positive vibrations) into the water. Visualize your negativity going down the drain when you are done. Go to your sacred space and use a black pen or marker to write down in as much detail as possible the problem you want to overcome or the emotions you wish to release. Light the black candle and draw an invoking pentagram over the candle, saying:

Dark Goddess
Raven Queen
Creation and destruction follow in your wake
You are the spark of creation
The Devourer of life

Creator and destroyer
Ever renewing and reshaping the universe,

Wise Crone
Phantom Queen
Devourer
Creatrix
Destroyer
Empower me
Strengthen me
Enlighten and awaken me
Let me rise from the ashes of
(whatever the situation is) *and be reborn!*

Light the piece of paper using the black candle and put it in the fireproof bowl. Bury the ashes away from your property.

An herbalist friend of mine did a variation of this spell using a mortar and pestle. She rolled out a flat square piece of modeling clay, let it dry, then wrote what she wanted to banish in marker on it. She smashed and pulverized the clay tablet with the mortar and pestle while visualizing the problem being ground to pieces and disappearing.

Washer at the Ford Ritual

Death and transformation are a part of life. We experience death and rebirth when we move from one phase of life to another. Sometimes this transition is smooth, other times it is fraught with difficulties. This ritual calls upon the Washer at the Ford as a goddess who guards transitions and change. Use this ritual during times of change and to help you move on to a new phase in your life's path. It can be used after a divorce or breakup, when starting a new career, or when one simply needs to bring change into one's life. A friend of mine used it to help her quit smoking and to help dedicate herself to a healthier lifestyle.

You Will Need:
Patchouli incense
1 large cauldron or bowl
Pomegranate tea
Warm filtered water

This ritual is best performed in your bathroom or outside if the weather permits. You will be washing water over your body, so the larger the bowl or cauldron, the better. If you can't find pomegranate tea, use any kind of tea that will make the water a dark-red color. You could use hibiscus or strawberry tea as a substitute, but pomegranate with its association with the Underworld would be ideal.

Light the incense and pass the bowl through the smoke, saying:

In the name of the Phantom Queen
I bless this cauldron of change

Fill the bowl with the tea bags or herbs and warm water, letting it sit for a few minutes until the water begins to darken. While you are waiting for the tea to steep, sit and meditate about what it is you wish to shed from your life or what new phase you wish to begin.

When the water is dark, dip your hands into the bowl and swirl the water around. Imagine you are the Washer at the Ford, washing the remnants of your old life in the cauldron of change in order to bring about renewal and a new phase and bring new purpose into your life. When you are ready, call upon the Washer at the Ford by saying:

Washer at the Ford
Lady of change
Of death and rebirth
It is you who guides us past the boundaries of this life
And leads us to healing and renewal
Queen of Phantoms
Who is both the Crone and the Maiden
Guide me toward healing

I move past this phase in my life
I shed the old, as a snake sheds its skin
and welcome new and better things
Phantom Washerwoman,
guide me through this time of change!

Using your fingers, run the tea along your body, visualizing your old self washing away, leaving you renewed.

When you are done, thank the Washer at the Ford and pour the water in the bowl outside.

Phantom Queen Invocation

Fata Morgana
Goddess of Fate
Draw back the Veil and step forth from your shadowed lands
Raven-haired Goddess picking at the loom
Weaving the threads of life
Cutting the cord at life's end
Keening, shedding crimson tears
As you wash the shrouds of the dead
As a Phantom you guide the soul in its journey across the Veil
And take us into your cauldron womb to be reborn
Goddess of the shadowed realms
Phantom Queen
Come tarry here with me
Teach me the wisdom in death and decay,
And the mysteries of creation and rebirth!

Crow and Crone Invocation

(If working with a group, the coven members can repeat the refrain "Crone Goddess, Crow Goddess.")

Morrigan, Queen of the Sidhe
Crone Goddess, Crow Goddess

Morrigan, I call thee from Avalon's fair shores
Crone Goddess, Crow Goddess

Morrigan, mistress of battle
Crone Goddess, Crow Goddess

Morrigan, chooser of the slain
Life's beginning and its end
Crone Goddess, Crow Goddess

Morrigan, enchantress
Weaver of fate
Crone Goddess, Crow Goddess

Your battle cry stills the hearts of men
Crone Goddess, Crow Goddess

Morrigan, Crone Goddess
Morrigan, Crow Goddess

Phantom Queen Incense

1 tbsp. juniper berries
2 tbsp. cypress
2 tbsp. rosemary
1 tbsp. comfrey

14
Mistress of Magick

Morrigan out of the cave of Cruachu ... chanted over her ... every spell of power; she was full of guile.
—*Edward Gwynn,* The Metrical Dindshenchas

You find yourself on a barge moving across a placid lake. It is quiet save for the sound of the barge as it glides through the still lake waters. A heavy mist hangs over the water, and you are uncertain how the bargeman knows where he is going. Just as you are about to ask him if he is lost, the mist breaks and you see before you a lush green island more beautiful than you could have imagined. Green slopes are covered with apple trees, heavy with ripe fruit. Everything is green and growing, and the isle seems to glow with a soft otherworldly light. You know why men have called this place the Fortunate Isle and why those who live here are thought to be immortal.

The barge glides to the shore and you step out. Your arrival has not gone unnoticed, and a small procession of women walks toward you. They are all very beautiful, like the isle, and they seem to have an otherworldly glow about them. All eight women have similar features and the same raven-black hair, and you realize they must be sisters. The closest one steps forward and greets you. "Greetings, traveler. I am Gliton, and these are my sisters Moronoe, Mazoe, Gliten, Glitonea, Cliton, Tyronoe, and Thiten." Each woman nods in your direction as her name is spoken. "We welcome you to Avalon, the Land of Women, that some call the Fortunate Isle."

You greet her in return and tell her you have come seeking their sister, the Mistress of Magick, Morgan le Fay. Gliton nods. "Many come seeking her. She is upon the Tor. We will take you there, but be warned: if you seek our sister's wisdom, you may be tested along the way."

The sisters lead you through the greenery of Avalon, stopping among the trees of an orchard to gather large ripe apples. The sisters chat merrily with you and sing along the way to the Tor. Soon you see the rise of the Tor and the spiraling processional way that has been carved into the ground around it in the distance. One does not simply walk up the Tor, but must take the serpentine path that circles up and around it.

Gliton tells you that the rest of your journey must be alone, and the sisters leave, wishing you well. Alone you begin walking the processional way, certain you will quickly reach the top. But soon you come to a part of the processional way that is blocked. Large pillars of stone a little taller than you block your progress. Expecting a challenge, you have brought with you magickal tools—strapped to your back is a golden sword and at your side a willow wand. You draw the magickal sword and confidently approach the stones. Raising the sword above your head you strike the pillars, but they do not crumble as you expected. They remain completely unmarked. You try again without results. You decide to go around the pillars but as soon as the thought crosses your mind, a heavy mist forms and covers either side of the path. If you step off the path now, you are certain to lose your way.

Realizing you are getting nowhere with the magickal sword, you put it on the ground. Taking a deep breath, you ground and center. You raise your hands and summon the powers of earth, willing the stones to break apart. You feel the elemental power of earth flowing up through your body. In your mind's eye you see your desire and will it into existence, making it take form in the fabric of the universe. You feel the energy peak, then settle into the material world. Hearing the stones begin to crack, you open your eyes to see them crumbling to dust.

You step over the powdered remains of the stones and continue on. The path is clear, but the mist still hangs heavy. You continue on, making your way almost halfway up the hill. Just when you think you will make it to the top of the Tor, something streaks across the sky and lands a few feet ahead of you. Then another and another fall in a long arc around you. They look like tiny meteors of red and orange flame. When the objects hit the ground, they continue to burn. Immediately you reach for your willow wand and make a long arching motion to create a magickal barrier of protection. You continue forward but another meteor flies past your face, through the protective shield and much too close for comfort. The meteors begin to fall much faster now. Quickly you put the wand on the ground and hold your hands in the air. Again you call upon the elements, this time air, drawing its energy to you and willing the meteors to be blown away. When you open your eyes, the path is clear and nothing else falls from the sky.

You continue on and soon reach the end of the path. The mist thickens and you feel like you are floating in a sea of clouds rather than standing high upon the Tor of Avalon. With no more magickal tools, you realize the only thing you needed this whole time to wield magick was yourself. You close your eyes and draw on the elemental power of fire. You will the mist to clear, seeing the fire draw the moisture from the air. When you open your eyes, the mist is completely gone. In the center of the Tor stands a woman. She wears robes of red and purple, and the braids in her hair are decorated with crystals and raven feathers. At her feet is a large copper cauldron and you know you have found the chief of the sisters of Avalon, Morgan le Fay.

"I have been called Morrigan, Modron, Morgan le Fay, Sorceress, Witch, and Enchantress. I have wielded my magick upon battlefields of mist, woven charms of healing, spun spells of destruction and creation. I know the secrets of the earth, herbs used to curse or cure. I shift shape, flying across the land as a raven or crow. The secrets of magick are mine, but I tell you this: magick is nothing without the Will to wield it. Sometimes we forget the greatest power dwells within us. We rely on props and tools, when the power of Will is what gives life and form to magick. Your sword and your wand could not aid you on your journey, only your Will brought you here."

She gestures for you to come closer and places a hand on your shoulder. The instant she touches you, the world around you changes. Everything becomes woven of brilliant threads of glistening light. You can still see the outline of the Tor, the cauldron at your feet, and Morgan le Fay, but they are made of woven threads of energy. You realize you are seeing the world as Morgan le Fay does.

"My magick had always been woven of the elements. When concealing myself from enemies in a shroud of mist, I draw upon water. Through earth I raised the pillars of battle so the Fir Bolgs could not flee the swords of the Túatha De Danann. I have called upon air to soar as the raven above the din of battle. I have called upon showers of blood and fire to hinder my enemies. I have changed my companions into the stones of the earth to hide them from those who foolishly pursued us. All things are made of the elements of life. Woven in these threads are fire, water, earth, and air. All these things form the fabric of the physical world, pull a thread, reweave it, shape it into another pattern, and the design is altered to your Will."

She reaches out with her other hand and pulls a glowing thread from her other arm. You watch as smooth flesh changes to feathers, then transforms back to human flesh once again. "The Witch weaves and unweaves, shapes and bends the world around her. Magick is not wielded by magick swords or wands, they are extensions of yourself. The real magick lives within you."

With these words she and the Tor vanish, and you find yourself back in your body.

Whether it is used for shape-shifting, casting spells to curse, or healing others, magick is at the heart of all the Morrigan's myths. She is a sorceress, the patroness of Witches, and an enchantress using her magick to reshape the world around her. From her incarnation as a goddess to her later appearance in folklore as Morgan le Fay, her connection to magick remains central to her mythology. As the Morrigan, she used spells to bring victory in battle; as Morgan le Fay, she could weave enchantments to heal or cause mayhem.

Whether it is for transformation or warfare, the Morrigan's magick manifests through the elements of nature. As an earth goddess it seems fitting for her magick to draw upon the elements that make up the natural realm that she holds sway over. In *The First Battle of Moytura* she traps the Fir Bolgs by summoning showers of fire and blood-colored rain (fire and water). She sings spells over Odras, transforming her into a river (water). During the final battle between the Túatha Dé Danann and the Fir Bolgs, she used pillars of stone (earth) to mark the battlefield, preventing anyone from deserting. Her battle cry (air) kills Cúchulain's enemies and fuels the hero's battle frenzy. Like a Witch calling upon the elements within sacred space, the Morrigan draws on the elements that form all life to weave her magick, bending and shaping these creative forces to give form to her will.

As a goddess the Morrigan's magick is related to warfare, but as Morgan le Fay her magick fills a different role. As a sorceress she is the ultimate woman of power, controlling the forces of nature and shaping reality to her will, yet more often than not she is vilified for her use of magick. Merlin, a male who commands powerful magick, is connected to knowledge and wisdom. Morgan, on the other hand, is seen as wild and out of control, simply because it was taboo for women to hold such power. Despite this, Morgan le Fay has become a sort of trickster goddess within the Arthurian saga. Using cunning and illusions to test the valor of Arthur's knights, she has evolved into a figure akin to Coyote, the Native American Trickster, causing mischief in service to the greater good. She tests Sir Gawain's honor by sending the Green Knight to challenge him, and imprisons Lancelot in her castle to test his devotion to Guinevere.

In *Sir Gawain and the Green Knight,* Morgan le Fay sends the Green Knight to Arthur's court to test the courage of his knights. He challenges Arthur's knights to behead him, but only on the condition that he may return in a year and a day to behead the knight in turn. Gawain agrees, not expecting the knight to be able to hold him to the bargain. To everyone's astonishment, after being beheaded by Gawain the Green

Knight promptly picks up his head and leaves the court very much alive! Gawain then embarks on a quest to find the Green Knight and keep his end of the bargain. Along the way Gawain is given a magickal girdle that prevents the Green Knight from beheading him. At the end of the story, the Green Knight reveals that the whole encounter was instigated by Morgan le Fay as a means to test the worthiness of Arthur's knights. She uses her magick both to test Gawain, through the Green Knight, and to save the knight's life by giving him the means to survive an impossible task. Through illusions and deceptions she assesses the knight's worthiness.

In the *Vita Merlini,* Morgan le Fay's magick is primarily used for healing. She was said to know the use of all healing herbs and plants, as well as have the ability to change shape. When Arthur is mortally wounded, Morgan le Fay brings him to Avalon to be healed. "There nine sisters rule by a pleasing set of laws those who come to them from our country. She who is first of them is more skilled in the healing arts, and excels her sister in the beauty of her person. Morgan is her name, and she has learned what useful properties all the herbs contain, so that she can cure sick bodies. She also knows an art by which to change her shape, and to cleave the air on new wings like Daedalus... and when she will she slips down from the air onto your shores."[106] Although her magick can cause chaos and is used to challenge heroes, it brings balance and comfort when used for healing.

According to Malory's *Le Morte d' Arthur,* Morgan was trained to use her magick in a nunnery. "Morgan le Fay was put to school in a nunnery, and there she learned so much that she was a great clerk of necromancy."[107] A Christian nunnery is a rather odd place for Morgan le Fay to learn magick. The mention of necromancy also seems out of place. While Morgan's magick does cause strife in Arthur's court, there is never any mention of her using it to raise the dead. Indicating necromancy as her particular form of magick may instead point to her original functions as a goddess. *Necromancy* comes from the Greek (nekrós), meaning "dead," and μ (manteía), meaning "divination." The term originally indicated the art of calling on spirits or ancestors to divine the future. It wasn't until the Renaissance that necromancy became associated with black magick and raising corpses. Taking into consideration the original meaning of *necromancy* and that Morrigan the goddess is associated with both the art of prophecy and gathering the dead, Morgan le Fay's connection with necromancy begins to make sense. When demoted to a mortal woman, she retained abilities similar to the

106. Parry, *Vita Merlini,* p. 28.
107. Malory, *Le Morte d' Arthur,* p. 8.

goddess. While she does not care for the dead, she instead calls upon them to predict the future.

The Morrigan uses her magick to heal, instigate change, and create balance. She challenges both the Túatha Dé Danann and Arthur's knights. When she forces the Túatha Dé Danann to fight the Fir Bolgs, she compels them to face their enemies in order to inherit Ireland. She forces Gawain to keep his word, even when it could cause his own death, and to grow from his experiences during his quest. When Arthur lies dying she brings him to her magickal isle, promising to heal him with her magick. As the enchantress, the Mistress of Magick, she is a force of transformation and change. She wields the power of the elements and uses her magick to shape the world around her.

Embracing the Inner Witch

Morgan le Fay is synonymous with enchantment and magick. She is the ultimate Witch, Sorceress, and Wise Woman. She teaches us to embrace our inner "Witchy" nature. She dares us to take action and step into an active role in our destinies rather than letting others control us. When we embrace the Sorceress archetype, we embrace our ability to shape and control our lives and tap into our own innate magick.

As the Mistress of Magick, the Morrigan teaches us that magick is everywhere. It is not something relegated solely to full moon rituals, Sabbats, and Esbats. This is partly for practical reasons: we don't always have access to our sacred space or have time to cast a circle when we need to create magick. I've cast spells while waiting in line at the bank, looking for a parking spot, and at work. Ultimately the most important magickal tool is yourself, and this is the Morrigan's lesson. I'm not saying to go throw away your wand or any of your magickal tools, only that they are just that—*tools*, vessels for your own magickal power. A magick sword does not power and create a spell—you do. Your tools simply channel your own innate magickal energy.

Embracing the Inner Witch Spell

The first step to embracing your magickal nature is to feel magickal! For this spell you will need something that makes you feel especially "Witchy." This could be jewelry, clothes, or even makeup. Ideally it should be something you can wear. Take the object or objects to your sacred space. If you wish cast a circle, but it is not necessary. Burn your favorite incense and pass the object through the smoke, saying:

Morrigan, patroness and Queen of Witches
Weaving the elements one by one into a spell of power
Whispering enchantments to the wind
Sorceress, Witch, Mistress of Magick, I feel your call
I bless this _________ in the name of the Morrigan
That it may help me embrace the power of my inner Witch

Change into the clothes, apply your makeup, or put on the jewelry you have selected. Close your eyes and see the Morrigan in her guise as the Mistress of Magick standing before you. Maybe she appears as the sorceress Morgan le Fay or in triple form leaning over a cauldron whispering a spell. See her form and your own merge, filling you with the power of the Queen of Witches. Chant:

Whenever I wear this _________
I will be filled with the power of the Queen of Witches
And embrace my magickal nature
Whether I am in the mundane world
Or between the worlds within a magick circle
I am a Witch
I shape and bend my reality
I forge my life's path through my will
I am one with air, fire, water, earth, and all the forces of nature
My life is filled with magick, enchantment, and mystery!

When you are ready thank the Morrigan for her blessing. Wear the object you have blessed whenever you need to feel magickal.

Connecting to the Elements

The Morrigan's connection to the elements is clear through her magick. She can harness air, fire, water, and earth to manifest her will. Part of connecting to the Morrigan as the Mistress of Magick is working with the elements. For this exercise, take a week (or longer, if you wish) to connect and work with each element. In your journal create a heading for each element and write down your experiences or simply what each element means to you throughout the week. For example, if you are working with the element of earth, try to spend some time outside that week. Visit a park, plant some flowers or herbs. Keep in mind the gifts each element gives you in both your mundane and magickal lives. The earth gives us sustenance, a place to live, and raw materials to create our homes, buildings, and roads.

Spend a few minutes meditating on the element you are working with each day. The following affirmations can be used prior to meditating or as a daily devotion to help you connect to each element.

Earth Affirmation:

Hold a stone or crystal in your hand, or stand outside with your bare feet on the ground and say:

I am one with the element of earth
I am stable, strong, and filled with prosperity

Air Affirmation:

Take a deep breath and slowly release it, then say:

I am one with the element of air
I am filled with inspiration and creativity

Fire Affirmation:

Light a candle or take a moment to sit where the light of the sun can warm your body and say:

I am one with the element of fire
My inner flame burns bright
I bring my passions and dreams into reality

Water Affirmation:

Turn on the faucet in your kitchen or bathroom and let the water run over your hands for a few moments, or make a cup of your favorite tea and drink it slowly, then say:

I am one with the element of water
I am filled with compassion, healing, and intuition.

Magick without Props

For this exercise you will need a quiet place where you will not be disturbed. Decide beforehand what it is you wish to manifest. You could be drawing love into your life or prosperity—as long as you have a clear goal in mind, it can be whatever you want. You will be casting a circle, calling the elements, and casting a spell to manifest your desire. The catch? You won't be using any tools except yourself. The point of the exercise is to become more familiar with the energy that fuels your magick. The more aware you are of energy and how to shape it to your desire, the more effective your magick will be.

Ground and center. When you are ready, cast the circle by pointing the index finger on your dominant hand (the one you write with) at the ground and visualizing pure white energy flowing from your hand to form the boundary of the circle. When you are done, take a minute to clearly see the circle in your mind's eye. You do not have to say anything to confirm that the circle is cast. (This whole exercise does not require any chants at all, only your own force of will and the power of visualization.)

When you are ready, go to each quarter, hold your arms crossed over your chest, then slowly open them to an invoking position. As you do so, visualize the power of each element filling you and the circle. I usually visualize each element as a vortex of power that flows from each quarter. When you have called all four elements, stand in the center of the circle. See the energy from the quarters flow from each direction to meet and meld together in the circle's center to form the element of spirit. Raise your hands, with your palms up, as if you are holding the energy between your hands. In your mind's eye, shape the energy into your desired goal. See your goal manifesting, becoming a part of reality. Your ability to visualize what you want to manifest is essential here, as that is what shapes and fuels your magick. Take as much time as you need, until you have a clear image of what you wish to manifest in your mind.

When you are ready, begin to lower your hands, seeing the energy you have raised move slowly down as well, until you touch the floor. Visualize your desired goal moving from the ethereal realm down into the physical realm. See the energy merging with the fabric of the material plane, manifesting and becoming a part of reality.

Return to the four quarters. To close them, hold your arms in an invoking position and then slowly close your arms until they are crossed against your chest. Visualize the element departing from the circle. Finally, walk counterclockwise around the circle, pointing your index finger at the circle's boundary. See the energy returning to you and opening the circle.

Casting a Crystal Circle

Crystals are excellent sources of energy. Most likely you have already used crystals during spellwork, but they can also be used to cast and raise energy within a circle. To cast a crystal circle, lay six to nine crystals on the ground along the boundary of your ritual circle. If you wish to use candles to mark the cardinal directions, place crystals in between the candles. Some healers use a similar procedure when using crystals for healing. The person being healed lies down and crystals are placed on their chakras and then stones are placed a few inches away from the person's head, feet, shoulders, and hips, essentially encircling them with crystals to raise their energy vibrations. Instead of raising the energies of a particular individual, you are raising the energy vibrations within your circle.

Ideally you should use several of the same type of crystal to outline the boundaries of the circle rather than many different ones. For general ritual work, use clear quartz. For rituals involving the Morrigan or during the new moon, use obsidian. For rituals during the full moon, moonstone would be ideal.

Before using the crystals, soak them in a mixture of salt and water to get rid of any negative vibrations. When you cast the circle, visualize a white light connecting the crystals to form a circle of brilliant energy.

Mistress of Magick Ritual

This ritual can be used when calling on the Morrigan for any kind of spellwork or when working with her in her guise as the Mistress of Magick.

You Will Need:
1 black or purple candle
Cauldron
Sword or athame
Mistress of Magick Incense (see page 302)

Place the candle in the cauldron, then put the cauldron in the center of your altar. The cauldron is one of the quintessential symbols of the Witch, representing the womb of the Great Goddess and the act of creation. For this ritual, it will symbolize your ability to create and transform the world around you through your magick.

Cast the circle with your sword or athame, saying:

I cast this circle of magick in the name of the Morrigan
Great sorceress of the Túatha De Danann
That it may be a boundary between the worlds
A place of power, magick and mystery
In the name of the Queen of Witches, this circle is sealed!

Light the incense. Carry the incense clockwise around the circle to bless the area. Then return to the altar and waft the smoke over your body. When you are ready, go to each quarter, saying:

East:
Crow Goddess
Sorceress and Shape-Shifter
Milky skin changing to black feathers
Weave your magick here with me this night!

South:
Cunning sorceress of the Tribe of Danu
On the battlefield you wove your charms and sang your spells

Bringing victory, fueling the heat of battle
Weave your magick here with me this night!

West:
Otherworldly One
Stirring your mist-filled cauldron
Queen of Witches, Lady of Night
Who walks between the worlds
Weave your magick here with me this night!

North:
Lady of the Holy Isle
Skilled healer, cunning Witch
Who knows the use of all the herbs of the earth
Weave your magick here with me this night!

Light the candle inside the cauldron, saying:

Queen of Witches
Sorceress
Lady of Magick and Witchery
You are the Morrigú
Laughing with abandon, weaving the threads of magick
Amongst the clash of swords and the rattle of chariots
And you are Morgan le Fay
Priestess, Witch, and Enchantress of the Sacred Isle
Changing your shape,
Weaving charms of healing from the herbs of the earth
Escorting kings to your mist-filled realm
And you are Badb of the cauldron
Stirring your Otherworldly brew like a Witch stirs her cauldron
You claim the power within
You are the mistress of your own world
Shaping the patterns of your life through your Will
Lady of Magick, Queen of Witches
Let my hands weave your magick
Let my voice be your own
Let my will be one with yours
That all I will shall come to be!

Visualize the Morrigan (or Morgan le Fay, if you prefer) standing before you. Take a moment to clearly see her form, then see her merge with your own. Feel the power of the Queen of Witches filling you. Perform any planned pathworking or spellwork. When you are ready, thank the Morrigan and extinguish the candle. Close the quarters by saying:

Depart in peace, Queen of Witches
and powers of air/fire/water/earth

Cut the circle with your sword or athame, saying:

The circle of the Morrigan is now open
but her power and magick ever remain a part of me

Magickal Tool Blessing

Over time you may acquire ritual tools that you will only use for rituals and spells involving the Morrigan. These tools should be set aside from your other magickal tools or placed on the Morrigan's altar when not being used. These tools should be blessed and consecrated before you use them.

You Will Need:
Sage incense
Dragon's blood oil

Sit in front of your altar and take a few deep breaths. See the Morrigan standing before you and visualize her energy filling you. When you are ready, light the incense and pass the tool being blessed through the smoke, saying:

In the Morrigan's name I bless this _________
My ally in magick and an extension
Of my own magickal energies
May the Morrigan's blessings and strength
Flow through it and me whenever I use it
So mote it be!

Hold the tool in your hands. See the Morrigan's energies filling the tool. When you are ready, anoint the tool with the oil and leave it on the Morrigan's altar (or at the foot of the altar if it is too large to fit on the altar) overnight.

Nine Morgans Invocation

The following invocation calls upon the nine sisters Geoffrey of Monmouth attributed to the Isle of Avalon. We can see these sisters as representations of the Morrigan's many aspects, all containing a part of a single goddess. Call upon the sisters of Avalon to strengthen your magick, for any type of earth magick, and to charge herbs.

Nine Morgans
Sisters, Healers, Fates
Morgan le Fay, Moronoe, Mazoe, Gliten, Glitonea,
Cliton, Gliton, Tyronoe, and Thiten

Nine Morgans
Ladies of Avalon
Keepers of the Holy Isle
Mistresses of all magickal arts
Morgan le Fay, Moronoe, Mazoe, Gliten, Glitonea,
Cliton, Gliton, Tyronoe, and Thiten

Nine Morgans
Who know all the secrets of the herbs and plants
Who can change shape, flying on the wings of a raven
Morgan le Fay, Moronoe, Mazoe, Gliten, Glitonea,
Cliton, Gliton, Tyronoe, and Thiten

Nine Morgans who stand upon the Holy Isle
Nine sisters, Nine healers, Nine fates
Goddesses of magick and mystery
Guardians of the Fortunate Isle
Guide me toward your wisdom

Bless me with your healing touch
Fill me with your might and strength
Morgan le Fay, Moronoe, Mazoe, Gliten, Glitonea,
Cliton, Gliton, Tyronoe, and Thiten

Morgan le Fay's Shield

You Will Need:
Marker and construction paper
Incense burner and incense charcoal
Angelica root
Dragon's blood resin
Rue
Lavender
Bay leaves

For this spell you will be creating a talisman or shield to protect your home. On a piece of construction paper draw a shield with a pentagram within it. You may also wish to incorporate other symbols or runes of protection into the design as well. In your sacred space put a pinch of each herb listed on an incense burner. Pass the shield in a clockwise motion over the smoke while saying:

Angelica to guard against evil
Dragon's blood for strength and protection
Rue to banish
Lavender to cleanse
Bay for victory!

I call upon thee Morgan le Fay
Lady of Avalon
Mistress of the Sidhe
Bless this shield with your power
That it may deflect from me all harm
A magickal barrier of strength
Of protection
Of will
That none of ill intent may pass!

Hold the shield above the altar. Visualize Morgan le Fay standing in front of you. She reaches out and touches the shield, and it pulses with a brilliant white light. Visualize the shield creating a barrier around your home that only those who wish you well may pass through. Hold the image in your mind, and say:

In Morgan's name, so mote it be!

Place the shield by your front door or under your welcome mat.

Morgan le Fay Poppet Spell

For this spell you will need a poppet to represent the person being healed. A poppet can be as simple as a paper cutout of a person or can be made from fabric and stuffed with healing herbs. In a pinch, a picture of a person can be used in place of a healing poppet.

You Will Need:
Angelica incense or an incense of your choice
1 small bowl of water
1 red candle
1 bowl of earth (large enough to place the poppet in)
1 poppet or picture of the person being healed

Go to your sacred space. Cast a circle if you wish. On your altar arrange the incense, bowl of water, candle, and bowl of earth to correspond with each of the four directions. When you are ready, invoke Morgan le Fay by saying the following:

Morgan le Fay
Lady of the Holy Isle
Chief among your sisters
Wise in the ways of healing
Add your blessing to this spell!

Hold the poppet in your hand and visualize the person you wish to heal merging with the image of the poppet, while you say the following three times:

Though you were separate
Now you are one, (person's name)

Move the poppet through the incense. Visualize the power of air moving through the person, blowing away the illness while you say:

I call upon the power of air
To sweep away all illness and pain from _________

Pass the poppet over the candle, visualizing the fire burning away the illness and restoring strength and vitality to the person's body while you say:

I call upon the power of fire
To burn away all illness and pain from _________

Sprinkle some water over the poppet, visualizing the water washing away the illness and cleansing the body while you say:

I call upon the power of water
To wash away all illness and pain from _________

Place the poppet in the bowl of earth and visualize the illness passing from the person's body and into the earth while you say:

I call upon the power of earth
To stabilize and give strength to _________

Keep the poppet in a safe place, or give it to the person being healed.

Mistress of Magick Invocation

Use this invocation to call upon the Morrigan in her guise as the sorceress Morgan le Fay.

Queen of Witches weaving your spells
Faery woman of shadow-filled lands
Black-winged enchantress
Summoning phantoms and magickal mist
Bringing strength, conjuring victory

Wise woman whispering your charms to the wind
Wild sorceress enticing kings and noble knights
Raven-haired Morrigu, Morgan of the faeries
Goddess of Witches, Queen of Night
From the Otherworlds give my magick form and shape
Breathe life into my spell
Lend your power to my work!

Mistress of Magick Incense

This incense can be burned to honor the Morrigan as the Mistress of Magick and Queen of Witches. Dragon's blood in particular is known for adding energy to magickal workings, and this incense can also be burned to add power to any kind of spellwork.

2 tbsp. dragon's blood resin
1 tbsp. myrrh
½ tbsp. hawthorn berries
½ tbsp. vervain
½ tbsp. mullein

Morrigan House Cleansing

Our homes accumulate the energy of those who live there. Stress, emotional upheaval, and arguments leave negative energy behind that needs to be routinely cleansed. Your sacred space or any area where you routinely perform spellwork should also be cleansed on a monthly basis.

You Will Need:
Glass bowl
Filtered water
Rosemary
Rue

To banish negative energy from your home or ritual space, fill a large glass bowl with filtered water. Place equal parts rosemary and rue in the water and allow it to sit for an hour, preferably in a sunny area. (*Caution: Do not drink the water or ingest the rue, as it is poisonous.*) Walk clockwise around the rooms in your home or your sacred space. Use your fingers to sprinkle the water around the room while saying:

Lady of the Sidhe
Lady of the faery mound
Cleanse and bless this space
In the Morrigan's name, so mote it be!

15
Lover

She is the Raven and she is the Dove
The ecstasy of battle and of love.
—*Diana L. Paxton,* Ravens of Avalon

It is the night of Beltane. In the sky above, stars glisten through a cloudless sky. A warm breeze blows across you, bringing with it the scent of wildflowers. In the distance you see a massive balefire lit atop a grass-covered mound. People dance around the fire and you long to join them.

You make your way to the mound, taking a spiral path to its top. You find others are joining the celebration. Men and women shed their clothes and dance with abandon, their naked bodies moving in time to the beat of a drum. Their dancing mesmerizes you; it is sensual and filled with a joyful abandon and a lust for life. You want to join the dance, but something holds you back and you stand along the edge of the revelries just watching. Nearest the balefire two masked figures dance with one another. A tall regal woman wears a mask adorned with flowers and bright feathers. Red spirals are painted along her bare arms and stomach, and twisting painted serpents coil around her shapely legs. The man next to her wears a mask adorned with leaves and ivy vines, with two antlers sprouting from each side. They dance closer to one another than the rest, their bodies moving in sensual tandem, their thrusts mimicking lovemaking. But what captures your attention is the look of absolute adoration and love that fills their eyes. The love and lust that fills their dance makes them glow with joy and the promise of passion, and you know you are gazing upon the Great Goddess and God, and that the love you see in them birthed all that exists in the world. As you watch the lovers, the woman turns to you. She smiles, whispers something to the God, then walks toward you.

"Here we celebrate the dance of life, the ecstasy and passion that renews the soul and ushers in new life. All that lives is a part of the dance." You tell her you wish to join the dance,

but still are unable to move. She seems to understand and takes your hand. "At times we lose sight of our passions; we give up on our dreams and ourselves. The inner fires become banked, cooling to mere embers. It is then that we must seek the Lover and stoke the fires of our inner passion. To do this we must shed that which has suffocated our inner fires and let our fires consume the old to leave us purified. Before you can join the dance, you must seek purification."

The woman leads you to the far side of the mound, away from the fires and dancers and into a small cluster of trees. In the center of the small grove there is a well, full to the brim, almost overflowing with water that reflects the golden-red lights of the nearby balefire. Sitting on the edge of the well is a large chalice made of hammered gold, etched with intricate spirals and knotwork.

"To drink from the Cup of Truth, you must shed the masks that you have built around your spirit. The power of the Lover is in connection, the bonds forged between lovers, the love shared between family and friends, our connections to the Divine that exists both within and outside of ourselves. The Lover is the ecstasy and joy we feel when we become one with the mysteries, and when we gaze upon and love our true selves. The Lover brings all things together, weaving the web of life."

She comes closer to you and lifts the flower mask from her face. She radiates with an inner golden glow, her spirit shining from within brighter than any balefire. She puts the mask back on and gestures for you to approach the well.

You can see a worn path around the well's base and instinctively follow it, walking in a sunwise circle around the well. As you do so, you lift your shirt and toss it aside. You circle the well three full times, removing articles of clothes as you go until you stand before the well naked and unmasked.

Leaning over the waters you gaze into the well, and the face and form that reflect back to you, although familiar, are not that of your physical body. It is your True Self. You take a few silent moments to study the image.

"In the guise of the Lover, I guard the secrets of the True Self. As you must seek me both within and without, so too must you direct your love toward yourself before your desires and passions can be fulfilled with another. I am the Great Queen, regal and assured in her self-confidence. I am a lover's passionate caress. I have been called the Maiden, the Lover, the divine whore. I am passion and love, desire at its most sacred. It is to me that you call out when lost in the ecstasy of a lover's embrace. Joy, laughter, wild abandon, and inspiration are all mine. My temple is the flesh, my offering a loving caress, a love-filled gaze, a knowing smile. But know you must love yourself before you can fulfill your dreams and desires. I am the deep

and abiding love that dwells in the heart, I am sudden inspiration, the conception of new ideas and new life."

She dips the chalice into the well and offers its cool liquid to you. As you drink the sacred water, you feel your body, mind, and spirit come alive, your inner fires and passions reigniting. You feel as if you could accomplish anything; your dreams and goals seem more attainable than ever. You feel alive with a fire and joy for all life.

The drumming seems louder now and you become aware once again of the joyous dance around the balefire. Smiling, both you and the Great Goddess join the dance. This time you do not hesitate, and your body moves and sways to the pulse of the drum. As you dance, you feel filled with all the joy and ecstasy life has to offer.

The Morrigan flies cross the pages of Celtic mythology like a fierce whirlwind, uncontrollable and untamable, shape-shifting from myth to myth, changing the tides of battle, choosing who would live and who would die and who would share her bed.

Her love affairs and sexuality are a potent part of her personality. Who would have triumphed in the *Táin* if she had not lusted after Cúchulain? If she had not lain with Dagda, would the Túatha Dé Danann have defeated the Fir Bolgs? The Morrigan's passions are not simply feelings of lust, but instead become a powerful creative force within her stories. Her passion can change the outcome of battles or summon prophetic vision in the throes of ecstasy. As a woman in control of her own personal power, she channels this force just as surely as she channels her magickal energies.

Female sexuality is often seen in a negative light. Women who take several lovers are "sluts," while men who do the same are "studs." Even in our modern world there are still countries that allow the mutilation of female genitalia, believing that if a woman cannot feel pleasure during sex, she will be a faithful wife. All of these practices revolve around curbing and suppressing a woman's sex drive, either through physical mutilation or social ridicule. The need to suppress these urges indicates that we feel such forces are uncontrollable and unclean. There are many reasons why a culture that gives males a higher social standing would want to suppress such emotions. Being in control of one's sexuality—and, in turn, of one's body—is empowering and gives women (and men) a sense of control over their lives. Losing that sense of personal power is akin to losing control over one's life.

The attempt to control female sexuality can also be seen as an attempt to control the power of creation, something that is inherently female. Sexuality is closely linked to the power of creation and procreation. If females were not sexual beings, there would be no new generations to replace the old, no new life or the capacity for rebirth; the wheel of life would come to a grinding halt. By attempting to control women's sexuality and their bodies, men have tried to claim the power of creation—and the power of the Goddess—for themselves.

While many other Celtic goddesses take numerous lovers and participate in illicit affairs, the Morrigan's sexuality is often described as uncontrolled, her sexual appetite "sexual gratification for its own sake."[108] While the Morrigan takes both gods and mortal men as lovers (and has several different husbands depending on the aspect she appears in), her sexuality is no different or perverse than her contemporaries'. Her sexuality only appears out of control by the standards of a patriarchal culture. The intentional vilification of this part of her personality reflects the differing religious mores between the Celtic Pagans and their Christianized descendants, rather than a sinister aspect to the Morrigan's nature.

As we discussed in the Goddess of Sovereignty chapter, kings ritualistically gained the right to rule through a sexual union with the goddess of the land. When the king became too weak to rule or unworthy, the goddess could choose another man to take his place, usually a younger/stronger version of the old king. In the realm of mythology these two kings, younger and older, are really the same person, but if we view these stories as literal fact, they lose their original significance and become love triangles created by unfaithful women. The image of the sovereign goddess eventually became debased into that of a wanton adulterous woman. With their connection to sovereignty and the land severed, their escapades became stories of uncontrollable sexual urges. The Morrigan's right to choose her lovers went against the new social morals of Christianity, where a woman's body and sexuality was not her own but the property of her husband. An independent woman in control of her body was a dangerous and immoral archetype, and stories once pertaining to sovereignty and conferring the right of kingship were twisted into moral lessons against giving in to the urges of the body, making the story work with the morals of the new religion.

The Morrigan is mentioned as the wife of several gods, depending on which of her faces she is wearing. In her unified form as the Morrigan or Morrigu, she is

108. Blamires, *Magic of the Celtic Otherworld,* p. 160.

coupled with Dagda and is named as his wife in the *Dindshenchas*. Dagda, a god of fertility and plenty, complements the Morrigan's darker connections to death and destruction. Dagda possessed a club that killed with one end, while the other could bring a warrior back to life, showing a duel nature similar to the Morrigan's. Their union at Samhain is a joining of opposite forces, of life and death. Here her sexuality is a reaffirmation of life. Their sexual union symbolically ensured the continued fertility of the clan, crops, and livestock for the coming year. While Samhain was a festival to honor the dead, women called on their deceased loved ones to enter their wombs to be reborn into the clan during this festival, honoring the close connection between death and rebirth. The Morrigan's sexuality and ability to bring forth life balances the darker aspects she embodies. According to Moyra Caldecott, "Her twin appetites for sexual gratification and for bringing about violent death are a travesty of the very necessary and natural forces of creation and destruction that keep the universe functioning, an imbalance of which brings about disaster."[109]

As Badb and Nemain, the Morrigan is the wife of Neit. There is very little known about Neit, other than that he is a god of war. *Cormac's Glossary* describes them as a "venomous" pair. As Anu and Danu, she is paired with the god Bile, also a god of the Underworld. When she appears in her lighter aspects as a mother goddess, such as Anu and Danu, she is paired with gods representing her polar opposite, just as Dagda (a god of fertility) is paired with the Morrigan in her darker aspect as a goddess of death.

Rather than allowing the men in her life to pursue her, the Morrigan initiates relationships with her lovers. This can clearly be seen in her interactions with Cúchulain. While Cúchulain never becomes her lover, she tries to seduce him, not the other way around. As Macha the faery, she simply appears in Crunnchu's house one day and takes over all the household duties—including warming his bed—as if she had always been there. Although Crunnchu is more than pleased with her rather bizarre entrance into his life, Macha doesn't exactly give him a choice about their union. She just shows up and takes over. While he does not spurn her as Cúchulain does, his boasts about his wife's abilities lead to the end of their union and her death. Like most stories about faeries who marry mortal men, the union is dissolved if the mortal partner committed a certain taboo, in this case boasting about his wife's abilities when he was warned against such actions. This taboo is similar to the geis kings and

109. Condren, *The Serpent and the Goddess*, p. 35.

heroes were bound to, which ended their reign or caused their death when broken. Since Crunnchu broke his word, Macha's death may be symbolic of her returning to the Faery Realm.

As the Faery Queen Áine, we find a similar theme in her mortal love affairs. When Áine took the Earl of Desmond as her husband, she made him promise to never be surprised by anything the children she bore him could do. They lived happily for a time until the day their son displayed his Otherworldly nature by shrinking and jumping in and out of a bottle. The earl gasped with surprise, breaking his promise, and Áine and their son turned into birds and flew away. As in Macha's tale, Áine's relationship starts and ends on her own terms. She is not bound to remain with an unworthy man, but free to leave and dissolve the union when she desires. Áine had several other lovers, including the hero Finn mac Cool, and because of her large sexual appetite, she eventually became known as one of the Leanan Sidhe. The Leanan Sidhe, or Faery Lover, was somewhat akin to a sexual vampire. While they granted their lovers the gift of inspiration, their sexual unions drained the men of their life essence, eventually killing them. Again we see a woman's sexuality being described as dangerous, even deadly, when not held in check.

In the *Vita Merlini,* Morgan le Fay and three other queens happened upon Lancelot as he slept under an apple tree. The four women saw how handsome the knight was and immediately began to argue over who would take him as their lover. Unable to come to an agreement, Morgan cast a spell over Lancelot so he would not wake, and they carried him off to Morgan's castle. The queens imprisoned the knight, telling him he must choose one of them as his lover or forfeit his life. Refusing to betray his love for Guinevere, he tells them he would prefer death. Later he is rescued by one of Morgan's servants, who offers to free the knight if he will help her father in a tournament. Again the Morrigan asserts her right to choose her lovers, in this case literally abducting one and locking him up as a love slave. She uses her magick to take him captive and offers him a choice: bend to her will or die. As in the rest of the Morrigan's myths, refusing her love has dire consequences, just as it did for Cúchulain.

Morgan le Fay's sexuality in general is viewed in a negative light in Arthurian myths. When she wasn't imprisoning knights who refused to be her lover, she was sleeping with her own brother. Morgan le Fay conceives a son with Arthur, a son who eventually fights against his own father, leading to the king's demise. Her sexuality is viewed as dangerous, something Arthur falls victim to rather than retaining any blame for the union. Her lover Accolon also fights Arthur when she plots to overthrow the king. Both these stories twist sexuality into an evil thing. When the characters give in to their baser instincts, it comes with disastrous consequence: Arthur's death and his attempted dethronement.

These are both corrupted versions of stories that deal with the goddess of the land conferring sovereignty on the king. By mating with both Accolon and Arthur, Morgan gives them the right to rule over the land. She initially sleeps with Arthur, in effect granting him the right to be king; then she initiates a union with a younger man, Accolon, when she feels Arthur's time is at an end. Unfortunately Accolon was defeated by Arthur. This may be an attempt to show that the goddess of the land was no longer needed to make a king and thus vilifies her inherent power, a power deeply connected to her sexuality.

As the Lover, the Morrigan challenges us to embrace our own sexuality, to see it as a potent natural force that connects us to the power of creation. She appears to us as the faery lover, the lusty lady of the land, a temptress-goddess secure in her right to choose her lovers. She is a woman empowered, whose sexual energy brings renewed life to the land and adds to her own pleasure and vitality.

Harnessing the Power of the Lover

Sex and sensuality is a natural part of our lives. Harnessing the power of the Lover doesn't mean you have to go out and have a lot of sex; it is about viewing sex as a divine act instead of something dirty. It is also about honoring our own bodies and seeing ourselves as sensual beings, no matter how young or old we are or how thin or voluptuous we are. Both men and women struggle with body image. We are shown ideals of the human form on TV and in magazines, ideals that are reached by unhealthy diets, surgical procedures, or air brushing. Our bodies are temples for the Divine; they are sacred, and we should honor the forms Spirit gives us to wear during our lives rather than worry about what is wrong with their appearance.

Spend time in front of the mirror for the next few days and list at least five things you love about your body. Yes, there will always be something you want to change, but by making a habit of seeing the beauty in your body, you are honoring the Lover within yourself as well as your own sensual power. The union of Goddess and God, male and female, the sensual energy of joy, pleasure, and absolute ecstasy that formed the universe and everything in it exists within each of us. It is the power behind creation, the fire that drives life onward. The power of the Lover is sacred, not dirty or unnatural; in fact, it is the most natural energy possible!

As Pagans we see sex as a sacred act, the joining of Goddess with God, the Great Rite. Now that sex is beginning to become less of a taboo subject in our culture, researchers and scientists are finding that sex affects our overall health, and that a rigorous romp under the sheets can improve your physical and psychological wellbeing. Research has found that regular sexual activity can increase longevity, boost the immune systems, lower cholesterol, and may even lower cancer risk. "Researchers have suggested that sexual expression may lead to a decreased risk of cancer because of the increase in levels of oxytocin and DHEA, which are associated with arousal and orgasm in women and men. A 1989 study found increased frequency of sexual activity was correlated with a reduced incidence of breast cancer."[110] Having sex one to two times a week has been linked to high levels of the antibody immunoglobulin, which increases your body's natural defenses. On the other hand, prolonged abstinence has been linked to increased stress and even depression.

The lesson of the Lover is learning to love yourself, to honor your body as a sacred temple of the Divine. The Lover reminds us to look at the temptresses and wild women of mythology and see them not as immoral or out of control but as archetypes of personal power.

Exercise 1: Honoring the Temple of the Body

Have you ever looked into the mirror after getting dressed up for an important event and felt powerful? Or gazed at yourself in the mirror when primping for a date and felt more confident because you knew you looked sexy? A business suit, a little black dress, or a fresh manicure can make us feel different, empowered, and beautiful. Beauty is often considered vain, but taking care of our earthly bodies and honoring our individual beauty is a sacred act. Too often we are forced to accept someone else's version of beauty. We worry we are too short or too tall, too thin or too heavy. To honor the temple of our bodies and to see ourselves as vessels of the Divine is part of the power of the Lover. We must learn to see our own inner beauty.

For this exercise, take a day to honor your own unique beauty. In the morning, take a cleansing bath, then stand in front of the mirror

110. Amen, *Sex on the Brain*, p. 16.

in the nude. Instead of seeing your imperfections, say out loud at least five things you love about your body. Spend the rest of the day pampering yourself, wear something that makes you feel sexy, get a massage, or plan a romantic date with your significant other.

Áine's Love Spell

You Will Need:
Meadowsweet
Yarrow
Cinnamon
1 red candle
Vanilla oil
Paper and pen

Mix the meadowsweet, yarrow, and cinnamon in bowl with three strands of your hair. Anoint the candle with vanilla oil from the wick to the base and roll it in the herbs. Before you begin, write down what kind of love you want to attract on a piece of paper. What are the person's traits, personality, and so on? When you get to the last line of the spell, *"Let my lover be . . . ,"* you will read the traits and qualities you have written down. Concentrate on the type of person you wish to draw toward you, and the type of relationship you are looking for. Do not visualize a specific person! Love spells that attempt to manipulate a person's feelings always, always backfire. Instead let the universe bring the right type of person to you.

Light the red candle, saying:

Áine of the green earth and holy well
Bring your blessings onto this spell
Mistress of faery fire
Passion, melody, and the heart's desire
Bring to me the love that I require
Let my lover be _________
In Áine's name, so mote it be!

Morrigan Fertility Spell

You Will Need:
1 blue or pink candle
Raspberry leaf
Red clover
Nettle leaves

To help conceive a child, hold a pink or blue candle (blue if you want a boy, pink for a girl; use white if you have no gender in mind) in your hands while concentrating on your desire. Burn equal parts of raspberry leaf, red clover, and nettle (all herbs associated with fertility) as incense, leaving a small portion of the herbs aside to be sprinkled outside as an offering to the lady of the land and goddess of fertility.

Light the candle, saying:

Great Morrigan
Lady of the land
Whose womb is the fertile earth
Mother of the innumerable gods and mortal men
Bring to me your blessings this night
Bestow upon me your creative power
Fertility of the land is my desire!

Let the candle burn out. If you can't burn it in one sitting, light it each night for a short time until it burns out. Sprinkle the remaining herbs outside as an offering.

Self-Love Spell

Acknowledging the power of the Lover requires more than loving another person. Self-love is the true power of the Lover. If we can't love ourselves, we can't fully love another person or maintain a healthy relationship. The following spell can be used after ending a relationship, when you feel depressed, or if you want to honor both your inner and outer beauty.

You Will Need:
Pen and paper
Pink or red rose petals
Pink candle
Your favorite love incense
Rose oil or perfume

Before beginning this spell, write a list of things that you love about yourself, anything and everything you can think of, from your physical body to more abstract personality traits.

Sprinkle the rose petals around your ritual area if you are casting a circle or around the pink candle if you do not wish to cast a circle. I like to begin this spell by reading Patricia Monaghan's poem "Maeve Prepares for Beltane." Maeve was infamous for her love affairs and in the poem as she prepares for a new tryst amidst the Beltane fires, she honors her own inner fire, knowing this is the most important part of her lovemaking. You can use any poem or prose that reminds you of self-love.

Light the pink candle and your favorite love incense. Take a few moments to see a beautiful pink light surrounding your body and filling your spirit. When you are ready, read aloud the poem or prose you have selected.

Take a moment to inhale the sweet smell of the incense and concentrate on the pink energy surrounding your body and spirit. Use the rose oil to anoint each of your chakras, seeing the rose-colored light filling each energy center, spreading loving energy throughout your mind, body, and spirit. When you are ready, say:

I honor myself
The love I share with others
I shine upon myself!

Take out your list. Say "I honor my . . . " then read a trait from the list. Continue until you have read everything on the paper. If you do this as a group ritual, go around the circle, having each person read one thing from their list, and continue until everyone has read everything on their lists. This can almost turn into a kind of chant, speeding up the more each person reads and ending with exuberant shouts! Alone or in a group, the more energy you put into it, the better you will feel afterwards.

Extinguish the candle. Relight it for a few minutes for the next three days and take a few moments to concentrate on what you love about yourself, visualizing the loving pink light around you.

Lover's Draft

You Will Need:
Rose petals
1 small bowl
1 bottle of your favorite wine
Rose oil
Vanilla oil
2 wine glasses

Use this spell to enhance love and to bring you and your lover closer together. Place the rose petals in a bowl and hold your hands over it, charging them with loving energies. Concentrate on love and harmony within your relationship. Place the petals in the wine bottle and let them sit for at least an hour. Next mix together a few drops of vanilla and rose oils in the bowl. Using your finger, dab the oil around the base of each wine glass so you will breathe in the scent of the oil as you drink the wine. Share the wine with the one you love.

A Kundalini Spell

Kundalini is the tantric term for vital sexual energy. It is described as a coiled serpent at the base of the spine (root chakra) that rises to energize the rest of the chakras when awakened. Kundalini energy can be raised during ritual to power our spellwork and as a means to raise energy. If you were raised to view sex and sexuality as "dirty" or "sinful," using sexual energy in magick may be awkward at first. Once we can learn to shed this misconception, sex magick can be a very potent part of our spiritual practice. The energy raised during orgasm is just as valid as drumming, chanting, or any of the other methods Witches use to raise power in a circle. While most people assume that sex magick requires a partner, sex magick can be practiced solo. Using Kundalini energy can be a private practice and does not have to be part of a group setting. If you do wish to practice sex magick with a lover, both participants should be familiar with the practice. It is not something that should be done with a lover who is unaware of what you are attempting to do.

Begin with a cleansing ritual bath. If you want to enhance the sensual mood, light some candles in your bathroom. If you do not have a lot of privacy where you live (roommates and such), you may wish to do the entire spell in your bathroom, with a candle, bowl of water, incense, and a stone or crystal to represent the elements.

Go to your sacred space, ground and center, and call the elements. Take a few minutes to visualize what you wish to manifest. The trick will be to hold that image in your mind while you are raising Kundalini energy. When you have the image of what you want clearly in your mind, begin to masturbate. Hold the image in your mind. This may prove difficult, but your concentration will pay off! When you reach peak, visualize the energy you have raised moving through your body beginning in your base chakra and moving up through your crown, then out into the universe to manifest.

Morrigan Lover Invocation

Lusty Morrigan, Goddess of sex
Lady of the flame and of the heart's desire
Wild, sensual Goddess
Flesh your sacred temple
Your seat of power the heart
You unite with the God to bring balance, healing, and vision
Your passions fuel your will,
bringing form and shape to your desires
You are the Lady of Fertility,
Goddess of the lush green earth
Lady of Life, stoke the fires within me
Let me burn with your light!

Lover Incense

1 handful of rose petals
½ tsp. musk root
1 tsp. cinnamon
2 tsp. orris root
9 drops ylang-ylang oil

Lover Oil

Add the following essential oils to ¼ cup of base oil and mix together:

9 drops rose essential oil
3 drops musk essential oil
5 drops ylang-ylang essential oil

Part Four
Ancient Goddess, Modern Worship

We live in the midst of invisible forces whose effects alone we perceive. We move among invisible forms whose actions we very often do not perceive at all, though we may be profoundly affected by them.

—Dion Fortune

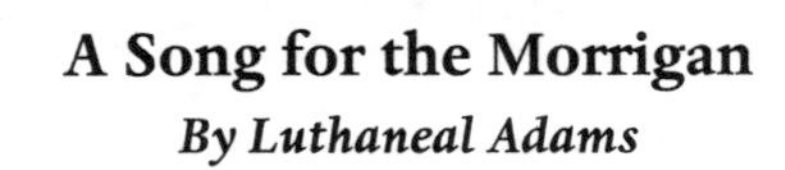

A Song for the Morrigan

By Luthaneal Adams

Of Holy power, sing to the Morrigan
She of battle, of beauty and strength
Sing to the Morrigan daughter of legend
Live in her grace, in absence of friends

Heart of the Goddess, beat in your chest
Fill your blood with courage and strength
Hear her cry and know you are mighty
Be warriors when needed, in absence of friends.

Worshipping the gods, the Morrigan included, is a personal experience for each of us. When I first began working with the Morrigan, I found very little information about her worship, ancient or modern. My own practices evolved through trial and error, and eventually I found what worked the best for me. It is my hope that my experiences will help you on your personal way to honor the Morrigan and build a meaningful relationship with her. While we will discuss modern worship as it pertains to the Morrigan, the information in this section can be applied to working with any deity. We will explore how to incorporate the Morrigan and her energies into our everyday lives by creating altars, leaving offerings, learning the art of aspecting, and connecting to her through seasonal rituals and moon rites.

When we seek to honor and connect to the gods in our daily lives, we can forge a relationship with the Divine that extends far beyond a cast circle. We learn that the gods are everywhere. They are always within reach. You could be in a line at the bank, driving your car, or at your desk at work—whenever you need their presence in your life, they are there. Our gods aren't "somewhere up there" in the clouds, they are all around us, hidden in the land beneath our feet, in the air we breathe, and—most important—within each of us.

16

Altars & Offerings

The first altars were places in nature: caves painted by our Paleolithic ancestors, sacred groves, and hilltops. Later our ancestors began creating temples and shrines, making a given place sacred by the items and statues placed there. Altars have served as places of worship, meditation, and comfort for people of all religions, and creating altars and sacred space is a concept found in virtually every religion.

Creating an altar sets aside a space for you to communicate with the Divine, meditate, pray, ask for advice, and petition the gods. In general there will be two types of altars you will use: The first is a "working altar," which is usually a permanent altar in your sacred space that is used during rituals and spells. I keep most of my magickal tools on my working altar, as well as a cauldron and a deer antler to represent the God and Goddess. I also add certain items to my working altar for seasonal rituals. The second type of altar is a "deity altar," which is dedicated to a specific goddess or god, and is a place you can go to commune with that deity and experience their energies outside of ritual.

An altar can be something as simple as the top of a dresser, a low wooden table, or a flat stone. The altar I use for the Morrigan is a large flat stone that emerged out of the stream in my backyard after a heavy storm. Given the Morrigan's connection to rivers and water, I knew it would make the perfect altar for her. If you wish to create a stone altar, you can also buy a piece of flagstone from your local garden center. You may wish to have your altar facing a certain direction. Since the Morrigan is an earth goddess, facing the altar toward the north, which is connected to the element of earth, would be appropriate.

A statue of the Morrigan will most likely be the centerpiece of your altar. Your statue will act as a representation of the Morrigan and her energies. In the Hindu religion, the statue of a god is treated as a living thing; the statue literally *is* the god.

I have always liked this idea, and whenever I bless a statue, I visualize part of that god or goddess entering the statue, connecting it to the source of the deity's energies. There are several beautiful statues of the Morrigan that can be found online or through companies that specialize in Pagan statuary, such as Sacred Source. I started with a single statue of the Morrigan that depicted her holding a spear with a raven perched on her shoulder. I eventually added two other statues to represent her triple nature. In this chapter you will find a statue-blessing ritual that you can use to bless your altar statue.

If you cannot be open about your spiritual beliefs with your friends and family, you may want to have a very simple altar. The Celts did not use statues to represent the gods until Britain was invaded by the Romans in the first century CE and Roman practices mingled with Celtic ideology. Instead of a statue, you may want to use a red or purple candle to represent the Morrigan. You can inscribe her name on the side or base of the candle. You could also decorate your altar with a red or black cloth or crystals that correspond with the Morrigan. You may use a poster or art print from your favorite artist to represent the Morrigan in place of a statue. Jessica Gilbert, Brian Froud, Amy Brown, and several other artists sell prints depicting the Morrigan or Morgan le Fay. No one would have to know that your taste in art is a private way of honoring this goddess.

An altar bowl or dish to place offerings in is another essential to a deity altar. On my altar I have a ceramic bowl that has Celtic spirals along the rim. If you choose to leave offerings that will spoil, such as wine, milk, or any kind of food, your libation bowl should be emptied on a regular basis. If possible find a spot outside where you can bury the offerings. Never put offerings in the trash. If you leave items that will not spoil, empty your libation bowl on each new moon. Since you may also wish to leave incense as an offering, an incense burner would also be a good addition to your altar. Over the years you may also add other objects of personal significance. After working with the Morrigan, you may be gifted with crow or raven feathers. I usually place these on the Morrigan's altar and use certain ones to waft incense over the altar. You can also purchase black feathers at most craft stores, to be used for the same purpose or simply as decorations for your altar.

It is a good idea to bless your altar periodically. Some Witches prefer to do this on Sabbats or Esbats; others only do so when they feel the need to renew the blessing on the altar. Dust will inevitably accumulate and pet hair or scales (if you have reptiles) may find their way onto your altar. Pets seem to take a particular interest in altars of any kind. My cats have always had an odd obsession with my working altar. One in particular likes to take cat naps underneath or occasionally on top of it! I also have a ball python who is aptly named after Loki, the god of mischief. Loki lives up to his name and makes a habit of escaping from his cage no matter what kind of locks or weights are there to deter him. While he never has taken an interest in my working altar (probably because the cats have already claimed that one), he likes to coil underneath the Morrigan's altar. Animals are very sensitive to energies and if you have pets, either make sure your altar is in an area that your pet does not have access to or make certain there aren't any items on the altar that can be dangerous or poisonous to your animals.

Morrigan Statue Blessing

You Will Need:
White sage
Sandalwood
Crow or black feather
Statue you wish to bless
Dragon's blood oil

Put the white sage and sandalwood on the incense burner, then use the crow feather to waft the incense over the statue. Hold the statue in front of the altar and visualize the statue and the Morrigan becoming one. When you have this image clearly in your mind, say:

Though you were separate now you are one
Morrigan, Morrigan, Morrigan!

Anoint the top, middle, and bottom of the statue with the oil, saying:

I bless you that you may be a holy vessel
Of the Morrigan's divine essence
In the Morrigan's name, so mote it be!

Place the statue back on the altar.

Morrigan Altar Blessing

Milk was believed to have both healing and blessing qualities. It also reminds us of the Morrigan's connection to the earth, and comes from one of her totem animals. Here we will be using it both to bless and to consecrate your altar and as an offering. As the Morrigan is an earth goddess, you may wish to keep a small dish of earth from your property on your altar to help you connect with the energies of the land around you.

You Will Need:
Milk
Patchouli incense
Crow or black feather
Small amount of earth from your property
Salt
1 white votive

Clear all items from the altar and physically clean the items and the altar surface if need be. Put your altar items on the side for the time being. Dip your fingers into the cup of milk and sprinkle it on the altar, saying:

Mother's milk
Sustenance of life
Ever-flowing
Enrich and sustain us
Mother of the life-giving waters
I honor you!

Light the incense and use the crow feather to waft the incense over the altar, saying:

Dark raven
Mistress of night and change
Ferrier of souls to the Otherworlds
Morrigan
Phantom Queen
I honor you!

Mix the dish of earth with three pinches of salt, then sprinkle some of the mixture on each of the four corners of the altar, saying:

Earth Mother
Hallowed and dark
Your mysteries I would keep
Creation and destruction are but one
Cycles of change
Light and dark
A sacred balance you keep
Lady of the land
I honor you!

Pass any items that will be kept on the altar through the incense, then place them on the altar. If you keep a candle on the altar to represent the Morrigan, light it. If you do not normally have a candle on the altar, place a white votive candle in the center of the altar and light it, saying:

Morrigan, Raven Mother
Morrigan, Earth Mother
Morrigan, Phantom Queen
Queen of the Sidhe
And the Túatha Dé Danann
I honor thee
Goddess of the land and rivers
Warrior Queen
I welcome your energies to this place
Morrigan, I honor you!

Pour the remaining milk into the offering bowl, saying:

Morrigan, I honor you!

Put the remaining earth and salt mixture into the offering bowl.

Morrigan, I honor you!

Put the rest of the herbs on the burner and waft more incense over the altar, saying:

Morrigan, I honor you!

Spend a few minutes sitting by the altar communing with the Morrigan. When you are done, pour the contents of your offering dish outside.

Offerings

Offerings will differ depending on the ritual or reason you are petitioning the Morrigan. Offerings you leave for Macha will be different from those you may leave Anu. In this section you will find different types of offerings I have used to honor the Morrigan over the years, along with their significance and which aspect of the Morrigan they correspond to.

It is often assumed that blood is a required offering for the Morrigan because of her "bloodthirsty" reputation. While I have used blood as an offering to her, you should only use blood if you are comfortable with this type of offering. Blood, especially menstrual blood, represents the vital life force that flows through us. While I do not use blood often, the times I have used this type of offering have all been very moving experiences. Only use your own blood, never another person's. *Safety should also be your first consideration.* Using a thumb pricker, while less dramatic, is much safer than using an athame or knife to cut your palm or finger. If you associate offering blood with violence or aggression, it would be best to use another type of offering to honor the Morrigan; the spirit in which you give an offering is more important than the actual thing being offered.

While offerings can be left outside, you should consider keeping a libation bowl on your altar. It can be a simple glass dish or something more elaborate. Before leaving an offering, hold the item in your hands, seeing your love and devotion for the Morrigan flowing from you to the object.

Wine, Spirits, and Liquid Offerings

Red wine: Reminiscent of blood, this can be used to honor the Morrigan in any of her guises and in any type of ritual.

Beer: Beer, especially Guinness, is sometimes given to horses to give their coats a healthy sheen. Guinness or other dark beers are appropriate offerings to Macha, to whom horses are sacred.

Whiskey: If you plan to burn a petition or do fire scrying, pour some whiskey into a fireproof container or cauldron and light it during your ritual. Whiskey is made from fermenting grains and is an appropriate offering to the Morrigan in her guise as the goddess of the land.

Mead: Mead is a sweet wine made from honey. The Celts considered mead the drink of the gods. It can be used for fertility rituals and summer rites. The full moon in June is called the Mead Moon, and mead can be used in place of red wine for rituals done during this month. This is an appropriate offering for Áine, Anu, and Maeve.

Milk: Milk was believed to have restorative properties and was left on doorsteps for the Fairy Folk. Milk can be used for healing and fertility rituals. It is an appropriate offering for Anu, Áine, Macha, and the Morrigan in her guise as Queen of the Faeries. Mix a cup of milk with a tablespoon of honey and use it in place of wine in rituals invoking Morgan le Fay or the Fair Folks.

Water: Morrigan is connected with rivers and water in many of her myths. Filtered spring water or water from a holy well can be placed on her altar or used as an offering. It is a simple but meaningful offering and is appropriate for any of the Morrigan's guises. Water from the ocean would also be appropriate.

HERBAL OFFERINGS

Apple: Apples are connected to the Isle of Avalon (which means "Isle of Apples"). It was a symbol of immortality and the Otherworlds. The apple has also been traditionally used in love spells. Apples were buried at Samhain as food for the dead. Use them as decorations for your Samhain altar or as offering to the Phantom Queen who rules over death and rebirth. Apples are appropriate offerings to Modron, Morgan le Fay, Áine, and the Morrigan in general.

Oats: Oats make up a large part of the diet of horses and cattle. Oats are an appropriate offering to the horse goddess Macha and to the earth goddess Anu. Organic oatmeal, Quaker Oats (not the instant kind or ones with flavor additives), or any of the many breakfast oatmeals sold at supermarkets work well as offerings.

Juniper berries: Juniper is associated with protection and psychic powers. The berries take three years to mature, making it sacred to the Triple Goddess. Use in rituals to Badb and Nemain, and in divination or protection rituals.

Elderberries: Elderberry bushes were believed to have protective properties, and the berries can be used to bless or protect objects. All aspects of the Morrigan.

Dragon's blood resin: This resin adds power to any magickal working. Oil made from the resin can be used to anoint candles. The resin can be ground into powder and added to magickal blends or left as an offering. All aspects of the Morrigan.

Grain: Like oats, any type of grain can be used as an offering to Macha and Anu.

Hazelnuts: When the Morrigan appeared to Cúchulain, she was accompanied by a faery man holding a hazel staff. She is also connected to the number nine, and the hazel is represented by the ninth letter in the Ogham. Hazelnuts are notoriously hard to crack. They can be offered whole or placed in the oven for 20 to 30 minutes at 275 degrees until the skins crack. These nuts are good for outdoor rituals, as they will serve as a food source for local wildlife. Leave hazelnuts as offerings to attract wealth and wisdom. Use when working with Macha, Anu, and the Morrigan in general.

Meadowsweet: Áine was said to have given this herb its lovely scent. This herb is often used in love spells and can be used in incense or as an offering to Áine.

Mugwort: Medically, mugwort can help regulate menstruation and can be used when working with the Morrigan in her Mother or fertile aspects. It is also used to aid in psychic workings and for washing crystal balls and other divination tools. Mugwort tea can be used as an offering to Macha or Badb before performing divination. Pour some of the tea into a libation bowl or outside, then sip the remaining tea during your divination session.

Oak: Acorns from the oak were a source of food for Celtic animals and people. Use acorns or oak leaves in rituals dedicated to Macha or Anu. The leaves were burnt to purify an area and for general health and longevity. Use a permanent marker to draw a symbol of what you wish to manifest on an acorn and leave it as an offering to the Morrigan. Acorns are also an appropriate offering for the Morrigan as the Queen of Battle. After the battle was over, the Morrigan would gather severed heads from the battlefield, and these heads were also called "the Morrigan's Acorn Crop." Appropriate offering for Macha, Anu, and the Morrigan as the Queen of Battle.

Lavender: Lavender is used to attract love and create peaceful energies. Mix with meadowsweet for incense honoring Áine.

Rue: Rue was used to protect against the "evil eye" and to banish evil spirits. Early physicians used the pungent odor of this herb to repel fleas. Use rue for protection and banishing spells and with the goddess Badb and Nemain. *Caution: Do not ingest, as rue is poisonous.*

COLORS

Using the appropriate color candles, altar cloth, or decorations can enhance your rituals and spell work. Each color holds a specific vibrational energy and also acts as a symbolic representation to your subconscious of an idea, element, or concept.

Black: Black is the color of the abyss, the place were all energy gathers before taking shape and form. Use black to represent the Crone or Badb, and to banish negative energies or people. While we associate black with death, the Celts connected black with the earth and with rich fertile soil (white was connected with death).

Brown: Dark, earthy brown can be used for earth and prosperity magick. Use it to represent Anu, Macha, and the Morrigan in her guise as an earth goddess.

Dark blue: Connected to healing, water, and calming energies. Use this color to represent the Morrigan's connection to water, rivers, Danu, and the Queen aspect of the Morrigan.

Green: Represents the earth and growth. Use green for prosperity and Earth Mother rituals. Use when working with Macha and Anu. Green is also connected to the faeries. Use green candles when practicing faery magick or when invoking Morgan le Fay.

Purple: Purple is the color of royalty and spiritual development. Dark purple can be used in place of black to represent the Crone aspect of the Morrigan. Use in rituals to learn about past lives, developing psychic talents, and invoking the Morrigan as the Mistress of Magick.

Red: Red is the Morrigan's favorite color, representing sex, passion, blood, and the life force. This color can be used with all of the Morrigan's faces and guises.

White: White can be used to represent Anu or any of the Morrigan's aspects if you cannot find a candle of an appropriate color. While black contains all colors, white is absent of color and is a good generic color to use if nothing else is available. White (not black) represented death to the Celts, possibly because it is the color of bone. White animals, such as white cattle and horses, were connected to the goddess of death and can be used when calling upon the Crone aspect of the Morrigan.

Gems and Crystals

Gems and crystals can be used as offerings or can be used to add power to spells involving the Morrigan's different aspects.

Amethyst: This is a highly spiritual stone that calms and enhances positive vibrations. Use it with spells or rituals invoking the Morrigan as the Mistress of Magick and Morgan le Fay.

Jet: This black, glasslike stone is actually the remains of fossilized wood. Use to enhance herbal spells or Ogham magick. Use in spells invoking Badb and Anu.

Obsidian: Often used to make stone knives and arrowheads, this stone is excellent for rituals invoking the Morrigan's warrior aspects. Use in protection spells and for scrying rituals.

Garnet: This stone adds energy to any ritual and is worn to increase energy and vigor. It is a stone of protection and dispels negative energies. Use in rituals and spells involving Macha and the Morrigan in general.

Clear quartz: This stone is a general all-purpose stone that can be used in any magickal working. Use with any aspect of the Morrigan.

Emerald: Associated with love and earth energies, emerald rings can be used in spellwork invoking Áine and Anu to bring love and prosperity into your life.

17

Patron Deities

When I first started practicing Witchcraft, I hadn't intended to incorporate a patron deity into my spiritual practice, and for several years, I didn't. While some would argue that it is up to the Witch to choose a patron, my personal experiences indicate that you're not the one doing the choosing—your patron goddess or god chooses you. A patron may make his or herself known through dreams or pathwork, or you may simply feel drawn to information about that deity or their culture. You may feel that you should invoke a certain deity during a seasonal ritual or Sabbat and have a moving encounter with them. You may encounter symbols or animals associated with your patron deity in unexpected places. However your patron makes him—or herself known, you will perceive if the connection is right.

Your patron god or goddess resonates with the lessons you have incarnated in this life and with your own personal energies. They act as your personal spiritual guide and protector and will be a great source of wisdom and knowledge along your spiritual path. Dedicating yourself to a patron deity and becoming their Priest or Priestess is not something to be undertaken lightly. It is a transformative experience and not one you can go back on.

Ironically, when a patron does make their presence known, many practitioners resist the connection. A friend and fellow Priestess of the Morrigan told me she had initially decided she wanted Aphrodite as her patron. After a few months of attempting to work with the goddess of love, the goddess of war showed up instead! The more she ignored the Morrigan, the more persistent she became. The Morrigan appeared to her in dreams. For several days in a row, a crow decided to use her bedroom window sill as a perch, tapping at the window until she woke up. At the time she was going through a messy divorce and fighting to keep custody of her children. Eventually my friend realized the Morrigan's strength and warrior attitude was really what she needed in her life, rather than Aphrodite's loving persona.

While your relationship with your patron will be the strongest, you may acquire what I call "secondary patrons." Secondary patrons are deities that you have cultivated a relationship with, and who you work with on a regular basis, but are not as deeply connected to as your patron. These deities and your patron make up your personal pantheon. You may feel the influence of these gods in your life at particular times, during a seasonal ritual, or during a crisis in your life where their energies can be beneficial. They may also make their presence known in similar ways as your patron, just not in as pronounced a fashion.

My secondary patrons are Brigid and Lugh. While they entered my life in a less dramatic way than the Morrigan, they made it clear that they would play a role in my life. I had several vivid dreams about each deity over a number of years, and found myself calling on them during rituals often. While the Morrigan remains a constant presence, Lugh and Brigid are there as well, lending their strength and guidance when need be. Your secondary patrons will not necessarily be from the same culture as your patron, and (as with my personal pantheon) they will not always include exclusively male or female deities. Your patron can be either gender regardless of what gender you are, as can your secondary patrons. We all need to work with both male and female energies to be whole and balanced in our spiritual practices. Although there are some traditions that feel women must have a female patron and males a male patron, there is no reason why a woman cannot have a patron god, or a male have a patron goddess.

When the Morrigan first made her presence known to me, I wasn't looking to adopt a patron deity—or rather, to be adopted by one. The Morrigan's presence came at a pivotal juncture in my life; she didn't simply make all my problems go away, but she guided me through a challenging time in my life and helped me reshape my circumstances for the better. You may be surprised who your patron is when you discover him or her, but trust that welcoming them into your life and spiritual practices will be a powerful and rewarding experience.

The Modern Priest & Priestess

In my opinion, what defines a Priest or Priestess is *service* to one's chosen deity. Your path as a Priest or Priestess will be as individual as you are. A Priestess of Bast may have different experiences than a Priest of Freya, but our connection to the Divine and dedication to the gods unites the path of all Priests and Priestesses. Being a Priest or Priestess is about cultivating a deep ongoing relationship with the Divine. For most Pagans, it begins with encountering a patron deity who resonates with their own personal energies and with the lessons each of us has incarnated on this earth to experience. By becoming a Priestess, you become a vessel for that deity's wisdom and energies. Being a Priestess is a way of life; it is not something you can dedicate yourself to, then forget about. It is about connecting to the Divine and seeing the Divine in yourself and others every single day.

Much of your work as a Priestess may begin with your own transformation. Your patron deity may present challenges to you that force you to grow or release things in your life that are harmful or no longer serve your spiritual growth. This inner transformation is an ongoing process, but the lessons you learn will help you later when sharing the wisdom or talents you have mastered in the service of others. A friend of mine who was called by the goddess Brigid to be her Priestess at first found herself challenged by the goddess to heal herself. She had been battling depression at the time and dedicated herself to studying herbalism and Reiki. After undergoing the process of becoming whole and making many life-changing decisions, including divorcing an abusive husband and going back to school for a degree in psychology, she is now a marriage counselor and a Reiki teacher, passing on her experiences in healing herself for the benefit of others.

A Priest serves both his gods and his community. Here *serve* is the primary word. When you dedicate yourself to a deity, you are promising to work with the god's or goddess's energies and learn their mysteries, to better both yourself and the world around you. Honoring the Divine also requires that you honor and recognize the Divine within yourself. You may choose to donate time to a charitable cause, pick up trash from a local park, or perform a random act of kindness for someone in need. Furthermore a modern Priest isn't just a Priest on Esbats or at the Saturday night coven gathering—he is a Priest every day of his life and can channel the power and energies of the goddess into every aspect of their lives.

The legitimacy of Pagan clergy is often debated. To some, a license legitimizes a Priest; others feel initiation into a coven makes a Priest credible. I personally feel it should make no difference whether a person is self-initiated or initiated by a coven. The vows you make to the gods are just that—to the gods. Not to a particular coven or organization. Of course, if you plan to perform handfastings, you may wish to become a licensed clergy member in your state, so any marriage ceremonies you officiate over will be legally recognized. There are several non-denominational organizations you can go through to become ordained, such as the Universal Life Church. Again, becoming ordained and being able to perform legal marriages is only a legality; it is how you choose to serve the gods and live as a Priestess that will define your role as a part of Pagan clergy.

Morrigan Priestess Dedication Ritual

At some point you may wish to become a Priest or Priestess of the Morrigan. By dedicating yourself as a Priestess you are making a commitment to work with the Morrigan on a more intimate level, furthering and enriching your spiritual practice. Before dedicating yourself to the path of a priesthood, take some time to consider if you are ready for this step in your spiritual path.

You Will Need:
Your favorite incense
1 black feather
Sword
Dragon's blood oil
Red wine

Go to your sacred space. Light the incense. Using the black feather, waft the incense over your body, beginning with your head and moving down to your feet. Visualize the wings of a raven brushing over you, blessing you and scattering any negative energy to the winds. Then walk clockwise around the circle with the incense, saying:

In the Morrigan's name, I cleanse and bless this space
Let darkness flee and light remain
So mote it be!

Use the sword to cast the circle, saying:

In the Morrigan's name, I cast this circle
A boundary between the worlds
Where creation and destruction, life and death are one.

Call the directions:

From the East I call upon the Morrigu!
The three in one
Woman cloaked in the black feathers of the raven and crow
The gentle breeze is your loving embrace
The fierce storm winds, a reminder of your power and strength
Morrigu, bear witness to my vow!

From the South I call upon Macha!
The light of the sun is a reflection of your brilliance
The heat of your forge shapes and molds the spirit
You are the hearth fire, the sudden flame of inspiration,
The rage of a warrior's wrath
Macha, bear witness to my vow!

From the West I call upon Badb!
The rivers and holy well waters are your blood
The crashing ocean waves,the churning waters of your cauldron
Spear in hand you guard the shores of your mist-shrouded isle
Badb, bear witness to my vow!

From the North I call upon Anu!
From you all life came
The earth and soil are your flesh and bone
Your spirit nourishes the soul as earth's bounty nourishes our bodies
Anu, bear witness to my vow!

Take a few moments to meditate on why you wish to dedicate yourself as a Priestess and what becoming a Priestess means to you. When you are ready, raise your hands in an invoking position, saying:

Morrigan, Great Queen of the Túatha Dé Danann
You who ride the winds of night in the shape of a raven
Queen of the Sidhe and mist-filled lands
Weaving magick and uttering prophecies
Shadowed woman washing armor and mail astride the river
Bold warrioress, Lady of the Blade who bows to no one
To your children you bring strength and might

Threefold Goddess of life, death, and rebirth
You are the lusty Maiden, ripe Earth Mother, cunning Crone
All life mirrors your reflection

Today I dedicate myself as a Priest/ess of the Morrigan
From this day forward I will be known as _________
A Priest/ess of the Morrigan
May you walk ever at my side, Great Queen
And guide me along life's path
May the Morrigan witness my words and accept my oath!

Anoint your lips with the oil, saying:

In the Morrigan's name, my vow is sealed
I will speak with the voice of the Goddess!

Anoint your heart, saying:

In the Morrigan's name, my vow is sealed
I will love courageously and seek the wisdom of the Goddess!

Anoint your womb/phallus, saying:

In the Morrigan's name, my vow is sealed
I will bring harmony and beauty into the world!

Anoint your feet, saying:

In the Morrigan's name, my vow is sealed
I will walk the path of the Priest/ess from this day forward
Until the Morrigan brings me to her shadowed lands

Take a few moments to sit quietly and connect with the Morrigan. You may wish to write down any messages or words of wisdom she imparts to you.

When you are ready, circle the wine three times with the feather, saying:

Hail Morrigan
Goddess of life, death, and rebirth!

Take a sip of the wine. Pour the remaining wine on the ground outside after the ritual. When you are ready to end the ritual, go to each quarter, saying:

Depart in peace, Morrigu/Macha/Badb/Anu

Cut the circle with the sword.

Aspecting

Often considered a form of divine possession, aspecting is when a person channels the presence of a goddess or god, literally becoming that deity for the duration of a ritual. The Priest or Priestess takes on the deity's persona, acting as the deity and speaking for them. This is also referred to as invoking (as opposed to evoking, which is when a deity is welcomed into a cast circle rather than drawn into the body of a person). Aspecting is not play-acting and is not the same as ritual drama. A sure sign of false aspecting is when the person channeling a deity starts using words like *thee* and *thou*. In my experience, gods speak in the language and dialect that those worshiping them understand, not the flowery speech of the Renaissance. During true aspecting, the Priestess or Priest literally becomes the god or goddess incarnate—their normal speech patterns, personality, demeanor and even body posture are no longer the same. Sometimes they may even appear taller, or their facial features, hair, or eye color may seem altered. If this happens, what you are seeing is the deity's essence that has merged with the person's aura, rather than a physical transformation.

Aspecting can be a powerfully moving experience and can enhance any ritual work. When working with a coven, it gives the Priest or Priestess and participants the ability to experience the presence of the gods in a physical way. While it is a type of divine possession, this is not the same as the possession we are familiar with in horror movies. Spirit possession is when someone is unwillingly manipulated by a spirit and unable to remove the spirit from their body. This has nothing to do with aspecting. If at any time during aspecting you wish to release the deity, you can do so. The deity is not going to force you to do anything or cause you any harm.

There are two types of aspecting: "light" aspecting and "deep" aspecting. Light aspecting is the most common and the most useful. During light aspecting you are fully aware of your actions, your consciousness and the deity's merge, and you are aware of their presence within you. The deity may speak through you, but you will still be able to consciously direct their energies toward a given task. This can still be a very intense experience and can be practiced within or outside of a cast circle. Light aspecting is the most common, since there is no reason for the Priestess or Priest to be unconscious during a ritual.

Deep aspecting is when a person is no longer aware of what occurs after drawing a deity into him—or herself. This will not happen by accident; the human willingly relinquishes control. Sometimes the person will have an out-of-body experience or will simply not remember anything that occurred.

A common misconception is that aspecting can only be done within a coven setting. This is not true. A solitary practitioner can also practice aspecting. In fact, it may be an even more moving experience for a solitary. Your first attempts at aspecting should be done within a cast and sealed circle. As your skills improve, you will be able to draw on the essence of a deity anytime you wish, with or without a circle.

It is imperative that you do not attempt to aspect a deity that you have not researched or meditated upon. Take time to get a feel for the god's or goddess's energies through meditation and pathwork before taking the next step. If you have trouble connecting with a deity through pathworking or if the deity is resistant to attempts at aspecting, do not work with that deity.

Drawing in the Morrigan

When practicing aspecting, the only tool necessary is yourself. Whether you are practicing within a cast circle or not, it is essential to ground and center yourself prior to beginning. You will be incorporating the energies of a specific goddess or god with your own. Not being in a centered and clear state will affect how successful your aspecting will be.

You Will Need:
Dragon's blood incense
Dragon's blood oil (or another oil of your choice)

In this exercise we will be calling on the Morrigan to lend you her energies for a specific task and for a specific duration of time. Go to your sacred space, ground and center, and light the incense.

I prefer to use dragon's blood incense since it adds power to any working and the Morrigan is particular to the resin, but you can use any incense that is appropriate to the situation you wish to channel the Morrigan's energies for. Perform a self-blessing by anointing your chakras with the oil. Ground and center. Cast the circle and call the elements. When you are ready, close your eyes and visualize the Morrigan standing in front of you. See her in as much detail as possible. Hold the image, while saying:

Morrigan
Great Queen of the Túatha Dé Danann
I call upon you this day/night
To fill me with your strength and power
Your wisdom and cunning
For the purpose of _________
Morrigan
Great Queen
May we be one in spirit
Until this task is done

See the Morrigan step forward and into you, filling your body with her divine spirit, becoming one with you. You may feel a rush of energy or a warm sensation throughout your body.

Do not release the Morrigan as you would in a normal ritual. Her energies will remain with you until you release them or until the task you called upon her for is done. When you are ready to release her energy, see the Morrigan stepping out of your body and her energies and yours separating.

Aspecting Outside of a Ritual Circle

At some point you may feel the need to draw on the Morrigan's energy or that of another deity outside of a cast circle. When dealing with a problem person or coping with a crisis of any sort, you don't always have the luxury or time to cast a circle.

To aspect outside of a cast circle, ground and center, then visualize the deity you are aspecting standing in front of you bathed in a halo of white crystalline light. See the deity stepping into your body, merging and becoming one with your spirit. Some people see the deity entering through the crown chakra or visualize themselves "stepping" into the deity. Use whatever visualization works best for you. When you wish to release the deity, ground and center, then see the deity "stepping" out of your body. Thank the deity, then see them vanishing.

18

Seasonal Rituals

A few weeks before each of the Sabbats, I go to my sacred space and open myself to whatever deities or energies wishes to work with me for that particular ritual. I find that particular deity's energy playing a part in my life in the days leading up to the Sabbat and come across their symbols and animal totems in unexpected places. Some years I will only tweak the ritual I used the previous year, and other years I will write a completely new one. Sometimes the most meaningful part of the Sabbat might be the pathwork I do with that deity, rather than the actual ritual itself.

I honestly never expected to incorporate the Morrigan into any seasonal ritual other than Samhain. Her energies are the most potent at Samhain, and the holiday is connected to her mythology, marking her yearly union with Dagda. It's also the most obvious holiday to work with her energies and for many years it was the only seasonal ritual I incorporated the Morrigan into. But the Morrigan is persistent, and no matter how I resisted, she kept calling to me in her different aspects during times of the year I had never seen associated with her energies. Once I learned more about her threefold nature and began working with her Maiden and Mother aspects, what she had been telling me all along finally made sense. At Midsummer she appears as the fiery sun goddess Áine and the bountiful Earth Mother Anu. During the harvest season she is Macha the Mare Mother; at Samhain she is the Phantom Queen, the goddess of death and new beginnings; and in December she is the Winter Hag, midwife of the sun. Her energies are present throughout the wheel of the year, her changing faces and roles expressed through the turning of the seasons. You should not feel that you have to incorporate the Morrigan into all of these holidays simply because she is your patron deity; other deities may wish to work with you on these days as well. But if you feel drawn to the Morrigan during the Sabbats, don't be afraid to explore her varying energies.

The rituals in this section can be used as a guideline for your own seasonal rituals. Feel free to add to them or use the bits and pieces that appeal to you. Seasonal rituals are not meant to be exactly the same every year, and they will change and evolve as your spiritual self and practices progress. Paganism is not dogmatic—there are many ways to explore the themes of each holiday, and no one way is correct. The rituals are not meant to conform to the usual eight-Sabbat form, as the Morrigan's energies do not fit into all eight of these holidays. Thus we will be skipping Imbolc, Ostara, and Lammas. In addition to the seasonal rituals, I have also included a Feast of the Morrigan, a day during the year to honor the Morrigan in all her many forms and guises.

Samhain

October 31

Also called: Halloween, All Hallows' Eve

Samhain marks the end of summer and the beginning of the dark half of the year. It is a time to honor the dead. On Samhain the Veil between the worlds is thinnest, allowing for communication with the ancestors and those who have passed on. On Samhain we see the Morrigan in her role as a death goddess. It is also when she unites with Dagda. The union of the death goddess with the god of life reaffirms the continuation of life in the season of death.

Morrigan's Samhain Ritual

You Will Need:

Cauldron

1 each of red, white, and black candles to represent the Morrigan

1 green candle to represent Dagda

1 white candle to represent the ancestors and departed dead

Your favorite Morrigan or Samhain incense

1 black feather

Sword, athame, or wand

Chalice of water

Dish of salt

Place the cauldron in the center of the altar, with the red, white, black, and green candles surrounding it. The three candles representing the Morrigan should be placed close together around the top half of the cauldron, and the candle representing Dagda should be on the opposite side of the cauldron. Place the white candle inside the cauldron.

Light the incense and use the black feather to waft some of the smoke in each direction—east, south, west, north, above, and below—to bless the ritual space.

Use your sword, athame, or wand to cast the circle, saying:

In the Morrigan's name, I cast this circle
A boundary between the worlds
Where creation and destruction, life, and death are one

Return to the altar and circle the chalice three times with your sword, saying:

Blessed is the water of the Morrigan
Wellspring of life
From her waters I came, and shall one day return

Put the dish of salt on the altar and circle it with your sword, saying:

Blessed is the salt of the earth
The body of the Morrigan
From which all life grows and is sustained
From her I came forth and to her I shall someday return

Put three pinches of the salt in the water and stir it three times clockwise. Perform a self-blessing by anointing yourself with the water and use your fingers to sprinkle a few drops around the circle.

Call the quarters in whatever manner you choose, then return to the altar. While saying the following invocation, make a circling motion over the cauldron and candles with your hand or sword. You could also use a black feather, if you wish.

Anu, Macha, Badb
The three in one
Anu, Macha, Badb
I call thee Morrigan, come!

Light the white candle.

Anu
Wisdom of the deep
And fertile earth
I call thee Morrigan, come!

Light the red candle.

Macha
Mare Mother
Warrior Queen
Sword ready for battle
I call thee Morrigan, come

Light the black candle.

Badb
Cauldron Mother
Life and death
Are in your keeping
I call thee Morrigan, come!

Triple Goddess
Of sovereignty's power
I call thee Morrigan, come!

Cúchulain's bane
Dagda's wife
Nine braids in your hair
I call thee Morrigan, come!

Faery Queen
Prophecy your natural tongue
I call thee Morrigan, come!

Lady of Avalon
Mistress of fate
I call thee Morrigan, come!

Shape-shifter Goddess
Battle Crone
I call thee Morrigan, come!

Anu, Macha, Badb
I call thee Morrigan, come!

Anu, Macha, Badb
I call thee Morrigan, come!

Anu, Macha, Badb
I call thee Morrigan, come!

Take a few moments to feel the Morrigan's presence and listen to any wisdom she might offer you. When you are ready, light the green candle representing Dagda, while saying:

Dagda
Good God, All-Father
Bearer of the cauldron of plenty
Your club both destroys and restores life
Your harp moves the season, each in turn
You bless and sustain your people
Father God, hail and welcome!

Take a few moments to feel Dagda's presence and listen to any wisdom he might offer you.

Finally, light the white candle you have placed inside the cauldron. This candle represents your ancestors and friends and family members that have passed beyond the Veil.

I light this candle in honor of _________

Say the names of the loved ones you wish to honor, or you may simply say "in honor of my ancestors" if there is no one specific you wish to honor. You may wish to simply remind them that they are not forgotten or speak at length to a particular person who has passed on.

You may feel the presence of loved ones who have passed on within the circle; be aware of their energies, but don't be afraid. This can be a very profound moment, especially if there is any unresolved business between you or if you did not get a chance to say goodbye to the individual in life. Take all the time you need, as communication with those who have passed on is easiest on this night.

If you are planning on doing any divination or spellwork, do so now. On Samhain I re-bless my Tarot cards and other divination tools. This blessing can be done on cards you have used for years to recharge them or on a new deck. Place the cards or other divination tools on the altar and circle them with your sword, saying:

In the name of the Morrigan
Great Lady of Prophecy and Magick
I summon forth the gift of second sight
From your lips to my ears
These cards shall bring forth the information I require
In the name of the Raven Mother, you are blessed!

When you are ready to close the ritual, raise a chalice of wine above the altar. Slowly lower the sword into the wine, saying:

Astride the river Unius
The Morrigan and Dagda do yearly mate
God of life
Mother of death and rebirth
Dark and light
Male and female
Goddess and God
Unite and be one
A cycle fulfilled and another newly begun!

Take a sip of the wine and pour some into your libation bowl or put the chalice aside and pour the remaining wine outside after the ritual. Thank the Morrigan and Dagda, then extinguish their candles. Close the quarters and open the circle.

Samhain Seer Invocation

Use the following invocation when performing any divination on Samhain:

Summer's end
All hallows' night
I ask now for second sight!

Winter Solstice

December 21/22
Also called: Yule, Alban Arthuan

The Winter Solstice marks the longest night of the year. The sun god is reborn on this night, and the hours of sunlight increase in the coming days. It is a day to honor the dark part of the year that yields new life and rebirth and to honor deities associated with the sun. There are several sun goddesses in the Celtic tradition, and you may want to call upon the female aspect of the sun on this day as well.

The following ritual calls upon three goddesses associated with winter and the Cauldron of Rebirth. While the Crone guards our death, she also initiates our rebirth. The Winter Solstice is a time to begin new endeavors and to take time to recognize the lessons you have learned during the dark half of the year. Belenos or another sun deity of your choice can be substituted in place of Lugh. Lugh is also part of my personal pantheon, and his energies seems to complement the Morrigan's very well, but you can call upon another sun deity if you wish.

Ritual of the Cauldron Mothers

You Will Need:

Winter Solstice Incense (see page 352)
1 cauldron
1 black feather

1 tsp. each angelica, elderberries, and oak leaves
1 white or gold floating candle
1 bottle of spring water

Cast the circle and call the quarters. Go to the altar and light the incense. Pass the cauldron through the incense or waft the smoke over the cauldron with the black feather, saying:

By air I bless the cauldron of the Morrigan
Raven Mother, Wise Crone
Ferrier of souls from this life to the next
Here is the cauldron of the Morrigan!

Drop the herbs into the cauldron, saying:

By the roots and herbs of the earth
I bless the cauldron of Cailleach
Dark Crone
Blue Hag of Winter
Mistress of change, rebirth, and the turning of the seasons
Here is the Cauldron of Cailleach!

Pour the water into the cauldron. Stir the waters sunwise three times with your fingers, saying:

By water I bless the cauldron of Cerridwen
Lady of Transformation
Who stirs the waters of inspiration
Keeper of inner wisdom
Pour your blessings forth
Here is the cauldron, the womb, of Cerridwen!

Draw an invoking pentagram over the cauldron, saying:

Cailleach, Cerridwen, Morrigan
Crones of winter and rebirth
Cauldron keepers, spell weavers
All must bow to you in the end

Cailleach, Cerridwen, Morrigan
From Crone to Maiden easily you shift
Keepers of the gates of death
Midwives of rebirth
Your destruction brings creation
A spark of light in the pregnant darkness

Cailleach, Cerridwen, Morrigan
Forebearers of Spring
From your cauldron bring forth new light
Rebirth and change, transformation and might
Hail and welcome, Dark Mothers!

Cailleach, Cerridwen, Morrigan
Cailleach, Cerridwen, Morrigan
Cailleach, Cerridwen, Morrigan!

A floating candle would work best to represent the god; if you can't find one, a candle that is tall enough to remain lit after you have poured the water into the cauldron can be used as well. Light the candle and place it in the cauldron, saying:

Born out of the darkness of the Mother
Shining One
Sun king
Luminous and reborn
Divine child of light
Lugh, god of many skills
Champion of the Túatha Dé Danann
I welcome your light to this circle
Hail and welcome, Sun Lord!

Do any planned spellwork or pathwork. I tend to call on renewed prosperity during the Winter Solstice. Asking for a new venture to be blessed, or any work regarding new beginnings would also be appropriate. The following is a simple spell calling on prosperity that I often use during the Winter Solstice.

Take three sticks of cinnamon, equal parts ground ginger and orange peel, and place them in a gold or white bag. With your finger, sprinkle three drops of the cauldron water onto the herbs. Circle the bag with your wand three times, saying:

Lugh, Lord of light
Bring to me your abundance and might
My prosperity grows in your newborn light
As I will so shall it be!

Thank the Cauldron Mothers and Lugh. Close the quarters and the circle. Pour the cauldron water and herbs outside after the ritual.

Winter Solstice Incense

2 tbsp. frankincense
2 tbsp. myrrh
1 tbsp. juniper berries
½ tbsp. echinacea root
1 tbsp. angelica
2 tbsp. orange peel

Feast of the Morrigan

January 7, or any day you wish

I first came across this date in connection to the Morrigan in Edain McCoy's book *Celtic Women's Spirituality*. There is no historic backing that I have been able to find for the date, but the point is to take a day to honor the Morrigan and her mysteries, and to thank her for the aid and wisdom she has imparted on us. You can celebrate the Feast of the Morrigan on any day you wish; I only list January 7 since that is the day I have adopted for this feast.

You can honor the Morrigan with a full ritual or by simply lighting a candle on her altar and leaving her an offering. What matters is that you connect with her energies. A simple altar devotion can be as powerful as a complex ritual drama. Follow your intuition and go with what feels right to you. My own celebration changes every year and is a reflection of the lessons I've learned and my journey with the Morrigan through the previous year.

The following ritual is an example—feel free to add to it or change anything you wish. Your celebration should be a reflection of your connection to the Morrigan. If you are doing a group ritual, take time at some point in the ritual for everyone to share an experience they have had with the Morrigan that year.

Feast of the Morrigan Ritual

You Will Need:

1 red candle
Charcoal brick for the incense
Cauldron
Soil or salt (enough for a thin layer inside the cauldron)
Wand or black feather
Feast of the Morrigan Incense (see page 355)
Wine or mead
Libation bowl

Place the red candle in the center of the altar to represent the Morrigan. Light the charcoal brick and put it in the cauldron. Make sure to put a layer of salt or soil in the cauldron so the cauldron is not too hot to hold. Circle the incense with the black feather or wand three times, then put some of the incense on the charcoal. Carry the cauldron around the circle. Return to the altar and perform a self-blessing by using the black feather to waft the smoke over each chakra, starting at the crown of your head and moving down to your feet. If working in a group, choose one person to go around the circle and smudge the other participants. Put the cauldron back on the altar. Cast the circle and call the quarters.

Return to the altar and light the red candle. Raise your hands in an invoking position, saying:

Lady of Enchantment, Mistress of faeries
Raven Goddess on black wings
Anu, Macha, Badb,

Lady of Mysteries
Both dark and bright
Anu, Macha, Badb,

Lady of the Sea
Rivers and holy wells
Mother of the life-giving waters
Anu, Macha, Badb,

Earth Mother of sacred mounds and faery hills
who protects clan and hearth
Opener of doorways between life and death,

Great Queen of prophetic visions
Declarer of victories
Sovereignty is yours to bestow,

Raven of Battle
Red Queen
Washer at the Ford
Dark Crone on black wings,

Many are your names
Anu, Macha, Badb
Áine, Modron, Badb Catha, Cathubodva
Morrigna, Morrigu,

Morrigan
I honor you this night in all your name and guises!

The following blessing is based on the prophecy the Morrigan spoke after the defeat of the Fomorians. Circle the wine with the black feather three times, saying:

A cup very full
Full of honey
Mead in abundance

Summer in winter
Peace high as heaven
Heaven to the earth
Earth under heaven
Strength in each
Morrigan may your blessings flow through me!

Raise the chalice above the altar, pour some of the wine into the libation bowl, then take a sip. Say:

I am one with the Morrigan!

Now is the time for guided meditations, pathworking, or sharing your experiences of the Morrigan. Take a moment to thank the Morrigan for the lessons and wisdom she has granted you over the previous year. If you are just starting your journey with the Morrigan, ask for her aid in a specific task or throughout the coming year.

Thank the Morrigan and close the circle. Pour the contents of the libation bowl outside.

Feast of the Morrigan Incense

2 tbsp. dragon's blood resin
1 tbsp. vervain
1 tbsp. mullein
1 tbsp. patchouli
½ tbsp. musk
3 drops of your blood (menstrual blood, if you are female)

Beltane

May 1

Also called: May Day or Lady's Day

Unlike our modern concept of four distinct seasons, the Celts divided their year in two: a dark half and a light half. The dark half of the year began on Samhain, which marked the beginning of the season of cold and winter. Directly opposite Samhain on the year wheel, Beltane marked the beginning of spring and the fruitful half of the year. Meaning "balefire," Beltane is primarily a fire festival. Balefires were lit atop hills and the clan's herds were driven past the fires to bless them and ensure their fertility. On Beltane cattle were moved to their summer pastures. Young people spent the night in the wood "a-maying"—making love in the woods and fields as an act of sympathetic magick to encourage fertile crops. These trysts were sometimes referred to as "greenwood marriages," and children produced through such unions were considered especially lucky.

Beltane is a time to honor the union of the Great Goddess and Great God, the renewed fertility of the earth, creativity, and sexuality. What better holiday to honor the lusty earth goddess of Connacht, Maeve, and the sultry Faery Queen Áine?

For me, Maeve's connection to the Morrigan comes from her seat of power in Cruachan. In some stories, Maeve is the daughter of Crochan, the mysterious red woman and handmaiden to the goddess Étain. Crochan, although never said to be the Morrigan in another form, seems to bear a resemblance to the Great Queen and incidentally gives birth to Maeve in the Cave of Cruachan, the same cave that was said to be the home of the Morrigan. On some Beltanes I honor Maeve as a daughter of the Morrigan and a goddess of the earth and sexuality in her own right. Other years I honor Áine, as the Maiden aspect of the Morrigan who is well known for her love affairs with mortal men and heroes, and for her passion for life.

Áine's Faery Beltane Ritual

You Will Need:

Lavender
Meadowsweet (fresh if possible)
Wand
1 bottle or spring water
Cauldron or glass bowl
1 red or pink candle to represent Áine
1 green candle to represent the Lord of the Wild
Chalice of mead or wine
Athame

Mix the lavender and meadowsweet together. With your wand in one hand, cast the circle while sprinkling the herbs along the boundary of the circle with your other hand. Say:

In Áine's name this circle is bound
Lady bless this holy ground

Pour the water into the cauldron or bowl along with any remaining meadowsweet. Hold your hand over it, seeing the golden rays of Áine's sun fill and bless it. Walk around the circle sunwise, using your fingers to sprinkle the water around the circle, saying:

Waters of Áine bless and cleanse this place

Go to the east and use your wand to draw an invoking pentagram. Say:

Sylphs and Fae of the air
I call you to this faery rite
Bring to this circle the power of inspiration and creativity!

Go to the south and draw an invoking pentagram. Say:

Drakes and Fae of fire
I call you to this faery rite
Bring to this circle passion and power!

Go to the west and draw an invoking pentagram. Say:

Merrow and Fae of the sea and sacred waters
I call you to this faery rite
Bring to this circle your healing and cleansing touch!

Go to the north and draw an invoking pentagram. Say:

Gnomes and Fae of the earth
I call you to this faery rite
Bring to this circle strength and stability!

Return to the altar. Light the red or pink candle, while saying:

Queen of the Faeries
Lusty Queen of May
Áine of the faery hill
Come dance round the Beltane fire

Fill me with your gentle love and laughter
Hail Áine!

Light the green candle, saying:

Wild Lord of the Woodland
King of Faery hill and mound
Come, O Lord of the Wild
To the Witches' round
Raise our passions higher and higher
Dance with us around the Beltane fire

Continue with any planned spellwork. This would be an ideal time to attract a new love into your life or to ask for inspiration for creative projects.

Lower the athame into the mead, saying:

On Beltane the Lord and Lady unite
Two become one, and bring new life

Remove the athame and hold the chalice above the altar, saying:

To the Lord and Lady!

Drink some of the mead and pour the rest onto the ground. If you are working inside, pour the mead outside on the ground after the ritual.

When you are ready to close the circle, thank Áine and the Lord of the Wild and snuff the candles, then go to each quarter, saying:

Depart in peace, Fae and spirits of air/fire/water/earth

Open the circle.

Maeve's Beltane Ritual

You Will Need:
½ cup whiskey
1 fireproof bowl or cauldron
1 red candle to represent Maeve
Honey

Cinnamon
Nutmeg
Rose petals
Matches or a lighter
1 gold or yellow candle to represent Lugh
Pen and paper
Chalice of mead
Athame

As a fire festival, the element of fire plays a central role in any Beltane celebration. Pour the ½ cup of whiskey into a fireproof bowl; this will be lit during the ritual to represent the Beltane fire. If you are celebrating outside, you may wish to make a balefire for the ritual instead.

Maeve's name is connected to mead, a wine made of honey, and her name means "drunken woman." Honey and mead are excellent offerings to her. Take the candle you will be using to represent Maeve and pour some honey on a plate. Gently roll the candle in the honey, making certain not to get any on the wick. A light coating of honey is all that is needed, as too much will make the candle hard to handle. Place the cinnamon, nutmeg, and rose petals on a separate plate and roll the candle in the herbs. Let the candle set for ten minutes or place it in the refrigerator for ten to fifteen minutes (either in a candle holder or suspended by the wick so it doesn't stick to the plate).

Cast the circle and call the quarters. Go to the altar and hold your hands over the cauldron of whiskey that will be your Beltane fire, saying:

The sun has warmed the earth with its fiery caress
The air is heavy with the scent of flowers
And Beltane has come again.

Maeve, Lusty Queen of May
Keeper of sovereignty and passion

Fire in the head and loins
In your name, I light this Beltane fire

Carefully light the whiskey by dropping a match into the cauldron, saying:

Flame of creation, passion, and desire
Bless me now, O Beltane fire!

Take a moment to meditate on the element of fire; see the fire flow through you as you breathe in and out, purifying you and igniting the creative forces within you.

When you are ready, light the red candle, saying:

Maeve
Lusty Queen of May
Intoxicating one, insatiable one
Fair-haired wolf Queen, proud in posture[111]
Keeper of sovereignty and the mysteries of the earth
Who rules over our inner passions and strengths
Mistress of all things green and growing
Spark of life, spark of desire, creation and holy fire
Be here now, most lovely Goddess of the land
I drink deep of your honey-sweet spirit
Let your fiery power and mine be one!

Light the gold candle representing Lugh, saying:

Lugh, Lord of Light, Lord of fire
Shining bright like the Beltane fire
Hail Lord of the shining sun
Bless me now with your sacred fire!

On a pieces of paper write what it is you wish to draw to you in this season of light and abundance: a new love, creativity, inspiration, etc. Fold the paper and burn it in the fire, while concentrating on your desire manifesting.

When you are ready, hold the chalice above the altar, saying:

111. Maeve is given this description in the *Dindshenchas*.

This is Beltane
The night when the Goddess and God become one
From their union all life flows
I honor the Lord and Lady of life
And ask as they bring forth new life
That I too may bring my dreams and desires to fruition!

Lower the athame into the chalice of mead, saying:

Chalice to blade
Man to woman
Goddess to God
Flesh to spirit
All become one
And create life anew!

Thank Maeve and Lugh, close the quarters, and open the circle. Any ashes from the Beltane fire should be saved and can be used in any spellwork used to bring prosperity or for a general blessing.

Beltane Incense

1 handful of rose petals (red or pink)
1 tbsp. ground cinnamon
1 tbsp. ground nutmeg
1 tbsp. sandalwood
½ tbsp. musk
9 cloves

Summer Solstice

June 21 or 22

Also called: Midsummer, Litha, and Alban Heruin

The Summer Solstice marks the longest day of the year and the height of the sun's power. Balefires were traditionally lit to honor the sun and bring its fertile power to the fields and herds to ensure a plentiful harvest. The Faery Folk are thought to be especially active on this day, and offerings were left outside for the Good Folk.

In the following ritual you will be calling on Áine as a sun goddess rather than calling on the sun as a male force. The Celts saw the sun as both a male and a female force, having several sun goddesses and gods. This ritual only calls on the female aspect of the sun. Since we are more accustomed to seeing the sun as a male force, it is important to take time to experience the sun as the Mother Sun. If you wish you can call upon a sun god as well (Lugh or Belenos would be good choices). My own Summer Solstice rituals change from year to year. Sometimes I only invoke Áine, and other years I also call on Lugh, another of my patrons. Go with whatever feels right.

Áine Litha Ritual

You Will Need:
1 red or yellow candle
Glass container

On Midsummer balefires were lit on Cnoc Áine, and torches lit from that fire were carried through the fields to bless them. In this ritual you will carry a candle around your house or apartment to bring Áine's blessing into your home.

Cast the circle, then go back to the altar. Circle the candle with your wand three times, saying:

Áine
Faery Maid of fiery power
Bless now this sacred fire

Call the quarters, starting in the east:
Áine of the gentle wind
Playing upon your Faery Lyre
Inspiration's sweet melody
To me and this circle bring your quick wit and joyful banter!

South:
Áine of the midday sun
Life's spark, passion and desire
Bright phoenix rising ever higher
To me and this circle bring the cleansing touch of fire!

West:
Áine of the holy well waters
Ebbing, flowing
Wisdom growing
To me and this circle bring your water's healing touch!

North:
Áine of the faery mound
Spiral path upon the ground
Mistress of bud and root and growing things
To me and this circle the earth's abundance bring!

Return to the altar and raise your hands with your palms up, saying:

Áine who is Anu
Who is Danu
Who is the Morrigan
Goddess of the sun
Who rules over
Passion and fire
Love and desire
Lady of the Wisps
And holy well water
Fair-haired poet
Inspiration's muse
Fill within me inspiration's cup
Stir within me passion's flame
Nurture within me life's vital spark!

Do any planned pathworking or spellwork. Litha is an excellent time to call upon Áine's healing power, do spellwork to find love, and general prosperity. When you are done, light the candle in the glass container. (If you do not have a glass container, place the candle in something that will prevent wax from dripping onto your hands or the floor.) Say:

I gather Áine's light into this candle
That it may bless those it shines upon

See Áine's blessings and energies filling the candle. Put the candle to the side for now. Thank Áine, close the quarters, and open the circle. Do not blow out the candle; the ritual is not over yet! Walk around each room in your home in a sunwise direction with the candle, saying the following chant as you do so:

Áine's light bless me and mine
Bring to this place your fiery presence divine

Leave the candle in a safe place and let it burn out. For group rituals, each participant should have an individual candle. A tealight in a glass holder would be ideal, minimizing your chances of spilling wax. Have each person light their candle from a central candle on the altar. These candles can be brought home and relit on the participant's personal altar and walked around the home to bring Áine's blessings to their house or apartment.

Feast of Áine

Early August

The Friday, Saturday, and Sunday after the Festival of Lughnasadh (Lammas) were sacred to the goddess Áine. Physicians would not perform any sort of bloodletting on these days, fearing that the patient's life essence, which Áine ruled over, would leave the body and cause the patient to die.

One of the meanings of Áine's name is "pleasure," and taking time to enjoy life and indulge in your favorite activities can be a fun and playful way of honoring Áine. As a goddess of love and fertility, this would also be an excellence time to perform love and fertility spells. Since all three days were sacred to Áine, you may choose to honor her on all three days or choose one day in particular to work with her.

Áine Candle Petition

You Will Need:
Marker and a piece of paper
1 red or gold candle
Fireproof bowl

On a piece of paper, write down what you wish to manifest. Light the red or gold candle, saying:

Flame and fire
Wick and wax
Áine's flame burning fast
Bring now, what I ask!

Light the paper in the candle's flame and let it burn out in the fireproof bowl. Sprinkle the ashes outside. Let the candle burn out as an offering to Áine.

Mabon

September 21 or 22

Also called: Autumn or Fall Equinox, Second Harvest

Mabon marks the second harvest festival in the Celtic year. It is a time of balance, when day and night are equal. Mabon is sometimes referred to as "The Witch's Thanksgiving," and it was a time to give thanks for the harvest and to store away food for the cold winter months. The last sheaf of the harvest was dressed up to represent the Great Goddess as the queen of the harvest and placed on the mantle to encourage her blessings.

Mabon is a time to reap the lessons of the past and to work toward bringing balance into your mundane and spiritual lives. During this time of the year wheel, I always feel the most connected to the Celtic horse goddesses. You will find here both a ritual that invokes Macha's bountiful nature and a ritual to call upon Epona, Macha, and Rhiannon—all goddesses connected to the earth and horses.

Macha Equinox Rite

You Will Need:

Sword
Macha Herbal Blend (see page 65)
Crow feather
Salt
Cauldron of water

3 acorns or hazelnuts
Green marker
1 apple
Chalice of wine or apple cider

Cast the circle using the sword, saying:

I mark the boundaries of this sacred space
As Macha marked the boundaries
Of Emain Macha with her broach
In Macha's name this circle is sealed!

Light the herbal blend as incense and circle it three times with the crow feather, saying:

Winged one, Crow woman
Bless this circle with the cleansing power of air!

Walk around the circle clockwise with the incense. Return to the altar, use the crow feather to waft some of the incense over the altar, then perform a self-blessing by wafting the incense over your body with the feather. Put three pinches of salt in the water and stir it with your athame, saying:

Salt and water
Blood and body of the Goddess
Bring your blessings to this place
In Macha's name, I call you purified!

Go around the circle clockwise, sprinkling the salt water around the circle with your fingers. Then sprinkle some of the water on the altar, saying:

Here is the altar of Macha
Lady of the brilliant sun
Horse Goddess
Crow woman and faery seeress
In her name may this place be blessed
Hail Macha
Know that you are honored here!

Go to the east and draw an invoking pentagram with your sword, saying:

Crow Goddess
Black feathers gliding upon the wind
Swift-footed mare
Untamable, wild, and free
Macha, now hear me
Macha, be near me this day!

South:
Macha of the red tresses
Sun of womanhood
Fierce and cunning Queen
Riding upon your chariot, spear in hand
Macha, now hear me
Macha, be near me this day!

West:
Seeress, Lady of visions and far-reaching sight
Mistress of realms seen and unseen
Between the worlds you walk
Macha, now hear me
Macha, be near me this day!

North:
Lady of the Masts
Of the ripe and fertile plain
Marking the boundaries of your realm in earth and stone
Macha, now hear me
Macha, be near me this day!

Take the crow feather and circle the cauldron three times in a clockwise motion, saying:

Hail Macha
Mare Mother
Crow Goddess
Mother, Warrior, Queen

Sun of Womanhood
Lady who blesses and keeps the land
Great Queen of Battle
I give you honor, as the men of Ulster would not do,

On this day of balance between night and day
When light stands equal with dark
Come now, O mighty Queen
Who holds sovereignty over the land
Macha, now hear me
Macha, be near me this day!

Perform any additional spellwork or pathwork. When you are ready, pass the acorns or nuts through the incense. Use the marker to draw symbols representing something you wish to manifest. Hold the nuts in your hands and visualize your desire manifesting. When the image is clear in your mind, say:

Masts of Macha
Forest harvest
Seeds of the earth
Bring form and shape to my desire
In Macha's name, manifest!

Place the acorns in your cauldron. Circle the apple with the feather three times, then cut it in half with your athame, saying:

I honor you Macha
For the bounty that you bring
Harvest Queen
May your blessing of prosperity flow unending!

Take a bite from one of the apple halves and place the other in the offering bowl. Then circle the chalice of wine with the crow feather three times and hold it above the altar, saying:

Fiery Macha
Lady of the sun
Unbridled, untamable

In the end all warriors must give you your due
Macha, I give you honor, as the men of Ulster would not do!

Take a sip of the wine, then pour the remaining liquid in your libation bowl or put it aside to be poured outside after the ritual.

When you are ready to close the ritual, go to each of the quarters and draw a banishing pentagram, saying:

Depart in peace, powers of the east/south/west/north

Open the circle by cutting it with your sword, saying:

Macha's circle is now unbound

Bury the acorn or nuts on your property.

Ritual of the Mare Mothers

You Will Need:
Macha Herbal Blend (see page 65)
1 brown candle
1 yellow candle

Cast the circle and call the quarters. Go to the altar and say:

Equality of day and night
Balancing point of dark and light
Now are night and day equal, standing in perfect balance
May I too be guided toward a sacred balance

Light the herbal blend as incense. Light the brown candle, saying:

Epona, Macha, Rhiannon
White Mare, Dark Raven, Mighty Queen
Swiftly moving
Hoof beats drumming on the ground

Epona, Macha, Rhiannon
White Mare, Dark Raven, Mighty Queen,

The sharp spear, the field ripe with wheat
The sun's golden rays your mighty crown

Epona, Macha, Rhiannon
White Mare, Dark Raven, Mighty Queen
Abundance, Movement, Sovereignty
Your gifts grant to me,

Epona, Macha, Rhiannon
White Mare, Dark Raven, Mighty Queen
You keep the balance
Light and dark
Life and death,

Epona, Macha, Rhiannon
White Mare, Dark Raven, Mighty Queen
Swift as wind, flashing hooves
Wild, uncatchable, untamed
I honor you, Mare Mothers,

Epona, Macha, Rhiannon
White Mare, Dark Raven, Mighty Queen
Hail and be welcome!

Light the yellow candle, to represent the god, saying:

Lugh
Sun King
Wide shield of protection
Bestower of riches and well-being
Lord of the Harvest
I call upon your mighty spirit to descend upon this circle
Infuse it with your many blessings
And cloak me in your mantle of fiery power
Hail and welcome, Lugh!

If you have any spellwork planned, do so now. Then take a few minutes to meditate on your own personal balance in life. What is off balance, how can you correct the imbalance? Ask the Mare Mothers and Lugh for advice and aid.

When you are ready, close the quarters and thank the Mare Mothers and Lugh. Open the circle.

19

Moon Rites

The following moon rites can be used with the Basic Morrigan Ritual found on page 380 or with a circle casting of your choice. While the Morrigan is not specifically a moon goddess, the new moon is an excellent time to work with her darker aspect, do any psychic work, or call upon her to discover past lives. During the waxing and full moon, call upon the Morrigan's brighter faces for healing and abundance.

Morrigan Full Moon Ritual

You Will Need:

1 white candle
3 pieces of clear quartz or moonstone
Wand or athame

Place a white or light-colored candle in the center of the altar to represent the Morrigan. Place the clear quartz or moonstone pieces around the candle. Using your wand or athame, cast the circle, saying:

In the Morrigan's name
I cast this circle of moonlight
May Badb guard it, may Anu give it strength,
may Macha fill it with her magick!

If you wish, perform a self-blessing. When you are ready, call the elements. For the following quarter calls you can replace *Goddess* in the last line with *Divine* or something similar if you're working with a mixed-gender group. As you call each element, imagine yourself being filled with the power of that element.

East:
On this full moon night I invoke the Raven Mother
Winged one whose voice can be the gentle breeze
Or contain the power of a raging storm
Fill my words with the force of your Will
That I may speak with the voice of a Goddess!

South:
On this full moon night I invoke the Lady of Fire
You are the lover filled with passion
Or the mighty Queen filled with battle rage
Your power consumes and destroys
Yet can also raise our passions higher
Fill me with your sacred fire
That my spirit may shine with the light of a Goddess!

West:
On this full moon night I invoke the Phantom Queen
You who are both the alluring sea nymph and the wailing banshee
Lady of sacred waters, river guardian, and Sea Queen
You rule the shadowy realms of the seen and unseen
Fill my sight with the power of vision
That I may pierce the Veil and see with the sight of a Goddess!

North:
On this full moon night I invoke the Mother of the Land
You are both young and old, changing as the seasons
Yet enduring as the stones of the earth
Fill me with your unending strength
Let my flesh and yours be one,
That my body may be the temple of the Goddess!

Return to the altar. Light the candle, saying:

Morrigan
Lady of Ravens
Both Dark and Bright
Wise healer
Cunning warrior

Lady of magick
Weaving your spells
I call you here this night
Sing to us of victory
Of deep and powerful magick
As the full moon rises
Come to us who gather here
This night in your honor
Hail Morrigan!

Complete any spell work you have planned. When you are ready to end the ritual, thank the Morrigan and close the quarters by saying:

Depart in peace powers of air/fire/water/earth

To open the circle, cut it with your wand or athame, saying:

The circle of the Morrigan is now open
But her strength and power ever flows through me!

Morrigan New Moon Ritual

You Will Need:

1 black or dark-colored candle
Cauldron

The new moon is a time to look within, do spellwork to banish negative habits or people, and start new projects. Choose a black or dark-colored candle to represent the Morrigan for this ritual and place it in the cauldron. If working with a coven, the refrain *"Morrigan, Dark Morrigan"* can be chanted by the rest of the coven members as the Priestess speaks the rest of the invocation.

Cast the circle and call the quarters, then go to the altar and say:

The moon is hidden and dark
Her light shines within
Morrigan of the new moon
Guide me through the darkness

Light the candle, saying:

Dark Goddess
You who instigate change
Morrigan, Dark Morrigan,

Ancient and young
Shifting shape, changing form at will
Raven Woman
Maiden and Crone
Morrigan, Dark Morrigan,

Mistress of battle
Spear at your side
Your victory assured
Morrigan, Dark Morrigan,

Faery Woman
Enchanting one
Noble and wise
Morrigan, Dark Morrigan,

Teach me your mysteries
That destruction and creation are but one
Morrigan, Dark Morrigan,

Guardian of Avalon
Mistress of rebirth
Morrigan, Dark Morrigan,

Hooded crow
Grey-red wolf
Morrigan, Dark Morrigan,

I seek change
I seek transformation
I seek your strength

I seek inner illumination
Morrigan, Dark Morrigan,

Be here this night
Morrigan, Dark Morrigan
Morrigan, Dark Morrigan
Morrigan, Dark Morrigan!

Complete any spellwork you have planned, then thank the Morrigan and close the quarters.

New Moon Scrying Ritual

You Will Need:
Scrying tool, such as a dish of water or a scrying mirror
Black candle
Scrying incense of your choice

On the new moon, take your scrying mirror or a bowl of water to your sacred space. Light a black candle to represent the Morrigan and light your favorite scrying incense. Pass your hands over your scrying tool three times in a clockwise motion, while saying:

Morrigan of the dark moon
Whose eyes pierce the night
And see all that is hidden
Cast aside the Veil this night
Let me see with a Goddess's sight!

Gaze into the water or mirror. Eventually images will appear. Sometimes these images will be within your mind's eye rather than on the surface of the scrying tool. Take your time, sit comfortably, and do not strain your eyes. Eventually the answer to your question will come. When you are done, pass your hand over the tool three times in a counterclockwise motion and thank the Morrigan.

New Moon Ritual

By Meryt-Meihera

You Will Need:

Altar decorations: bloodstone, smoky quartz, raven feathers, black candles (or elemental colors)

Divination tools if you are planning on any scrying or divination work

Wine or other offering (I've used strawberries)

Incense, optional (I'm fond of sandalwood, rose, or lavender)

Mystery of the earth
Airy light of moon
Power of the flowing water
Warmth of the burning flame
Purity of the eternal essence
We call to thee in Morrigan's name

Righting of wrongs
Healing of ills
Cleansing of impurities
Desiring of truths
Sensing of harmony
In Morrigan's name, we call to thee

Speed of the wolf
Silence of the bird
Sight of the cat
Sensuality of the dragon
Sincerity of the spirit
We call to thee, Morrigan the starlit

Grant us your blessings this moonless night
May we always walk the path of delight
Aid our magick and hear our plea
As we will, so mote it be

With the Mystery of the earth
The airy light of the moon
The power of flowing water
The warmth of the burning flame
And with purity of the soul
We call to thee, in Morrigan's name

The New Moon is a time of Righting of wrongs
Healing of ills
The cleansing of impurities
Our desiring of truths and sensing of harmony
In Macha's name, we call to thee

Tonight, we tread the night with the Speed of the Wolf
We ride the wind with the Silence of the Bird
We stalk through the night with the Sight of the Cat
We savor one another with the Sensuality of the Dragon
And with the sincerity of spirit
We call to thee, Badb the starlit
Grant us your blessings this moonless night
That we may begin anew
And always walk the path of delight
By the powers of our Great Queen
May we all blessed be

Threefold Morrigan Invocation

The following invocation can be used for invoking the Morrigan in any type of ritual. You will need three candles: one white, one red, and one black. Hold your arms up in an invoking position, while saying:

Anu, Macha, Badb
Morrigan, dark and wild Goddess
Whose cries shatter earth and sky

For thee I raise my sword and vow eternal troth[112]
Hail threefold one of life, death, and rebirth!

Light the white candle.

Hail Goddess of Life!
You who are the fertile land
Keeper of clan and kine
Queen of the Sidhe,
Mistress of faery hill and mound
Hail Anu!

Light the red candle.

Hail Goddess of Death!
You who walk the mist-filled battlefield
And claim the dead
Great Queen, Raven of Battle
Sword dripping with the blood of the slain
Hail Macha!

Light the black candle.

Hail Goddess of Rebirth!
Dark Crone who stirs the cauldron of rebirth
You are the tomb, Goddess of night and endings
You are the womb, Goddess of new life and beginnings
Hail Badb!

Basic Morrigan Ritual

You Will Need:
Incense of your choice
Black feather
Sword or athame
1 red candle

112. Based on lyrics by Suidakra.

This ritual can be used as the framework for any type of spellwork or ritual, whether it be a full/new moon ritual or when you wish to call upon the Morrigan in any of her many guises.

Light the incense and carry it clockwise around your sacred space, using the black feather to waft the smoke, saying:

I bless this place in the name of the Raven Mother
In the Morrigan's name, let all negative energies depart!

When you are done, perform a self-blessing by using the black feather to waft the incense over your body, beginning with the crown of your head and ending at your feet, saying:

Lady of Magick
Lady of Might
Bless and cleanse me this night!

When you are ready, cast the circle using your sword while saying:

I cast now the circle of the Morrigan
A circle of mist and standing stone
A boundary between the worlds of gods and men
A place of magick and power
In the Morrigan's name, this circle is sealed!

Go to each quarter and draw an invoking pentagram with your sword or athame while saying:

East:
I call upon the black-winged Morrigan
Cunning raven-woman
Flying above the heads of warriors
Inspiring deeds of valor, promising victory
I call thee Raven Goddess, come!

South:
I call upon the Queen of Battle
Red Mare Macha
Sun of Womanhood
You are the sharp blade of a sword

The forge that shapes and tempers
I call thee Lady of Battle, come!

West:
I call upon the Phantom Queen
Shape-shifter Goddess
Form fluid and changing as water
Banshee who rules the realm of shadows
Washing away the blood of the dead and the sorrows of the soul
Badb, stirring the Cauldron of Life and Death
I call thee Queen of Shadows, come!

North:
I call upon the Mother of the Gods and Tribe
Lady of the Mounds
Cattle-raiding Goddess, red-eared heifer
Where you walk the land becomes fertile with new life
I call thee Earth Mother, come!

You can use the following chant to call the Morrigan into the circle or one of your choosing. Light the red candle, saying:

Morrigan
Mother both bright and dark
Lady of power, wisdom, mystery, and might
Cattle-raiding Faery Queen
Shape-shifting Goddess of the Apple Isle
Weaving moonlit spells, full of guile
Spear and shield in hand
To guide or guard
Come now, O Morrigan
I call thee Morrigan, come!

Perform any planned spellwork or pathwork. When you are done, circle the chalice three times with the feather. Then hold the chalice above the altar, saying:

Mistress of magick
Lady both dark and bright
Weaving spells, raven taking flight
Guardian of Magick
Mystery and Might
I give you honor and thanks this night!

Take a sip of the wine, then pour some into your libation bowl or outside on the ground after the ritual.

When you are ready to end the ritual, thank the Morrigan and draw a banishing pentagram in each quarter with the sword while saying:

East:
Depart now black-winged Morrigan, with my thanks and blessings.

South:
Depart now Queen of Battle, with my thanks and blessings.

West:
Depart now Phantom Queen, with my thanks and blessings.

North:
Depart now Earth Mother, with my thanks and blessings.

Cut the circle with your sword, saying:

The Morrigan's circle is now open!

Conclusion: Answering the Call

Somewhere the Morrigan is smiling secretly to herself. We are beginning to rediscover the power and magick of the Dark Goddess. She has never really left us, remaining hidden in the folklore of the faeries and the myths of the banshee; but now more than in any other time, I think we can fully perceive the scope of her power. She is not just a goddess of war, but a goddess of strength. She tears us apart and leads us to rebirth and renewal. She shatters our egos and hands us the cup of truth, allowing us to gaze upon our true selves. She is the spirit of justice and the maker of heroes. As with Cúchulain, she is ready to guide each of us toward our destiny, willing to aid us and bring us victory in our personal battles if we are brave enough to accept her aid.

The Morrigan has become an inseparable part of me, guiding me toward healing and strengthening my resolve. She is my Mother, my Goddess, and an inseparable part of myself. She calls to each of us in her own way, challenging us, tempering our spirits as a smith tempers a blade. Ancient warriors and kings revered her; in modern times, she seeks new champions. The Morrigan is calling to us once again. Will you answer her call?

Pronunciation Key

Celtic names can be relied on to sound very different than their spellings would suggest, and often frustrate practitioners who are not familiar with their pronunciation. In general "ch" is pronounced as a hard *k*, "si" as "shee," "dh" as a *v*, "ú" as "oo" (as in *zoo*), and "á" as "aw" (as in *paw*).

Ailill (AY-ill)

Ain (Awn)

Áine (AWN-yah)

Anu (AN-new or AHN-new)

Badb (BAH-v); also (BYE-v) being the modern Irish pronunciation, with a hard v at the end

Cailleach (ky-lee-ACK)

Cnoc na mBan-Laoch (KUH-nock nah mawn-lee-OCK)

Cruachan (KROO-a-khawn)

Crunnchu (CROON-hoo)

Cúchulain (KOO-cull-en)

Danu (DANN-oo)

Dindshenchas (din-HEN-ah-kus)

Emain Macha (eh-MAN MAH-kah)

Fir Bolg (FEAR-bolic)

Fomorian (fo-MORE-ee-ahn); also (foy-MOY-ra) in modern Irish

geasa (GEE-ass-ah)

geis (gesh)

Grainne (GRAHN-yah)

Iaine (Ea-AWN-ah)

Leannan Sidhe (lee-ANN-nan shee)

Macha (MA-ka)

Madb (may-v)

Morrigan (MORE-ee-gan)

Morrigú (MORE-i-goo)

Moytura (MOY-tour-ah)

Nemain (NEE-vuhn)

Ogham (OH-gum or OH-um)

Oweynagat (UAIGH-nah-g-cat)

Sidhe (shee)

Táin Bó Cúalnge (toyn bow coo-ahln-ee)

Túatha Dé Danann (TOO-ah-thah day-DAHN-ahn)

Glossary

Aided Con Culainn: *The Death of Cúchulain.* A story relating the events that led to the hero Cúchulain's death.

Andraste: A battle goddess favored by Queen Boudicca. Her totem was the rabbit, as she was a goddess of both fertility and war.

aspecting: Another term for invoking. Drawing a deity into your body rather than into a cast circle. In most cases, the deity will act and speak through the person; this is sometimes considered a form of divine possession.

Ath de Ferta: The Ford of the Two Chariots Poles. The place Cúchulain encounters the Morrigan in *The Táin Bó Regamna.*

augury: Also called ornithomancy. Divination involving the movements and songs of birds.

bandruaid: Also *banfhlaith* and *banfhilid.* A name used for a female Druid and means "Druid woman."

banshee: An Irish faery believed to protect a particular family. Her wails are an omen that someone in the family will soon die. She most likely evolved from the Washer at the Ford, another female death messenger.

Bean Nighe: A female faery who washed bloody clothes is desolate rivers. Seeing her was usually an omen of one's death, although some tales claim she would grant wishes if she was approached with respect.

The Book of Ballymote: An Irish manuscript created around 1390 CE. It contains genealogies of Irish kings, a version of the *Lebor Gabála Érenn,* bardic tracts, and information about the Ogham alphabet.

The Book of Leinster: Written sometime between 1151 CE and 1201 CE, it was used as a source book for later Irish manuscripts, such as *The Yellow Book of Lecan.* It contains *The Book of Invasions,* the most complete version of *The Cattle Raid of Cooley,* and the *Dindshenchas.*

The Boyhood Deeds of Cúchulain: Stories concerning Cúchulain's childhood exploits. These are usually included in *The Cattle Raid of Cooley*. The stories explains how he was given his name and how he came to be fostered by King Conchobar at Emain Macha.

The Cath Maige Tuired: Also called *The Second Battle of Moytura*. It chronicles the war between the Túatha Dé Danann and the Fomorians.

The Cath Muighe Tuireadh: Also called *The First Battle of Moytura*. It chronicles the Túatha Dé Danann's arrival in Ireland and their war with the indigenous gods, the Fir Bolgs.

Cathubodva: A Gaulish goddess known only through a single inscription on a stone in Mieussy, France. Her name means "Battle Raven," and she is often compared to Badb, who is given a similar name, Badb Catha, or "Battle Crow."

Cnoc Áine: A hill in the province of Munster that was sacred to Áine. At midsummer the faery folk were believed to roam the hill.

Cnoc na mBan-Laoch: The Hill of the Woman-Heroes located at Tara.

Conchobar mac Nessa: The king of Ulster during the time of *The Cattle Raid of Cooley*. He was Cúchulain's uncle and fostered the hero when he was a boy.

Connacht: The western province of Ireland. Home of Queen Maeve.

Cormac's Glossary: Also *Sanas Chormaic*. An early Irish glossary that contains references and etymologies for Irish words. It was a kind of encyclopedic dictionary of its time. Its creation is credited to Cormac mac Cuilennain, a bishop-king of Munster.

Crochan Crogderg: The Red Woman of the cave of Oweynagat. She was a maid servant of the goddess Étain and is described as having red skin and hair. In some stories she was said to be the mother of Queen Maeve.

Dagda: Called the "Good God," he was said to be the Morrigan's husband. He was known for his immense appetite for both food and sex. He possessed a cauldron called Undry, which was bottomless, making him a god of plenty and prosperity. He also had a club that could kill nine men with one blow, while the handle could reanimate a warrior and bring him back to life. He also owned an oak harp that changed the seasons and could turn the tide of battle when played.

Danu: The mother goddess of the Túatha Dé Danann. She was associated with water and fertility. She is often equated with the goddess Anu, another mother goddess.

Daughters of Calatin: Three sorceresses sent abroad by Queen Maeve to learn magick. They helped kill the hero Cúchulain in order to take revenge for their father's death.

deity altar: An altar dedicated to a specific goddess or god.

The Destruction of Da Derga's Hostel: Also called *Togail Bruidne Dá Derga.* An Irish epic tale that recounts the life and death of Conaire, a legendary High King of Ireland. After breaking his geasa, he is killed at Da Derga's Hostel.

Dindshenchas: A series of 176 poems and prose works concerning the origins of Irish place-names. One version of the *Dindshenchas* can be found in *The Book of Leinster,* which dates back to the twelfth century. Several partial versions also exist within thirteen different manuscripts.

Echtra Nera: Also called *The Adventures of Nera.* Dates back to the eighth century and relates the adventure Nera had when he traveled to the Otherworlds on the night of Samhain.

Emain Macha: The mythical capital of Ulster. It was said to have been named for the goddess Macha. She was said to have outlined the dimensions of the fort with the pin of her broach. In other versions of Macha's myths, this is the place she is forced to race the king of Ulster's horses.

Epona: Pan-Celtic goddess of horses.

evoking: To summon or call an energy, spirit, or deity into a cast circle or sacred space.

Fir Bolgs: The race of gods that lived in Ireland before the Túatha Dé Danann. They are described as ugly and misshapen. They represent the forces of chaos, while the Túatha Dé Danann represented order.

Fomorian: A race of gods who fought with the Túatha Dé Danann. Their name comes from the Gaelic *faoi-mhuir,* which means "beneath the sea," and they were thought to live underneath the waves. Though they fought with the Túatha Dé Danann, they also intermarried with them as well. The gods Lugh and Bres were half Túatha Dé Danann and half Fomorian.

The Gallic Wars: A series of military campaigns waged by Julius Caesar against the Gallic tribes from 58 BCE to 51 BCE. Caesar's book *Commentarii de Bello Gallico (Commentaries on the Gallic War)* was a firsthand account of the wars and one of the most important historical sources regarding the conflict.

geis: Also *geas,* plural *geasa.* A prohibition or taboo that was placed on a hero or king by either a goddess or an Otherworldly female. Breaking a geis would bring bad luck and in most cases caused the hero or king's death. Cúchulain's geis was never to refuse food offered to him and never to eat the flesh of his animal namesake, the dog. Shortly after breaking one of his geis by eating dog flesh, he was killed in battle.

Glean-na-Bodhar: "The Deaf Valley." The place Cúchulain was taken in the *Aided Con Culainn* so he would not hear the sounds of a phantom battle the Daughters of Calatin conjured to lure him to his death.

gressacht: The use of ridicule to incite heroic deeds.

Grian/Grainne: An Irish sun goddess. She was the sister of another sun goddess, Áine. Together they represented the seasonal cycle of the sun, with Grian ruling the dark half of the year and Áine ruling the bright half.

invoking: Summoning or drawing the essence of a deity into your body.

Lavandieres de Nuit: "Laundresses of the Night." The spirits of women condemned to haunt rivers and bodies of water as penitence for their sins, which ranged from committing suicide (usually by drowning) to infanticide to having the misfortune of dying unbaptized.

Leannan Sidhe: Also known as the "Faery Sweetheart." A faery woman who took mortals as lovers and drained their life energy. She gave her suitors the gift of inspiration.

Lebor Gabála Érenn: Also called *The Book of Invasions* or *The Book of the Taking of Ireland.* A collection of poems and prose that details the origins of the mystical races of Ireland. It was compiled during the eleventh century, although the stories date back to the ancient Irish oral tradition. In it, several different races invade Ireland and claim it as their own including the Fig Bolgs, the Túatha Dé Danann, and the Milesians.

Leinster: The easternmost province in Ireland. Tara, Ireland's sacred center, was located in this province.

Le Morte d' Arthur: A compilation of Arthurian legends by Sir Thomas Malory, published in 1485. In Malory's version of Arthurian lore, Morgan le Fay was Arthur's half-sister.

Mabinogion: A collection of Welsh legends written somewhere between 1382 and 1410 CE. It was compiled from *The White Book of Rhydderch* and *The Red Book of Hergest.*

Macha Mong Ruad: Translates to "Macha of the Red Tresses." A name given to one of Macha's incarnations as a mortal warrior-queen.

Masts of Macha: Also called "Macha's Acorn Crop" and *Mesrad Machae.* The severed heads of men who have been slaughtered on the battlefield. The Celts believed that the soul resided in the head, and the severed heads of enemies were often displayed on war chariots.

Milesians: The mythical ancestors of the Irish people. They conquered Ireland and banished the Túatha Dé Danann into the faery hills and mounds.

Mogh Roith: A legendary Druid who may have been an early Irish sun god. He was trained by the female Druid Banbhuana.

Morgans: Also called mari-Morgans, these were Breton sea sprites, similar to mermaids, that lured sailors to their deaths. Their singing was irresistible, drawing sailors to the source of the sweet melody; unfortunately, as soon as the Morgan touched the enamored sailor, he died instantly.

Munster: The southern province of Ireland. Home of the goddess Áine.

Oweynagat: Also called the Cave of Cruachan, the Cave of Cruachu, and the Hell Mouth Cave. It is near Queen Maeve's legendary fortress in Connacht. It was said to be an entrance to the Otherworlds and the home of the Morrigan. Queen Maeve was also said to have been born in the cave.

Queen of Elphame: Another term for the Queen of the Faeries.

riastradh*:* A type of battle frenzy that made a warrior unconquerable in battle. When a warrior enters riastradh he or she is described as transforming, their limbs swelling, their eyes bulging, and being granted inhuman strength. When Cúchulain entered riastradh he was able to kill one hundred of Maeve's warriors in a single battle.

Saint Adamnain: An Irish bishop who was said to have drafted a law banning women from participating in warfare. It is said he did so at the request of his mother, who had been disturbed by the sight of dead female warriors upon a battlefield.

Sidhe: Another term for the Faery Folk, and for the mounds they were said to live in.

Táin Bó Cúailnge: Also called *The Cattle Raid of Cooley*, or simply the *Táin*. An Irish epic tale detailing the war between Connacht and Ulster over the possession of a magickal bull. The most complete version can be found in *The Book of Leinster*.

Táin Bó Regamna: A story found in *The Yellow Book of Lecan*. It gives background information regarding *The Cattle Raid of Cooley*. In it Cúchulain angers the Morrigan, and she vows to attack the hero during battle.

Trioedd Ynys Prydein: Also called the Welsh Triads. The *Trioedd Ynys Prydein* is a collection of triadic sayings regarding events, places, and characters found in the *Mabinogion* and dates back to the thirteenth century. It is believed that these triads were used by bards in order to learn large amounts of traditional lore.

Túatha Dé Danann: Literally means "The Children of the Goddess Danu." Originally the title of the Irish pantheon of gods, this term was eventually used to describe the Faery Folk.

Ulster: One of the four provinces of Ireland. Ulster is the northernmost province and the home of the hero Cúchulain. Ulster and the western province of Connacht were often at war against one another.

Vita Merlini: Also called *The Life of Merlin.* Written in 1150 CE by Geoffrey of Monmouth and centers around the life of Merlin and the reign of King Arthur. It is the first work to mention the enchantress Morgan le Fay. In this work Morgan was a healer and one of nine sisters who ruled the Isle of Avalon. Here Morgan le Fay uses her powers to aid King Arthur.

working altar: An altar that is in your sacred space and is used during rituals and spells.

The Yellow Book of Lecan: A medieval Irish manuscript compiled sometime around 1390 CE. It contains versions of *The Cattle Raid of Cooley, The Wooing of Étain,* and *The Destruction of Da Derga's Hostel.*

Bibliography

Amen, Daniel. *Sex on the Brain: 12 Lessons to Enhance Your Love Life*. New York: Harmony Books, 2007.

Andrews, Ted. *Animal Speak: The Spiritual & Magical Powers of Creatures Great & Small*. St. Paul, MN : Llewellyn Publications, 1993.

Ardinger, Barbara. "Why We Need to Claim The Queen." *SageWoman Magazine*, Issue 74.

Blamires, Steve. *Magic of the Celtic Otherworld: Irish History, Lore & Rituals*. St. Paul, MN: Llewellyn Publications, 2005.

Bonewits, Isaac. *Bonewits' Essential Guide to Druidism*. New York: Kensington Pub., 2006.

Briggs, Katharine M. *A Dictionary of Fairies: Hobgoblins, Brownies, Bogies, and Other Supernatural Creatures*. London: Allen Lane, 1976.

Davis, Elizabeth, and Carol Leonard. *The Women's Wheel of Life: Thirteen Archetypes of Woman at Her Fullest Power*. New York: Penguin Books, 1996.

Carr-Gomm, Philip, and Stephanie Carr-Gomm. *The Druid Animal Oracle*. New York: Fireside, 1994.

Clark, Rosalind. *The Great Queens: Irish Goddesses from the Morrigan to Cathleen ni Houlihan*. Savage, MD: Barnes & Noble Books, 1991.

Condren, Mary. *The Serpent and the Goddess: Women, Religion, and Power in Celtic Ireland*. San Francisco: Harper & Row, 1989.

Conway, D. J. *Celtic Magic*. St. Paul, MN: Llewellyn Publications, 2004.

Corr, Charles, Donna Corr, and Clyde Nabe. *Death and Dying, Life and Living*. Belmont, CA: Cengage Learning, 2009.

Cowan, Thomas. *Yearning for the Wind: Celtic Reflections on Nature and the Soul*. Novato, CA: New World Library, 2003.

Cross, Tom Peete, and Clark Harris Slover. *Ancient Irish Tales: edited by Tom Peete Cross and Clark Harris Slover.* New York: H. Holt, 1936.

Dunn, Joseph, trans. *The Ancient Irish Epic Tale Táin Bó Cúailnge.* London: David Nutt Publishers, 1914.

Ellis, Peter Berresford. *Ancient World of the Celts.* Uniform title: *The Celts: a History.* New York: Carroll & Graf, 2004.

———. *A Brief History of the Druids.* New York: Carroll & Graf Publishers, 2002.

———. *Celtic Women: Women in Celtic Society and Literature.* Grand Rapids, MN: William B. Eerdmans Pub. Co., 1996.

Epstein, Angelique Gulermovich. *War Goddess: The Morrigan and Her Germano-Celtic Counterparts.* Ph.D. dissertation. Los Angeles: University of California Press, 1998.

Evans-Wentz, W. Y. *The Fairy-Faith in Celtic Countries.* Mineola, NY: Dover Publications, 2002.

Faraday, L. W. *The Cattle Raid of Cualnge.* London: David Nutt, 1904.

Franklin, Anna. *The Illustrated Encyclopedia of Fairies.* London: Vega, 2002.

Fraser, J., ed. and trans. "The First Battle of Moytura." *Ériu,* volume 8. Dublin: Royal Irish Academy, 1915.

Gardner, Gerald. *The Meaning of Witchcraft.* London: Aquarian Press, 1959.

Gray, Elizabeth A., trans. "The Second Battle of Mag Tuired." http://www.sacred-texts.com/neu/cmt/cmteng.htm (accessed March 2010).

Green, Miranda. *Animals in Celtic Life and Myth.* New York: Routledge, 1992.

Gregory, Lady Augusta. *Cúchulain of Muirthemne: the story of the men of the Red Branch of Ulster.* New York: Oxford University Press, 1970.

———. *Gods and Fighting Men.* London: J. Murray, 1904.

Gwynn, Edward, trans. *The Metrical Dindshenchas.* Dublin: Royal Irish Academy, 1903.

Hennessy, William M. "The Ancient Irish Goddess of War." *Revue Celtique.* Paris: F. Vieweg, 1870.

Hutton, Ronald. *The Pagan Religions of the Ancient British Isles: Their Nature and Legacy*. Cambridge, MA: B. Blackwell, 1991.

Jones, H. L., trans. *The Geography of Strabo*. London: Loeb Classical Library, 1927.

Jones, Noragh. *Power of Raven, Wisdom of Serpent: Celtic Women's Spirituality.* Edinburgh: Floris Books, 1994.

Kinsella, Thomas, trans. *The Táin: translated from the Irish epic Táin Bó Cualinge.* New York: Oxford University Press, 1970.

Koch, John. *Celtic Culture: A Historical Encyclopedia.* Santa Barbara, CA: ABC-CLIO, 2006.

Leahy, A. H. *The Courtship of Ferb.* BiblioLife, 2009.

———. *Heroic Romances of Ireland.* London: David Nutt, 1905.

Lucas, A. T., trans. *Cattle in Ancient Ireland.* Ireland: Boethius Press, 1989.

Lysaght, Patricia. "Aspect of the earth Goddess in the Tradition of the Banshee in Ireland." *Concepts of the Goddess*, ed. by Sandra Billington and Miranda Green. London: Routledge, 1996.

MacAlister, R. A. S., trans. *Lebor Gabála Érenn: The Book of the Taking of Ireland.* Dublin: Irish Text Society, 1956.

Malory, Thomas. *Le Morte d'Arthur: Sir Thomas Malory's book of King Arthur and of His Noble Knights of the Round Table.* London: Macmillan & Co., 1925.

Marcellinus, Ammianus, and Charles Yonge, trans. *The Roman History of Ammianus Marcellinus: During the Reigns of the Emperors Constantius, Julian, Jovianus, Valentinian, and Valens.* London: H. G. Bohn, 1862.

Markale, Jean. *Women of the Celts.* Rochester, VT: Inner Traditions International, 1986.

Matthews, John, and Caitlin Matthews. *The Encyclopedia of Celtic Myth and Legend: A Definitive Sourcebook of Magic, Vision, and Lore.* Guilford, CT: Lyons Press, 2004.

———. *Taliesin: The Last Celtic Shaman.* Rochester, VT: Inner Traditions, 2002.

McColman, Carl, and Kathryn Hinds. *Magic of the Celtic Gods and Goddesses: A Guide to Their Spiritual Power.* Franklin Lakes, NJ: New Page Books, 2005.

McCoy, Edain. *Celtic Women's Spirituality: Accessing the Cauldron of Life.* St. Paul, MN: Llewellyn Publications, 1998.

Meyer, Kuno, trans. "The Adventures of Nera." *Revue Celtique,* vol. 10. Paris: F. Vieweg,1889.

Meyer, Kuno. "The Wooing of Emer." *Archaeological Review,* vol. 1. London, 1888.

Moorman, Charles. *The Works of the Gawain-Poet.* Jackson, MS: University Press of Mississippi, 1977.

O'Donovan, John. *The Banquet of Dun na N-Gedh and The Battle of Magh Rath.* Dublin: The University Press, 1842.

Parry, John, trans. *Vita Merlini: Latin text by Geoffrey of Monmouth Bishop of St. Asaph Translated by John Jay Parry.* Urbana, IL: The University of Illinois, 1925.

Penczak, Christopher. *The Temple of Shamanic Witchcraft: Shadows, Spirits, and the Healing Journey.* St. Paul, MN: Llewellyn Publications, 2005.

Ragan, Willow. "Wisdom on Black Wings." *The Temple of Danann.* http://www.danann.org/library/myth/blackwing.html (accessed March 2010).

Rankine, David, and Sorita D'Este. *The Guises of the Morrigan: Irish Goddess of Sex & Battle.* London: Avalonia, 2005.

Rolleston, T. W. *Celtic Myths and Legends.* New York: Dover Publications, 1990.

Ross, Anne. "The Divine Hag of the Pagan Celts." *The Witch Figure: Folklore Essays by a Group of Scholars in England Honoring the 75th Birthday of Katharine M. Briggs.* Venetia Newall, ed. London: Routledge and Kegan Paul, 1973.

Skye, Michelle. *Goddess Alive: Inviting Celtic & Norse Goddesses into Your Life.* Woodbury, MN: Llewellyn Publications, 2007.

Stewart, Virginia, trans. "Orphic Hymn to Gaia." *Sibylline Order,* http://www.sibyllineorder.org (accessed March 2010).

Stokes, Whitley, trans. "The Death of Cú Chulainn." *Revue Celtique,* vol. 111. Paris: F. Vieweg, 1887.

———, trans. "The Destruction of Dá Derga's Hostel." *Revue Celtique,* vol. 22, Paris: F. Vieweg, 1901.

———, trans. "The Second Battle of Moytura." *Revue Celtique,* vol. 12. Paris: F. Vieweg, 1891.

———, ed. *Sanas Chormaic: Cormac's glossary. Translated and Annotated by the late John O'Donovan. Edited, with Notes and Indices, by Whitley Stokes.* Calcutta: O. T. Cutter, 1868.

———, ed. *Three Irish Glossaries. Cormac's Glossary Codex A. O'Davoren's Glossary and a Glossary to the Calendar of Oingus the Culdee; with a Preface and Index by W. S.* London: Williams & Norgate, 1862.

Stone, Brian, trans. *Sir Gawain and the Green Knight: Translated with an Introduction by Brian Stone.* Harmondsworth: Penguin, 1974.

Tacitus, Cornelius. *The History Germania and Agricola.* Chapman Press, 2007.

Index